Threshold Concepts in Practice

WITHDRAWN

EDUCATIONAL FUTURES
RETHINKING THEORY AND PRACTICE

Volume 68

Scope

This series maps the emergent field of educational futures. It will commission books on the futures of education in relation to the question of globalisation and knowledge economy. It seeks authors who can demonstrate their understanding of discourses of the knowledge and learning economies. It aspires to build a consistent approach to educational futures in terms of traditional methods, including scenario planning and foresight, as well as imaginative narratives, and it will examine examples of futures research in education, pedagogical experiments, new utopian thinking, and educational policy futures with a strong accent on actual policies and examples.

Threshold Concepts in Practice

Edited by

Ray Land
Durham University, UK

Jan H. F. Meyer
The University of Queensland, Australia

and

Michael T. Flanagan
University College London, UK

SENSE PUBLISHERS
ROTTERDAM/BOSTON/TAIPEI

A C.I.P. record for this book is available from the Library of Congress.

ISBN: 978-94-6300-510-4 (paperback)
ISBN: 978-94-6300-511-1 (hardback)
ISBN: 978-94-6300-512-8 (e-book)

Published by: Sense Publishers,
P.O. Box 21858,
3001 AW Rotterdam,
The Netherlands
https://www.sensepublishers.com/

All chapters in this book have undergone peer review.

Cover image: Detail from 'Eve offering the apple to Adam in the Garden of Eden and the serpent' c.1520–25. Lucas Cranach the Elder (1472–1553). Bridgeman Images. All rights reserved.

Printed on acid-free paper

TABLE OF CONTENTS

Thresholds talk, good food and excellent company at the 5th International Biennial Threshold Concepts conference dinner in Durham Castle, England, June 2014.
(© 2016, R. Land)

FOREWORD

The editors of this volume, in their preface, remind us that threshold concepts were first launched as an idea some fourteen years ago. I recall that one participant at the founding threshold concepts conference at Strathclyde University, Glasgow reproached those of us who were exploring this idea as offering nothing new. He was right in that no idea is formulated on virgin soil but there is much that is distinctive about threshold concepts and the chapters in this book testify to this. They offer a particularly advanced set of explorations from both education researchers and subject specialists. Indeed, the reach of the threshold concept framework has been developed significantly in this book; this extends to the transdisciplinary, doctoral studies, the question of variation, elaborated approaches to liminality and to studenthood and refinements or extensions to the very notion of a threshold concept. There are also fresh excursions into postmodern concerns for uncertainty, stuckness, risk, positionality and ambiguity. This is not a framework that has congealed into an orthodoxy.

In the early days, threshold concept theory could have taken an objectivist and technicist path, offering fixed definitions of a subject's constituents and purportedly aligned pedagogies. But the threshold concept framework has become so much more interesting than this. It has restored difficulty to learning. In particular, threshold concept proponents have always insisted that the cognitive and affective are enmeshed and the inquiry into how this may be so marks out this field as distinctive. Troublesome knowledge and liminality remain two of the most fruitful challenges to a simple cognitive framework or to the untroubled notion of learning outcomes. Meant originally to introduce transparency and clarity in curriculum design and delivery, the notion of outcomes and its siblings (performance criteria, learning aims and objectives) arguably generate a codified, contractual teacher-student relationship that inhibits a dialogic one.

In their preface, Land, Meyer and Flanagan propose threshold concepts as an alternative to the 'student experience' culture permeating many systems of higher education. In resisting the market call for 'satisfaction surveys', threshold concept researchers do not ask students 'Did you like my teaching?' Rather their question is more likely to be 'What did you find difficult?' They seek a conversation with students about mastery, which does not yield to a Likert scale survey but promises instead to build a mutually productive relationship. Indeed, a key strength of the threshold concept framework is that it draws in the interest and participation of subject experts, educationalists and students in transactional ways.

In proposing the value of subject-based threshold concepts fourteen years ago, Meyer and Land (2002) set a very important ball rolling. In matters of university pedagogy, they turned students and academic colleagues into producers rather than consumers of educational theory and practice. They disturbed the expert posture of faculty or educational developers and the idea that pedagogy needs to be taught within bounded courses. They offered instead a sustained invitation to create research and development partnerships using seminars, laboratories, lectures etc. as sites of empirical inquiry. The array of disciplinary experts contributing to this volume show the extent to which this invitation has been accepted. Quite simply, Meyer, Land and Flanagan have built an impressive international, resource-rich R&D community.

To use the phrase of architects in Chapter 24, threshold concepts prompt a 'big rethink' about the structure of subjects, the cognitive and affective difficulties of mastery and how best to learn and teach a subject. Moreover, the chapters in this book, very different in many respects, all have in common a commitment to university education as transformative and to the view that a threshold concept approach offers a transformative curriculum. The reader will not find easy answers or prescriptions in the following chapters but they will find thoughtful, insightful, empirically grounded explorations to inspire the making of such a curriculum.

REFERENCE

Meyer, J. H. F., & Land, R. (2002, September 6). Threshold concepts and troublesome knowledge: Linkages to ways of thinking and practising within the disciplines. In *Improving student learning theory and practice – Ten years on*. Paper presented at the Symposium Enhancing Teaching-Learning Environments in Undergraduate Courses (ETL), ISL Conference, The Sheraton Hotel, Brussels, Belgium.

Glynis Cousin
University of Wolverhampton

PREFACE

Threshold Concepts in Practice

INTRODUCTION

'In the middle of difficulty', Albert Einstein is alleged to have once remarked, 'lies opportunity'.[1] We are now in a time when, in the higher education sectors of many countries, increasing marketisation and high tuition fees risk creating consumerist expectations that the student experience will be relatively comfortable, with the university operating much in the mode of a service provider. The Threshold Concepts Framework, on the other hand, assumes that significant learning will be *transformational*. It is worth recalling, in such a climate, that it is often through encounters with conceptual difficulty or troublesome knowledge that we are obliged to revise our prevailing conceptions, consider matters differently, think otherwise and see anew. This can be exhilarating, and liberating, but is just as often, or perhaps more likely, to prove unsettling and uncomfortable. Yet as even President Obama has recently commented 'coddling' students is 'not the way we learn' (Sherlock, 2015). Without a certain amount of anxiety and risk, Lee Shulman has argued, there's a limit to how much learning occurs. 'One must have something at stake. No emotional investment, no intellectual or formational yield' (Shulman, 2005).

It is now fourteen years since Ray Land and Jan Meyer presented the first paper on threshold concepts[2] at the 10th *Improving Student Learning* (ISL) conference held in Brussels in 2002 (subsequently published as Meyer and Land, 2003). In the time since there have been five international biennial conferences, in Glasgow, Kingston Ontario, Sydney, Dublin and Durham England. These have generated a now considerable corpus of research and scholarship from over 1045 scholars in 45 countries. This valuable collection of resources has been carefully and expertly garnered in the excellent archive established at University College London by Dr Michael Flanagan and has since become established as the definitive international resource on this area of research (Flanagan, 2016).

Earlier volumes (Meyer & Land, 2006; Land, Meyer, & Smith, 2008; Meyer, Land, & Baillie, 2010) have explained the characteristics of threshold concepts in some depth. For the reader unfamiliar with this earlier work, however, the analytic framework used in thresholds concepts research maintains that there are particular concepts in a given discipline which cannot easily be assimilated or accommodated within one's existing meaning frame. Any aspect of the world, no matter how familiar, may, as Dewey noted (1991, p. 120), suddenly present an unexpected and incomprehensible problem. To accommodate such new and troubling knowledge will require not only a difficult reconceptualisation, but a reformulation of one's meaning frame. Schwartzman (2010), in an earlier volume on threshold concepts, has characterised a meaning frame as 'an orienting frame of reference' in and through which we are able to make meaning. It is 'a structure of assumptions within which one's past experience assimilates and transforms new experience, ... a habitual set of expectations' (p. 30). Such structures, she argues, 'embody the categories and rules that order new experience, shaping how we classify our encounters with the world: what we take in and how we act. They also dictate what we notice and what we ignore by selectively determining the scope of our attention ... informed by an horizon of possibility' (ibid). Citing Mezirow (1991, pp. 49–50) she notes that in this fashion they function 'as both lions at the gate of awareness and the building blocks of cognition'. Ironically our meaning frame is often the mechanism which brings the anomalous nature of a given phenomenon to light, but then proves inadequate to resolve the problems raised by its existence (Kuhn, 1996, p. 122) and must be reformulated.

The reformulation of such a powerful frame will clearly also effect a shift in the learner's subjectivity (Meyer & Land, 2005). It gives rise to a state of uncertainty 'in which the learner may oscillate between old and emergent understandings' (Cousin, 2006, p. 4). Learning thresholds are often the points at which students experience difficulty and are often troublesome as they require a letting go of customary ways of seeing things, of prior familiar views. This entails an uncomfortable ontological shift, as, in many respects, we are what we know.

Hence the superordinate and non-negotiable characteristic of a threshold concept is its *transformative* capacity. Moreover such concepts seem to have an integrating function in the sense of bringing what formerly appeared to be disparate elements into a coherent relationship, much as the addition of a particular jigsaw piece may bring other pieces together to provide a new and meaningful perspective.

The uptake of the Threshold Concepts Framework across some 259 subject areas in over 45 countries to date (Flanagan, 2016) has been both dramatic and gratifying. We would speculate that why the framework has had such resonance and appeal might be owing to the following factors. Firstly it is predicated on Perkins' (2000) idea of *Action Poetry*, the notion that for an idea to have traction it should have relatively straightforward main premises, it should be capable of translation into small-scale, low key research implementation quite quickly, and it should have both explanatory and actionable potential. In this regard it is likely to appeal to early career researchers. The framework, moreover, is strongly discipline-focused and hence taps into practitioners' own interests and identities. Part of its broader appeal may also be owing to its conceptually eclectic nature. It can provide a fresh analytic discourse, and vocabulary to be applied to new contexts of practice. It also addresses mainstream pedagogical and curricular issues within higher education and hence is often included within programmes of professional development for academic staff. Nonetheless, As Professor Peter Felten, the keynote speaker at the 5th International Biennial Threshold Concepts Conference wisely observed, the common endeavour is more concerned 'to provoke and suggest, not to prove and conclude'. There remains much work to be done.

The Flanagan archive vividly demonstrates how the study and analysis of threshold concepts has over the years become interwoven with that of cognate topics such as troublesome knowledge, liminality, transformational learning, conceptual difficulty, 'stuckness', students' prior knowledge, ways of thinking and practising (WTP), ontological shift, capability, and disciplinarity. The papers in this collection reflect this wider web of associated topics, and draw on them in their specific identifications, incorporations and contextualisations of threshold concepts across different disciplines and professional practices. They also address what students bring to the learning situation, in processes of 'transactional curriculum inquiry' (Cousin, 2009) and curriculum redesign.

The chapters in the current volume had their first airing at the 5th International Biennial Conference held at Collingwood College in the University of Durham from 9th–11th July 2014. In the rare sunshine of a Northern English summer, against the towering silhouettes of Durham's thousand year old Cathedral and Castle, 102 delegates from 18 countries presented their findings over an intensive three days in what, despite the troublesome nature of our deliberations, was a very happy social gathering. These selected chapters from the Durham conference add to the burgeoning collection of available resources in this field and seek to show how the Threshold Concepts Framework is now being used in contexts of practice – disciplinary, professional, pedagogical and curricular. They are organised in the pages that follow in relation to their contribution to new theoretical directions for thresholds research, or a specific concern with aspects of liminality, with the relation of threshold concepts to interdisciplinarity, to learning at doctoral level, and finally with aspects of thresholds in professional practice.

THEORETICAL DIRECTIONS

In his conference keynote *Peter Felten* (Chapter 1) reminds us that 'scholars and teachers should take seriously the experiences and insights of students as learners'. Much of the early work on thresholds was from the perspective of teachers. Felten demonstrates what insights we might gain into threshold concepts if we partnered with students as co-enquirers and co-explorers into the nature of thresholds and learning in higher education. In a series of three seminars held at Bryn Mawr College, just west of Philadelphia, students were invited to explore the idea of thresholds in relation to their own learning experience. Questions about affect, liminality, confidence, and disciplinarity emerged in these gatherings as the students described their experience with troublesome knowledge, focusing as much on the person doing the learning as the thing being learned. Many of these knowledge encounters were emotionally charged. Felten identifies *troublesome affect* as a particularly important area for further investigation for scholars of threshold concepts. One Bryn Mawr student, Sarah Jenness, observes that 'school militates against uncertainty' and questions why students would 'risk liminality in the classroom when certainty feels both personally and academically safer'. Students, it became clear, do not often come to higher education looking for, or appreciating, liminality in the classroom. In this regard, as James Atherton (2012) pointed out in his paper at the 4th Threshold Concepts conference in Dublin, liminality can become a liability. To counter this, Felten concludes, 'threshold concepts are not just about knowledge, they also are about confidence'. And to acquire threshold confidence, in order permanently to cross a threshold, the seminar students insisted, they needed to believe that they belonged 'on the other side'.

But even as we rightly celebrate the valued partnership roles that students have increasingly been playing in higher education over the last decade, with the Bryn Mawr students an exemplary case, nonetheless the language of partnership can become blurred unhelpfully with the discourse of student satisfaction. As *Ray Land* (Chapter 2) argues, a discursive shift has occurred over the last three decades from a language of education to that of 'the student experience'. This increasingly influential view sits uneasily with the idea that universities serve to offer programmes of a transformative nature. Universities are required simultaneously to produce satisfied consumers as well as develop graduates for the wider society who can act and exercise judgment in complex, uncertain, risk-laden and unpredictable environments. This shift has come about through a move to a marketised notion of higher education as principally a private good (and a primarily economic rather than educational transaction). A consumer logic of value for money, accountability and the need for increasingly rigorous protocols and standards of inspection then ensues, seeking certainty and 'crystal clarity' (Ecclestone, 2012). It can easily be deployed to put students and teaching staff in an oppositional stance, through the use, for example, of consumer satisfaction student surveys in which the student-as-consumer 'rates' the professor-as-service-provider. Learning gain is measured principally through measures of student satisfaction as opposed to learner *transformation*. Learning can come to be depicted within the organisation as an undertaking that has a high degree of certainty, is non-problematic, without any significant incurring of risk. It does not entail deep personal change or transformation, troublesome challenge or even, at times, engagement. Liminality becomes a liability (Atherton, 2012). Students, as organisational actors, need to be rendered differently, not as consumers, but as co-enquirers, co-creators, co-producers. In this way the discourse of thresholds is advocated as a counter-discourse to that of a neoliberal higher education, as a pedagogy of *un*certainty.

A new theoretical direction for thresholds scholarship is offered by *Jan Meyer* and *Julie Timmermans* (Chapter 3) who propose the construction of *Integrated Threshold Concept Knowledge* (ITCK). The empirical and social construction of ITCK, they argue, lies at the 'intersection' of specific transformational (and related) subject content with associated different 'types of knowledge'. Captured in ITCK is the dynamic interplay between different 'types of knowledge' arising primarily from analyses for, and of, threshold concepts. This includes consequent articulation of their 'critical features', knowledge of how these are experienced cognitively, affectively, and ontologically (in varying degrees) by students in the liminal state and, finally, how a fusion of these different forms of knowledge translates into in situ 'threshold concept representations', contributing in effect to a repertoire of student-centred 'responses'. The genesis of knowledge that is broadly of this form, they suggest, lies in the writings of Shulman and Marton in the mid- to late 1980s that were independently focused in that period on the need to develop a (subject) content-based amalgam of know-ledge, -how, and -why, to drive reforms in school teacher education and classroom practice. Three decades later their analysis of these writings provides an historical analogy and a foundation for contemporary arguments within the Threshold Concepts Framework. ITCK they propose, develops a new, or enriches an existing, learning and teaching philosophy that is personal and discipline-based. It is personal in emphasising attitudes and values: sense of self in relation to students, individual differences in their learning, and their learning wellbeing. It is discipline-based in emphasising sense of self (academic identity, 'being') in relation to discipline; thinking and practising that reflects its 'inner logic', its characteristic modes of discourse, reasoning, analysis and explanation.

Whereas previous research on threshold concepts in the classroom has tended to focus on upper-level seminars for majors (Middendorf & Pace, 2004; Land, Meyer, & Baillie, 2010), and hence comparatively small group sizes, *Susannah McGowan* (Chapter 4) investigates the embedding of threshold concepts in a large-scale lecture programme (450 plus students). As a baseline qualitative study of one large lecture course in History at the University of California Santa Barbara, her study contributes to three areas of research in higher education: application of threshold concepts at the course level; the application of threshold concepts in the humanities (and how it possibly contributes to current conversations about the survival of the humanities in higher education); and research on graduate student development and pedagogy in large lecture courses. This empirical study employed classroom observations, online surveys, interviews with the lead professor, teaching assistants, and students. Her initial findings were that, firstly, *conceptual threads* reinforce conceptual development: According to surveys, an explicit emphasis on concepts discussed in the professor's lecture and teaching assistant's discussion section, means that concepts are reinforced and practised, thus establishing a conceptual thread for the student. A second finding was that emphasis on concepts bolsters levels of engagement in discussion. Emphasis on *threshold actions* or the work involved that leads to the understanding of a historical threshold concept provides an avenue of engagement in the discipline. When the professor delivered his lecture on how historians analyse sources, two teaching assistants (two of nine) consistently employed these strategies subsequently in their own discussions with students. Finally it was found that *teaching assistants* play a vital role in imparting threshold concepts. This was a finding that the course professor had not taken into account in earlier offerings of the course. Moreover, in explaining these concepts to students in class, the professor realised he also had to make his intentions explicit to his nine teaching assistants. This was an unexpected outcome of the study yet one crucial to the development of teaching assistants as future professors.

A recurrent concern within thresholds research has been the question of how to identify, validate, and address threshold concepts within an individual discipline (Meyer & Land, 2005). Within a disciplinary context, individual instructors often identify threshold concepts based on their knowledge of their students' interaction with the content. Moreover, research methods for identifying threshold concepts vary widely to include interviews, case studies, Delphi techniques and other qualitative data (Meyer & Land, 2006; Davies, 2005). Hence *Beth White, Taimi Olsen* and *David Schumann* (Chapter 5) posed the question 'What can an instructor gain from considering student viewpoints and the experiences of other faculty?' They set out to test a method of disciplinary inquiry, using analysis of given circumstances, collecting data through multiple methods, and analysing results in a systematic approach. The study reported in their chapter focuses on one departmental sequence – a first semester composition and rhetoric course taught at a large research university in the Southern United States. (Future studies will expand to consider validity across disciplines). They discuss a method of identifying disciplinary threshold concepts within a course by using input from learners and instructors (surveys and interviews) as well as analysis of syllabi and instructional materials. They outline their research process, and present and analysis of their results that includes a comparison of student responses with instructor responses.

NEGOTIATING LIMINALITY

Since the 4th Threshold Concepts conference in Dublin there has been growing interest in the liminal dimension of the Threshold Concepts Framework and the number of papers at the 5th conference that drew attention to this topic merited a specific section within this volume.

We already know that not all learners experience threshold concepts in the same way and that the degree of troublesomeness associated with a particular threshold concept will vary between individual learners (Meyer & Land, 2006). The very willingness of learners to engage with the threshold concept itself and navigate the associated liminal space is equally varied (Meyer & Land, 2006). Some learners are willing, or even eager, to enter the liminal space in the hope of emerging transformed or coming to a new way of understanding whilst others pause at the entrance seemingly unable or unwilling to let go of their pre-existing understandings (Cousin, 2006). *Julie Rattray* (Chapter 6) points out that much of the work in this area has focused on intellectual or pedagogical explanations to explain the differential experiences of learners when they encounter troublesome knowledge (Flanagan, 2016). Her chapter explores another possible explanation for learners' behaviour when they encounter thresholds and more particularly are required to engage with liminality. This is the extent to which affective and psychological characteristics of the learner, such as resilience, might explain why some students are able to cope with liminality and persist in the face of uncertainty whilst others appear to withdraw from it and remain in an untransformed state. She draws on the work of Luthans et al.'s (2007) construct of Psychological Capital (PsyCap) as one measure of the affective dimension of learning. She explores firstly the potential relationship it has to academic performance before moving on to a consideration of any potential utility it might have as a means of explaining 'why some learners remain trapped in, or fail to enter, the liminal space and others emerge from the space to inhabit a new place of being'. Moreover, from a pedagogical perspective, she argues that 'the malleable nature of some psychological states render them meaningful in a learning and teaching context not only because of their explanatory function but as a potential source of intervention to support a positive learning experience'.

Liminality remains to some extent the 'black box' of thresholds research, given the evident intractability of attempting to access or represent this individual state in any reliable or accurate fashion. Much of the available data depends inevitably on self-reporting. Nevertheless *Ahmad Thamrini F. Syed Mohamed, Ray Land* and *Julie Rattray,* in their study of professional military education (Chapter 7) identify what they consider to be new possible responses to the liminal experience of transformation. Drawing on Homi Bhabha's (1994) notions of *ambivalence* and *hybridity* in their analysis of their empirical data, they find that certain learners do not necessarily follow a prescribed path of transformation to an established ontology (in this case military states of 'soldiership' and 'officership') but are capable of conforming to expected communal practices whilst simultaneously feeling 'empowered to intervene actively' by 'questioning and refashioning received ideas' (McLeod, 2000, pp. 218–219). The outcome is a state of ontological ambivalence, in which contrary (and sometimes contradictory) allegiances may be retained, and maintained, leading to the formation of hybrid identities. They suggest that experience of ambivalence in liminal states and subsequent adoption of hybrid identities may well be found in other processes of professional transformation, and that these lenses may prove fruitful in future inquiry.

Virginia Tucker (Chapter 8) further explores the novice-expert liminal space to study the threshold concepts involved in learning to become an expert. The professional practice site for this study is 'search expertise', and the study explores knowledge that could transcend both the particulars of an individual search engine (features, commands, and the like) and, second, the subject area of the database content. The study focuses on the liminality between the highly proficient novice and the expert searcher. 'Expert searchers' in today's information environment include reference librarians, information architects, university faculty who teach advanced search, and other professionals in a variety of information-intensive settings. Their experiences are characterized by a profound understanding of information concepts and content and they have an agile ability to apply this knowledge to both interacting with and having an impact on the information environment, often including having a role in the information experiences of others. The study closely examines novice-expert literature and considers practices relevant to the learning experiences of experts, such as how they structure knowledge, process ambiguous information, solve problems and use representations and reflection when learning. Emerging themes provide evidence of four threshold concepts: information environment, information structures, information vocabularies and concept fusion – the integration of the other three threshold concepts further defined by additional properties. In addition to the threshold concepts were findings that are not concept-based, including praxes and traits of expert searchers. A model of search expertise is proposed with the four threshold concepts at its core that further encompasses these traits and praxes. This allows the research to present an integrated model of the novice-expert space for the practice site of search expertise. In addition, melding understandings from novice-expert research and threshold concept theory literature (Meyer & Land, 2003; Cousin, 2010), the study finds ontological shift to be a critical component of the model, in addition to critical changes in discourse (Flanagan & Smith, 2008).

When confronted with troublesome issues and threshold concepts, students are obliged to choose *strategies* when faced with the prospect of liminality. *Terje Berg, Morten Erichsen* and *Leif Martin Hokstad* (Chapter 9), researching in the context of a Norwegian Business School, undertake a quantitative study to investigate the experience of undergraduate students, and their potential strategies (or lack thereof) in the liminal stage of their learning trajectory. The researchers identify two main strategies for the learners, either a strategy of fight or one of flight (e.g. procrastination, postponement, giving up easily), two typical psychological responses to liminality, expressed in stuckness (Cannon, 1929; Meyer & Land, 2006; Nolan, 2005). They choose to focus in this chapter on the fight strategies, as insights gained from study of coping strategies in general, and fight strategies in particular, give lecturers knowledge about how to conduct these strategies back to new students. The researchers identify specific potential threshold concepts based on a triangulation of the available data sources; interviews, questionnaires and discussions, observations, exam statistics, and an external researcher. They then investigate a range of fight strategies adopted to gain mastery of these concepts, which include extracurricular efforts, students' undertaking exercises by themselves, consulting the lecturer as an extra asset, joining a study group, consulting significant others and accessing the internet. Findings indicate that confidence is built from doing extracurricular efforts, doing exercises, and to some extent using the lecturer or the study group as extra assets. This self-confidence may give the student the necessary belief in how to overcome threshold concepts. Thus, next time the student is facing other threshold concepts, she has increased her ability to cope with these concepts. They suggest that what seems to be lacking in these students' learning trajectory and the course design 'is to facilitate the development of studenthood, how to become a student, which differs from being a pupil'. They point out, further, that components of a successful understanding on the learner's behalf are cultural as well as ontological. 'Parts of the underlying game lacking in many of the students', they observe, 'are the realisation of endurance, or the need for time on task, i.e. a slower, more meticulous learning process than experienced previously'. Or, in Cousin's words, the 'messy journeys' back, forth and across conceptual terrain' (Cousin, 2006).

THRESHOLD CONCEPTS AND INTERDISCIPLINARITY

As we increasingly find ourselves in an age of globalisation, uncertainty, risk and speed, the pressing scientific, social and economic problems of our times seem to demand more than one disciplinary lens to bring them more clearly into view, and to offer possibilities of resolution. As Roy (1979, p. 165) famously put it, 'the real problems of society do not come in discipline-shaped blocks'. Hence there has been an increasing emphasis in our universities, and from our funding agencies on the issue of interdisciplinarity. Two of the chapters in this volume consider this issue in relation to threshold concepts. *Jason Davies* (Chapter 10) points to the 'profound difficulties' for students on interdisciplinary programmes (particularly postgraduates) who face conflicting epistemological claims and/or threshold concepts. 'What do you do,' he asks, 'when your tutors or supervisors are *literally* arguing from different premises, with the implication that meaning-construction and intellectual reference points are as different as the physical buildings?' Furthermore he points to the often likely consequence that 'thinking outside the box' – a frequent mantra associated with interdisciplinary approaches – will require 'the immediate construction of a new box with a different design and a different set of understandings for what constitutes "success"'. Incommensurability, always anathema in interdisciplinarity, is, he argues, 'emphatically predicted by threshold concepts' given their: 'transformative', 'irreversible', 'integrative', 'bounded', and 'troublesome' nature. Much in the spirit of an ethnographer he examines the manner in which a discipline's threshold concepts 'feature in the building and maintenance of disciplinary integrity by "tribes" in academia', and points to the practice of *threshold guardianship*, where, far from the deployment of threshold concepts as enabling 'doorways' they might rather be seen to serve as locked doors 'to keep the disciplined in (or perhaps "safe")'. He helpfully advocates a possible way out of these dilemmas through the promotion of a culture of disciplinary distinction (identifying characteristic aspects) rather than definition (identifying dividing lines and borders). What all disciplines have in common, he reminds us, is that, 'for our heuristic purposes, they all operate with threshold concepts. These do not compete or invite competition, but are discrete: they are the site of incommensurability'. In this way, he proposes, threshold concepts are potentially a great leveller, 'and their articulation at some point, whether deliberately or piecemeal, is usually a necessary part of collaboration'. Such frankness about our practices of threshold guardianship might offer ways, he wisely suggests, for different 'tribes' to 'retain their integrity without impinging on others'.

Approaching interdisciplinary from a different perspective, *Aminul Huq, Marcia Nichols* and Bijaya *Aryal* (Chapter 11) consider threshold concepts in relation to interdisciplinary structures of learning. They undertook a retrospective quantitative examination of how a group of students approached and grappled with ambiguity and context in three courses: Introduction to Literature, Introduction to Physics, and

Calculus I. This would allow the researchers to determine if learning transfer is occurring across disciplinary lines and to provide a foundation for them 'to more deliberately imbed curricular points of integration that would better promote the transfer of learning and understanding on the TCs'. They suggest that 'ambiguity' and 'context' are *interdependent* threshold concepts, that is, those that are not only salient in multiple disciplines but that also can but taught across disciplinary lines. In contrast, *independent* threshold concepts are 'discrete concepts' at a specific learning stage within a discipline that do not require the previous mastery of another threshold concept, such as the concept of 'function' in Calculus, 'genre' in Literature or 'measurement uncertainty' in Physics. Independent threshold concepts can be applied to other concepts, but the concept itself does not depend upon learning other threshold concepts in near simultaneity. Finally *intradependent* concepts are those that are still at a particular learning stage within a single discipline, but that are dependent upon other concepts within that same discipline, like Symbolism in Literature or Limit, which depends on the concept of Function. The study reveals surprising, even counterintuitive, correlations between Literature, Physics and Calculus, for example that students may be more comfortable with ambiguity in physics than in literature. On the other hand high performers were found to perform well across all three disciplinary boundaries, suggesting that, despite common assumptions that students who are good at Maths and Science are not good with words and vice versa, this is simply not true. In fact, good analytical skills are not only necessary for success in all disciplines, but were found to transfer from STEM to Humanities and back again.

THE DOCTORAL JOURNEY

The experience of undertaking doctoral level study has for some time been recognised as one that requires powerful conceptual and ontological shifts, and frequent encounters with troublesome knowledge. Two chapters in this volume investigate the experience of doctoral students further. *Michelle Salmona, Dan Kaczynski* and *Leigh Wood* (Chapter 12) were concerned that doctoral degree non-completion rates have remained consistently high for the past 50 years, with, for example, approximately only 50% of Humanities candidates and 56% of Social Sciences candidates successfully completing their doctoral degrees in the United States (Grasso, Barry, & Valentine, 2009). They consequently undertook a survey to investigate this vexed situation in the United States and Australia. Particular attention was paid to the challenges of research methodology which they consider represents a key ingredient for the doctoral candidate completing the dissertation. As straightforward as the apparently linear sequence of topic selection, framing of problem statement, clarifying purpose and focus, and crystallising research questions might appear, the doctoral candidate, they maintain, 'is confronted with an overwhelming number of methodological decisions prior to implementing their research study which geometrically expand with each step taken'. They identify threshold concepts as a means to deconstruct and restructure teaching and learning of research methodology concepts for doctoral candidates. After developing a survey instrument to identify potential threshold concepts in research methodology (from the perspective of doctoral faculty and supervisors), they targeted members in the International Doctoral Education Research Network (IDERN) and a representative sample of supervisors at the universities which the authors are affiliated with. The scope of their inquiry explored such themes as: building a logical cohesive scholarly argument; recognizing when to bring theory into the study; gaining critical value from the literature to the study; progressing from description to analysis; credible evidence-based analysis and interpretation, and contributing trustworthy high quality research. The dissertation phase of learning and the critical role of supervision are prominent in this study, which stresses the critically important need to improve instruction in research methodology and to increase successful completion rates for doctoral students. The study acknowledges the importance of scaffolding learning and teaching which supports student mastery of concept knowledge. Conclusions examine strategies which promote the modelling of concepts beyond the procedural aspects of research methodology.

An internationally recognised author on doctoral supervision, *Gina Wisker* (Chapter 13) builds on her earlier work to address how doctoral students identify and deal with three kinds of blockage in their work: grappling with finding the appropriate methodology and methods; undermining by the supervisor, and a struggle with articulation. Students report silencing, loss of confidence and paralysis in their work with each of these blockages. Her chapter then focuses specifically on ways in which doctoral students deal with such transitional and troublesome moments in their learning journeys, considering their awareness of how and when they identify and engage with transformational knowledge, challenges in the supervisory relationship and writing blocks. It focuses on their recognition of these troublesome, transitional moments, and the ways in which they take ownership and agency, cross conceptual thresholds, articulate their research projects and the contribution of their findings, often through the supportive work of supervisors, and sometimes through engagement with the research literature. Re-scrutiny of the data from three earlier projects (2007–2010, 2009, 2012) and new data gathered for this study – involving face-to-face and email interviews leading to two case studies – offers insights into the ways in which doctoral students identify, meet and cross these conceptual thresholds in their work. It indicates how they evidence and articulate their awareness of moving forward to the achievement of their doctoral learning journeys and identities as researchers and writers, through ownership, agency and articulation.

THRESHOLD CONCEPTS IN PROFESSIONAL PRACTICE

In recent years the insights gained from threshold concepts, liminality and troublesome knowledge have been increasingly applied in areas of professional education and development. Nokia and Siemens Europe have used the idea in 'serious games' design for Management education, in the €9.4 million EU Cordis collaborative project.[3] In the USA the Association of College and Research Libraries (ACRL) have established a new national American Libraries Association Framework for Information Literacy for Higher Education. This has replaced an earlier standards-based approach with one that employs threshold concept-derived 'frames'.[4] In Trondheim, Norway the innovative TRANSark project has adopted threshold concepts as one of its five informing principles for the future transformation of architectural education.[5] In 2015 it received 1 million NOK from the Norwegian Government to further develop this programme. In Australia the Australian Council of Engineering Deans supported a national workshop series on TCs, one of the outcomes being the University of Western Australia (UWA) Faculty designing a new curriculum for engineering courses introduced in 2012. On the other side of the continent the University of Queensland's Occupational Therapy Department identified five threshold concepts, designed their curricula around them and flagged their importance to students by describing them in their Student Guide. In the 2014 United Kingdom Research Excellence Framework (REF) an impact case study submitted by Durham University on the impact of threshold concepts on higher education pedagogical practice worldwide was rated equal first in the UK.

This tendency is reflected in many chapters of this volume. Reference has already been made to the professional education of military officers and that of information search specialists. Further chapters address the application of TCs to the practice of engineers, medics, nurses, computer scientists, lawyers, teachers and architects. Hence the acknowledgment of this strong emphasis in the title of this volume. *Anthony Parker* and *Daniel McGill* (Chapter 14) discuss the implementation of a fully module-based Engineering programme in an undergraduate degree at Macquarie University in Australia. The implementation of threshold concepts in the design of this modular format is discussed as a singularly important influence in this design. The innovation of *threshold concept modules* is introduced and considered as a potentially significant contribution to the practice of a threshold concepts approach to Engineering pedagogy. The innovation of these concept modules is intended to allow space within a unit for a module to provide the focus of a specific threshold concept to be developed. The anticipated advantage of this approach is to ensure clarity of overall outcomes and the particularly the significant threshold themes of the unit. The concept module requires that the development of the relevant threshold concept is covered appropriately and comprehended by all participants. It further ensures that all key concepts in a unit and program of study are covered within the curriculum and understood by both staff and students, and that they are presented with a clear focus on the process with minimum distractions. The intention is to workshop one core notion, the threshold concept, from a variety of contexts, hence providing students multiple views of the fundamental learning threshold, with all the contingencies, variabilities and structures of a professional Engineering project.

Also in Australia, a team based at Queensland University, *Jan Meyer, David Knight, Tom Baldock, David Callaghan, Julie McCredden* and *Liza O'Moore* (Chapter 15), investigated how 'critical flow' was identified as a threshold concept in a third-year civil engineering course on 'open channel hydraulics'. The team also considered how responses to associated variation in student learning and metalearning led to the development of new forms of sustainable pedagogy. The methodology employed is transferable to other contexts, while the pedagogy targeting 'structural complexity' in student understanding is adaptable as appropriate to other threshold concepts. A starting position acknowledged the status of a threshold concept being of limited use in the absence of responsive pedagogy, and that such pedagogy in relation to that concept must proceed from knowledge of how students vary in their learning of it (Meyer, 2010). Thus emphasised, 'variation in student learning' is important for three reasons: First, conceptually discrete patterns of learning within such variation establish a basis for pedagogical responses including mechanisms for increasing students' metalearning capacity in relation to that concept (Meyer et al., 2009). Second, these patterns partially explain why a particular threshold concept will be apprehended and experienced by students in varying degrees attributable to individual differences. And in doing so a basic premise is reinforced: the epistemological, epistemic, discursive, and ontological shifts associated with threshold concepts constitute dimensions of inter-individual variation, not conformity. Third, when exhibited in a professional development context (informally and collegially so in the present case) such variation is catalytic; it serves as a threshold concept in its own right in reconceptualising teaching practice (Meyer, 2012).

The threshold status of 'critical flow' emerged from a triangulation of three sources of evidence: (a) expert conceptual analysis, (b) students' experiences and, (c) statistical analyses of students' answers to past examination questions (Knight et al., 2013a). Also empirically determined, in accordance with theoretical expectations, was clear evidence of variation in students' learning of, and capacity for metalearning engagement with, this concept (Meyer et al., 2012). 'Quality' in students' understanding (in answers to examination questions involving 'critical flow') was interpreted as variation in 'structural complexity' after the work of Biggs and Collis (1982). With a precursor of metalearning activity focussed on 'critical flow', associated follow up pedagogy of the concept centred on activity to directly alter students' learning behaviour by altering assessment practices and students' perceptions of task demands. 'Metacognitive assessment activities' based on 'critical flow' have accordingly been developed and trialled with outcomes consistent with theoretical expectations, as evidenced in demonstrably improved student engagement, satisfaction, and performance (Knight et al., 2013b).

In Engineering the student is often confronted with 'contrasting representations or models' (Entwistle et al., 2005, p. 9), which Entwistle explores as 'ways of thinking and practising' (ibid). These contrasting representations might take the form, in electric circuits, of graphs, mathematical models, drawings of circuits or the real circuits. In their research in Electrical Engineering in Sweden *Anna-Karin*

Carstensen and *Jonte Bernhard* have found that exploring the relationships – links – between these different representations, in the theory/model domain as well as in the object/event domain (Tiberghien, 2002), is of the utmost importance. In their chapter (Chapter 16) they explore how the learning of two-terminal equivalents may be facilitated by integration of small practical tasks within a lecture setting. In a contribution to an earlier volume on threshold concepts the authors described how a tool developed for investigation of 'the learning of a complex concept' was employed to find critical aspects, which they called 'key concepts', in the sense of a key unlocking the portal of understanding of threshold concepts (Carstensen & Bernhard, 2008). In their chapter in this volume they explore these links further. In continuing their work on how students make links between the different 'islands' of single concepts, in order to make a whole of the complex concept, they have noted that the links between these islands are of different kinds. They discuss what kinds of relationships these links consist of, how they differ in the ways students might need to cope with them, and how teachers may notice and highlight these relationships in their instruction. By analysing video-recordings of students' interactions during lab-work in accordance with Marton and Tsui's (2004) Theory of Variation, the authors are now able to make a more detailed analysis of what the links are, and hence a further contribution to the understanding of the nature of a threshold concept.

Learning in the health professions is profoundly ontological – it is about 'becoming' a practitioner. As *Andy Wearn, Anne O'Callaghan* and *Mark Barrow* observe (Chapter 17) 'In this process of "becoming", students and trainees can often recall significant moments when they felt stuck, challenged or enlightened. At these times they may be compelled to think differently about their practice and themselves as practitioners'. This team of medical researchers from Auckland in New Zealand undertook a study of the transformation that doctors experience during their Palliative Care training. Anecdotally, registrars undertaking a Palliative Care attachment as part of their specialist training identify this as a transformative process – making them think differently about medical practice and themselves as doctors. Their role in this setting is significantly different from that of other specialist areas. Dealing with the patients and their family or *whanau* where death is expected provides a range of challenges that may not have previously been consciously addressed. These observations resonate with the framework of threshold concepts and troublesome knowledge. Comparatively little research on TCs has been conducted within medicine, although it has been applied in other health professional contexts. In this study the research team chose to collect data from the learners rather than the tutors or content experts. The aims were: to explore the palliative care training experiences of doctors, identifying the aspects that they found transformative and/or troublesome; to identify a series of TCs in the area of Palliative Care, from the perspective of the learner; to use these TCs to inform teaching and learning in Palliative Care and medical education more broadly. This was a theory-testing qualitative study using a deductive and then inductive approach to coding. Purposive sampling was used to recruit medical registrars who had undertaken a six month Palliative Care run as part of their postgraduate training. Two focus group interviews (eight participants in total) were held using a semi-structured guide, and were audiotaped and transcribed verbatim. All defining features of the TCs framework were found repeatedly in the data. Eight tentative TCs were identified and stood up to comparison with the theoretical framework. The two which stood out most prominently were *Recognising and managing strong emotions in self or others*, and *Reframing communication – 'ask' before 'tell'*.

Also within the Health Professions a narrative research study was undertaken in Scotland by *Linda Martindale, Ray Land, Julie Rattray* and *Lorraine Anderson* (Chapter 18) to investigate research learning in undergraduate nursing education using threshold concepts as a framework. Research skills and methods are an integral part of the undergraduate nursing curriculum, underpinning the use of research evidence in practice. Understanding the research process and research methods are thresholds which students need to pass through to support their development into evidence-based practitioners. However research evidence suggests that undergraduate nursing students find research skills and methods troublesome and this is a significant barrier to learning. Troublesome research knowledge can be readily aligned with existing understanding of troublesome knowledge, as identified by Perkins (1999). For example Ax and Kincade (2001) identified counter-intuitive knowledge in the term 'research' because of the everyday usage of research as being simply to find out about something. In the threshold concepts literature, aspects of research learning have been found to be troublesome in other disciplines, such as Taylor's (2006) work on hypothesis development in biology and Kiley's (2009) study of research learning in doctoral students. Seventeen nursing students were interviewed in depth about their experiences of learning about research. Learning narratives were gathered and these were analysed using a thematic narrative analysis, specifically focusing on difficulties encountered by students. The analysis identified troublesome knowledge through the way in which students conceptualised the terms research and evidence based practice, as well as how they used (or avoided) specific research terms and concepts. However other troublesome elements were also apparent: the learning environments; the perceptions about what research means to a nursing student; and the anticipation of research learning being difficult. These findings point to troublesome areas in threshold concepts which are not necessarily intrinsic to the subject or concept itself, but which are linked to the culture and environments in which the students are learning and to their perceptions of the topic. In nursing this seems to be particularly problematic because of the need to learn within a higher education institution as well as in a range of healthcare settings. Understanding the range of factors which may make a threshold concept troublesome can help to explain students' challenges in learning. This understanding has the potential to influence curriculum design to address these problems more overtly.

An interesting debate has arisen within Computer Science in terms of approaches to the identification of threshold concepts within this discipline and the efficacy and reliability of the methods used to attain this. In Ireland *Dermot Shinners-Kennedy* (Chapter 19), though acknowledging that devising an effective methodology for identifying threshold concepts 'would represent an important milestone in the evolution of threshold concept scholarship', nonetheless concludes that 'For the most part the strategies deployed by researchers to date have yielded tentative proposals only and the uncertain nature of the outcomes has been a frustrating experience for investigators'. The retrospective nature of the methods employed come in for criticism. The author identifies what he sees as shortcomings inherent in the commonly-used approaches. Typically, he argues, the source of the evidence has been discipline experts and would-be discipline experts in the guise of learners. The belief is that experts can validate the inclusion of concepts in a classification because they 'know' their discipline and this knowledge provides them with the tools to dissect and analyse the body of knowledge to identify the appropriate concepts. A variant of this approach seeks empirical data gathered from students at various stages of completion of their programmes of study. Their lack of competence or gaps in their knowledge are viewed as sources of evidence to support or confirm the assignation of a particular status to a given concept. Both of these sources he considers unreliable. He identifies a list of shortcomings in prevailing methods that includes: the effects of basic level concepts; expert blind spot; hindsight bias; the illusion of memory; the influence of language and the effects of emotion. These issues, he argues, 'actually militate against the discovery of the type of data that is sought by investigators'.

A team of computer scientists from the Netherlands, *Bert Zwaneveld, Jacob Perrenet*, and *Roel Bloo* (Chapter 20), are not convinced by Shinners-Kennedy's reasoning. Hindsight bias, they contend, refers to prediction of events in the past with known outcome and overestimating its probability. Impaired memory, they point out, because of emotional load, refers to severely traumatic experiences. Moreover their own research into Computer Science threshold concepts 'obtained interesting and opposite results to those of Shinners-Kennedy and Fincher' (2013). Their approach was to involve students (about 60) as well as their teachers (about 20) from Computer Science. The student task, digital paper-and-pencil, was presented at the end of the BSc programme as a compulsory reflection assignment. The threshold concept was explained, including the characteristics drawn from Meyer and Land's (2006) original characterisation and with some non-Computer-Science examples. Students were asked for examples from their experience and to indicate the applicability of the characteristics. Preliminary results were that almost all students explained 1 to 3 concepts and declared the characteristics applicable most of the times. So, at least, in the view of these authors, the threshold concept has proved to be fruitful to stimulate reflection by students. They used the list of 27 computer science threshold concepts from Shinners-Kennedy and Fincher (2013) for comparison. Their results showed much more variety compared to this list. Only 50% of the time concepts were mentioned that were on Shinners-Kennedy and Fincher's list, with 'object orientation' most frequent (15%). Outside the latter list 'logics' was most frequent (10%). The Dutch team state that they will seek an explanation by analysing the differences between Computer Science curricula. Another aspect for further investigation is the variation in specificity level in the threshold examples. They also plan to show the teachers the student task and ask them for concepts they think the students mentioned. This team also eschew Shinner and Fincher's expressed preference for the use of Shulman's pedagogical content knowledge (PCK) to construct individual teacher's concept representations (CoRe's). PCK is defined by Shulman (1986) as that expertise that allows experienced teachers to effectively represent the subject to their students; it is the special amalgam between general and specific pedagogical knowledge and content knowledge. The Dutch team, however, point out that their experience with PCK and construction of CoRe's with groups of teachers (Saeli et al., 2012) leads them to the conclusion that this is an interesting research method, uncovering many aspects of teaching within a discipline, but time-consuming if only directed at the threshold phenomenon. Moreover, focusing on teachers as a source gives only indirect information.

In the practice of Law *Marianne Dickie* and *Ilona Van Galen* (Chapter 21) sought to redesign their existing programme of legal education into an online mode that would involve new ways of teaching which moved beyond the lecture room and tutorial to asynchronous discussion forums and podcasts. Though they had carefully sought to provide a space for a community of learning based on the community of inquiry model (Garrison et al., 2001), they had not anticipated the prevailing perceptions and expectations that their law students entertained in relation to studying online. Assumptions were held that online study was informal, would be self-paced, and equalled a small time commitment. Students expected that they would not need to participate regularly and interpreted 'asynchronous' learning as meaning that teachers were always available. It was expected, further, that normal university policy and rules would not apply, and that online study could not include a practical component. Because of these perceptions students found it hard to engage with complex legal theoretical and practical work within the required time constraints. Whilst the providing team attempted to rectify any impediments to engagement, they initially believed the problem was predominantly one-sided, with feedback indicating that students did not 'consider themselves to be postgraduate law students'. This consideration inevitably impacted on their ability to grasp essential concepts needed to complete the course successfully. A review of the team's approach, however, found that what they had considered to be a threshold concept for students was in fact caught up in a threshold problem they were facing themselves as both designers and academics. 'We realised that in order to create an online learning community, we needed to embrace aspects of traditional campus life and infuse these into the course design. This ground breaking realisation radically altered our site design and curriculum. The very nature of online learning required us to become architects of the environment in which our students learnt'. They subsequently transformed their thinking, utilising architectural and communication principles to reinvent physical spaces in a virtual world, and treating the electronic interface as both a campus and a workplace that students must enter and navigate in order to engage with their learning experience. The way students 'see and understand their learning environment' is now one of the central pillars of their curriculum design. The team were brought to the McLuhanesque[6] realisation that 'Ultimately our commitment to achieving positive student outcomes led us to the troubling, transformative, integrative and irreversible realisation that, for online study, the medium also matters'.

The Scholarship of Teaching and Learning (SoTL) is an important international movement, which contributes to the quality of teaching and learning in higher education, as well as to a growing body of educational literature (Hubball, Pearson, & Clarke, 2013). With a focus on student learning in diverse educational contexts, SoTL encompasses a broad set of practices that engage educational leaders in examining curriculum and pedagogy in a methodical and rigorous way (Hutchings, Huber, & Ciccone, 2011). In Chapter 22 *Andrea Webb* argues that by providing a literature-informed, peer-reviewed justification for programme and policy changes, SoTL offers 'a practical and complementary undergirding for research in teaching and learning'. However, she adds, many institutions lack internal SoTL expertise to effectively develop and evaluate curriculum and pedagogical practices and consequently there is a need for better and more integrated theoretical work in designing SoTL programs (Kandlbinder & Peseta, 2009). Recent studies illustrate that threshold concepts have proved useful for initiating cross-disciplinary discourses (Carmichael, 2010); acting as a starting place for curriculum making (Carmichael, 2012). The ultimate purpose of her chapter is to identify the threshold concepts in SoTL in order to facilitate the adoption and widespread use of SoTL by faculty members in diverse contexts. She draws on the theorisation in threshold concepts in the seminal Meyer and Land papers (2003; 2005; 2006) 'as a lens with which to investigate SoTL and as a frame to consider curriculum for SoTL programs'. Focusing on the 'stuck places' in SoTL programs, her research considers the experience of faculty members previously and currently enrolled in a SoTL program at a research-intensive university in Canada. Semi-structured responsive interviews were conducted with 14 current SoTL program members and 20 past graduates to explore their experience of learning the ways of thinking and practising SoTL. These interviews revealed a variety of troublesome concepts and coping strategies to navigate the liminal space. Participants noted the challenging epistemic shift required when designing and conducting SoTL research in an educational frame. Most of the interviewees expressed that participation in the SoTL programme transformed their understanding of teaching and learning in higher education. She concludes that given the potential institutional benefits afforded by the adoption of SoTL for pedagogical and curricular investigations, an understanding of SoTL that includes threshold concepts will help to facilitate the requisite cultural shift within departments and institutions. 'The troublesome nature of threshold concepts in SoTL provokes the uncomfortable, liminal spaces that are a necessary feature of learning to do SoTL. It will push the educational research in higher education into a new place for both faculty and students'.

Also within the practice of teaching, *David Moroney, Eugene McKendry* and *Ann Devitt* (Chapter 23) present a study of pre-service and practising language teachers in the Republic of Ireland, within the Threshold Concepts Framework (Land et al., 2010), to explore the core but troublesome knowledge and practices of language teaching and the conditions that facilitate the integration and implementation of these concepts over a teaching career. Their project draws on previous work on threshold concepts in teacher education (Devitt et al., 2014) and considers the interplay of knowledge, belief and practice at initial teacher education, and beyond, for language teachers. The Threshold Concepts Framework, they suggest, holds the promise of providing a new lens through which to explore the notion of teacher cognition, defined by Borg (2006, p. 1) as "what teachers think, know and believe". The potential of threshold concepts as catalysts in the restructuring of not only learners' knowledge systems but also their beliefs and even identity, they argue, resonates with a model of teacher knowledge which encompasses dimensions of thought from experiential to theoretical knowledge and personal belief to objective 'truths' (Woods & Çakir, 2011). This qualitative case study had an initial exploratory phase with eight practising language teachers in Ireland to identify threshold concepts underlying good language teaching. A follow-on study consulted pre-service language teachers to explore their experience of identified TCs as part of their initial teacher education programme.

Phase 1 found, from the perspective of professionals in the field, that facilitating meaningful language use in the classroom and fostering learner autonomy are the key elements underlying good language teaching. This essential knowledge is often expressed as a belief system, one which is in place since initial teacher education or participants' language learning history. However, the degree to which teachers can teach in accordance with these beliefs is expressed as contingent upon local and broader policy contextual factors. Preliminary analysis of the blogs suggest that while the student teachers are primarily focused on more technical aspects of teaching, such as planning and classroom management, these aspects are oriented towards core principles of language teaching, such as bringing real language use into the classroom by using the target language. Participants also expressed a tension between knowledge and beliefs about teaching and their ability to teach in accordance with these beliefs, through a lack of skills in this case rather than contextual factors. This tension appears to contribute to a sense of *impostorship* (Brookfield, 2006) where they report that they do not feel like a teacher as their practice is behind their state of knowledge and their beliefs.

Architecture is a highly interdisciplinary field. At its base is the need to deal with complexity; to oscillate between details and 'the big picture', and to move across discipline borders in search of patterns and intersections. In the concluding chapter of this volume (Chapter 24) a research team from Trondheim in Norway, *Leif Martin Hokstad, Gro Rødne, Bjørn Otto Braaten, Steffen Wellinger* and *Fredrik Shetelig*, discuss the TRANSark project, a proposal to rethink architecture with a threshold concept-centred methodology for curriculum (re)design for the education of architects. In architecture leading voices have called for a 'big rethink' to develop new ways of thinking and practising in the discipline, and also in the education of future architects (Buchanan, 2012). Among the challenges for the education of architects is now to prepare students for multiple frameworks and competing values, ill-defined problems and open-ended situations (Barnett, 2000). Architecture is a knowledge domain where aesthetic, tactile experience is crucial, and creative practice is a way of thinking and a way of understanding. These perspectives align well with the Threshold Concepts Framework, and it has been suggested that architecture engages with liminality, being the threshold between 'old' paradigms and values and the 'new' which are as yet not clear (Meyer & Land, 2005). It requires a period of indeterminacy prior to the crossing of the threshold (Cousin, 2006). The educational trajectory of TRANSark is organised into four components. *Making is Thinking* acknowledges that architecture belongs to the 'making disciplines' (Pallasma, 2009) and the connection between mind and body. Students undergo an embodied experience by working in full scale from the very beginning of their study. *Live Studios*, a PBL-based methodology, is designed to challenge the students, bring them out of the academy into real-world situations that enable them to gain insights, skills and understandings that cannot easily be academically 'taught'. *Complexity and Change* assumes that the overall context of design and building processes is continually changing and developing into ever higher levels of complexity. The Integral Approach provides a possible map and a method (Integral Methodological Pluralism) that can be used as a tool of orientation in complex matters (Wilber, 2007). The components listed above challenge the learners considerably and position them in a daunting liminal phase that is necessary to grasp the 'underlying game' (Perkins, 2006). TRANSark frames these challenges of redesign within the lens of the fourth component, the *Threshold Concepts Framework*, and focuses on how liminality is expressed and experienced among students, how patterns and integration may be made possible for them, and how 'the underlying game' can be rendered accessible.

CONCLUSION

As with previous volumes in this series on threshold concepts, we sincerely hope that the chapters that follow will convey something of the commitment, passion and engagement that characterised our time together at the Durham conference, where colleagues from around the world first presented these ideas and opened them to debate and critique. It is encouraging to see the uptake of the Threshold Concepts Framework in many areas of practice, and in an increasing number of institutions and countries. The continually burgeoning repository of material in the splendid Flanagan archive (Flanagan, 2016) closely monitors migration into new sectors and fields. We owe a debt of gratitude, as always, to the many authors included in this volume, and to the generosity of their colleagues and students in contributing their time, thoughts and feelings to an exploration of learning thresholds in a common endeavour to gain better insights into student learning and conceptual difficulty.

As we go to press with this volume plans are already well under way for a sixth international Thresholds Concepts conference, entitled *Thresholds on the Edge*, to be held at Dalhousie University in Halifax, Nova Scotia from June 15–17, 2016. We look forward with great anticipation to further engagement around this continually intriguing theme, to renewing discussions with old friends and embarking on future explorations with new ones.

NOTES

[1] Einstein, A. cited by Wheeler, J.A., interviewed in *Cosmic Search*, Vol. 1, No. 4 (Fall 1979). (Wheeler does not indicate in the interview whether he is quoting Einstein verbatim, or offering his own description of how Einstein worked).
[2] There is an amusing anecdotal account of the inception of Threshold Concepts in Meyer, J. (2014) *Foreword to the Waikato Journal of Education Special Edition: Emergent learning and threshold concepts in tertiary education*, Waikato Journal of Education (Te Hautaka Mātauranga o Waikato), Special Edition: Emergent learning and threshold concepts in tertiary education, *19*(2), 5–6 http://www.wje.org.nz/index.php/WJE/article/view/94
[3] EU Cordis project and partners http://cordis.europa.eu/search/index.cfm?fuseaction=proj.document& PJ_RCN=10389771
[4] American Libraries Association (ALA) Framework for Information Literacy for Higher Education http://www.ala.org/acrl/standards/ilframework
[5] TRANSark (Transforming Architecture), Norway. http://www.ntnu.edu/transark
[6] Marshall McLuhan (1964) *Understanding Media: The Extensions of Man*; 1st Ed. McGraw Hill, NY; reissued by MIT Press, 1994. This text contains McLuhan's often-quoted phrase that 'the medium is the message'.

REFERENCES

Atherton, J. (2012). *Liminality as liability*. Paper presented at the 4th Interntional Biennial Threshold Concepts Conference, Trinity College, Dublin.
Ax, S., & Kincade, E. (2001). Nursing students' perceptions of research: Usefulness, implementation and training. *Journal of Advanced Nursing, 35*(2), 161–170.
Barnett, R. (2000). *Realising the university in an age of supercomplexity*. Buckingham: Society for Research into Higher Education & Open University Press.
Bhabha, H. K. (1994). *The location of culture*. London & New York, NY: Routledge.
Biggs, J. B., & Collis, K. F. (1982). *Evaluating the quality of learning: The SOLO taxonomy*. New York, NY: Academic press.
Borg, S. (2006). *Teacher cognition and language education: Research and practice*. Norfolk, VA: Continuum.
Brookfield, S. (2006). *The skilful teacher: On technique, trust, and responsiveness in the classroom*. San Francisco, CA: Jossey-Bass.
Buchanan, P. (2011–2012). *The big rethink*. 12 Essays. Retrieved from http://www.architecturalreview.com/home/the-big-rethink
Cannon, W. B. (1929). *Body changes in pain, hunger, fear and rage*. New York, NY: AppletonCentury Crofts.
Carmichael, P. (2010). Threshold concepts, disciplinary differences and cross-disciplinary discourse. *Learning and Teaching in Higher Education: Gulf Perspectives, 7*(2), 53–71.
Carmichael, P. (2012, June 28–29). *From this curriculum to that which is to come*. NAIRTL Conference 2012, Trinity College Dublin. Retrieved July 10, 2013, from www.nairtl.ie/index.php?pageID=634

Carstensen, A.-K., & Bernhard, J. (2008). Threshold concepts and keys to the portal of understanding: Some examples from electrical engineering. In R. Land, J. H. F. Meyer, & J. Smith (Eds.), *Threshold concepts within the disciplines* (pp. 143–154). Rotterdam, The Netherlands: Sense Publishers.

Cousin, G. (2006, December). An introduction to threshold concepts. *Planet* [online], *17*, 4–5. Retrieved June 17, 2012, from http://www.gees.ac.uk/planet/p17/gc.pdf

Cousin, G. (2009). *Researching learning in higher education.* New York, NY: Routledge. (Chapter 12)

Cousin, G. (2010). Neither teacher-centred nor student-centred: Threshold concepts and research partnerships. *Journal of Learning Development in Higher Education, 2*, 1–9.

Devitt, A., Kerin, M., & O'Sullivan, H. (2014). Threshold concepts and practices in teacher education: Professional, educator and student perspectives. In *Threshold concepts: From personal practice to communities of practice* (pp. 129–133). Cork: NAIRTL.

Dewey, J. (1991 edition, originally published 1929). *How we think: A restatement of the relation of reflective thinking to the educative process.* Amherst, NY: Prometheus Books.

Ecclestone, K. (2012). Instrumentalism and achievement: A socio-cultural understadning of tensions in vocational education. In J. Gardner (Ed.), *Assessment and learning* (2nd ed.). London: Sage Publications.

Einstein, A. cited by Wheeler, J. A., interviewed in *Cosmic Search*, Vol. 1, No. 4 (Fall 1979). (Wheeler does not indicate in the interview whether he is quoting Einstein verbatim, or offering his own description of how Einstein worked).

Entwistle, N., Hamilton, A., Kelly, R., Nisbet, J., Chapman, R., Hayward, G., & Gachagan, T. (2005). Teaching and learning analogue electronics in undergraduate courses: Preliminary findings from the ETL project. *International Journal of Electrical Engineering Education, 42*(1), 8–20.

Flanagan, M. (2016). *Threshold concepts: Undergraduate teaching, postgraduate training and professional development: A short introduction and bibliography.* London: UCL. Retrieved from http://www.ee.ucl.ac.uk/~mflanaga/thresholds.html

Flanagan, M. T., & Smith, J. (2008). From playing to understanding: The transformative potential of discourse versus syntax in learning to program. In R. Land, J. H. F. Meyer, & J. Smith (Eds.), *Threshold concepts within the disciplines* (pp. 91–104). Rotterdam, The Netherlands: Sense Publishers.

Garrison, D. R., Anderson, T., & Archer, W. (2001). Critical thinking, cognitive presence, and computer conferencing in distance education. *American Journal of Distance Education, 15*(1), 7–23.

Grasso, M., Barry, M., & Valentine, T. (2009). *A data-driven approach to improving doctoral completion* (Occasional Paper). Washington, DC: Council of Graduate Schools.

Hubball, H. T., Pearson, M., & Clarke, A. (2013). SoTL inquiry in broader curricula and institutional contexts: theoretical underpinnings and emerging trends. Invited Peer-reviewed Essay for inaugural issue. *International Journal for Inquiry in Teaching and Learning, 1*(1), 41–57.

Hutchings, P., Huber, M. T., & Ciccone, A. (2011). *The scholarship of teaching and learning reconsidered: Institutional integration and impact.* San Francisco, CA: Jossey-Bass.

Kandlbinder, P., & Peseta, T. (2009). Key concepts in postgraduate certificates in higher education teaching and learning in Australasia and the United Kingdom. *International Journal for Academic Development, 14*(1), 19–31.

Kiley, M. (2009). Identifying threshold concepts and proposing strategies to support doctoral candidates. *Innovations in Education and Teaching International, 46*(3), 293–304.

Knight, D. B., Callaghan, D. C., Baldock, T., & Meyer, J. H. F. (2013a). Identifying threshold concepts: Case study of an open catchment hydraulics course. *European Journal of Engineering Education, 39*(2), 125–142. Retrieved from http://dx.doi.org/10.1080/03043797.2013.833175

Knight, D. B., Meyer, J. H. F., Baldock, T. E., Callaghan, D. P., & McCredden, J. (2013b, December 8–11). *Embedding metacognitive exercises in the curriculum to boost students' conceptual understanding.* AAEE Conference proc., Gold Coast, Australia. Retrieved from http://www.engineersaustralia.org.au/australasian-association-engineering-education/2013-annual-conference

Kuhn, T. S. (1996). *The structure of scientific revolutions* (3rd ed.). Chicago, IL: University of Chicago Press.

Land, R., Meyer, J. H. F., & Baillie, C. (2010). Threshold concepts and transformational learning. Rotterdam, Boston & Taipei: Sense Publishers.

Luthans, F., Avolio, B. J., Avey, J. B., & Norman, S. M. (2007). Positive psychological capital: Measurement and relationship with performance and satisfaction. *Personnel Psychology, 60,* 541–572.

Marton, F., & Tsui, A. B. M. (Eds.). (2004). *Classroom discourse and the space of learning.* Mahwah, NJ: Lawrence Erlbaum.

McLeod, J. (2000). *Beginning postcolonialism.* Manchester: Manchester University Press.

Meyer, J. H. F. (2010). Helping our students: Learning, metalearning, and threshold concepts. In J. Christensen Hughes & J. Mighty (Eds.), *Taking stock: Research on teaching and learning in higher education* (pp. 191–213). Montreal & Kingston: McGill-Queen's University Press.

Meyer, J. H. F. (2012). 'Variation in student learning' as a threshold concept. *The Journal of Faculty Development, 26*(3), 8–13.

Meyer, J. H. F., & Land, R. (2003). Threshold concepts and troublesome knowledge: Linkages to ways of thinking and practising within the disciplines. In C. Rust (Ed.), *Improving student learning: Improving student learning theory and practice–Ten years on.* Oxford: Oxford Centre for Staff and Learning Development.

Meyer, J. H. F., & Land, R. (2005). Threshold concepts and troublesome knowledge (2): Epistemological considerations and a conceptual framework for teaching and learning. *Higher Education, 49,* 373–388.

Meyer, J. H. F., & Land, R. (2006). Threshold concepts and troublesome knowledge: An introduction. In J. H. F. Meyer & R. Land (Eds.), *Overcoming barriers to student understanding: Threshold concepts and troublesome knowledge* (pp. 3–18). London: Routledge Falmer.

Meyer, J. H. F., Ward, S. C., & Latreille, P. (2009). Threshold concepts and metalearning capacity. *International Review of Economics Education, 8*(1), 132–154.

Meyer, J. H. F., Knight, D., Baldock, T., Kizil, M., O'Moore, L., & Callaghan, D. (2012). *Scoping metalearning opportunity in the first three years of engineering.* Proceedings of the 23rd annual conference of the Australasian Association of Engineering Education, Melbourne. Retrieved April 2, 2013, from http://www.aaee.com.au/conferences/2012/documents/AAEE-Conference-proceedings-2012.pdf

Mezirow, J. (1991). *Transformative dimensions of adult learning.* San Francisco, CA: Jossey-Bass.

Middendorf, J., & Pace, D. (2004). Decoding the disciplines: Helping students learn disciplinary ways of thinking in new directions in teaching and learning. In *New directions in teaching and learning series* (Vol. 98). San Francisco, CA: Jossey-Bass.

Nolan, M. (2005). The emergence of global stability in local interaction in a consulting practice. In R. Stacey (Ed.), *Experiencing emergence in organizations. Local interaction and the emergence of global pattern.* New York, NY: Routledge.

Pallasmaa, J. (2009). *The thinking hand.* Southern Gate: Wiley.

Perkins, D. (1999). The many faces of constructivism. *Educational Leadership, 57,* 6–11.

Perkins, D. (2000). *Minding the gap.* Presentation to the ESRC Enhancing Teaching-Learning Environments (ETL) Project, Edinburgh University, Edinburgh.

Perkins, D. (2006). Constructivism and troublesome knowledge. In J. H. F. Meyer & R. Land (Eds.), *Overcoming barriers to student understanding: Threshold concepts and troublesome knowledge.* Abingdon: Routledge.

Roy, R. (1979). Interdisciplinary science on campus: The elusive dream. In J. J. Kockelmans (Ed.), *Interdisciplinarity in higher education* (pp. 161–196). University Park, PA: Pennsylvania State University Press.

Saeli, M., Perrenet, J. C., Jochems, W. M. G., & Zwaneveld, B. (2012). Programming: Teachers and pedagogical content knowledge in the Netherlands. *Informatics in Education, 11*(1), 81–114.

Schwartzman, L. (2010). Transcending disciplinary boundaries: A proposed theoretical foundation for threshold concepts. In J. H. F. Meyer, R. Land, & C. Baillie (Eds.), *Threshold concepts and transformational learning* (pp. 21–44). Rotterdam, Boston and Taipei: Sense Publishers.

Sherlock, R. (2015, November 28). How political correctness rules in America's student 'safe spaces'. *The Telegraph.* Retrieved from http://www.telegraph.co.uk/news/worldnews/northamerica/usa/12022041/How-political-correctness-rules-in-Americas-student-safe-spaces.html

Shinners-Kennedy, D., & Fincher, S. A. (2013). Identifying threshold concepts: From dead end to a new direction. In *Proceedings of the ninth annual international ACM conference on International computing education research* (pp. 9–18). ACM. Retrieved from http://www.telegraph.co.uk/news/worldnews/northamerica/usa/12022041/How-political-correctness-rules-in-Americas-student-safe-spaces.html

Shulman, L. (1986). Those who understand: Knowledge growth in teaching. *Educational Researcher, 15*, 4–14.

Shulman, L. (2005). Pedagogies of uncertainty. *Liberal Education, 91*(2), 18–25.

Taylor, C. (2006). Threshold concepts in biology: Do they fit the definition? In J. H. F. Meyer & R. Land (Eds.), *Overcoming barriers to student understanding: Threshold concepts and troublesome knowledge*. Abingdon: Routledge.

Tiberghien, A., Vince, J., & Gaidioz, P. (2009). Design-based research: Case of a teaching sequence on mechanics. *International Journal of Science Education, 31*(17), 2275–2314.

Wilber, K. (2007). *Integral vision* (pp. 347–363). Boston, MA: Shambahala Publications Inc.

Woods, D., & Çakir, H. (2011). Two dimensions of teacher knowledge: The case of communicative language teaching. *System, 39*, 381–390.

ACKNOWLEDGMENTS

The editors of this volume would like to express their thanks to Peter de Liefde at Sense Publishers and Michael Peters (series editor) for their support and encouragement in the production of this volume. They would also like to express their appreciation to Jolanda Karada, Production Coordinator at Sense, and Jane Read of Read Indexing, for their professional expertise and careful attention to detail.

PART 1

THEORETICAL DIRECTIONS

PETER FELTEN

1. ON THE THRESHOLD WITH STUDENTS

INTRODUCTION

The idea of threshold concepts emerged from and has evolved through communities of scholarly teachers and researchers talking with each other about disciplinary learning. In this chapter, I will approach thresholds from a different angle. Drawing on threshold concept seminars that I conducted with undergraduate students at three US colleges, this chapter considers what we might understand about threshold concepts if we partnered with students to explore the nature of thresholds and learning in higher education.

PARTNERING WITH STUDENTS

While the literature on threshold concepts has mushroomed over the past decade, undergraduate student voices have largely been absent from this conversation. Questions about student learning, of course, are at the heart of the threshold concept framework. However, students are much more likely to appear as objects of study than as partners in these inquiries.

In 2012–2013, I co-facilitated a pair of semester-long seminars on threshold concepts with undergraduate students at Bryn Mawr and Haverford Colleges, two highly selective liberal arts institutions in suburban Philadelphia, Pennsylvania. The following year, I co-facilitated a similar seminar at Elon University, a mid-sized liberal arts institution in North Carolina. Each seminar included between eight and fifteen undergraduate students. The seminar began with students reading foundational literature such as Meyer and Land's (2006a) chapter 'Threshold concepts and troublesome knowledge: An introduction'. After thoroughly discussing this literature, students spent the remainder of the seminar's meetings reflecting on their own experiences with threshold concepts in higher education. For instance, students wrote about times when they had encountered particularly troublesome knowledge, and how the threshold concepts literature did (or did not) help them understand their own learning experiences. These reflections prompted spirited discussions about the nature of troublesome knowledge, threshold concepts, and learning in higher education. Questions about affect, liminality, confidence, and disciplinarity emerged in all three seminars, and this chapter will reflect on these four themes.

R. Land et al. (Eds.), Threshold Concepts in Practice, 3–9.
© *2016 Sense Publishers. All rights reserved.*

My analysis here represents a synthesis of my experience with students in these seminars. I am able to cite some of the seminar students because a handful have written about their perspectives for a special issue of the journal Teaching and Learning Together in Higher Education (Felten, 2013). The remainder of my claims here are based on my own notes from the seminars, which unfortunately do not allow me to credit individual students by name. Because my reflections emerge from seminar discussions and writings, I cannot make grand claims about either undergraduate learning or threshold concepts. Everything I offer here is provisional. I hope to provoke and suggest, not to prove and conclude. And I am deeply grateful to the students and colleagues, particularly Alison Cook-Sather of Bryn Mawr and Jessie Moore and Greg Honan of Elon, who joined me in these seminars.

TROUBLESOME AFFECT

From the beginning, David Perkins' framework of 'troublesome knowledge' has been a central facet of threshold concepts theory (Meyer & Land, 2003). According to Perkins, knowledge can be troublesome because it is conceptually difficult, alien, inert, tacit, or ritual (2006). Some scholars have raised questions about this framework, such as McCormick's commentary on how 'students' everyday worlds' intersect with disciplinary concepts (2008, p. 55), and Meyer and Land's reflections on the variation in student experiences with troublesome knowledge in the academy (Meyer & Land, 2006a). Still, Perkins' definition of troublesome knowledge is a defining feature of threshold concepts.

Students' reflections on troublesome knowledge, however, suggest that this framework is missing at least one essential element. When seminar students wrote about their own experiences with threshold concepts, they universally described their learning as troublesome, but some of the most frequent words they used did not fit neatly into Perkins' categories. Students often described their own learning process as 'stressful,' 'debilitating,' 'frustrating,' and 'intensely emotional'. They reported that they were 'shocked,' 'upset,' 'hopeless,' and 'very anxious' .Sophia Abbot, a Bryn Mawr undergraduate, captured this common sentiment when she reflected on a pivotal moment in her learning: 'After class, I was not sure whether I wanted to cry or scream. I did not know how to face the privileged existence I have had, and I felt utterly helpless in terms of how to move forward' (2013). In fact, students in all three seminars consistently used at least some emotional language to explain their encounter with troublesome knowledge.

The difference between scholars and students in this case seems to be one of perspective. Perkins and other researchers focus on characteristics of the knowledge itself that is troublesome. In other words, certain knowledge is alien or tacit, making it challenging to learn no matter who is doing the learning. Students in the seminars, on the other hand, describe their experience with the knowledge, focusing as much on the person doing the learning as the thing being learned. In this way, students echoed the analysis of Blackie, Case, and Jawitz:

If we are to take the idea of the person of the student seriously, we need to begin to pay attention to the emotional side of education. Knowledge may be emotionally neutral. There is no obvious emotional content to the concept of chemical bonding, for example. However, the manner in which an individual interacts with knowledge is emotionally charged. (2010, p. 641)

Questions of 'troublesome affect' seem to be a particularly important area for further investigation for scholars of threshold concepts. A few researchers already have begun to open this door. For instance, Leah Shopkow's study of threshold concepts in the discipline of history suggests that 'affective issues' such as 'maintaining emotional distance' and 'dealing with ambiguity' are frequent bottlenecks for student learning (2010, p. 328). Exploring this emotional terrain would return threshold concepts to an early claim by its founders that too often higher education scholars and teachers tend 'towards the disembodiment and genericisation of the learner, and an assumed lack of an affective and social dimension to their subjectivity' (Meyer & Land, 2006b, p. 31). As the seminar students remind us, we would be wise to recognise that both knowledge and affect can be troublesome.

LOCATING LIMINALITY

As the word 'threshold' suggests, this framework presumes learning is a dynamic experience that moves a student from one state to another. During this passage, the student is in a liminal position that exists 'betwixt and between' established categories, such as novice or expert (Turner, 1964). While a student is in this 'liquid space' the potential for learning, experimentation, and growth are maximized; Meyer and Land call liminality a 'transformational state' (Meyer & Land, 2005, p. 380).

Students in the seminars resonated with the concept of liminality. Many of them described their own powerful learning experiences as rites of passage as they moved, often awkwardly and unexpectedly, from 'before' to 'after' a threshold. Yet the stories of these transitions rarely centred on a discipline or a classroom. The undergraduate curriculum, students insisted, privileges having the correct answers and demonstrating competency, rather than asking questions and exploring ambiguity. In the words of Bryn Mawr student Sarah Jenness, 'student anxiety is raised in [the classroom], though, because it is not only about knowing the right answer, but also wondering what the professor expects and what students need to know to do well in the class. In other words…school militates against uncertainty' (2013).

This common student perspective presents a significant barrier to considering the classroom a liminal space. Not only is nearly any threshold concept affectively and cognitively troublesome, which may lead students (and other humans) to approach it cautiously, but the classroom as a site of liminality may seem to be contrary to what school is all about. Throughout their schooling students have been trained to look for answers and have been rewarded for being right. Why risk liminality in the classroom when certainty feels both personally and academically safer?

Scholars of threshold concepts should confront that question directly. Students may be deliberately not crossing thresholds in a classroom or a discipline because their prior educational experiences have taught them to value being correct and concrete. To persuade students to willingly enter a liminal space, they need to understand the value of doing so – not only in an abstract way ('This uncertainty is essential for you to learn something important') but also in a pragmatic way ('Stepping into this liminal space will be rewarding for you academically'). Students often do not come to higher education looking for or appreciating liminality in the classroom.

THRESHOLD CONFIDENCE

After hearing a number of peers recount stories of their own encounters with threshold concepts, one student seminar participant observed: 'One thing that I have noticed is that threshold concepts are not just about knowledge, they also are about confidence'.

Reflecting on their own encounters with threshold concepts, many seminar students noted that their learning could not be disentangled from their sense of confidence related to that learning. Because threshold concepts are difficult to master, because they are troublesome, the learning process is characterised by struggle and difficulty. Haverford College professor Laura McGrane describes her students' narratives of threshold concepts as an experience with 'punctuated equilibrium – we climb, we plateau, we slip, we plateau, we climb again' (2013). McGrane's student Ryan Rebel wrote:

> I've often felt like I've been faking a certain discipline until that mysterious ethereal retrospective moment when I realise I have crossed the threshold and am actually doing it. But is there any threshold after all? Is there only a continuous scale of less and less and less faking until you're the person in the world who is faking the least and so nobody can call you on it anymore? That's kind of depressing. Or liberating, maybe. (quoted in McGrane, 2013)

Repeatedly in the seminar, students (like Rebel) emphasised that crossing a threshold involved both mastering the concept and also feeling comfortable in their new knowledge. This common student perspective echoes research by Terrell Strayhorn on the importance of an undergraduate 'sense of belonging' for learning in college (2012). Strayhorn defines belonging as 'the experience of mattering or feeling cared about, accepted, respected, valued by, and important to the group' (2012, p. 3). To permanently cross a threshold, seminar students insisted, they needed to believe that they belonged on the other side.

DISCIPLINING THRESHOLDS

Meyer and Land take as a given that threshold concepts are disciplinary. Many seminar students, however, expressed a more capacious view. Esteniolla Maitre, for instance, initially found the Meyer and Land framework appealing, but as she and her peers talked further, she 'began to dislike the definition – not because of its inaccuracy but because of its limitation. It became clear that while threshold concepts were explored in the classroom, the crossing of such thresholds seemed confined to and rooted in the classroom as well' (2013).

In all three seminars, students expanded the definition of threshold concepts to including learning that reached across or beyond academic disciplines. One student perceptively noted that faculty may locate thresholds within particular disciplines because, as experts, they are deeply embedded within a field:

> Something I noticed about how the conversation ended up was that a lot of the professors ended up going back to their own discipline. That felt different [from what students in this seminar are saying]. We all do have our own majors and interests but I don't think we bring disciplines up to the extent that they do. It's probably because they've spent years in their discipline and we are still discovering our own and still very much in an inter-disciplinary mindset. So it's interesting to see that they think threshold concepts are different by discipline. (personal notes, 2013)

Students, as seminar participant Hannah Bahn wrote, wanted to explore 'what threshold concepts could be' (2013). This nearly always involved using the threshold concept framework as a tool, a heuristic, to consider learning that reached beyond individual disciplines – what one student called 'non-academic learning'. Indeed, students in the seminars found the threshold concepts so useful as a tool for reflecting on their own learning that they resisted bounding it within disciplines. Esteniolla Maitre argued that 'Failure to account for a more holistic definition of a threshold concept—and, ultimately, learning—threatens to perpetuate a classroom environment where there are discrepancies among students because of their failure to understand versus a failure to understand them' (2013).

ON THE THRESHOLD WITH STUDENTS

The perspectives of students in three seminars likely will not (and should not) reframe the literature on threshold concepts. Still, scholars and teachers should take seriously the experiences and insights of students as learners (Cook-Sather et al., 2014; Healey et al., 2014).

My experiences with student seminars on threshold concepts suggest that higher education teachers and scholars would do well to more carefully attend to:

- the affective experiences of learning;
- the classroom and curriculum as troublesome sites for liminality;
- the sense of confidence and belonging necessary for crossing thresholds;
- the disciplinary and the trans-disciplinary nature of thresholds in learning.

Inviting students to partner with us in our research and practice would be a major step toward enhancing our understanding and teaching of threshold concepts. As a student told me in an interview nearly a decade ago, 'Faculty…are so focused on getting stuff done that they don't pay attention to their students, who I think are the most valuable assets [in a classroom]' (Mihans et al., 2008, p. 8).

REFERENCES

Abbot, S. (2013). Understanding privilege. *Teaching and Learning Together in Higher Education, 9*. Retrieved from http://teachingandlearningtogether.blogs.brynmawr.edu/archived-issues/ninth-issue-sprin-2013/understanding-privilege

Bahn, H. (2013). Why the process of learning matters: Expanding my own definition of threshold concepts. *Teaching and Learning Together in Higher Education, 9*. Retrieved from http://teachingandlearningtogether.blogs.brynmawr.edu/archived-issues/ninth-issue-sprin-2013/why-the-process-of-learning-matters-expanding-my-definition-of-threshold-concepts

Blackie, M. A. L., Case, J. M., & Jawitz, J. (2010). Student-centredness: The link between transforming students and transforming ourselves. *Teaching in Higher Education, 15*(6), 637–646.

Cook-Sather, A., Bovill, C., & Felten, P. (2014). *Engaging students as partners in learning and teaching: A guide for faculty*. San Francisco, CA: Jossey-Bass.

Felten, P. (2013). Introduction: Crossing thresholds together. *Teaching and Learning Together in Higher Education, 9*. Retrieved from http://teachingandlearningtogether.blogs.brynmawr.edu/archived-issues/ninth-issue-sprin-2013/introduction-crossing-thresholds-together

Healey, M., Flint, A., & Harrington, K. (2014). *Engagement through partnerships: Students a partners in learning and teaching in higher education*. Retrieved from https://www.heacademy.ac.uk/sites/default/files/resources/engagement_through_partnership.pdf

Jenness, S. (2013). Being comfortable with uncertainty. *Teaching and Learning Together in Higher Education, 9*. Retrieved from http://teachingandlearningtogether.blogs.brynmawr.edu/archived-issues/ninth-issue-sprin-2013/being-comfortable-with-uncertainty

Maitre, E. (2013). Expanding the definition of 'Threshold Concept'. *Teaching and Learning Together in Higher Education, 9*. Retrieved from https://teachingandlearningtogether.blogs.brynmawr.edu/archived-issues/ninth-issue-sprin-2013/expanding-the-definition-of-threshold-concept

McCormick, R. (2008). Threshold concepts and troublesome knowledge: Some reflections on the nature of learning and knowledge. In R. Land, J. H. F. Meyer, & J. Smith (Eds.), *Threshold concepts within the disciplines* (pp. 51–58). Rotterdam, The Netherlands: Sense Publishers.

McGrane, L. (2013). Topographies of knowing in 299B: Junior seminar. *Teaching and Learning Together in Higher Education, 9*. Retrieved from http://teachingandlearningtogether.blogs.brynmawr.edu/archived-issues/ninth-issue-sprin-2013/topographies-of-knowing-in-299b-junior-seminar

Meyer, J. H. F., & Land, R. (2005). Threshold concepts and troublesome knowledge (2): Epistemological considerations and a conceptual framework for teaching and learning. *Higher Education, 49*, 373–388.

Meyer, J. H. F., & Land, R. (2006a). Threshold concepts and troublesome knowledge: An introduction. In J. H. F. Meyer & R. Land (Eds.), *Overcoming barriers to student understanding: Threshold concepts and troublesome knowledge* (pp. 3–18). Abingdon & New York, NY: Routledge.

Meyer, J. H. F., & Land, R. (2006b). Threshold concepts and troublesome knowledge: Issues of liminality. In J. H. F. Meyer & R. Land (Eds.), *Overcoming barriers to student understanding: Threshold concepts and troublesome knowledge* (pp. 19–32). Abingdon & New York, NY: Routledge.

Mihans, R., Long, D., & Felten, P. (2008). Power and expertise: Student-faculty collaboration in course design and the scholarship of teaching and learning. *International Journal for the Scholarship of Teaching and Learning, 2*(2), 1–9. Retrieved from http://digitalcommons.georgiasouthern.edu/ij-sotl/vol2/iss2/16/

Perkins, D. (2006). Constructivism and troublesome knowledge. In J. H. F. Meyer & R. Land (Eds.), *Overcoming barriers to student understanding: Threshold concepts and troublesome knowledge* (pp. 33–47). Abingdon & New York, NY: Routledge.

Shopkow, L. (2010). What decoding the disciplines can offer threshold concepts. In J. H. F. Meyer, R. Land, & C. Baillie (Eds.), *Threshold concepts and transformational learning* (pp. 317–332). Rotterdam, The Netherlands: Sense Publishers.

Strayhorn, T. L. (2012). *College students' sense of belonging: A key to educational success for all students.* New York, NY: Routledge.

Turner, V. (1964). Betwixt and between: The liminal period in rites de passage. In *The Proceedings of the American Ethnological Society, Symposium on New Approaches to the Study of Religion* (pp. 4–20). Seattle, WA: University of Washington Press.

Peter Felten
Elon University

RAY LAND

2. TOIL AND TROUBLE

Threshold Concepts as a Pedagogy of Uncertainty

Break on through to the other side.
                    (Jim Morrison)[1]

INTRODUCTION

A powerful discursive shift has occurred within higher education globally over the last three decades in which higher education teaching is rendered as the facilitation of 'the student learning experience', and as a primarily economic rather than educational transaction (Apple, 2000). This corporatist, consumer discourse has arisen from intensified global competitiveness, and is creating tensions within traditional modes of organisation of teaching and learning. In this pervasive discourse the learner is constructed as a consumer of services, 'a situation in which the learner has certain needs and where it is the business of the educator to meet these needs' (Biesta, 2005).

Yet this increasingly influential view sits uneasily with the idea that universities serve to offer programmes of a transformative nature. Universities are required simultaneously to produce satisfied consumers as well as develop graduates for the wider society who can act and exercise judgment in complex, uncertain, risk-laden and unpredictable environments. The latter entail radically different forms of curriculum, student-staff relationships and student encounters. The former Director of the Carnegie Center for Teaching and Learning, Lee Shulman, emphasised this point when characterising the education of professionals:

> it's ... insufficient to claim that a combination of theory, practice, and ethics defines a professional's work; it is also characterized by conditions of inherent and unavoidable uncertainty. Professionals rarely can employ simple algorithms or protocols of practice in performing their services. How then does a professional adapt to new and uncertain circumstances? She exercises judgment. One might therefore say that professional education is about developing pedagogies to link ideas, practices, and values under conditions of inherent uncertainty that necessitate not only judgment in order to act, but also cognizance of the consequences of one's action. In the presence of uncertainty, one is obligated to learn from experience. (Shulman, 2005, p. 1)

R. Land et al. (Eds.), Threshold Concepts in Practice, 11–24.

Shulman is concerned with the complexity of professional practice, as is much of this volume. The Threshold Concepts Framework – with its emphasis on transformation through troublesome knowledge and shifts in subjectivity 'under conditions of inherent uncertainty' – shares many of the characteristics of what Shulman terms 'pedagogies of uncertainty'. It will be argued here, further, that the Threshold Concepts Framework can also serve as a counter-discourse to the commodification of learning.

LEARNING AS CONSUMPTION

The discursive shift under discussion has come about through a range of factors including the erosion of welfarism, and a move to a marketised notion of higher education as principally a private good. Learning increasingly gains prominence in policy documents as a far more individualistic activity (Field, 2000). To ensure consumer satisfaction, a consumer logic of value for money, accountability and the need for increasingly rigorous protocols and standards of inspection then ensues. The discourse of 'the student experience' becomes to a great extent an empty signifier which is difficult to argue against. It can, however, easily be deployed to place students and teaching staff in an oppositional stance, through the use, for example, of consumer satisfaction student surveys and module evaluation scores in which the student-as-consumer 'rates' the professor-as-service-provider. In public and marketing documentation the discourse becomes interwoven with narratives of excellence, images of graduate success and student happiness, a sense of student entitlement and the friendliness and helpfulness of (providing) staff. In its strongest rendition this representation can depict learning within the organisation as an undertaking that is non-problematic, without any significant incurring of risk. It does not entail deep personal change or transformation, troublesome challenge or even, at times, engagement.

In this way teaching to satisfaction ratings sets different parameters for what counts as education, and as quality. The discourse is antithetical to critical or transformative notions of pedagogy. In such climates, teaching, worryingly, can become risk-averse, formulaic and comfortable. Worst of all, learning is depicted as easy, non-problematic, without risk, requiring minimal commitment. As Jenkins and Barnes (2014) argue, students' pedagogic entitlement to transformation, hard work and challenge, confusion even – where liminality and uncertainty trigger different ways of thinking, different modes of knowledge and deep personal change – are curtailed. Teaching in higher education is increasingly rendered as the '*delivery*' of learning opportunities or experiences (Barber et al., 2011). A 'student experience', however defined – socially, culturally, aesthetically, as a particular lifestyle, or more prosaically perhaps in terms of services, quality of accommodation, technological environment and even catering – is more easily rendered as a commodity, and more open to marketisation. In a search for satisfaction and certainty, and in a flight to security, the language of transformation and innovation may be lost.

EDUCATION AS CONTRACT

Interestingly, in a response to a report from the consumer magazine *Which?* that had investigated universities' compliance with consumer law, the Chief Executive of Universities UK (UUK) pointed out that 'In relation to consumer protection law, it is important to recognise that the relationship that exists between a student and their university is *a distinctive relationship to do with learning and teaching, rather than a standard consumer contract*' (UUK, 2015) [Author italics].

This form of response from higher education sector representatives (of all persuasions) is often a positioning statement for negotiating with government, reminding the latter of their limited governance of the sector and the autonomous nature of universities. However, it points to a lack of clarity in, and the unresolved nature of, the contractual nature of what students might reasonably expect and be entitled to when entering a university programme of study. The high trust of the market inherent within a consumer model of learning will place emphasis on the *satisfaction* of the individual (student) consumer. The sector generally, however, appears uneasy with the idea of a straight seller-consumer relationship. Granted, it is clearly beneficial to have an easily understandable, straight-forward way of knowing what redress is available (under consumer law if necessary) when things go obviously wrong. For example, a specific course might be advertised as guaranteeing entry to an accelerated postgraduate course at a subsequent stage, and turn out not to. A doctoral programme might guarantee access to training facilities or teaching opportunities that, in the event, do not materialise. A module advertised at the time of enrolment may subsequently be withdrawn.

Since students started paying for their tuition increased attention has been paid to satisfying student expectation in relation to quite reasonable assumptions, through mechanisms such as the National Student Survey (NSS). This might monitor the extent of receiving useful feedback on coursework, reliably and on time, though practice in these respects remains still far from exemplary. The current UK government, like an increasing number of other similarly inclined educational administrations around the globe, is clearly interested in the value proposition of what higher education offers for substantial student tuition fees. This might be expressed through possible metrics such as contact hours, access to learning resources, availability of staff, staff-student ratios, retention and employability rates. Metrics are currently under consideration to measure 'learning gain' and 'value for money'. This value proposition is to be instated formally through legislation currently before the UK Parliament to establish a Teaching Excellence Framework which will monitor, quantify and measure educational quality. It will subsequently rank institutions as excellent, in return for proportional institutional eligibility to raise tuition fees in line with inflation. The legislation also includes measures to deregulate higher education and to intensify market competition through the accelerated entry of private 'new providers'.

The debate takes us directly to the heart of what we are attempting to achieve in university study. Is it entry to disciplinary or scientific communities? Skilled employees? Critical citizens? Fulfilled self-actualising individuals? Somewhat glib analogies occasionally surface contrasting gym membership with hotel service to emphasise the client-centred nature of higher education, and client obligation in regard to commitment, effort and engagement. Others see Argyris' (1960) notion of a 'psychological work contract' – existing as a tacit entity outside formal market relations unlike a legal consumer contract – as a more generative idea for higher education. Analogies take us so far, but the experience of higher education seems to remain resolutely multi-faceted, complex and individualised, difficult to reduce to contractual aspects. It would seem, rather, to be *sui generis*. A proper entity – itself, and not really like anything else. But whatever constitutes that entity, it would seem to involve transformation – distinctive alchemy that takes what students are, what they aspire to become, what transforming experiences the academy can offer, and infuses these elements into a process that remains difficult to define and which is not fully manifest until many years and experiences later.

LEARNING AS TRANSFORMATION

In contradistinction to the consumerist sentiment, the notion of learning as transformation offers a powerful alternative discourse. According to Mezirow, (1997, pp. 5–12) transformative learning is the learning that affirms autonomous thinking and helps us understand our experience. Freire (cited in Wolf, 2014, p. 1) reminds us that 'No one is born fully-formed' and that 'it is through self-experience in the world that we become what we are'. Proust (1900/1987) argues that the only real voyage of discovery consists not in seeing new landscapes, but 'in having new eyes, in seeing the universe with the eyes of another'. But as the now sizeable research literature on threshold concepts in many disciplines indicates (Flanagan, 2015), such transformation frequently entails difficulty. Dewey (1933/1986) points to the difficulty entailed in such transformation. 'The path of least resistance and least trouble is a mental rut already made. It requires troublesome work to undertake the alteration of old beliefs'. The renowned economist Keynes (1936/1973, p. xxiii) suggests that this difficulty lies in the letting go of prevailing belief: 'The difficulty lies, not in the new ideas, but in escaping from the old ones, which ramify … into every corner of our minds'. And the novelist Pam Barker reminds us (Barker, 1991, p. 184) that the process of transformation consists 'almost entirely of decay'. The process of transformation is often triggered through encountering dissonance. The cognitive psychological and biological literature suggests 'to promote development, phenomena must somehow be troublesome enough, inharmonious enough for existing structures, to disturb balance and lead the organism to actively respond' (Timmermans, 2010, p. 10). Of course this can be uncomfortable for both the student and the teacher. As bell hooks (1994, p. 206) observed in regard to her own teaching:

> Students do not always enjoy studying with me. Often they find my courses challenge them in ways that are deeply unsettling. This was particularly

disturbing to me at the beginning of my teaching career because I wanted to be liked and admired. It took time and experience for me to understand that the rewards of engaged pedagogy might not emerge during a course.

When education is presented as personal *transformation* it becomes more difficult, indeed probably impossible, to commodify. Transformation is not consumed; it is undergone. It lends itself less easily to prediction, standardised outcome, pricing, comparison, monitoring and control. Moreover, as Julie Rattray points out (Chapter 6 this volume) transformative learning has a strong affective dimension. Shulman (2005, p. 1) observed that 'without a certain amount of anxiety and risk, there's a limit to how much learning occurs. One must have something at stake. No emotional investment, no intellectual or formational yield'. We see an example of this in the response of a Norwegian architecture student encountering challenging understandings of what architectural practice might become:

In the beginning we were thrown into something completely new and unknown that has been difficult to deal with. The feeling of not being clever enough, and not having control of what you are doing, have resulted in a lot of frustration and stress, and this has influenced the process to the extent that I have become exhausted and depressed, and I wanted to quit. (Hokstad et al., this volume)

At a later stage in the programme of learning this difficulty, frustration and stress have changed to a sense of new insight, exhilaration and meaningfulness as the student undergoes further transformation towards thinking and feeling as an architect.

Eventually it became clear that the project was about examining the edge/ridge, the exciting state of mind where meaningful and many faceted places may emerge. The architecture here on the edge/ridge is rich on senses, a delicate point of balance. It *is* senses. (ibid.)

In the following example a music student describes the awkward ontological shifts entailed in attempting to balance the demands of studying both anthropology and musical composition as 'a mental battle':

It was a sort of a mental battle between the side of me that is a slightly bigoted composer, a composer of art, that says: 'well this isn't art, this is how the composition world works', it's about taste, it's about subjectivity, and that's completely different from how anthropological research works. Of course I had a flavour of that from ethnomusicology, but actually being immersed in that it was the biggest mental battle for me... so it was a kind of split personality thing... I was treated as an anthropologist, being detached from my preconceptions and then I go back to composition and immediately you have to switch on your subjectivity.[2]

The superordinate and non-negotiable characteristic of a threshold concept is its transformative capacity. The Threshold Concepts Framework represents a way of thinking about curricula where specific elements that are challenging for students to understand have a transformational impact on their learning once they are understood. The integrative nature of threshold concepts represents the antithesis of the transmission and retention of large content volume, the 'stuffed curriculum' (Cousin, 2006). It is, rather, the relationships between aspects of knowledge that are seen as transformative, in opening up new ways of seeing. 'The power and value of the threshold concept can only be recognised by a student if they can see how it is able to act in an integrative way' (Davies, 2003, p. 6).

PEDAGOGIES OF UNCERTAINTY

Consumerist models of learning tend to stress certainty, clarity, straightforwardness and control. This fosters a sense of security and comfortableness that is likely to produce the satisfaction (of the paying customer) that is the aim of every course. However the social and professional world that the student will enter will not be so clear cut nor so manageable. And the nature of transformative learning rarely provides such comfort or security. It will present a continuing need for inquiry, for personal adaptation and further development. As Freire (1970, p. 21) emphasises:

> For apart from inquiry, apart from the praxis, individuals cannot be truly human. Knowledge emerges only through invention and re-invention, through the restless, impatient, continuing, hopeful inquiry human beings pursue in the world, with the world, and with each other.

Characterising consumerist pedagogy as the 'banking' concept of education, he points out that:

> Whereas banking education anesthetizes and inhibits creative power, problem-posing education involves a constant unveiling of reality. The former attempts to maintain the *submersion* of consciousness; the latter strives for the *emergence* of consciousness and *critical intervention* in reality. (Freire, 1970, p. 68)

Barnett (2004) argues that it would be irrational and self-defeating to assume that we can prepare a new generation of students to cope with uncertainty by establishing a new kind of certainty in the curriculum. Pedagogies of uncertainty, he suggest, cannot be technological in nature (i.e. framed tightly in terms of learning objectives and outcomes). They are framed rather through a transformation of human being – through ontological shift(s). In a four frame model of student development for future society (Barnett, 2004) he distinguishes between the acquisition of generic skills or graduate attributes for a world of no risk, where *fixed ontologies* are offered as a preparation for an unknown world, compared with a world of high risk where personal transformation will require *open ontologies* for an unknown world. This is the serpent's apple offered in Eden, heralding an unknown future self, heralding reinvention.

Through observations such as these we come to see what a pedagogy of uncertainty entails, and it seems to be characterised by the kind of 'ontological insecurity' that Giddens (1991) identified as a mark of late modernity.

Amid supercomplexity, the educational task is primarily an ontological task. It is the task of enabling individuals to prosper amid supercomplexity, amid a situation in which here are no stable descriptions of the world, no concepts that can be seized upon with any assuredness, and no value systems that can claim one's allegiance with any unrivalled authority. (Barnett, 2015, p. 224)

Within the curriculum and within pedagogy he maintains, concepts such as fragility, uncertainty and instability are also ontological states. A pedagogy of uncertainty comes to mean that learning *for* uncertainty means learning to live *with* uncertainty. Similarly, such pedagogies cannot dispel anxiety, but seek to provide students with perspectives that will enable them to live *with* anxiety. As Barnett puts it:

The ice is perpetually slippery but this says nothing about the individuals on the ice, only about the conditions of epistemological insecurity in which they now find themselves. But this epistemological slipperiness generates, in turn, ontological destabilisation. For if the world is radically unknowable then, by extension, 'I' am radically unknowable. (pp. 224–225)

This is a far cry from the sureties demanded within a consumer model. Here like the serpent's subversive entry into the stable and seeming-safe Eden, learning becomes 'subversive in the sense of subverting the student's taken-for-granted world'. Far from providing clarity and certainty, this, Barnett believes, will persuade students that, no matter how much effort are put in, 'there are no final answers' (Barnett, 1999, p. 155). Understanding comes to be seen as an *iterative practice* as opposed to an *isolated process* with a clear beginning and end point.

The practical considerations for these contrasting pedagogies are considerable. Whereas consumer models have an intrinsic orientation towards meeting the needs of the individual, within pedagogies of uncertainty this individualisation is destabilised. This is confirmed by Hay (2010, p. 264) who reports that

from a dialogic position, learners do not come to understand things in isolation, but meanings are shaped through the inter-animation of the different voices (or texts) of others, as students learn to see things from other perspectives. Here, it is an increasing inclusion of difference that leads towards more encompassing understanding.

Similarly, consumer models of learning imply acquisition and accumulation. By studying students' approaches to learning researchers have shed light on the different conceptions of learning that students hold. Dahlgren (1984, p. 31) found that deep approaches to learning, aimed at conceptual and theoretical understanding, were symptomatic of transformative conceptions, where learning 'is not a self-contained entity but one which has the potential of enabling individuals to consider afresh some part or aspect of the world around them'. Surface approaches, on the other hand, were associated accumulative conceptions of learning, with knowledge retained for short-term strategic purposes of meeting the requirements of assignments and examinations.

Consumer models place considerable emphasis on the need for timely formative feedback. But even here we find that feedback can trigger an emotional response and if misread, it can reinforce feelings of failure and incompetence (Brookhart, 2006). Feedback arguably can demotivate as well as motivate. Higgins, Hartley and Skelton (2001, p. 274) characterise feedback as a *'problematic* form of communication' involving relationships of power. Teachers use a particular academic discourse, which may not be understood by students who in turn lack the confidence to seek clarification, preventing them from making the most effective use of feedback.

LIMINAL EXPERIENCE

Disciplines give access to powerful knowledge (Young, 2008) but not just through epistemic access but through ontological shift. For powerful knowledge is frequently 'troublesome knowledge'. Threshold Concepts research (Flanagan, 2015) has drawn extensively on the notion of troublesomeness in the liminal space. Liminality is viewed as a transformative state in the process of learning in which there is a reformulation of the learner's meaning frame (Schwartzman, 2010) and an accompanying shift in the learner's subjectivity (Meyer & Land, 2005). Standard anthropological definitions of liminality – as a rite of passage in which the novitiate lacks social status, remains anonymous, has to demonstrate obedience, with intimations of humility, and perhaps humiliation – do not accord easily with the notion of the paramount influence of the consumer. The liminal state entails an envisaging (and ultimate accepting) of an alternative version of self, contemplated through the threshold space. Blackie et al. (2010) portray this as the learner's 'emergent being'. Ross (2011) speaks of a 're-authoring' of self, or 'undoing the script'. The American Buddhist nun, Pema Chodron recalling her most influential teachers, concluded that:

> My models were the people who stepped outside of the conventional mind and who could actually stop my mind and completely open it up and free it, even for a moment, from a conventional, habitual way of looking at things ...If you are really preparing for groundlessness, preparing for the reality of human existence, you are living on the razor's edge, and you must become used to the fact that things shift and change. Things are not certain and they do not last and you do not know what is going to happen. My teachers have always pushed me over the cliff ... (Chodron cited in hooks, 1994, p. 206)

PEDAGOGIC RIGHTS

Clearly such a transformative approach to learning sits uneasily with a neoliberal rendering of the learner as consumer of educational services. It is argued here that The Threshold Concepts Framework – with its emphasis on transformation through troublesome knowledge and shifts in subjectivity –can be considered as a counter-discourse to the commodification of learning. The obligation and commitment to be provoked into liminal states of learning, to experience troublesome knowledge, to undergo ontological shifts which can lead to different ways of thinking, different modes of knowledge and deep personal change are presented here – in keeping with the work of Jenkins and Barnes (2014) discussed earlier – not as consumer rights (satisfaction and entitlement) but as students' 'pedagogic rights', which offer alternative and, in our view, more valid effective notions of quality in higher education. As Barnett has observed: 'The student is perforce required to venture into new places, strange places, anxiety-provoking places. This is part of the point of higher education. If there was no anxiety, it is difficult to believe that we could be in the presence of a higher education' (Barnett, 2007, p. 147).

The notion of pedagogic rights originates in the work of Bernstein (2000) who envisioned learners as deserving a different kind of (threefold) entitlement: to enhancement, inclusion and participation. This, in turn, would give them access to confidence, group involvement and action at civic level:

The learner's pedagogic rights (Bernstein, cited in Mclean, Abbas, & Ashwin, 2011)

Enhancement	Individual	'The right to the means of critical understanding and to new possibilities.' (Bernstein, 2000, p. xx)	Confidence
Inclusion	Social	'The right to be included socially, intellectually, culturally and personally [including] the right [to be] autonomous.' (ibid., p. xx)	'Communitas' Belonging in group(s)
Participation	Political	'The right to participate in discourse and practices that have outcomes: to participate in the construction, maintenance and transformation of social order.' (ibid., p. xxi)	Civic discussion and action

So this offers an alternative discourse, a view of learning as an *educational* transaction that is concerned not simply with the student's acquisition of knowledge or consumption of services as with their 'coming into presence' (Biesta, 2005). This entails 'being challenged by otherness and difference', what Derrida terms a 'transcendental violence' (Derrida, 1978) that is persistent, presenting difficult demands and situations. In this mode the learner is not in a position to identify and state their learning needs, which are emergent and contingent. It requires an altered relation of trust with their teachers and fellow learners. Students, as organisational actors, are rendered differently, are *transformed*, as co-enquirers, co-creators, co-producers (Neary & Amsler, 2013). In this discourse, teachers, in turn, have to assume a different form of responsibility, operating within risk and uncertainty, which cannot be predicated on the assumed certainties of a conventional accountability protocol. It rests on mutual *trust*.

EINSTELLUNG EFFECT

One problem remains in regard to transformative learning. The serpent, bearer of troublesome knowledge, who engenders the process of transformation, can also carry a sting in its tail.

A successful transformative learning experience can lead, as has been discussed earlier, to acquisition of powerful knowledge and to significant shifts in ontology and identity. But there can be unintended consequences of successful transformation in that it can produce a state of what psychologists have termed 'functional fixedness', 'design fixation' or 'paradigm blindness'. This is a cognitive bias which restricts a person to using and perceiving an object only in the way it is traditionally used and perceived. The generally accepted formal term is taken from the German – the *Einstellung Effect*. The German term has a range of meanings, ranging from simply 'attitude', to the position of a needle on a dial, as in a radio receiver, to the idea of a precise 'focus'. However, in its psychological use, it means being caught within a particular way of seeing a problem, or design or solution. The effect tends to occur as a result of a previously successful resolution of an issue or coming to a clear understanding of something that had proved difficult. The problem arises when there is a need to resolve a subsequent issue of further complexity or of a different nature. What happens is that the previously successful approach, taken under one set of conditions, tends to be adopted again under different circumstances, as it has become a powerful and ingrained way of seeing and thinking. It becomes a case of 'thinking inside the box'. Our previous experience starts a self-fulfilling circle which begins with information consistent with the already activated schema being more likely to be picked up. Consequently the belief that the schema is the right one to deal with the situation is confirmed and alternatives are less likely to be considered (Keren, 1984).

The individual thinks that they are considering the evidence in an open-minded way, not realising that their attention is being selectively directed to only certain aspects of the problem or issue under consideration. Those things that they notice do indeed fit in with the activated schema and so confirm the view that the way they are dealing with the situation is the correct one. Things that do not fit in are either not noticed, or if they are, they are not integrated because they do not fit the activated schema.

Experts in any field, be they medical doctors, scientists, managers, chess players, airline pilots, designers, military strategists, tend not to make errors. When they do, however, the research suggests (Singley & Anderson, 1989; Reason, 1990) that one reason is because they recognise the situation as a familiar one, when it is not. Hence they apply their usual, but now inappropriate, methods to find a solution. The doctor misrecognises the subtly different symptoms in a new patient and prescribes a remedy that has been effective in earlier, seemingly similar cases. The military general assumes the conflict to be entered can be effectively approached through the use of tactics similar to the previous one. A chess player having reached checkmate successfully through a particularly elegant board play, assumes similar moves will be the appropriate solution in the next game. Chess players who had solved a particular chess challenge in five moves, when told it could actually be achieved in three, were found to be eyeing the same board squares as in their earlier successful approach. Chess players who had not previously engaged in the challenge and were unaware of how many moves constituted the optimal solution, were more likely to achieve the result in three moves than the previous group whose eye movements suggested they were still thinking in terms of the solution they had employed previously.

We show, by measuring players' eye movements, that the mechanism by which the first idea prevents a better idea coming to mind can be demonstrated. Crucially, we find that players believed that they were actively searching for better solutions when in fact they continued to look at aspects of the problem related to the first idea they considered.

The Einstellung effect is doubly pernicious. Firstly it arises from an experience of success, or a positive sense of achievement in an earlier task, which imbues the original (and, on that occasion, effective) mode of framing and analysing the problem, and the subsequent design or problem-solving methods with positive connotations and affective associations. Secondly, as with the chess players in the research study, the actors involved do not realise that it is influencing their thoughts and feelings (Bilalic et al., 2008). Research undertaken into the causes of Einstellung, or 'design fixation', suggest interesting affinities with aspects of transformation that are found within the Threshold Concepts research. For example, Crilly (2015) identifies a strong 'commitment to initial ideas' and 'sticking to a restricted set of solutions that are known to work' as dominant factors in Einstellung, which corresponds closely with the difficulty in letting go of prevailing beliefs in the liminal state which has been identified as barrier to the need to 'see differently' and integrate novel elements when crossing thresholds. This is linked to 'project constraints that prevent exploration' and 'organisational cultures that give people ownership of their ideas, which gives them the incentive to defend them'. This would align with notions of the 'defended learner' identified early in the Thresholds research literature as a contributing factor in troublesome knowledge. It also points to the dimension of subjectivity that operates within functional fixedness, as it does within the liminal state, and the necessity for this to change if performance is to be improved. The idea of functional fixedness derives originally from Gestalt psychology, which places emphasis on holistic processing. This corresponds well with the need to reformulate one's 'meaning frame', or even experience a 'rupture in knowing' as reported in the Thresholds research (Schwartzman, 2010, pp. 30–33).

So the powerful nature of experiencing transformation, changed perspective and ontological shift that often occurs as a result of liminal experience in learning may in the same process lead to successful threshold crossing and entry into new conceptual and ontological territory whilst at the same time introducing a new constraint that may impede or even prevent future threshold crossing. In effect, as Bilalic et al. (2008, p. 1) put it, 'good thoughts block better ones'. Writers on the Einstellung effect suggest potential strategies for combating functional fixedness or design fixation. These include the use of diverse teams, practical making and testing of models, the facilitation of learning or problem-solving sessions by tutors familiar with fixation risks. Learners themselves are encouraged to explore and reflect on the possibility of fixation (in themselves and/or in those they collaborate with) and to examine episodes of paradigm blindness (Crilly, 2015). Bringing 'strangers to the tribe', to challenge, extend and render existing perspectives 'strange' would be another strategy. These approaches may well merit further exploration as we seek effective pedagogies and curriculum designs to enhance our students' understanding of threshold concepts and their transformation as knowers.

CODA

The cover of this volume contains an image of the forbidden fruit from Lucas Cranach the Elder's painting of *Eve offering the apple to Adam in the Garden of Eden and the serpent* (c.1520–25). This chapter, and writing and presentations elsewhere on threshold concepts (e.g. Meyer & Land, 2006, p. xiv), have made use of the Eden story and its imagery to conjure notions of troublesome knowledge and the idea of teaching as transgressive. It is important to remember that the purpose of such trouble and discomfort is to help our students to move on, to find new spaces and possibilities, and new freedoms. No-one has expressed this better than bell hooks.

> The academy is not paradise. But learning is a place where paradise can be created. The classroom, with all its limitations, remains a location of possibility. In that field of possibility we have the opportunity to labour for freedom, to demand of ourselves and our comrades, an openness of mind and heart that allows us to face reality even as we collectively imagine ways to move beyond boundaries, to transgress. This is education as the practice of freedom.

NOTES

[1]   *Break On Through (To the Other Side)* is a song by Jim Morrison and The Doors released in the USA on Elektra Records, January 1, 1967.
[2]   Private communication with the author.

REFERENCES

Apple, M. W. (2000). *Official knowledge: Democratic education in a conservative age.* New York, NY & London: Routledge.

Argyris, C. (1960). *Understanding organizational behaviour.* Homewood, IL: Dorsey Press, Inc.

Barber, M., Moffit, A., & Kihn, P. (2011). *Deliverology 101: A field guide for educational leaders.* Thousand Oaks, CA: Corwin.

Barker, P. (1991). *Regeneration.* London: Penguin.

Barnett, R. (1999). *The idea of higher education.* Buckingham: Society for Research in Higher Education and Open University Press.

Barnett, R. (2004). Learning for an unknown future. *Higher Education Research & Development, 23*(3), 247–260.

Barnett, R. (2007). *A will to learn: Being a student in an age of uncertainty.* Buckingham: Society for Research in Higher Education and Open University Press.

Barnett, R. (2015). *Thinking and rethinking the university: The selected works of Ronald Barnett.* Abingdon & New York, NY: Routledge.

Barradell, S. (2013). The identification of threshold concepts: A review of theoretical complexities and methodological challenges. *Higher Education, 65,* 265–276.

Biesta, G. (2005). Against learning. Reclaiming a language for education in an age of learning. *Nordisk Pedagogik, 25,* 54–66.

Bilalic, M., McLeod, P., & Gobet, F. (2008). Why good thoughts block better ones: The mechanism of the pernicious Einstellung effect. *Cognition, 108,* 652–661.

Blackie, M. A. L., Case, J. M., & Jawitz, J. (2010). Student-centredness: The link between transforming students and transforming ourselves. *Teaching in Higher Education, 15*(6), 637–646.

Brookhart, S. M. (2007, December). Feedback that fits. *Educational Leadership, 65*(4), 54–59.

Cousin, G. (2006). An introduction to threshold concepts. *Planet, 17,* 4–5.

Crilly, N. (2015). Fixation and creativity in concept development: The attitudes and practices of expert designers. *Design Studies, 38,* 54–91.

Dahlgren, L.-O. (1984). Outcomes of learning. In F. Marton, D. Hounsell, & N. Entwistle (Eds.), *The experience of learning* (pp. 19–35). Edinburgh: Scottish Academic Press.

Davies, P. (2003). Threshold concepts: How can we recognise them? *Embedding Threshold Concepts Project* (Working Paper 1). Retrieved from http://www.staffs.ac.uk/schools/business/iepr/docs/etcworkingpaper(1).doc

De Groot, A. D., & Gobet, F. (1996). *Perception and memory in chess.* Assen, Holland: Van Gorcum.

Derrida, J. (1978). Violence and metaphysics: An essay on the thought of Emmanuel Levinas. In A. Bass (Trans.), *Writing and difference* (pp. 79–153). Chicago, IL: Chicago University Press.

Dewey, J. (1933/1986). How we think. A restatement of the relation of reflective thinking to the educative process. In J. A. Bodston (Ed.), *John Dewey, The later works, 1925–1953: 1933 Essays and how we think.* Carbondale, IL: Southern Illinois University Press. (Original work published 1933)

Field, J. (2000). *Lifelong learning and the new educational order.* Stoke on Trent: Trentham Books.

Flanagan, M. (2014) *Threshold concepts: Undergraduate teaching, postgraduate training and professional development: A short introduction and bibliography.* London: UCL. Retrieved from http://www.ee.ucl.ac.uk/~mflanaga/thresholds.html

Freire, P. (1970). *Pedagogy of the oppressed.* New York, NY: Herder and Herder.

Giddens, A. (1991). *Modernity and self-identity: Self and society in the late modern age.* Cambridge: Polity Press.

Hay, D. B. (2010). The imaginative function in learning: Theory and case study from third-year neuroscience. *Psychology: The Journal of the Hellenic Psychological Society, 17,* 259–288.

Higgins, R., Hartley, P., & Skelton, A. (2001). Getting the message across: The problems of communicating assessment feedback. *Teaching in Higher Education, 6*(2), 269–274.

hooks, b. (1994). *Teaching to transgress: Education as the practice of freedom.* New York, NY & London: Routledge.

Jenkins, C., & Barnes, C. (2014, June 24). *Student satisfaction negates pedagogic rights – Theirs and ours!* 13th Learning & Teaching Symposium, University of Westminster, Marylebone, London.

23

Keren, G. (1984). On the importance of identifying the correct 'problem space'. *Cognition, 16*, 121–128.

Keynes, J. M. (1973). *The general theory of employment, interest and money*. London: MacMillan. (Original work published 1936)

Luchins, A. S. (1942). Mechanization in problem solving – The effect of Einstellung. *Psychological Monographs, 54*(6), 95.

Mclean, M., Abbas, A., & Ashwin, P. (2011). *The use and value of Basil Bernstein's theory and concepts to illuminate the nature of (in)equalities in undergraduate social science education*. Retrieved from http://www.pedagogicequality.ac.uk/documents/Bernstein_and_inequality_JUNE_25_2011_001.pdf

Meyer, J., & Land, R. (2005). Threshold concepts and troublesome knowledge (2): Epistemological considerations and a conceptual framework for teaching and learning. *Higher Education, 49*(3), 373–388.

Meyer, J. H. F., & Land, R. (2006). Editors' preface: An introduction. In J. H. F. Meyer & R. Land (Eds.), *Overcoming barriers to student understanding: Threshold concepts and troublesome knowledge*. Abingdon & New York, NY: Routledge.

Mezirow, J. (1997). Transformative learning: Theory to practice. *New Directions for Adult and Continuing Education, 1997*(74), 5–12.

Mezirow, J. (2000). Learning to think like an adult: Core concepts of transformational theory. In J. Mezirow (Ed.), *Learning as transformation: Critical perspectives on a theory in progress*. San Francisco, CA: Jossey-Bass.

Neary, M., & Amsler, S. (2012). Occupy: A new pedagogy of space and time? *Journal for Critical Education Policy Studies, 10*(2), 106–138.

Proust, M. (1900/1987). On reading Ruskin. In J. Autret, W. Butford, & P. J. Wolfe (Eds., & Trans., with an introduction by R, Macksey) *Prefaces to La Bible d'Amiens and Sesame et les Lys with selections from the notes to the translated texts*. Newhaven, CT: Yale University Press. (Original work published 1900)

Reason, J. (1990). *Human error*. New York, NY: Cambridge University Press.

Ross, J. (2011). *Unmasking online reflective practices in higher education* (Unpublished Ph.D thesis). University of Edinburgh, Scotland.

Schwartzman, L. (2010). Transcending disciplinary boundaries: A proposed theoretical foundation for threshold concepts. In J. H. F. Meyer, R. Land, & C. Baillie (Eds.), *Threshold concepts and transformational learning* (pp. 21–44). Rotterdam, Boston and Taipei: Sense Publishers.

Shulman, L. (2005). Pedagogies of uncertainty. *Liberal Education* (Spring issue). Retrieved from https://www.aacu.org/publications-research/periodicals/pedagogies-uncertainty

Singley, M. K., & Anderson, J. R. (1989). *The transfer of cognitive skill*. Cambridge, MA: Harvard University Press.

Timmermans, J. A. (2010). Changing our minds: The developmental potential of threshold concepts: In J. H. F. Meyer, R. Land, & C. Baillie (Eds.), *Threshold concepts and transformational learning* (pp. 3–19). Rotterdam, Boston and Taipei: Sense Publishers.

Universities UK. (2015, October 23). *Universities UK response to* Which? *report on consumer law*. London: UUK. Retrieved from http://www.universitiesuk.ac.uk/highereducation/Pages/UniversitiesUKresponsetoWhichreportonconsumerlaw.aspx#.VjYMD7fhCM8

Wolf, G. (2014, March 7). Paulo Freire: Pedagogy between oppression and liberation. *ELM European Lifelong Learning Magazine*.

Young, M. F. D. (2008). *Bringing knowledge back in: From social constructivism to social realism in the sociology of education*. London & New York, NY: Routledge.

Ray Land
Durham University

JAN H. F. MEYER AND JULIE A. TIMMERMANS

3. INTEGRATED THRESHOLD CONCEPT KNOWLEDGE

INTRODUCTION

After more than a decade of flourishing international research on threshold concepts in the disciplines, we have reached a key point in the maturation of our field – a point where, as a community of scholars, we must ask ourselves questions, such as: How do we translate the rich findings of this research into a theoretically sound and actionable form, so that they are of use to instructors, students, and educational developers? And how may we do this in a way that brings unity to the approach while remaining non-prescriptive and adaptive to the various contexts in which threshold concept research and practice occur?

As a basis for translating findings into practice, we accordingly propose the construction of *Integrated Threshold Concept Knowledge* (ITCK); socio-empirically constructed knowledge that translates into *in situ* 'threshold concept representations', thus contributing to a repertoire of communicable student-centred pedagogic 'responses' relevant to the learning of threshold concepts. Such knowledge is constituted in a fusion of different 'types of knowledge' arising primarily from the following sources:

- Analyses *for*, and *of*, threshold concepts and consequent articulation of their 'critical features';
- Empirical evidence of how these critical features of threshold concepts are apprehended by students, and subsequently experienced cognitively, affectively, and ontologically (in varying degrees) in the liminal state;
- Exhibited patterns of variation in learning, metalearning, metacognitive, and assessment performance, activities associated with threshold concepts;
- Interpretations of the dynamics of apprehension and discernment that lead to 'learning challenges and stuck places'.

Historical examples of the genesis of such types of knowledge lie in the writings of Shulman and Marton c.1985 that were independently focused at that time on the need to develop a (subject) content-based amalgam of know-*ledge*, -*how*, and -*why*, to drive reforms in school teacher education and classroom practice. Three decades later, an analysis of these writings offers obvious analogies and a basis for developing both a student-centred pedagogy of threshold concepts, as well as foreshadowing an approach for advancing the professional development of university teachers, particularly within institutional educational development programmes.

R. Land et al. (Eds.), Threshold Concepts in Practice, 25–38.

TYPES OF KNOWLEDGE AT THE INTERSECTION OF
TEACHING AND LEARNING

In the mid 1980s, two generative ideas on 'types of knowledge', one of 'pedagogical content knowledge' arising from personal experience (Shulman, 1985, 1986), and one of knowledge of 'pedagogy of content' arising from research (Marton, 1986, 1989), were independently developed in essays addressing the need to reform teacher education programmes and classroom practice in, respectively, the United States (Shulman) and Sweden (Marton). Fuelled by a common concern – a perceived receded focus at that time on the content basis of teaching and learning in (mainly) secondary education – they both argued the imperative, from different but complementary perspectives, to address what were respectively referred to by Shulman as 'the problem of the missing paradigm' (of teaching content), and by Marton as 'five lost decades' of relevant educational research as a basis for teaching reform.

There is, however, a contrast in emphasis in these essays. Shulman's essays are expansive around a perceived and fundamental need to construct an 'elaborate knowledge base' for school teaching, and the need for teachers to thus develop personal expertise first and foremost at the 'intersection' of *content and pedagogy*. Marton's analysis and argument is more specific and emanates from a different perspective in seeing a 'special type' of research producing a relevant knowledge base for teaching practice, specifically 'research into how the pupils[1] learn the teaching content they are expected to learn' (1986, p. 5). Marton thus emphasises knowledge creation at the 'intersection' of *content and learning*, and the need, first and foremost, to conduct relevant research towards this end.

As we begin to develop our notion of Integrated Threshold Concept Knowledge, there is thus an initial interest in these two historical sources of distinguishable 'types of knowledge' sourced at the intersection of subject 'content' with, respectively, pedagogy and learning. In relation to 'content' the predominant focus in one source is on what *teachers* do with 'content' to transform it into pedagogical substance and, in the other source, the focus is on what *learners* do with 'content' (how they learn) as a basis for informing pedagogy. 'Content' is the centrepiece of both arguments. But how might it be productively (and optimally) conceptualised at these two critical 'intersections' in a manner relevant to academic practice in higher education?

SHULMAN'S TYPE OF KNOWLEDGE AT THE INTERSECTION OF
CONTENT AND PEDAGOGY

In addressing this question we first consider the perspective proposed by Shulman (1986) based on his presidential address at the 1985 annual meeting of the American Educational Research Association: 'Those who understand: Knowledge growth in teaching'. Shulman's basic argument was that 'teaching' requires more than a knowledge of subject matter[2] coupled with generally advocated 'good' teaching practice; in particular those practices, propositions, behaviours, procedures, and classroom management activities that are divorced from subject content. His vision was to redress a perceived imbalance between teachers' knowledge of subject content and their lack of specific knowledge of how to internally transform it into a repertoire of 'representational forms' in order to teach it in a manner expected to impact positively on comprehension learning outcomes.

Thus identified was the need to focus on those processes by which teachers *internally* transformed their subject knowledge into representational forms – the content of teaching – as well as an accompanying understanding of 'how particular formulations of that content related to what students came to know or misconstrue' (Shulman, 1986, p. 6). Shulman suggested three categories of 'content knowledge' *one* of which, *pedagogical content knowledge*, 'goes beyond knowledge of subject matter per se to the dimension of subject matter knowledge *for teaching* […] the ways of representing and formulating the subject that make it comprehensible to others. [It] also includes an understanding of what makes the learning of specific topics easy or difficult' (p. 9).

Pedagogical content knowledge is thus constructed by, and is for the use of, *individual teachers*; it is accessed as a personally developed repertoire of content-specific pedagogic practices that are responsive to pupil 'diversity' in the classroom. As Shulman (1987, p. 8) puts it, such knowledge is 'that special amalgam of content and pedagogy that is uniquely the province of teachers, their own special form of professional understanding; […] [i]t represents the blending of content and pedagogy into an understanding of how particular topics […] are organized, represented, and adapted to the diverse interests and abilities of learners, and presented for instruction'. Such knowledge is also 'most likely to distinguish the understanding of the content specialist from that of the [content] pedagogue' (p. 8). In this latter 'understanding', Shulman makes implicit and explicit references to knowledge about pupils' learning and the factors that influence it; for example, pupils' prior knowledge including, in particular, conceptions and misconceptions about the content to be learned. And while 'content' is of necessity referred to in the abstract in much of his general discussion, Shulman makes it clear that this 'understanding' can be constituted in particular subject contexts (such as mathematics and science) in which many pupils experience learning difficulty and perform badly. In higher education, 'subject' may be also be read here as 'discipline' for present purposes, thus embracing the discursive and ontological aspects of learning emphasised within the Threshold Concepts Framework.

Shulman (1987) refers to 'content' in finer grain as *inter alia* 'some form of "text"[3] […] or an actual piece of material' to be understood (p. 14). 'By focusing on the teaching of particular topics – […] quadratic equations, […] photosynthesis – we learned how *particular kinds* of content knowledge and pedagogical strategies necessarily interacted in the minds of teachers' (p. 5, emphasis added). Furthermore, in the following statement, Shulman presages the development of a substantial 'conceptual change' research literature in commenting on the fertility of cognitive research into student misconceptions for the benefit of teaching:

We are gathering [...] knowledge [...] about the instructional conditions necessary to overcome and transform those initial [mis]conceptions.[4] Such research-based knowledge, [another 'type of knowledge' in its own right] an important component of the pedagogical understanding of subject matter, should be included at the heart of our definition of needed pedagogical knowledge. (Shulman, 1986, p. 10)

ITCK INTERSECTION WITH PEDAGOGY AND LEARNING

Shulman's observations on 'teaching representations' of content specificity are of especial interest for present purposes. To begin with, and in general: In higher education, threshold concepts and a socially-empirically (rather than personalised) constructed understanding of the associated learning challenges and 'stuck places' that they present for students, constitutes one basis for ITCK. And, in this specific context, some propositions are arguably specific to the threshold concepts domain.

'Troublesomeness', for example, can be used deliberately to provoke the condition of a liminal state that captures inter-individual variation across cognitive, epistemic, and ontological dimensions. That is, variation in those critical features of threshold concepts that might be apprehended or experienced by students as weird, illogical, counter-intuitive, unsettling, and alien, leading to 'stuck places', or that might, in the 'Decoding the Disciplines' model of Pace and Middendorf (2004), characterise the presence of 'bottlenecks' in the curriculum. More deeply, 'troublesome' threshold concepts can unlock developmental progression, their power being that "they trigger dissonance not only at the cognitive and affective levels, but also dissonance at the epistemological level, calling upon learners to 'change their minds,' not by supplanting *what* they know, but by transforming *how* they know" (Timmermans, 2010, pp. 10–11).

A second proposition is that 'responding' to this concept-specific variation in 'stuck places' requires some detailed knowledge of how students vary in their (cognitive and emotional) experiences of *learning that concept*; knowledge that can be 'put on paper', disseminated between teachers and their students, discussed, socially constructed, and communicated to others. And 'experiences' are grounded here in learning, metalearning, and metacognitive activity. Resultant types of valid knowledge may emerge at the simplest untheorised level of analysis of students' written answers to examination questions, or evaluative comments on their learning experiences of specific course content. Theorised research evidence is more helpful as is next discussed.

MARTON'S 'TYPE OF KNOWLEDGE' AT THE INTERSECTION OF CONTENT AND LEARNING

Marton shares a common focus of expression (teacher education programmes c.1985) with Shulman's work. And although Marton's insights are complementary, they also provide a contrast to 'cognitive research', as espoused by Shulman, as the source for one particular 'type of knowledge'.

Marton's 1986 work (which does not reference Shulman) unambiguously encapsulates in its title a focus on an *alternative* form of educational research and the impact it can have on teaching practice. However Marton (1989) – substantively Marton (1986) expanded under a different title – acknowledged in a footnote that Shulman's presidential address 'advocated a view […] which is close to the one I promote. In both cases, the central role of content in the educational enterprise is stressed. […] My own interest is centred on content as a link between educational research and educational practice' (pp. 1–2).

In essence, Marton (1986, 1989) argued the need for a 'special kind' (or type) of knowledge generated from a privileged form of research (phenomenographic)[5] to impact on teacher education and 'praxis' – a term chosen by Marton (1986) as a synonym for 'practice' but one that in his mind at that time referred specifically to that part of a teacher's work 'that involves teaching the content they are expected to teach' (p. 6).

Marton's espoused type of knowledge – epitomised in contemporary work at that time undertaken by Dagmar Neuman[6] (one of his postgraduate students) – determines qualitative variation in students' 'internal' understandings of concepts. Marton's type of knowledge does *not* emanate from educational research that seeks to provide 'external' explanations to a question such as why some pupils do not learn the four rules of arithmetic; specifically explanations that are 'external' to pupils' experiences, that direct attention away from 'internal' explanations of how pupils actually 'do sums', and that provide an 'external' basis for why some students 'do sums' differently to others.

'External' explanations are held by Marton to arise from forms of research that, for example, methodologically approach the research question by obtaining valid and reliable measures that differentiate between pupils who respectively can, and cannot, 'do sums' correctly. 'External' would be resultant explanations of variation in between-subgroup differences typically captured in, for example, socioeconomic status variables that represent the basis of statistically significant subgroup differences and therefore explain why some subgroups do 'do sums' better than others. Marton's assertion is that this different type of knowledge is of no practical value to a teacher in a classroom with a pupil 'who has difficulty in the addition of two-digit numbers' (1986, p. 8).

In contrast, his espoused (phenomenographic-based) type of knowledge – which explains the qualitative variation in how pupils 'do sums' – emanates from their internally different *conceptions of numerals.* Simply put, pupils' different ways of 'doing sums' are 'not caused by but rather *expressed* in their conception of numerals' (1986, pp. 11–12, emphasis added).

ITCK INTERSECTION WITH RESEARCH

There are three points to be made here for present purposes. First, what Shulman and Marton were arguing for c. 1985 were benefits for teacher education in the future tense. Shared here is the importance of 'content' in shaping, in the present tense, the professional development and academic practice of university teachers and the learning wellbeing of their students. Second, both Shulman and Marton emphasised the value of types of (research-based) knowledge *operating at a discrete concept level*; for example 'photosynthesis'[7] (Shulman) and 'numeral' (Marton). Third, neither type of their respectively espoused types of research-based knowledge can lay exclusive claim to sources of explanatory variation in students' experiences of learning threshold concepts. The type of knowledge required for this purpose has less to do with the contrasting niceties of philosophical stance and methodology, and more to do with a spectrum of both qualitative and quantitative research perspectives that focus on the contextualised learning experiences of 'real people' rather than statistical abstractions of them; perspectives that focus essentially on (variation in) individual, or individual-similarity subgroup, cognitive processes, and ontological experiences.

BERTHIAUME'S 'TYPE OF KNOWLEDGE' AT THE INTERSECTION OF DISCIPLINARY CHARACTERISTICS AND PERSONAL EPISTEMOLOGY

Berthiaume (2007) provides another example of a type of knowledge for teaching that is relevant for present purposes because it is contextualised in the academic practice of higher education. He proposes 'Discipline Specific Pedagogical Knowledge' derived from three sources: The first of these, in familiar terrain already discussed, is a 'knowledge base' for teaching that includes knowledge structures for teaching (which subsumes Shulman's position); teachers' beliefs related to teachers and teaching, as well as to learners and learning; and teachers' goals related to teaching.

Another source related to discipline specificity integrates knowledge of the epistemological structure and socio-cultural characteristics of the discipline (see for example Donald, 2002), as well as the 'significant cultural dimensions such as norms, practices or rules' which make academic disciplines 'akin to specific cultural groups or tribes' (Berthiaume, 2007, p. 22; see also Becher, 1989; Becher & Trowler, 2001). A professor's knowledge for teaching may therefore be seen as rooted within, and closely reflecting, the knowledge structures of the discipline in question. Conferring the status of 'threshold' on a concept may thus be interpreted as a social act by a (bounded) disciplinary community in endorsing *ex cathedra* the transformative conceptual power of the concept.

A final source is that of 'personal epistemology' – the professor's 'view of knowledge and knowing, knowledge construction, and knowledge evaluation' (Berthiaume, 2007, p. 186). Within the Threshold Concepts Framework, this aspect of personal epistemology introduces a source of variation among disciplinary experts in interpretations of how learners construct understanding, and may be supported in constructing understanding, of a threshold concept.

Berthiaume's theoretical and empirical research suggests that relationships exist between the components of these sources, with professors developing knowledge of, and strategies for, teaching and learning that are related to (if not rooted in) their discipline's epistemic and socio-cultural structures and perhaps mediated by their personal[8] epistemologies. The notion that personal epistemologies may mediate the construction of knowledge for teaching cautions us against assuming homogeneity in the ways that disciplinary experts construct and therefore represent knowledge for teaching (Berthiaume, 2007, p. 191). One could therefore not assume that one biologist's representations of, and repertoire for, teaching a threshold concept such as 'photochemical response' would closely resemble another's. Thus admitted is the notion of variation in teachers' thinking about, and understanding of, threshold concepts.

ITCK INTERSECTION WITH PERSONAL EPISTEMOLOGY AND OTHER TYPES OF KNOWLEDGE

As described by Shulman, the pedagogical content knowledge 'amalgam' is not socially constructed, although it can clearly incorporate one such type of knowledge arising from cognitive research. The 'amalgam' represents rather a type of knowledge that is essentially internal to, and for the benefit of, *the individual teacher* – (and perhaps ambiguously) uniquely and idiosyncratically so. That Shulman's (1986, 1987) generative ideas subsequently found traction in the discourse of teacher education is well illustrated in the case of science education.

Little more than a decade later, van Driel, Verloop, and de Vos (1998) directly addressed the issue of developing, in particular, science teachers' pedagogical content knowledge and, in doing so, they anchored their argument in the notion of 'craft knowledge' – a term not explicitly used by Shulman. In setting aside concerns that craft knowledge has been perceived as *inter alia* non-scientific, a repository of 'magical tricks', and not a knowledge of propositions, van Driel et al. (1998) proposed a formulation of craft knowledge capable of rising above 'the idiosyncratic level of individual narratives' (p. 674) and 'restricted to types of knowledge which actually guide the teachers' behaviour during classroom practice' (p. 675). They further expressed an intention to identify 'common patterns' in this type of craft knowledge, therefore implying that such knowledge could be externalised and categorised.[9]

In retrospective contrast, Marton's early (1986, 1989) contribution to the 'knowledge' debate was not a reformulation of (pedagogical content) knowledge. In was, instead, an unambiguous and particular research-based assertion of (in his view) 'relevant' knowledge production; a type of knowledge that is neither craft-based, nor elusive – knowledge that can be clearly communicated in the language of educational research for teaching purposes, and that is amenable to organisation within a constructivist episteme.

It is unproductive for present purposes to unequivocally entertain the idea that the presence of some 'type of knowledge' can be asserted by emphasising its visible absence in the sense that it cannot be communicated and therefore contribute to a constructivist discourse. Shulman (1986), and in his later interview account as reported in Berry, Loughran, and van Driel (2008) does not, for example, explicitly refer to tacit knowledge. There is however an insightful passing reference to it in a footnote in Shulman (1987, p. 12) in which he observes that 'it is of limited value if the teachers are held responsible for explaining what they do and why they do it, to their students, their communities, and their peers'.

The problem here is that, notwithstanding the acknowledgement that pedagogical content knowledge constitutes 'an accepted academic construct' (Berry et al., 2008, p. 1272), teachers have difficulty in attempting 'to articulate the critical links between practice and knowledge' (p. 1271). There were, in fact (c. 2008), 'few concrete examples' (Berry et al., p. 1272) of this aspect of science teachers' 'professional' knowledge. One explanation for this paucity of examples at that time was that there was apparently no obvious reason for teachers to provide them as a priority above competing demands of 'doing teaching'. More to the point for present purposes is that, in general, the unique and tacit nature of (pedagogical content) knowledge was reaffirmed as something that teachers are unaware of, and elusive in the sense that its articulation is hindered by perceptions of both an apparently non-existent 'language' to express it and a conceptual structure within which to organise it.[10]

The conjecture that this type of knowledge *might* be expressible given a suitable conceptual structure and 'language' to do so is worth pursuing. And, in this respect then, the question remains open as to whether the Threshold Concepts Framework can accommodate this type of knowledge for inclusion within ITCK – that is, provide the means for expressing and organising what are essentially held to be internal 'pedagogic ways of knowing'.

INTEGRATED THRESHOLD CONCEPT KNOWLEDGE

The proposition presented here is that, in higher education, it is possible to construct *Integrated Threshold Concept Knowledge* for the benefit of student learning – knowledge that is empirically based, and socially constructed, at the 'intersection' of specific *transformational* subject content with associated different 'types of knowledge'; specifically knowledge of the following:

• The epistemological, epistemic, and ontological status of threshold concepts, in particular their 'critical' and possibly troublesome features. Knowledge of what it is about these features that provokes a liminal state, and creates 'stuck places'. Foregrounded here is an analytical process that seeks answers to questions like: Do threshold concepts exist in the curriculum? Why are they so? What is their personal epistemological status? How are they distributed? How do they contribute to communicable 'ways of knowing' (epistemes)? A separate type of knowledge addresses the nature of variation in the progression to *threshold capability* (Baillie, Bowden, & Meyer, 2013).

- How students *vary* in their experience of apprehending and learning threshold concepts in the liminal space. The dimensionality of this experience traverses cognitive, affective (emotional), and ontological domains. With a specific focus on threshold concepts, evidence of variation may be reflected in a wide range of qualitative and quantitative data sources. Obvious sources are interview, 'think aloud', and focus group transcripts. Equally productive are answers to scenario questions (Taylor, Tzioumis, Meyer, & Ross, 2014), reflective metalearning essays (Ward & Meyer, 2010), and data captured by psychometric instruments specifically designed to focus on the learning of just one particular threshold concept (Zimbardi et al., 2014), or more general instruments that are adaptable to such a specific focus of student-learning response context (Meyer, Ward, & Latreille, 2009). Also admitted are recorded expressions of embodied knowledge in for example architecture (Hokstad et al., this volume), and the performing arts (Rowe & Martin, 2014).

- The logic and theoretical underpinning of repertoire in the 'pedagogic response domain' enabling, in particular, access to strategies – including assessment protocols (Land & Meyer, 2010) – involving 'threshold concept representations' for learning and teaching purposes. 'Repertoire' is therefore reflected in the availability of access to, and choice from, a range of relevant and purposeful strategies developed within these perspectives by self *and others*. And specific examples of such strategies will typically traverse student learning, metalearning, metacognitive, pedagogic, assessment, and curriculum perspectives.[11]

Meyer et al. (2014; this volume) provide a multifaceted example of such repertoire, as well as a resultant 'threshold concept representation'– expressed within a pedagogic and formative assessment perspective – as a 'metacognitive assessment activity'. An example of repertoire from a curriculum perspective lies in the explicit design of 'threshold concept modules' within curriculum structure Parker and McGill (this volume). Also see Male and Baillie (2014).

In short, ITCK is essentially a fusion of 'different types of knowledge' arising primarily from activity following an analytical process *for*, and *of*, threshold concepts'. This activity includes subsequent articulation of their 'critical features', generating knowledge of how these are experienced cognitively, affectively, and ontologically (in varying degrees) by students in the liminal state as well as an understanding of how these different types of knowledge translate into *in situ* 'threshold concept representations' in contributing to a repertoire of student-centred 'responses'.

EDUCATIONAL DEVELOPMENT ACTIVITIES ROOTED IN ITCK

That university teachers generally have individual capacity to 'research' their own practice is well established. Less established is evidence that such often-idiosyncratic activity impacts on their students' learning. Were this not the case, there would be no need for institutionalised course evaluation procedures and educational development programmes. The challenge at whatever level of institutional structure is to harness and formalise individual capacity to develop and share ITCK for the common good of the student experience. Such endeavour transcends, and is in contrast to, the default 'one size fits all' that often characterises the provision of educational development programmes. Advocated here at the heart of ITCK development is a celebration rather than suppression of differences that arise in inter-disciplinary discourses about the contextualised nature of transformative learning, in particular the epistemic and ontological learning journey of 'becoming' and 'being'.

A question arises about what form of 'research' enquiry might support such development of ITCK, particularly as undertaken by individual university teachers. As one foundation for such development, the point has already been made that various forms of research, both qualitative and quantitative, can appropriately and validly illuminate the experiential world of individual differences in learning threshold concepts. And in the context of a UK educational development programme, the study by Meyer (2012) furthermore confirms the capacity of such activity to contribute positively to the development of a personal teaching philosophy.

The chapter by Meyer et al. (this volume) on the threshold concept of 'critical flow' provides a narrative on the development of ITCK in a manner that could conceivably have been substantively nurtured in *any* educational development programme at the institutional, or even 'in-house' departmental, level. Their narrative chronicles the development of ITCK in a manner available to all using a transferable (concept-free) methodology, rather than a technical discussion of the concept itself, which is presented elsewhere for the curious (cf. Knight et al., 2014).

Finally, the vision of ITCK in the context of academic practice is that of developing a new, or enriching an existing, learning and teaching philosophy that is personal and discipline-based: *Personal* in emphasising attitudes and values: sense of self in relation to students, individual differences in their learning, and their learning wellbeing; *Discipline-based* in emphasising sense of self (academic identity, 'being') in relation to discipline; thinking and practising that reflects its 'inner logic', its characteristic modes of discourse, reasoning, analysis and explanation.

NOTES

[1] In this chapter a distinction is made between school *pupils* and university *students.*
[2] Shulman (1986) elaborates in some detail on subject content knowledge as an understanding of how knowledge within the discipline may be organised in different ways. Internalised wisdom and logic may then drive a particular pedagogic choice in a given context – hence, the enactment of pedagogical content knowledge, which effectively subsumes subject matter knowledge.

[3] 'Text' in relation to defining, and therefore in the student apprehension of, a threshold concept may embrace various forms of natural, artificial, or mathematical expression.

[4] It makes no sense to argue *ab initio* for changing students' conceptions of a threshold concept that has yet to be apprehended and that lies beyond their conceptual and ontological horizon. Conceptual change theory may well be helpful in explaining how students find themselves in liminal 'stuck places' insofar as the 'critical features' of the threshold concept may be initially misapprehended. A further observation is that 'conceptual change' within the Threshold Concepts Framework is seen as distinctive.

> We turn now to the question of how to operationalise 'integration' and 'transformation' in ways that distinguish conceptual change in threshold concepts from conceptual change in other traditions. Practice in these traditions has examined different conceptions of the same phenomenon and the conditions – including those that arise from the learner's intentions and emotions – in which it is more likely that they will shift from a less complex to a more complex conception of the phenomenon. This focus on conceptions of one particular phenomenon is different from that suggested by 'threshold concepts'. Threshold concepts have been suggested as ways of thinking about a wide range of phenomena that fall within the scope of a particular discipline or mode of thought. The transformation that is suggested as an outcome of understanding a threshold concept should be seen in changes in conception of several (perhaps many) phenomena and this way of thinking about conceptual change is different from that suggested by other traditions. (Davies, 2010)

[5] Phenomenographic analysis has proved to be accessible to teachers in both school and university contexts and has contributed significant insights into 'learning' as experienced from the internal perspective of the learner.

[6] Her work is referenced in Marton (1989) as Neuman (1987) which is more accessible than the Marton (1986) reference to her work in Swedish.

[7] An example of content specificity that is 'troublesome knowledge' in both school and university contexts. In undergraduate biology courses 'photosynthesis' is apprehended by students as the more sophisticated idea of 'photochemical response', identified as a 'discipline concept' in plant systems by Ross, Taylor, Hughes, Kofod, Whitaker, Lutze-Mann and Tzioumis (2010), and one that is epistemically integrated within the threshold concept of 'energy transformation' across the biological sciences.

[8] The 'personal' is often constructed internally (Berthiaume, 2007, p. 21), but can be externalised and contribute to social-empiric construction. We are led to this conclusion by the design of Berthiaume's study itself, in which he conducted semi-structured interviews with university professors to examine the individual components (including personal epistemology) of Discipline Specific Pedagogical Knowledge (DPK), as well as their interaction. Questions in the interview protocol were constructed by drawing on the literature (theoretical and empirical) in personal epistemology and used to elicit an external expression of the internal beliefs and thinking of participants. The data generated through the study provide empirical evidence of the various components of DPK. Furthermore, the DPK research is intended to contribute to the practice of both university teachers and educational developers. 'The idea is that the DPK framework can serve as an outline of what can be present in the case of that university professor developing pedagogical knowledge in relation to his/her discipline. As such, it can serve to develop both guiding and diagnostic tools for the university professor wishing to develop his/her understanding of the most effective ways to teach in his/her discipline' (p. 193). Berthiaume notes that this would not be left to the individual university professor to struggle with alone, but through, for example, the support from educational developers.

[9] The interest here is in 'craft knowledge' for ITCK purposes. We note in passing that, notwithstanding its claimed validity, Pedagogical Content Knowledge is not a stable construct by virtue of definition. Many authors have proposed reformulations of Shulman's original expansive writing and generative ideas. In their intention to seek the 'common patterns' referred to, van Driel et al. (1998) were quite clear in their 'craft knowledge' reformulation of such knowledge. Less clear is the extent to which they succeeded in identifying such 'craft knowledge' patterns amenable to externalisation. Based on

semi-structured interviews, a small-scale, longitudinal, qualitative study by Henze, van Driel, and Verloop (2008, p. 1323) reported the identification of 'possible common patterns' in the development of Pedagogical Content Knowledge of nine experienced school teachers, but it did so in an apparent reformulated departure of the of the original 'craft knowledge' emphasis. In fact, twenty four years after the 'craft knowledge' reformulation, and citing the concept of 'force' in physics as an example, van Driel and Berry (2012) reconfirmed that pedagogical content knowledge is 'specifically related to topics *within* certain disciplines' (p. 26, emphasis in original), and they further assert its development is 'a complex process that is *highly specific* to the context, situation *and person*' (p. 27, emphasis added).

[10] An extant Pedagogical Content Knowledge literature is acknowledged that advocates a methodology that begins with (school) teachers, individually or in groups, identifying the 'big ideas' in a given subject domain. For each such idea answers to eight questions of the following form are then sought:

- Why is it important for students to know this idea?
- What are the intended student learning outcomes?
- What do you know about this idea that students do not yet need to know?
- What are the difficulties or limitations associated with the teaching of this idea?
- What do students need to know in order to learn this idea?
- How may students' understanding of, or confusion concerning, this idea be established?
- What factors influence your teaching of this idea?
- What are the teaching methods and their rationale?

In reading 'concept' for 'idea', the capacity of this methodology to generate an additional 'type of knowledge' (as part of ITCK) is considered to be insufficient for present purposes. Knowledge so produced is bereft, for example, of any epistemological analysis of the concept in question, or any research-based (or otherwise determined) knowledge of how students vary in their learning of it.

[11] As an aside Shulman (1986, p. 10) referred to 'curricular' knowledge (in a much narrower sense than intended here) as a repertoire of associated *materials* (or 'tools of teaching') that can be deployed to 'present or exemplify *particular content* and remediate or evaluate the adequacy of student accomplishments' (emphasis added).

REFERENCES

Baillie, C., Bowden, J. A., & Meyer, J. H. F. (2013). Threshold capabilities: Threshold concepts and knowledge capability linked through variation theory. *Higher Education, 2*, 227–246. doi:10.1007/s10734-012-9540-5

Becher, T. (1989). *Academic tribes and territories*. Buckingham, UK: Open University Press.

Becher, T., & Trowler, P. R. (2001). *Academic tribes and territories: Intellectual enquiry and the cultures of disciplines* (2nd ed.). Buckingham, UK: SRHE/Open University Press.

Berry, A., Loughran, J., & van Driel, J. H. (2008). Revisiting the roots of pedagogical content knowledge. *International Journal of Science Education, 30*, 1271–1279. doi:10.1080/09500690801998885

Berthiaume, D. (2007). *What is the nature of university professors' discipline-specific pedagogical knowledge? A descriptive multicase study* (Unpublished doctoral dissertation). McGill University, Montreal, Canada.

Davies, P. (2010, July). *Transforming knowledge structures: A procedure for developing students' understanding of threshold concepts*. Paper presented at the Third Biennial Threshold Concepts Symposium: Exploring transformative dimensions of threshold concepts, Sydney, Australia.

Donald, J. G. (2002). *Learning to think: Disciplinary perspectives*. San Francisco, CA: Jossey-Bass.

Henze, I., van Driel, J. H., & Verloop, N. (2008). Development of experienced science teachers' pedagogical content knowledge of models of the solar system and the universe. *International Journal of Science Education, 30*, 1321–1342. doi:10.1080/09500690802187017

Hokstad, L. M., Rødne, G., Braaten, B. O., Wellinger, S., & Shetelig, F. (this volume). *Transformational learning in architectural education: Re-thinking architecture and the education of architecture*.

Knight, D. B., Callaghan, D. C., Baldock, T., & Meyer, J. H. F. (2014). Identifying threshold concepts: Case study of an open catchment hydraulics course. *European Journal of Engineering Education, 39*, 125–142. doi:10.1080/03043797.2013.833175

Land, R., & Meyer, J. H. F. (2010). Threshold concepts and troublesome knowledge (5): Dynamics of assessment. In J. H. F. Meyer, R. Land, & C. Baillie (Eds.), *Threshold concepts and transformational learning* (pp. 61–78). Rotterdam, The Netherlands: Sense Publishers.

Male, S. A., & Baillie, C. A. (2014). Research guided teaching practices: Engineering thresholds; an approach to curriculum renewal. In A. Johri & B. M. Olds (Eds.), *Cambridge handbook of engineering education research* (pp. 393–408).Cambridge: Cambridge University Press.

Marton, F. (1986). Educational research: Then and now. Reflections on practices and impact. *The Australian Educational Researcher, 13*, 5–31. doi:10.1007/BF03219264

Marton, F. (1989). Towards a pedagogy of content. *Educational Psychologist, 24*, 1–23. doi:10.1207/s15326985ep2401_1

Meyer, J. H. F. (2012). 'Variation in student learning' as a threshold concept. *The Journal of Faculty Development, 26*, 8–13.

Meyer, J. H. F., Knight, D. B., Baldock, T. E., Callaghan, D. P., McCredden, J., & O'Moore, L. (2014). *What to do with a threshold concept: A case study.* Paper presented at the 5th Biennial International Threshold Concepts Conference, Durham, UK.

Meyer, J. H. F., Ward, S. C., & Latreille, P. (2009). Threshold concepts and metalearning capacity. *International Review of Economics Education, 8*, 132–154.

Neuman, D. (1987). *The origin of arithmetic skills: A phenomenographic approach.* Göteborg, Sweden: Acta Universitatis Gothoburgensis.

Pace, D., & Middendorf, J. (Eds.). (2004). *New directions for teaching and learning, 98. Decoding the disciplines: Helping students learn disciplinary ways of thinking.* San Francisco, CA: Jossey-Bass.

Parker, A., & McGill, D. (2014). Modularisation of learning outcomes in terms of threshold concepts. *Waikato Journal of Education, 19*(2), 105–114. doi:10.15663/wje.v19i2.102. Retrieved from http://www.wje.org.nz/index.php/WJE/article/view/102

Ross, P. M., Taylor, C. E., Hughes, C., Kofod, M., Whitaker, N., Lutze-Mann, L., & Tzioumis, V. (2010). Threshold concepts: Challenging the way we think, teach, and learn in biology. In J. H. F. Meyer, R. Land, & C. Baillie (Eds.), *Threshold concepts and transformational learning* (pp. 165–177). Rotterdam, The Netherlands: Sense Publishers.

Rowe, N., & Martin, R. (2014). Dancing onto the page: Crossing an academic borderland. *Waikato Journal of Education, 19*(2), 25–36. doi:10.15663/wje.v19i2.96. Retrieved from http://www.wje.org.nz/index.php/WJE/article/view/96

Shulman, L. S. (1985, April). *Those who understand: Knowledge growth in teaching.* Presidential address at the annual meeting of the American Educational Research Association (AERA), Chicago, IL.

Shulman, L. S. (1986). Those who understand: Knowledge growth in teaching. *Educational Researcher, 15*, 4–14. doi:10.3102/0013189X015002004

Shulman, L. S. (1987). Knowledge and teaching: Foundations of the new reform. *Harvard Educational Review, 57*, 1–22.

Taylor, C., Tzioumis V., Meyer, J. H. F., & Ross, P. (2014). Using a mixed methods approach to explore student understanding of hypotheses in biology. In C. O'Mahony, A. Buchanan, M. O'Rourke, & B. Higgs (Eds.), *Threshold concepts: From personal practice to communities of practice. Proceedings of the National Academy's Sixth Annual Conference and the Fourth Biennial Threshold Concepts Conference* (pp. 83–87).

Timmermans, J. (2010). Changing our minds. The developmental potential of threshold concepts. In J. H. F. Meyer, R. Land, & C. Baillie, (Eds.), *Threshold concepts and transformational learning* (pp. 3–19). Rotterdam, The Netherlands: Sense Publishers.

van Driel, J. H., & Berry, A. (2012). Teacher professional development focusing on pedagogical content knowledge. *Educational Researcher, 41*, 26–28. doi:10.3102/0013189X11431010

van Driel, J. H., Verloop, N., & de Vos, W. (1998). Developing science teachers' pedagogical content knowledge. *Journal of Research in Science Teaching, 35*, 673–695. doi:10.1002/(SICI)1098-2736(199808)35:6<673::AID-TEA5>3.0.CO;2-J

Ward, S. C., & Meyer, J. H. F. (2010). Metalearning capacity and threshold concept engagement. *Innovations in Education and Teaching International, 47*, 369–378. doi:10.1080/14703297.2010.518429

Zimbardi, K., Meyer, J. H. F., Chunduri, P., Lluka, L. J., Taylor, C. E., Ross, P. M., & Tzioumis, V. (2014). Student understanding of the critical features of a hypothesis: Variation across epistemic and heuristic dimensions. In C. O'Mahony, A. Buchanan, M. O'Rourke, & B. Higgs (Eds.), *Proceedings of the National Academy's Sixth Annual Conference and the Fourth Biennial Threshold Concepts Conference: Threshold concepts: From personal practice to communities of practice* (pp. 123–127).

Jan H. F. Meyer
School of Civil Engineering
The University of Queensland

Julie A. Timmermans
Centre for Teaching Excellence
University of Waterloo

SUSANNAH MCGOWAN

4. THE CAREER OF THRESHOLD CONCEPTS IN A LARGE-LECTURE HISTORY COURSE

An Examination of Uptake of Disciplinary Actions

INTRODUCTION

Borrowing Etienne Wenger's description of his own influential concept, *communities of practice*, as having a "career" of its own, this research examined the careers of threshold concepts within a large lecture history course (441 students) at an American research-intensive university in 2013 and 2014. In Wenger's terms, the advancement of concepts within a large system does not happen automatically, so how could threshold concepts move through large courses from the professor to the student? The only way a student can work on threshold concepts is if the concepts are mediated in some way by the professor or the teaching assistant through an instructional explanation (Leinhardt, 2004). Even the level of the mediation and the capabilities of the people involved play a role in whether or not a threshold concept moves through a system. In order for concepts to weave through the system seamlessly, the teaching of threshold concepts required an examination of the practices involved in doing so. Previous research on threshold concepts in the classroom focused on upper-level seminars for majors (Middendorf & Pace, 2004). This baseline qualitative study contributes to three areas of research in higher education: application of threshold concepts at the course level; what this application looks like in terms of practices at the discussion section level; and the important role of the teaching assistant (TA) in his or her own development as practitioners of the discipline and in teaching history.

This study centers on one professor who reflected on the threshold concept literature (Adler-Kassner, Majewski, & Koshnick, 2012) in order to enact changes in his large-lecture American history course over the course of two years (by "large," this means a class of 441 students). After much reflection on historical thinking (Wineburg, 1998, 2001) and the emerging literature on threshold concepts and what constituted "thresholds" in any given discipline like history (Meyer & Land, 2006; Anderson & Day, 2005), the professor chose to combine short lectures on threshold concepts in history (selected by him and his course) with strategic content (e.g., he discussed the concept of historical empathy before a unit on slave resistance in the American South). He decided to make important historical thinking concepts explicit for students within seven "mini- lectures" throughout a ten-week course.

R. Land et al. (Eds.), Threshold Concepts in Practice, 39–52.
© *2016 Sense Publishers. All rights reserved.*

He delivered these short lectures to all the enrolled students; then students were divided into discussion sections led by the professor's nine teaching assistants. The discussion sections provided a space where students had the opportunity to practice primary source analysis or as one teaching assistant phrased it, "do fingers-in-the-pie history" (McGowan, discussion transcript, 2013). For students to learn these threshold concepts within this big learning system, they had to be distributed – from the professor to his teaching assistants and then to the students. These discussion spaces provided a critical cross-section to view how these concepts were distributed based on the pedagogical actions of the teaching assistants.

CONTEXT

Many current conversations within U.S. higher education make the findings in this study relevant and timely. The potential for situating threshold concepts in history posed benefits for student learning but it also represented the potential for epistemological enculturation for the teaching assistants who were in their second or third year of their Ph.D. program. Two discussions of reforms for history graduate student training occurred in 2014, both stemming from the American Historical Association (AHA), one of the main disciplinary governing bodies in the U.S. One was in reaction to the threat of online education and the other in reaction to the lack of employment available to history graduate students. AHA called for the need to better prepare graduate students so that students would not opt for online courses. As one history professor described the problem:

> Better-preparing graduate students to teach history could help bridge an emerging cultural "schism" between research and adjunct faculty and help history departments better defend themselves against the enrollment-draining potential of the massive open online courses. Such changes also must be paired with a radical undergraduate curriculum reform that challenges traditional, content-pure perceptions of the major. (Jaschik, 2014, paragraph 3)

Challenging the "content-pure perceptions" of the discipline in order to repair the cultural schism between research and teaching within history departments described a second initiative out of AHA. "No More Plan B," aimed to develop alternative courses within programs geared towards expanding the skills of history graduate students. One university planned to offer a course specifically related to teaching where graduate students would translate historical content for instruction at all grade levels. Pairing better teaching assistant training for epistemological knowledge *and* for teaching with undergraduate reform complement the emphasis in this study on the crucial role of teaching assistants in large courses.

While the threshold concept framework offered potential to rethink the learning context wherein students acquire and utilize key ideas from the discipline, little work has been done to date as to what this looks like within large lecture courses in higher education. Research in teaching and learning in higher education in the last fifteen years addresses the importance of integrating disciplinary ways of thinking – i.e. an understanding of the ways that questions are asked and investigated within disciplines – in undergraduate courses. However, the application of the emergent threshold concept research varies in history departments and within these large-scale learning settings. The research represented here demonstrates the potential impact the threshold concepts framework holds for designing large systems of learning but more importantly, the research demonstrated the impact of threshold concepts on graduate student development and enculturation into the discipline; how the teaching students incorporated threshold concepts into their discussions related to how they saw themselves in their program and in their roles as teachers of disciplinary concepts.

METHODS FOR TRACING CONCEPTS IN LARGE LEARNING SYSTEMS

Wenger (2010) described the adoption of his own concept, communities of practice, as having a "career" that expanded in ways he and his colleague, Jean Lave, never anticipated. He described the concept as "simple, intuitive" and influential in many different fields, particularly educational and corporate organizations. In order to trace careers of concepts, Wenger recommended focusing on three parts of the learning system: its structure, its participants, and its practices (p. 179). In this case, the structure of a large lecture course contained the main lectures delivered by the professor three times a week in a movie theatre. Each of the nine teaching assistants assigned to the course led three discussion sections a week. Each discussion section contained eighteen students.

In order to capture the practices of this learning system, each "mini-lecture" on historical concepts within a lecture given by the professor was observed and recorded. The mini-lectures were:

Table 1. The seven historical thinking concept lectures given in 2013 quarter

Time of quarter	Subject
First week	Introduction to Historical Thinking
Second week	Analysing a primary source
Third week	Historical Empathy
Before first essay	How to write a thesis statement
Fourth week	How historians argue I (Presentation of professor's own research and the criticism related to his research)
Fifth week	Causation & counterfactuals
Seventh week	How historians argue (Contested narratives about Lincoln)
Tenth week	Summary of historical thinking lectures as they pertained to the final. He stressed to students they should be able to develop arguments, analyse narratives, and use evidence

It is crucial to note that these mini-lectures on historical concepts stemmed from the professor's own thinking and lengthy reflection on what he considered important for students to understand in history based on influential research on historical thinking and threshold concepts (Wineburg, 1998; Calder, 2006; Pace, 2008; Meyer & Land, 2005, 2006). This project did not set out to define threshold concepts in history; instead it focused on how the threshold concept framework provided an impetus to redesign a course based on disciplinary principles suited to the institutional context of this course. His reflections on the use of threshold concepts and historical thinking, however, was (and is) still in process – so the professor was learning about threshold concepts and while simultaneously incorporating them into his teaching. From the scholarly teaching perspective, this project could be categorized as an initial step at looking into what was possible to do in course design and what worked (Hutchings & Shulman, 1999). Understanding the structure of the course and the practices involved in the work of professor and his teaching assistants, helped to uncover the potential movement of the concepts contained in the mini-lectures and the associated practices and dispositions necessary to facilitate that movement (Brown & Duguid, 2000; Wenger, 2010).

Following the delivery of these lectures, four teaching assistants (TAs) volunteered to have one (out of three) sections observed each week. Online surveys were administered to all students to gather feedback on the mini-lectures and perceptions on how students would apply these concepts to other history courses and non-history courses.

Interviews with the professor, the four teaching assistants, and four students from observed sections rounded out the qualitative methodologies aimed to capture the movement of concepts within such a large, complex instructional system. Even though this research focuses on the actions of the teaching assistants, there is one important caveat of this study: the low response rate of student participation in the study. This could have been caused by the lack of efforts at the institutional level to address quality enhancement in large courses where students are simply unaccustomed to this type of "interventional" study. Despite the low number of student participation in interviews (n = 4 out of 441) and the final online survey (n = 50, who completed every question), there existed an initial connection between how students reported their perception of the effectiveness of the mini-lecture concepts and the TAs' efforts to emphasize those concepts in the discussions. More importantly, there were initial claims in student survey data indicating which concepts would help them in future history courses; indicating the career of the concept displayed viability beyond the confines of the course. Further research of students in large courses is needed to investigate these potential claims on student learning and transfer. While the initial focus of this study concerned student learning of threshold concepts, the focus quickly turned to the teaching assistants' capabilities to understand, adapt, and disseminate these concepts in their own teaching.

THRESHOLD CAPABILITIES OF TEACHING:
UPTAKE, TRANSLATION & FRAMING

At the onset of the study, an unintentional assumption on the professor's part led to the focus on the role of the teaching assistant within the structure of the course. While the professor focused on improving student learning through explicating historical thinking concepts, he did not make his plan to unveil seven "mini-lectures" on historical concepts explicit to his TAs prior to the start of the course; neither did he directly tell them to discuss the mini-lectures with students as the course progressed. This was an unintended outcome of the study yet it provided a new lens in which to describe how the TAs chose to embed concepts. Therefore, the discussion section provided the space to examine how the TAs took up the threshold concepts identified by the professor, translated them, or mediated those concepts to students. The actions of the TA, and in turn their own understanding of the concepts, determined the trajectory of the concepts in the course.

In looking at the discussion sections and the efforts of the TAs to include threshold concepts, the TAs displayed varying understandings of the concepts presented by the professor and varying abilities for introducing those concepts in their own teaching. To advance the careers of the threshold concepts introduced by the professor, the TAs needed to have what Baillie, Bowden, and Meyer (2013) described as "threshold capabilities," abilities that "define thresholds to professional learning in a defined area of knowledge" (p. 10). Baillie, Bowden, and Meyer used this term in the context of student learning, how students develop certain capabilities to encounter and to understand threshold concepts. In this context, the term was adapted to the context of teaching to describe the efforts of the TAs to embed the threshold concepts in their discussion sections. These threshold capabilities contributed to the ways in which TAs framed the concepts for students to learn and understand in relation to

Table 2. TA Stages of use of threshold concepts in discussions

	TA Stage 1: None No mention of concept	*TA Stage 2: Uptake:* Minimal reference	*TA Stage 3: Translation* of the concept or action	*TA Stage 4: Framing* the discussion
Historical thinking concept mentioned in professor's lecture	Explanation: No mention of the professor's lecture or terminology surfaced.	Explanation: One or two elements of the lecture surfaced in the discussion.	Explanation: The TA brought up the concept and incorporated it into the discussion.	Explanation: The concept provided a framework for the discussion and a place for students to apply the concept.

the course material. If students were to encounter threshold concepts in class to help them learn how historians practice, they needed the TAs to possess certain capabilities to mediate or embed those concepts in the discussion itself.

To understand the potential threshold capabilities of the TAs, their actions or instructional strategies addressing the concepts in the mini-lectures were coded as uptake, translation, or framing:

Uptake

Uptake is the act of selecting, defining, and representing an idea or concept in teaching. The idea of uptake (Freadman, 2002), borrowed from genre studies and from a study on teacher talk moves in the history classroom (Reisman, 2011), entailed either naming the concept itself (e.g., analyzing primary sources, historical empathy) or using it briefly referencing the concept within the discussion. Based on whether a teaching assistant decides to "take up" a term or concept, then it is important to look at how it is taken up and incorporated into the discussion.

Translation

One form of uptake is translation. Freadman's use of the term "translation" fits the idea of how the TAs incorporated the threshold concept into discussion. As she explains, translation is indicated when a concept is repurposed, a signpost used to point in a particular direction: "any subsequent sign translates the previous sign into a different language, a different conceptual framework, a different set of assumptions ... " (p. 43). The degree of distribution of a concept from the professor's lecture was a signpost indicating the particular stage in which the TA incorporated the concept, a moment in the concept's "career." At times, TAs' translation of a concept derived from the professor's concept lecture in addition to their prior knowledge on the topic or their prior way of teaching the concept (as in the case of the concept lecture on analyzing primary sources – a concept that contained multiple applications by TAs yet differed from the professor's own framework).

Framing

In terms of the final stage of uptake, framing the discussion, Reisman (2011) used the term "contextual framing" in the history classroom defined as a teacher's ability to provide historical contextualization for students through her discussion facilitation strategies. Stemming from this usage, the term "*conceptual framing*" defined the moments where the TAs advanced the careers of threshold concepts, using the concepts as the basis engaging students in discussion. While uptake and translation indicated the career of the concept at play in the discussion sections, the notion of "framing" indicated a more comprehensive approach to embedding the threshold concept in the discussion section. In these instances, not only did the TA translate the concepts for students, they solicited student involvement in practicing these concepts. Consistent focus and deliberate practice with the concept represented key signposts of conceptual framing, thereby advancing the career of the concept in how students used the concept to make sense of historical documents.

These concepts – uptake, translation, and framing – provided the necessary terms to describe the TAs' practices. The stages the TAs went through to apply threshold concepts in their discussions paralleled the process of stages of faculty professional development in understanding threshold concepts identified by Meyer (2012): engagement, description, interpretation, and action. In this study, the stages of uptake differed in the TAs' level of engagement with or understanding of the concepts and how their engagement with the concepts defined their actions in the discussion sections. Throughout this study, the role of the TA as the intermediary between the official course system and the students became an important space to analyse because of the range of uptake, translation, and framing capabilities with each concept.

THRESHOLD CONCEPTS IN ACTION

The challenges that arose out of this integration of threshold concepts in the course structure stemmed from trying to capture the moments when a TA decided to take up what the professor was trying to do and their approach to providing a framework (not necessarily the professor's framework) for students to incorporate concepts within their discussion sections. As data suggest, the farther along the trajectory of uptake the TAs were (Stages 3 and 4, Table 2), the more likely the concept travelled from professor to TA to student. The third mini-lecture on "historical empathy" will be used to illustrate how the concept functioned within the course.

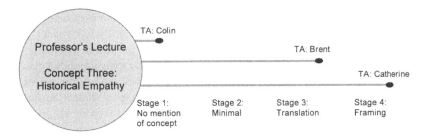

Figure 1. Concept lecture and its trajectory in the TAs' discussion sections. All TA names are pseudonyms

The professor chose to make "historical empathy' a threshold concept in his course due to the role empathy could play in reading primary sources and in anticipation of students' reactions to selected primary sources, "historians want to understand the perspective of historical actors, so it is vital that historians have the imagination to try to see the world from different perspectives" (Majewski, 2014). The professor introduced historical empathy prior to the start of a unit on slavery and slave resistance in the U.S. in the mid 1800s. He outlined strategies to analyse a primary source through the lens of empathy versus a presentist[1] view: "To be empathetic as an historian you have to be willing to put yourself in the shoes of lots of different people" (McGowan, recorded lecture, 2013). He also outlined the concept of empathy as "trying to understand the thoughts, beliefs, and actions of others;" "empathy does not mean agreement or applying judgment;" and "trying to understand others as humans." This type of historical lecture intended to offset the potential visceral reactions students might have had to the readings for that week that included pro-slavery arguments. Furthermore, he added, "To be empathetic as an historian you have to be willing to put yourself in the shoes of lots of different people" (McGowan, lecture, 2013). The following vignettes illustrate the stages of uptake among three TAs: Colin, Brent, and Catherine.

Stage 1: No Mention of Concept: Colin

Colin was in his third year of the program and in his fourth year of being a TA. While earning his master's degree in history at a different university, he served as a teaching assistant for two years. At the university in question, he had taught two years (including teaching this course once before). He was the most experienced teaching assistant of the nine.

In his discussion section, Colin demonstrated little involvement in extending the career of the concept to his own discussion section. In fact, key moments demonstrated a possible misinterpretation of the historical concept of empathy given that he started the discussion by asking who were the "good guys" and "bad guys" among the authors. Colin also led his discussion from an "either/or" or an "agree/ disagree" framework, "Let's say then, bringing our morals into play here, what do you say? Do you agree with what he is saying? Is this morally repugnant?" Colin resorted to prompting students to agree or disagree with the source using questions intended for yes or no answers. He encouraged students to apply presentist views on the sources when that was the opposite of what the professor espoused in his lecture. His explanation of the sources themselves were useful in helping students understand the author's argument; but situating them in a context and viewing them as they existed in their time were not evident strategies in his discussion facilitation. These problematic misinterpretations of the concept prevented the concept of historical empathy to even enter the conversation. For each concept unveiled in the course, Colin remained in Stages 1 and 2 in his discussion facilitations.

In Colin's interview after the course ended, when asked which of the mini-lecture concepts he felt he was struggling with in his own graduate work, he responded, "Still working on all of them … I mean it's nice to have them. I haven't even really given much thought to this idea of threshold concepts." It was possible that Colin did not integrate the concepts because he could not connect them or integrate them into his own understanding. Therefore, he stuck to what he knew from his prior knowledge and understanding about teaching. He appeared to dismiss the potential reflection on his own teaching that the concepts could have provided him even while admitting that he would like to improve as a teacher.

Stage 3: Translation to Framing of Historical Empathy: Brent

Brent was in his third year in the program. He had four quarters (roughly one year) of teaching assistant experience prior to the start of this course. Brent struggled to translate this concept of historical empathy at the onset of the discussion. Brent's initial struggle, however, yielded to a productive conversation towards the end showing the potential troublesome nature (Perkins, 2006) of this particular concept for TAs and its application to a discussion section. Brent's discussion sorted into three phases: he encountered a difficult introductory discussion on presentism where students' responses showed confusion as to what this meant causing frustration on the part of the TA. Second, he engaged students in a thorough analysis of the readings consistently returning to the text to direct the conversation and asking targeted questions about the argument and audience of the author. Third, he returned to the difficult topic of presentism, imbued with new language, to allow students to review or renew what they had discussed at the beginning of class. Within the timespan of fifty minutes, this TA showed a tremendous range of adaptation, flexibility and responsiveness to students in order to translate this concept for students.

In the first three minutes of the first phase of the discussion, Brent asked students to discuss what it meant to take a presentist perspective on the past. Students struggled with answering this question possibly due to the fact they had not delved into the sources or they did not know what "presentist" meant as the professor did not define explicitly in his lecture the need for historical empathy as a way to combat "presentism." Both students and the TA were frustrated in this initial discussion until a student specified a particular passage in a source to demonstrate a point she was making. This turn towards the text led the TA to abandon discussing what it meant NOT to apply a presentist view and focus instead on analytical reading and explanations. Brent prompted students to look for arguments, to identify the audience, and to question the degree of persuasion for the particular audience.

After fifteen minutes of a thorough analysis of the primary sources that ensued after the confusing introduction, the TA returned to the original issue of judgment in history. Brent then posed this question:

> Going back to the larger question that I started off with about values and judgments in history, how do you write or read about slavery? Is slavery an exception to value-neutral history? What do we … just tell the story and there is George Fitzhugh and there's Frederick Douglass and then the past is complicated and murky? *I'm asking how do we approach these five documents as historians?*

However, at this juncture, and in the way he referred to the students as historians, it appeared that the class was in a better position to answer this question than they had been at the beginning of class. It is possible that the primary source analysis neutralized the discussion to allow students to fully understand what the TA may have been asking at the beginning of class. Two student excerpts from the discussion indicated the type of response the TA sought at the beginning of the discussion; yet, for these students, the TA's effective guidance to read the sources through an empathetic lens allowed them to reassess their prior knowledge and attempt to understand the source within the particular context of the time:

Student A: It's hard to be open-minded because you've been taught that ever since you learned about the Underground Railroad that slavery is just inherently wrong, morally corrupt, and there is no bright side to it whatsoever. It was hard to read Fitzhugh [since] we're taught that factory workers brought us into industrialization, not slavery."

Student B: For someone who is brought up in the system [of slavery] and tell them that what they have seen their entire life is wrong. He's making a moral judgment to defend his way of life; that's the way I see it that he's on the defensive. (McGowan, Discussion transcript, 2013)

In Brent's interview discussing this moment, he explained how the historical empathy concept was one he struggled with in his own research on racial perceptions in eugenicists. Brent admitted that it was difficult to exercise empathy for these "pretty bad dudes" but he saw it as his "job" or professional responsibility as an historian to create an accurate representation of these historical actors. To use threshold concept terminology, this concept proved troublesome for the TA on two levels: applying it to his own research and in understanding how to use this concept in his discussions.

Brent's experience with incorporating historical empathy discussion revealed the troublesome nature of the concept for him and for the students. Yet he returned to his impressive capabilities for keeping the focus on the actions of analysing sources in order to steer the discussion back to the sources. In both instances, his identity as both a disciplinarian and teacher produced complex, rich discussions about the readings and the strategies to uncover what they were about. Translation and framing of threshold concepts often supported the "uncoverage" (Perkins, 2006) of content within his discussions.

Stage 4: Framing of Historical Empathy: Catherine

Catherine was in her second year in the program. She majored in Economics and French at a small, regional liberal arts university prior to coming to this research-intensive university. She had only ten weeks (one term) of teaching experience prior to this course. Where Colin displayed an outright struggle with this concept and Brent showed a similar struggle that led to a productive end, Catherine latched on to the concept of historical empathy in order to frame her discussion from the start. Catherine noted in her post-term interview that the historical empathy lecture affected her thinking and how she shaped her discussion section following the professor's lecture. She stated:

> I just remember that one standing out. Being like you can't … it really changed [my] perception of how to judge historical actors. Such as you can't impose your morals on the past, so I think that was good.

When asked if this lecture changed how she approached her discussion section, she replied,

> I think I chose to focus more on how we are going to categorize these people [all historical actors]. Or how should we be ok [with] categorizing these people or why can't we impose our standards on them? As opposed to being, what did he think? Who disagreed with him? More like the … it added a different element to section that week.

To illustrate how she added a new element to her discussion for that week, an excerpt from the start of her discussion section demonstrates how she chose to frame the discussion on slavery. She asked students to think about what future historians might say about current social problems in the US and what their responses would be to those future historians about why they could not solve these problems immediately. The excerpt below shows the steps she took students through to consider change within an institutional system:

> I want to talk about the importance of context when looking back at things. So I know a TA that has taught [this class] before. Apparently he got a thesis statement from a really good student on the first paper that said, "slaveowners were assholes." What would you say is wrong this statement?

> Let's say it is 2313 and we're looking back at the year 2013. What sorts of things will people 300 years in the future critique us about? Like what are we doing that is obviously terrible or they will be able to easily say this is obviously a bad thing why don't we fix it?

In order to frame their discussion on slavery, Catherine walked students through specific steps to think about the profound challenge of rethinking their current definitions of slavery in relation to how historical actors defined slavery in the past in the sources. Her goal in this exercise was for students to think about how difficult it is to change these issues in a short period of time. This connection between thinking about what students would want future historians to say about 2013 to their own thinking on conditions in the U.S. South in 1830s, 40s, and 50s provided an entry point to approaching the primary sources – through the lens of historical empathy. Catherine, the most novice TA in the group, showed another possible method for framing a concept thus demonstrating its movement from the professor to the discussion section. While the more experienced TAs displayed conceptual ambivalence around connecting concepts to the classroom (Colin and Brent), Catherine displayed the "dispositional aptitudes" (Cronin, 2012) necessary to merge her development in the discipline and her learning to become a teacher of the discipline.

THE ROLE OF THE TEACHING ASSISTANT

When Catherine reframed her discussion to include historical empathy, the professor's lecture affected her own thinking about how she viewed historical actors; therefore, she wanted students to shift their thinking as well. Bounded with the notion of uptake was the ability to see oneself in a certain way in order to demonstrate teaching capabilities needed to help students take up the concepts. While initial findings suggest particular actions to take to sustain the emphasis on threshold concepts in a large lecture setting, the most important result of the study showed that teaching assistants were a crucial link in promoting and sustaining the careers of the concepts within the large lecture learning system.

When looking at the TAs, it is important to understand how they perceive the concepts, because their belief in them – whether or not they agree or see them as being important – matters in terms of how much they spoke to those concepts. Recent research on threshold concepts within professional development speaks to understanding the liminal spaces of graduate student development as they move through this enculturation process. Cronin (2012) identified a threshold concept for graduate students as learning to view their discipline holistically, "attitudes and beliefs, about the discipline; about themselves as emerging academic teachers and about building capacity for empathy with their students as disciplinary novices" (p. 39). Cronin's concept of dispositional attitudes applies to the TAs' actions. Similarly, Devitt et al. (2012) argue that "the development of a student teacher's identity as a professional is of prime importance in negotiating the liminal space of the novice teacher, rather than solely the cumulative acquisition of concrete technical and organizational [sic] skills associated with effective classroom teaching" (p. 129). Devitt and colleagues found student teachers underwent an ontological shift in their understanding of teaching when "awareness raising through interactions with theory in lectures or reading" (p. 131) occurred.

Returning to the theoretical underpinnings of uptake, Freadman (2002) offers the image of uptake as crossing a boundary. According to Freadman, uptake and translation "is the mediation of a boundary, not its obliteration … uptake is the local event of crossing a boundary" (p. 43). But that boundary crossing into a discipline in both research and teaching is affected by a number of factors: prior knowledge, dispositions, and earlier experiences. Enculturation to the discipline and teaching involves crossing boundaries, adopting the disciplinary "worldview" and working through these liminal spaces to become full members of the discipline residing at the intersection of identity and knowledge.

CONCLUSION

The initial intention of the professor aimed to make course concepts explicit to students; while that may have happened, the benefits of this type of inclusion connected to the everyday work of a TA in a meaningful way. This new approach to history survey courses, and the means to delineate the stages of uptake in teaching concepts, provided a space for the TAs to consider what it meant to be a member of a discipline and teach within that discipline. When TAs took the time to reflect on these disciplinary considerations, positive strides towards good teaching connected to student learning. Cultivating the TA role, within this large university setting, provides the bridge between the disciplinary concepts, the curriculum of the course, and the students.

Threshold concepts spurred the professor in this study on a trajectory to redesign his course to connect students to core disciplinary concepts. Tracing the careers of these concepts yielded more information about what is needed within the system in terms of the types of processes that need to be in place to support the inclusion of the concepts in the course. In order to embed threshold concepts in a large course, the research pointed to an important participant in making certain that concepts travel in the learning system: the teaching assistant. Exemplary TA practices in discussions combined an understanding of the concepts and an understanding of how to integrate those concepts for students in meaningful ways. These teaching strategies helped students exhibit the actions of an historian when approaching primary sources. The historical thinking strategies, such as analysing primary sources, represented the particular threshold actions needed to support students in moving through thresholds to the discipline. The lens of looking at a course as a large system allowed an articulation of these distinctions in terms of what the effects of introducing threshold concepts in a course were and the actions and processes inherent to understanding these concepts not only on the part of students, but on the next generation of teaching faculty.

NOTE

[1] According to Wineburg (1998), presentism is the act of "viewing the past through the lens of the present" (p. 338).

REFERENCES

Adler-Kassner, L., Majewski, J., & Koshnick, D. (2012, Fall). The value of troublesome knowledge: Transfer and threshold concepts in writing and history. *Composition Forum, 26*. Retrieved from http://compositionforum.com/issue/26/

Anderson, C., & Day, K. (2005, November). *Subject overview report: History. Report from the Enhancing Teaching-Learning Environments in Undergraduate Courses Project.* Edinburgh: University of Edinburgh. Retrieved from http://www.etl.tla.ed.ac.uk//docs/HistorySR.pdf

Baillie, C., Bowden, J. A., & Meyer, J. H. F. (2013). Threshold capabilities: Threshold concepts and knowledge capability linked through variation theory. *Higher Education, 65*(2), 227–246.

Brown, J. S., & Duguid, P. (2000). *The social life of information.* Boston, MA: Harvard Business School Press.

Calder, L. (2006). Uncoverage: Toward a signature pedagogy for the history survey. *Journal of American History, 92*(4), 1358–1371.

Cronin, J. (2012, June). 'Doing' history: What may liminal space and transition time expose during the process. In C. O'Mahony, A. Buchanan, M. O'Rourke, & B. Higgs (Eds.), *Threshold concepts: From personal practice to communities of practice.* Paper presented at the Fourth Biennial Threshold Concepts Conference (pp. 38–43).

Devitt, A., Kerin, M., & O'Sullivan, H. (2012, June). Threshold concepts and practices in teacher education: Professional, educator and student perspectives. In C. O'Mahony, A., Buchanan, M. O'Rourke, & B. Higgs (Eds.), *Threshold concepts: From personal practice to communities of practice.* Paper presented at the Fourth Biennial Threshold Concepts Conference (pp. 129–132).

Freadman, A. (2002). Uptake. In R. Coe, L. Lingard, & T. Teslenko (Eds.), *The rhetoric and ideology of genre: Strategies for stability and change.* Cresskill, NJ: Hampton Press.

Hutchings, P., & Shulman, L. (1999, October). The scholarship of teaching and learning: New elaborations, new developments. *Change Magazine, 31*(5), 10–15.

Jaschik, S. (2014, March 20). A broader history Ph.D. *Inside Higher Education.* Retrieved http://www.insidehighered.com/news/2014/03/20/historians-association-andfour-doctoral-programs-start-new-effort-broaden-phd#sthash.QLRqpC6v.dpbs

Leinhardt, G. (2004). Instructional explanations: A commonplace for teaching and a location for contrast. In V. Richardson (Ed.), *Handbook of research on teaching* (4th ed., pp. 333–357). Washington, DC: American Educational Research Association.

Majewski, J. (2014). *The five keys to historical thinking* (Unpublished course handout) (S. McGowan, 2013). Discussion transcript.

Meyer, J. H. F. (2012). 'Variation in Student Learning' as a threshold concept. *The Journal of Faculty Development, 26*(3), 8–13.

Meyer, J. H. F., & Land, R. (2005). Threshold concepts and troublesome knowledge (2): Epistemological considerations and a conceptual framework for teaching and learning. *Higher Education, 49*(3), 373–388.

Meyer, J. H. F., & Land, R. (2006). *Overcoming barriers to student understanding.* London: Routledge.

Middendorf, J., & Pace, D. (2004). *Decoding the disciplines: Helping students learn disciplinary ways of thinking in new directions in teaching and learning. New Directions in Teaching and Learning Series (98).* San Francisco, CA: Jossey-Bass.

Pace, D. (2008). Opening history's 'Black Boxes': Decoding the disciplinary unconscious of historians. In C. Kreber (Ed.), *Teaching and learning within and beyond disciplinary boundaries* (pp. 96–104). London: Routledge.

Perkins, D. (2006). Constructivism and troublesome knowledge. In J. H. F. Meyer & R. Land (Eds.), *Overcoming barriers to student understanding: Threshold concepts and troublesome knowledge.* London: Routledge.

Reisman, A. (2011). *Beyond the binary: Entering the historical problem space in whole class text-based discussion.* Dissertation Chapter. Retrieved from https://stacks.stanford.edu/file/druid:vv771bw4976/Reisman_Dissertation_Readingli keHistorian-augmented.pdf

Wenger, E. (2010). Communities of practice and social learning systems: The career of a concept. In C. Black-more (Ed.), *Social learning systems and communities of practice* (pp. 179–198). London: Springer.

Wineburg, S. S. (1998). Reading Abraham Lincoln: An expert/expert study in the interpretation of historical texts. *Cognitive Science, 22*(3), 319–346.

Wineburg, S. (2001). *Historical thinking and other unnatural acts: Charting the future of teaching the past.* Philadelphia, PA: Temple University Press.

Susannah McGowan
University College London
Independent Learning Design Consultant

BETH A. WHITE, TAIMI OLSEN AND DAVID SCHUMANN

5. A THRESHOLD CONCEPT FRAMEWORK FOR USE ACROSS DISCIPLINES

Threshold Concepts Theory posits that learners are likely to encounter difficult "threshold concepts" whose acquisition is essential to their advancement in a given discipline. These concepts "can be akin to a portal, opening up a new and previously inaccessible way of thinking about something" (Meyer & Land, 2006, p. 3). Meyer and Land identified seven characteristics of threshold concepts applicable to multiple disciplines (Atherton, Hadfield, & Meyers, 2008; Meyer & Land, 2003; Meyer, Jan, Land & Baillie, 2010). These characteristics portray threshold concepts as: (1) transformative (a significant shift in the learner's perception of the content), (2) troublesome (a concept that is alien, tacit, counterintuitive, subversive, or conceptually difficult) (Perkins, 2006), (3) Irreversible (unlikely to be forgotten), (4) Integrative (awareness of the interrelatedness of concepts, beliefs, and theories), (5) bounded (constrains the boundaries of the subject), (6) constitutive (repositioning oneself in relation to the content), and (7) discursive (gaining language related to the content).

A critical question underlying the notion and characteristics of threshold concepts relates to the nature of "stuckness." Given the seven aspects above, students enter what is referred to as the "liminal state" (Adler-Kassner, Majewski, & Koshnick, 2012). Meyer and Land (2006) describe the liminal state as "a suspended state in which understanding approximates to a kind of mimicry or lack of authenticity" (p. 16). It is a way of "being in two states at the same time" or "between different states, not fully understanding, but being acquainted" (Tight, 2014, p. 255). They describe a great degree of movement back and forth between states. Similarly, Kiley and Wisker (2009) refer to the stage of liminality as "the period that precedes the actual threshold crossing" (p. 432). Students may mimic both language and behaviours at this stage until they cross the threshold into thinking as a scholar in their discipline.

In an effort to better understand the nature of this liminal space, this chapter begins to address the question of how to identify, validate, and address threshold concepts within an individual discipline (Meyer & Land, 2005) – moving beyond simple identification to examining and comparing student and faculty perceptions regarding threshold concepts. Within a disciplinary context, individual instructors often identify threshold concepts based on their knowledge of their students' interaction with the content. Our hypothesis is that instructors may—in the absence of dialogue

R. Land et al. (Eds.), Threshold Concepts in Practice, 53–63.

with students about the curriculum—misunderstand or simplify the liminal state and the complex processes that underlie how students engage with their field of study.

Our study also responds to the necessity for further exploration of research design around the threshold concepts theory in higher education. Noting the wealth of research related to the nature and process of conceptual change necessary for good curriculum design and implementation in K-12, Lucas & Mladenovic (2007) point to the relatively limited literature related specifically to conceptual change in higher education. They suggest that the emerging threshold concepts framework provides a new conceptual change model that needs significant empirical examination. Early research on threshold concepts focused attention on identifying specific concepts within a discipline, (Meyer & Land, 2005) a task since denounced in favour of looking at the cognitive processes involved in navigating the liminal spaces of any discipline (Meyer, 2010). With this broader scope, conversation moves from threshold concepts within a discipline to threshold concepts in learning in higher education generally. To move from specific, disciplinary knowledge to aspects of threshold concepts such as "transformative nature" or beyond, to questions of "why a concept might be 'transformative' and to 'the nature of the misconception surrounding it'" is the strength of Lucas's argument (Lucas & Mladenovic, 2007, p. 240). This argument looks into the "why" and the "nature" of "beliefs" that students carry, and it leads to discussions with students themselves. While instructors possess disciplinary knowledge, and their discipline influences what they teach, the process of leading students through the liminal space can be informed by identifying, through dialogue with students, how their students construct knowledge (Lucas & Mladenovic, 2007, p. 241).

Conceptual change happens through navigating liminality during the learning process. Early in their studies, students give "explanations that are far from coherent and quite difficult to understand containing inconsistencies and misunderstandings" (Lucas & Mladenovic, 2007, p. 241). It is in this place of liminality that students mimic and approximate knowledge (Cousin, 2006; Meyer, & Land, 2006). Indeed, when instructors are unaware of their own underlying assumptions about a concept (for instance, their own tacit knowledge) and do not convey complete explanations of a concept, students may remain in the state of mimicry.

The authors of this chapter take the perspective that a multi-faceted approach to further research is necessary to fully understand threshold concepts as they are enacted in the classroom. Such research can lead to better understanding of student learning in higher education disciplines and can help faculty who teach in these disciplines. If research only considers the instructor's interpretations of the difficult concepts in a course, then this means of identification of concepts reflects assumptions of accuracy. Yet, these assumptions often underlie current literature in single discipline studies of faculty perceptions (Kiley & Wisker, 2009; Land, Cousin, Meyer, & Davies, 2005; Lucas & Mladenovic, 2007). A less prominent trend in the literature is comparative (mixed methods) studies, which seek to balance student and instructor data and voices. Furthermore, in the existing literature, research methods for identifying threshold concepts vary widely to include interviews, case studies, and other qualitative data (Davies & Mangan, 2005; Meyer & Land, 2006). While individual experience may be valid from a disciplinary perspective, the question of full inclusion of both the teacher and student perceptions with regard to accuracy needs to be addressed. Quinlan and her colleagues (Quinlan et al., 2013) report that most studies in threshold concepts employ qualitative methods, with little or no attention paid to quantitative approaches. She is also critical of the lack of methods and protocols, for example, criticizing Lucas' work by questioning who decides if a threshold concept is really a threshold concept.

This program of research focuses on multiple disciplines. This first study within the program, as reported here, considers the content within a single course in a specific discipline to identify specific threshold concepts and to check student perceptions of their confidence related to mastering these concepts, as well as their comfort level with each concept. Furthermore, it attempts to ascertain beliefs that instructors have about their students' comfort levels with each concept to determine if there are inconsistencies in perceptions. Finally, and perhaps most critically, students' perceptions of this "liminal" space–specifically, what is occurring in this space–are examined. Thus, this proposed process begins to address both Meyer's (2010) concerns about cognitive processes as well as Lucas's reinforcement of emotional impact as it exists within this liminal space.

Given that this project is in process, the following pages provide the outline of a mixed methods study for examining threshold concepts. This sampling strategy, which employs both students and instructors as samples, makes use of both qualitative and quantitative methods to provide a more comprehensive picture. This process is guided by the following questions:

- Which concepts within a course do students find difficult (potential threshold concepts)?
- Which concepts do instructors identify as core/threshold concepts, the understanding of which are key to progress in the discipline?
- To what degree is student confidence (self-efficacy) regarding duly identified threshold concepts consistent with their comfort level (affective response)?
- To what degree do students and teachers agree with the level of comfort that students have about threshold concepts?
- To what degree does the theory behind threshold concepts match the actual perceptions of students?

METHODOLOGY

The methodological process described here employs a multi-method approach. First, a team of faculty developers and disciplinary instructors is created. This provides perspectives both from the instructors of record but also from faculty developers familiar with threshold concept theory and literature as well as curriculum design, student behaviours (from observation, as well as the literature) and pedagogical practices. Second, this team analyses syllabi and other course materials such as the textbook to identify concepts taught within the course which may meet the criteria set forth above as "threshold concepts " (Meyer & Land, 2003) and to create surveys for students and instructors. This involves an iterative interpretation stage. Third, students are surveyed to identify their understanding and comfort levels with these concepts. Again, the understanding measures reflect a level of confidence with the concept while the comfort items reflect affective responses associated with the realized learning of these concepts. Fourth, course instructors are surveyed to identify their perceptions of the comfort level that students have with each concept. Fifth, students are interviewed regarding difficult concepts and why they have found these concepts to be difficult. Finally, all data is analysed and synthesized to provide a comprehensive picture that is interpreted by the team. The analysis of quantitative data employed SPSS while the analysis of qualitative data employed NVivo software. The intent is to use the results not only to identify threshold concepts and their navigation within the discipline, but primarily to provide the team's disciplinary instructor with information that can inform curricular and pedagogical choices. In other words, the course itself—the pedagogy, organization, materials and other aspects—is the focus, and the information is used to inform instructional faculty towards improved design and delivery for better student learning.

EXAMPLES OF OUTPUT

This multi-method approach provides multiple outputs. For purposes of this chapter, a test of this approach was conducted with a First Year English Composition course using multiple sections of the course, taught by different instructors. A set of 20 potential threshold concepts were identified by the research team of instructors and faculty developers (see Table 1) and corresponded with concepts students identified as troublesome. Although the results below are not fully analysed in this chapter in terms of the extensive research literature in composition and rhetoric studies, some findings are presented below in order to discuss the pilot project in terms of its strengths and weaknesses and to present next steps.

The results of the student survey provided interesting findings on students' beliefs about applying the concepts. Three options were provided ("can you do the following"—yes, no, not sure). For purposes of analysis, answers in the uncertain category and in the negative were grouped together to compare with answers in the "yes" column. Both sets were then compared with the second half of the survey, which asked about comfort. The first column of data in Table 1 reflects the percentage of respondents who stated that they could complete the task. The data in column two reflect those who felt comfortable (= or > than 4 on a 5 point differential scale anchored by not at all/comfortable/very comfortable). A differential index score was created in the third column of data to gain a

Table 1. Potential threshold concepts in English composition

Concept	Column A	Column B	Column C
	% Who agree they can complete the task	*% Who say they are comfortable with the task**	*Difference Index* (Column A – Column B)
Analyse a writing task	87.6	71.4	16.2
Write a thesis statement	99.1	85.9	13.2
Figure out the writing situation	77	53.1	23.9
Recognize the characteristics of the writing situation	66.4	46.9	19.5
Write the main idea	99.1	91.2	7.9
Identify the genre in which I am writing	84.1	63.4	20.7
Understand how to write in a specific genre	65.5	45.9	19.6
Decide on a format for my writing (format/organization)	80.4	69	11.4
Understand how to write in a specific academic discipline/major (in a discourse community)	61.9	43.4	18.5
Decide my message in the writing task	96.4	80.5	15.9
Decide how to organize a paper (organization)	95.6	85	10.6
Decide my purpose for writing task	92	79.7	12.3
Determine the audience(s) for a piece of writing	90.3	70.6	19.7
Determine the needs of the audience for a piece of writing	72.6	54	18.6
Decide on evidence to use in writing for a specific task	87.6	73.5	14.1
Decide how to revise a paper (revision)	80.5	67.2	13.3
Identify and use parts of an argument	87.6	70.8	16.8
Write an argument	93.8	79.7	14.1
Write with an authentic academic voice	61.9	55.8	6.1
Decide on writing style	74.3	60.3	14

* Comfort was judged to be = or > 4 on a 5 point scale

57

perspective on the consistency level of the two scores. As noted above, the greatest inconsistencies between beliefs that they could complete the task and their comfort level appeared for the following:

- understanding how to write in a specific situation, such as in an academic
- discipline;
- identifying genres, and understanding how to write in a specific genre;
- determining an audience and the needs of the audience for a piece of writing;
- identifying and using parts of an argument.

In the table above, those items with the highest discrepancy (over 16 points) are shown, whereas students stated that, on the whole, they could do and were comfortable doing tasks such as writing a thesis statement and a main idea.

Also of interest in the quantitative results is the comparison of the instructors' perceptions of student comfort level with the students' actual recorded comfort levels for each concept. Although one should be statistically concerned about analysis employing "between group" difference scores using aggregate data, nevertheless, what these scores reflect is of some interest from an exploratory nature. Across all the comparisons, students perceived themselves to be more comfortable with all the concepts than their instructors perceived them to be. This could reflect an over-confidence on the part of the students, a healthy scepticism on the part of the teachers, or possibly some combination of both.

The qualitative interviews revealed information about the liminal state of students in this course, which was, overall, not resolved. All 15 (100%) student interviewees reported learning a difficult concept and becoming confident in their own knowledge. 9 of the 15 (60%) students discussed the process of becoming unstuck. 13 (87%) students discussed using peer, teacher, or their own resources to overcome difficulties with class work. 8 of 15 (53%) students reported being very "stuck" with one or more concepts. Of these 8, 3 (37%) of students indicated "transformative" understanding as evidenced by firm statements of confidence. In this sense, these three students seem to be indicating the presence of threshold concepts, given the seven aspects of the model. (However, it was beyond the scope of this study to pinpoint concepts as threshold for the discipline-or the course-without further research into the literature of rhetoric and composition.) Said one student of the broad concept of rhetorical analysis (and related ideas such as ethos and pathos):

I understand it very well … I don't get scared when I see it. It's weird now. We're writing a fourth paper on it now and I kind of like jumped right in and I know what they are and I've used plenty of examples with them.

A second student remarked:

It was just … I understood it. After I understood it, I was like ok. I'm ok with this. It was just a matter of hitting that point where you understand what you're doing and what point you're getting to.

Of the 8 (53%) students who were "stuck," the other 5 (63%) indicated being in the liminal state, somewhat confident but not entirely. In discussing a persuasive writing assignment, the student commented:

> [the teacher] was saying that, you'll use those types of persuasive techniques to make people ..., so that part makes sense, but I think sitting down and thinking, 'there's a step by step process to do this', is a new thing for me.

Another student discussed the concept of academic voice:

> I think this paper I did was supposed to be for an academic audience and that was hard for me from public to academic because I feel like I have only one internal voice and I don't think it sounds too childish, but I don't think its super academic either.

Regardless, for several students, there was a sense of learning but also hesitation about that learning.

Of the threshold concept descriptions listed at the start of the paper, most students did not—of course—tell interviewers that their understanding was "transformative" or that they now had an "integrated" sense of concepts. Two figures are employed below to depict these themes. Figure one describes the liminal state of students, as they got "stuck" on a concept and then moved through the process of getting "unstuck" to resolution, with variance in their confidence in the resolution. The language of "being stuck" was used by interviewers. As the protocol did not invite such experiences to be addressed, there were no findings at this point on how these experiences were transformative or not.

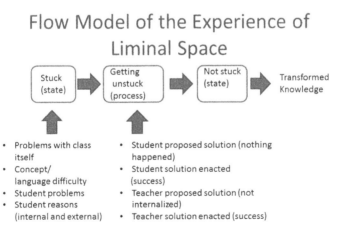

Figure 1. Students' experience with liminality

Figure 2 represents a model aligning the findings from the qualitative data—as well as the quantitative data—with the aspects of threshold concepts according to theory. As stated above, the one area needing further, focused research is the "transformative" nature of student learning.

Preliminary Theoretical Implications

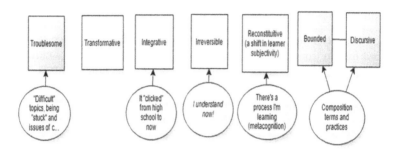

Figure 2. Preliminary implications

MOVING FORWARD

This process has several advantages as compared to previous research methods. First, it combines the thinking of both instructors and faculty developers in a team approach to the research. While instructors may have significant insights into difficult concepts as a result of disciplinary expertise and repeated experiences teaching a course, faculty developers contribute through their knowledge of the threshold concept literature and theory. Second, the multi-method approach relies on both qualitative and quantitative methods by employing samples of course content, instructor input, and student input to provide a more comprehensive picture of how these concepts are being perceived within the learning process. Third, this methodology allows for direct comparisons of instructor and student perceptions. Identification of differences can help instructors better understand where students (or faculty) may not have a realistic perspective regarding the concept or where students may not have mastered concepts even though students perceived they did. Finally, employing this process across multiple courses and disciplines will provide opportunities for disciplinary/course comparisons as well as generalizations about threshold concepts, thus advancing Land's beliefs regarding research on this topic (i.e., moving from identification with one discipline to generalizations across disciplines).

The process has limitations as well. Students and instructors may not be willing to openly discuss difficult concepts within their curriculum when they participate in an interview. The faculty focus group format may have exacerbated this problem, and the results were not used due to low participation (whereas the faculty survey was used). Low participation may have occurred from a lack of time or, more critically, a concern about how they would be perceived by the researchers.

Another limitation comes from the discipline itself. The concepts studied in the composition course are theoretical as well as process (skills). Students work on applying concepts, yet they are "tested" holistically. In this pilot, the actual products (essays) could have been analysed, yet such analysis would involve another set of research validity questions (norming and standards for essay writing) and decisions about whether all the concepts are clearly revealed through the essay product. And finally, interview protocols that probe the transformative nature of student learning should be added for a more thorough investigation.

Regardless, the results from this first demonstration of the process (employing English composition tasks that students find difficult) yielded some important findings. First, student confidence level as reflected in the belief they could complete a task, and their respective comfort level, differed for certain tasks. This is intriguing in that, while students report a certain level of confidence, at the same time, they typically report a lower level affective comfort. Combining this finding with the fact that teachers consistently related comfort levels lower than students may suggest that students have a false sense of confidence and teachers sense this from actual performance in classes. This finding has two implications. First, teachers may need to focus more on mastery of concepts with all their students to elevate their own perceptions of their students' comfort levels. In other words, course redesign may help instructors determine points in the course to assess and more clearly affirm when mastery – or a stage towards mastery – is achieved.

Second, the process employed here did not use an actual performance test for each concept. Future versions of this process will do so. Comparing confidence and comfort with actual performance in the moment might be quite revealing. If the instructors are correct in their perceptions, students will answer inconsistently with what they believe to be their ability to complete tasks. Given the conclusions reached in this chapter, the new team is surveying faculty and students and will conduct interviews but will also include concept testing results to measure students' actual knowledge.

CONCLUSIONS

At this time, this project has entered a second stage. A new team is formed with representation from instructional faculty and faculty development, in a new subject area. The project continues to involve (1) a team approach (2) with consideration of concepts taught in a disciplinary class (3) using a mixed methods approach with information from both students and faculty (4) to create an understanding of both achieved knowledge and affective responses to learning. (Lucas & Mladenovic, 2007) were among the first to examine the relationship of the affective domain to threshold concepts, suggesting that students may reject or otherwise defend their current beliefs several times before considering other options. Bradbeer (2005) adds that, in addition to the "intellectual effort required for the transformation to understanding of a threshold concept, there is individuality in the timing of the threshold crossing, which can be seen as a "'Eureka' moment but is also frequently sighted and rejected on several occasions and only gradually accepted, if at all" (p. 3). This response was evident in the data of the pilot phase of this project.

As the project continues in its second phase, researchers (in a newly formed team) will again look at the comparison data and intersections with qualitative data. The goal, as in the pilot phase, is to uncover information that is useful in a particular higher education situation for the purpose of participating with instructional faculty in gathering useful information. Rather than being concerned with uncovering *apriori* threshold concepts, the questions continue to be:

- Which concepts within a course do students find difficult (core concepts)?
- To what degree is student confidence (self-efficacy) regarding threshold concepts consistent with their comfort level (affective response)?
- To what degree do students and teachers agree with the level of comfort that students have about threshold concepts?
- To what degree does the theory behind threshold concepts match the actual perceptions of students?

The generalizability of this study for others in higher education will be less about specific threshold concepts (although the likelihood is that many of the same concepts cause students some difficulty); rather, the focus is to help instructional faculty utilize a process to better understand their own students, to examine how students learn within a course structure, and to better meet their needs. There are implications as well for the transference of knowledge to upper-level courses in the discipline, when students are going through a liminal state of understanding and expressing some uncertainty. The research process as well as the data yielded may advance the understanding of student learning in relation to aspects of a course design and delivery.

REFERENCES

Adler-kassner, L., Majewski, J., & Koshnick, D. (2012). The value of troublesome knowledge: Transfer and threshold concepts in writing and history. *Composition Forum, 26*(Fall), 1–17.

Atherton, J. S., Hadfield, P., & Meyers, R. (2008). Threshold concepts in the wild. *Practice*, (June), 1–13. Retrieved from http://www.doceo.co.uk/tools/Threshold_Concepts_Wild_expanded_70.pdf

Bradbeer, J. (2005). Threshold concepts and troublesome knowledge in the GEES disciplines. *Planet, 15*(3). Retrieved from http://dx.doi.org/10.11120/plan.2005.00150003

Cousin, G. (2006). Section 1: An introduction to threshold concepts. *Planet, 17*, 4–5. doi:10.11120/plan.2006.00170004

Davies, P., & Mangan, J. (2005, August 23–27). *Recognising threshold concepts: An exploration of different approaches.* Paper presented at the European Association in Learning and Instruction Conference (EARLI) Nicosia, Cyprus. In *Recognising threshold concepts: An exploration of different approaches* (Vol. 44, pp. 1–18). Nicosia, Cyprus: Staffordshire University.

Kiley, M., & Wisker, G. (2009). Threshold concepts in research education and evidence of threshold crossing. *Higher Education Research & Development, 28*(4), 431–441. doi:10.1080/07294360903067930

Land, R., Cousin, G., Meyer, J. H. F., & Davies, P. (2005). Threshold concepts and troublesome knowledge (3): Implications for course design and evaluation. In C. Rust (Ed.), *Improving student learning, diversity and inclusivity* (pp. 53–64). Oxford: Oxford Center for Staff and Learning Development.

Lucas, U., & Mladenovic, R. (2007). The potential of threshold concepts: An emerging framework for educational research and practice. *London Review of Education, 5*(3), 237–248. doi:10.1080/14748460701661294

Meyer, J. H. F. (2010). Helping our students: Learning, metalearning, and threshold concepts. In C. Hughes & J. Mighty (Eds.), *Taking stock: Research on teaching and learning in higher education* (pp. 191–214). Montreal, QC & Kingston, ON: McGill-Queen's University Press.

Meyer, J. H. F., & Land, R. (2005). Threshold concepts and troublesome knowledge (2): Epistemological considerations and a conceptual framework for teaching and learning. *Higher Education, 49*(3), 373–388. doi:10.1007/s10734-004-6779-5

Meyer, J., & Land, R. (2003). *Threshold concepts and troublesome knowledge: Linkages to ways of thinking and practising within the disciplines* (Occasional Report 4). ETL Project, Universities of Edinburgh, Coventry and Durham.

Meyer, J. H. F., & Land, R. (2006). *Overcoming barriers to student understanding: Threshold concepts and troublesome knowledge*. Abingdon: Routledge.

Meyer, J. H. F., Land, R., & Baillie, C. E. (2010). *Threshold concepts and transformational learning. Educational futures: Rethinking theory and practice, 42*. Boston, MA: Sense Publishers. Retrieved from http://www.lamission.edu/learningcenter/docs/1177-threshold-concepts-and-transformational-learning.pdf

Perkins, D. (2006). The underlying game: Troublesome knowledge and threshold conceptions. In J. H. F. Meyer & R. Land (Eds.), *Overcoming barriers to student understanding: Threshold concepts and troublesome knowledge*. Abingdon: Routledge.

Quinlan, K. M., Male, S., Baillie, C., Stamboulis, A., Fill, J., & Jaffer, Z. (2013). Methodological challenges in researching threshold concepts: A comparative analysis of three projects. *Higher Education, 66*(5), 585–601. doi:10.1007/s10734-013-9623-y

Tight, M. (2014). Theory development and application in higher education research: The case of threshold concepts. *International Perspectives on Higher Education Research, 10*, 249–267. doi:10.1108/s1479-3628(2014)0000010018

Beth A. White
Tennessee Teaching and Learning Center
University of Tennessee, Knoxville

Taimi Olsen
Tennessee Teaching and Learning Center
University of Tennessee, Knoxville

David Schumann
Haslam College of Business &
Tennessee Teaching and Learning Center
University of Tennessee, Knoxville

PART 2

NEGOTIATING LIMINALITY

JULIE RATTRAY

6. AFFECTIVE DIMENSIONS OF LIMINALITY

INTRODUCTION

Threshold transformations foster ontological shifts that are associated with both cognitive and affective changes in the individual. They cause the individual to view and experience the world differently in terms, not just of the intellectual understanding of an idea but also in the way they feel about, or experience, the world. It is difficult to imagine how coming to understand the notion of 'other', identified as a threshold concept by Cousin (2006), would not be experienced as both an intellectual and emotional transformation. In addition to being associated with affective outcomes the very process of transformation associated with the acquisition of a threshold concept itself has been described as a highly emotive experience (Felton this volume). Felten notes that students frequently talk about their encounters with threshold concepts as 'scary' or 'frightening'. By their very nature threshold concepts involve learners engaging with knowledge that is believed to be difficult or troublesome (Perkins, 1999; Meyer & Land, 2005) implying that they are something to be approached with caution or trepidation. Much of this fear comes from the necessity to let go of existing understandings or ways of viewing the world and enter the liminal space, a place associated with uncertainty, as the new concept is grappled with (Meyer & Land, 2005). The current chapter considers the affective dimension of the Threshold Concepts Framework (TCF) by considering the extent to which liminality might be experienced as both a cognitive and affective state that is more easily navigated by some students than others.

We already know that not all learners experience threshold concepts in the same way and that the degree of troublesomeness associated with a particular threshold concept will vary between individual learners (Meyer & Land, 2006). The very willingness of learners to engage with the threshold concept itself and navigate the associated liminal space is equally varied (Meyer & Land, 2006). Some learners are willing, or even eager, to enter the liminal space in the hope of emerging transformed or coming to a new way of understanding whilst others pause at the entrance seemingly unable or unwilling to let go of their pre-existing understandings (Cousin, 2006). Much of the work in this area however, has focused on intellectual or pedagogical explanations to explain the differential experiences of learners when they encounter troublesome knowledge (Flanagan, 2015). The current chapter explores another possible explanation for learners' behaviour when they encounter thresholds and more particularly are required to engage with liminality. It considers

R. Land et al. (Eds.), Threshold Concepts in Practice, 67–76.

the extent to which psychological characteristics of the learner, such as resilience, might explain why some students are able to cope with liminality and persist in the face of uncertainty whilst others appear to withdraw from it and remain in an untransformed state. Building on Luthans et al.'s (2007) construct of Psychological Capital (PsyCap) as one measure of the affective dimension of learning, the chapter explores firstly the potential relationship it has to academic performance before moving on to a consideration of any potential utility it might have as a means of explaining why some learners remain trapped in, or fail to enter, the liminal space and others emerge from the space to inhabit a new place of being. It argues that the malleable nature of some psychological states render them meaningful in a learning and teaching context not only because of their explanatory function but as a potential source of intervention to support a positive learning experience.

AFFECTIVE DIMENSIONS OF LEARNING

Before considering the potential link between affect and liminality it is important to take a moment to consider the place of affect within the context of learning more generally. Within the domain of learning research primacy has typically been given to the cognitive processes associated with learning and learners' behaviour (Baker, Andriessen, & Järvelä, 2013). Research has explored the psychological factors associated with learning but there has been a tendency to focus on cognitive processes such as motivation, self-regulation and use of cognitive strategies (see Gębka, 2014 for a detailed discussion of this research). Gębka (2014) notes that researchers have started to build complex models integrating a range of psychological, but still largely cognitive, factors to explain differentiated learning behaviours (Fenollar, Roman, & Cuestas 2007; Phan, 2010). Whilst this work continues to shed light on the relationship between motivation and performance it tells us little about the affective experience of learning and how that might influence subsequent learning behaviour and engagement. In comparison relatively little is known about how affective psychological states such as hope or optimism might relate to the same set of learning behaviours (Baker et al., 2013; Cozolino, 2014; Davidson et al., 2012; Day et al., 2010). In this section we will consider what is known about the place of affect in learning

HOPE

Much of the work exploring the affective dimensions of learning has been carried out within the domain of positive psychology (Lopez & Snyder, 2003; Seligman, 2006; Seligman, Ernst, Gillham, Reivich, & Linkins, 2009) and it stems, at least to some extent, from Albert Bandura's socio-cognitive theory of behaviour (Bandura, 1977, 1997, 2000). In addition researchers have become increasingly interested in the link between affect and learning due to an increased concern about the mental health and emotional well-being of learners (Davidson et al., 2012).

Research in the domain of positive psychology and learning has tended to focus on the relationship between psychological states such as hope, optimism or resilience and learners subsequent academic performance. The findings from this research suggest, for example, that hope, which is associated with an individual's belief in their own ability to follow identified pathways as a means of achieving future goals through personal agency, is a good predictor of future academic success (Snyder, Shorey, Cheavens, Pulvers, Adams III, & Wiklund, 2002), whilst Chang (1998) argues that a learner's ability to cope with academically challenging situations and to solve problems effectively is mediated by their level of hope. Davidson et al. (2012) explored the specific role of hope as it relates to undergraduate students' learning and performance. They utilised the salutogenic paradigm developed by Antonovsky (1987), which focuses on the extent to which individuals can develop coping strategies and resilience behaviours which promote emotional well-being in a range of contexts, including educational ones (Margalit, 2010). They reported that students who had participated in a workshop designed to enhance their hope, academic self-efficacy and sense of coherence showed more improvement in their grades in the semester following the workshop compared with students who had not participated in such a workshop. In another study Day, Hanson, Maltby, Proctor and Wood (2010) found that, when they controlled for intelligence, prior academic performance and personality characteristics, hope was a reliable predictor of academic success.

OPTIMISM

A second affective dimension that has been considered in relation to learning and academic performance is optimism, which can be thought of in terms of the desire to attain specific goals by attributing their potential achievement to positive outcome expectations and engagement in goal-oriented actions (Scheier & Carver, 1985). Optimism in a learning context is associated with learner autonomy and self-determination in relation to the accomplishment of learning tasks and goals (Shogren, Lopez, Wehmeyer, Little, & Pressgrove, 2006). The optimistic learner believes in the possibility of positive outcomes and that these can be attained through personal effort or persistence (Bryant & Cvengros, 2004).

EMOTIONAL SECURITY AND RESILIENCE

Both hope and optimism relate to an individual's view of their own agency and autonomy within a learning situation and the extent to which they believe they can utilise multiple pathways and strategies to effect a positive outcome in the learning situation. They are associated with the setting and attainment of specific future learning goals and as such will be influenced and shaped by previous learning experiences. We are more likely to make positive attributions about the possibility of future success (optimism) if we perceive ourselves to be responsible for past successes. Emerging work on attachment-based teaching (Cozolino, 2014) capitalises on these ideas and proposes an approach to teaching which is much more attuned to the affective dimension of learning and how it could support teaching practices. It combines the idea of the importance of emotional security and the development of resilience with states such as hope and optimism to propose an approach to teaching and learning that has learners' emotional security at its centre (Cozolino, 2014). In this context resilience refers to the ability of an individual to cope with, and adapt to, negative experiences and to minimise the damaging long-term emotional consequences of these experiences (Rutter, 2006). Resilient learners can cope with negative learning experiences, irrespective of whether they are perceived to have an internal or external locus of control, as they are able to minimise the negative effects of the experience and adapt to the adverse experience to find alternative outcomes or cope with the delayed success.

PSYCHOLOGICAL CAPITAL

Drawing on work from organisational psychology that explored the effectiveness of individuals within an organization, Luthans and Youssef (Luthans & Youssef, 2004; Luthans, Youssef, & Avolio, 2007) propose that instead of considering individual psychological factors we might think of them as acting together to form a kind of 'psychological capital' (PsyCap) which cumulatively operates to influence human behaviour. PsyCap has its roots in the area of positive psychology and refers to rs to o efers to in the area of positive pate of development' (Luthans et al., 2007, p. 3). It is represented as a higher order multi-dimensional factor that encompasses the three affective components (hope, optimism and resilience) discussed previously with self-efficacy (Bandura, 1997), and is associated with an individualacy (Bandura, nd refers to rs to o efers to in the area of pos's belief in their own ability to accomplish a specific task and the links between self-efficacy and learner behaviour are well established (Pajares, 2005; Schunk, 1991; Zimmerman, 2002). Learners with high self-efficacy typically are more willing to engage in appropriately challenging learning tasks and will persist with a learning task until they complete it, whereas learners with low self-efficacy typically show less persistence, particularly in the face of challenge, and are more likely to give up when they encounter difficulties (Bandura, 1986, 1997, 2000; Pajares, 2005; Schunk, 1991). Luthans et al. (2007) argue that whilst the individual factors that constitute PsyCap influence human behaviour individually it is in combination that their influence is greatest; the whole is greater than the sum of its parts (Luthans, Youssef, & Avolio, 2007; Searle, 2010).

Much of the work on PsyCap to date comes from the field of management and organisational psychology and studies considering its direct application in educational contexts are scarce (Searle, 2010). One study which has crossed the boundaries of organisational and educational contexts reported that an intervention designed to enhance the psychological capital of a group of management students showed that improved PsyCap was associated with higher academic performance

(Luthans, Avolio, Avey, & Norman, 2007). Given the scarcity of studies exploring the relationship between PsyCap and a range of cognitive and affective factors already associated with learning and learner behaviours. In a small-scale study undertaken with a cohort of 46 undergraduate education students, this author (Rattray, 2014) found evidence of a modest relationship between PsyCap and academic performance (0.75). Students complete a modified PsyCap inventory (Luthans et al., 2007) prior to the submission of a written assignment that explored their understandings of the relationship between theories of how people learn and their application within an educational context to determine what, if any, relationship exists between PsyCap and academic performance. Whilst this is a small-scale study it suggests that future work exploring this issue merits a place within educational research.

LIMINALITY AND AFFECT

In Meyer and Land (2005) described liminality as a fluid or liquid state of understanding or being. They note that learners who occupy the liminal space can often move back and forward within this fluid state as they grapple with the threshold they are attempting to cross. Others have described liminality as akin to a kind of 'no man's land' (Hokstad, Rødne, Braaten, Wellinger and Shetelig, this volume) or even as a labyrinth or maze that learners need to navigate their way through (TRANSark, 2015). Vivian (2012), applying a semiotic framework to liminality, likens it to a cognitive tunnel that one must enter and pass through in order to emerge transformed (see Figure 1). Vivian's conceptualisation of liminality as a tunnel represents a useful metaphor here reflecting as it does the idea of entering a dark and foreboding place where the final outcome, and indeed the path to achieving it, is as yet uncertain or initially at least out of sight (Land, Rattray, & Vivian, 2014). Whether we think of liminality as a liquid state, a labyrinth or a tunnel we cannot deny that it is this element of the threshold concepts framework that has proved to be challenging, or troublesome, to researchers, representing as it does the less well understood part of the transformation. We know that learners pass through the liminal space or tunnel en route to being transformed (Land, Rattray, & Vivian, 2014; Land, Vivian, & Rattray, 2014) but quite what supports or facilitates this passage is less clear. If we characterise mastery of a threshold concept as representing the end point of a particular learning cycle (as well as being the point of departure for another) then we might think of the mastery of the threshold concept as becoming the learning goal to be attained. Work from the field of motivation tells us that motivation is an 'important aspect of the learning experience and consequently it is an integral part of any conceptual change' (Pintrich, Marx, & Boyle, 1993). Motivation can be thought of as 'the process whereby goal-directed activity is instigated and sustained' (Schunk, Pintrich, & Meece, 2008, p. 4). Motivation therefore is associated with a learnereby goal-directed persist with learning to attain mastery of a threshold. The question then for us as researchers is what might explain why some learners persist in their efforts to grasp a threshold concept sufficiently to negotiate the liminal space, and why others either do not embark on the journey at all, or give up part way through and remain stuck in the liminal tunnel.

THE LIMINAL TUNNEL

The metaphor of the liminal tunnel has utility both in terms of the conceptual and ontological transformations that are brought about by the acquisition of a new threshold concept. Not only does it resonate with the idea of modular curricula that are based on a linear sequencing of disciplinary knowledge but, if we think of it as a cognitive and affective tunnel, it brings the affective dimension of the ontological shift into much sharper focus emphasising as it does the idea of an intimidating or unseen place that must be entered and passed through if transformation is to occur.

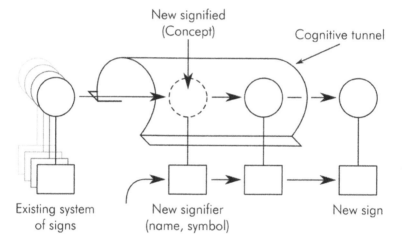

Figure 1. The Liminal Tunnel (Reproduced from Vivian, 2012)

EMOTIONAL CAPITAL

The affective dimension of threshold concepts has not been entirely neglected by researchers. Cousin (2006) has argued that what she terms 'emotional capital', might provide an explanatory framework for categorising students into different affective typologies. In her work addressing students understanding of 'n her wor' – which she argues is a threshold concept – she found that students' level of emotional capital influenced their willingness to engage with and subsequently understand this threshold, which might itself be considered an emotive concept. Emotional capital is, according to Cousin (ibid) an accumulation of the affective assets or resources which are the result of varied life experiences. Emotional capital is the affective relation of social capital (Bourdieu & Passeron, 1997), and it represents one way of thinking about the affective dimension of learning. Whilst Cousin applies the idea to one very specific threshold, her acknowledgement that negotiating the liminal tunnel includes an affective component reflects an increasing shift towards a consideration of this aspect of learning and learner behaviour (Weatheral, 2012).

EFFORT AND AGENCY

If a cornerstone of threshold transformations is persistence then the individual needs to be resilient. They need to be able to cope with their own oscillating behaviour within the liminal space as they strive for understanding. They need, further, to believe that the threshold will be crossed and that they are capable of crossing it. They need to be able to envision themselves, even if not clearly, occupying a new space beyond the threshold. In short, they need to have the psychological coping strategies that enable them to deal with the difficult and uncertain liminal phase and to accept that it will take time and effort to find their way through it. Cousin (2006) argues, as we have seen, that threshold transformations might be facilitated by a student's 'emotional capital' and others have established clear links between positive psychological constructs such as hope, (Sneider et al., 2002) self-efficacy (Bandura, 1997, 2000), optimism, (Seligman, 2006) and resilience (Borman & Overman, 2004). In relation to learning, these psychological characteristics are associated with a willingness to engage and take ownership of the learning and with awareness that learning does not simply happen but, rather, it requires effort and agency (Seligman, 2006; Sneider et al., 2002). The notion of agency is of particular importance here as threshold transformations, involving, as they do, changes in individual subjectivity, could not occur without individual agency. The learner needs to come to see the threshold concept as a learning goal to be mastered and to accept that, whilst they can be supported in their mastery of the threshold by a tutor or peer, ultimately the transformation is theirs.

CONCLUSION

In considering what might explain this persistence we could explore the aspects of pedagogy that might support the conceptual shifts involved in the threshold transformation or we can look at the psychological factors that help to bring about the perseverance that is needed to cope with liminality.

The four factors constituting PsyCap might explain why some learners are able to pass through the liminal tunnel and acquire a new conceptual framework and others, despite having the intellectual capacity, are unable to make the same transformation. As we have seen, a learner who believes they are capable of understanding new ideas (self-efficacy), who makes positive attributions in relation to their potential for success (optimism), who can monitor and re-align goals and the pathways to attaining these goals (hope) and who does not give up in spite of the difficulties they encounter with the new knowledge (resilience) may be able to cope with liminality more effectively than those who lack these affective assets. Cousin (2006) argued that students with less emotional capital might experience greater levels of discomfort with troublesome knowledge and this might result in their being unwilling to enter the liminal tunnel at all and leave them permanently in the pre-liminal space (Meyer & Land, 2005). Cousin argues further that just as social capital is acquired in a cumulative way, emotional capital can be developed through onemulative inal space. This renders it a useful idea in education as, rather than reflecting a fixed set of learner attributes or pathologies, it represents something more changeable. In a similar way PsyCap is considered to be a malleable state rather than a fixed trait (Luthans et al., 2007) and this gives it potential utility in a learning context. Educators who want to facilitate learners' motivation to embark on the negotiation of the liminal tunnel, and engage in the process of ontological shift, might consider embedding the principles of positive psychology in their pedagogy and curricula as a means of enhancing their students' PsyCap and facilitating the engagement they seek.

REFERENCES

Antonovsky, A. (1987). *Unraveling the mystery of health: How people manage stress and stay well.* San Francisco, CA: Jossey-Bass.

Baker, M., Andriessen, J., & Järvelä, S. (2013). Introduction: Visions of learning together. In M. Baker, J. Andriessen, & S. Järvelä (Eds.), *Affective learning together. Social and Emotional dimension of collaborative learning.* Abingdon: Routledge.

Bandura, A. (1977). Self-efficacy: Toward a unifying theory of behavioral change. *Psychological Review, 84*, 191–215.

Bandura, A. (1986). *Social foundations of thought and action: A social cognitive theory.* Englewood Cliffs, NJ: Prentice-Hall.

Bandura, A. (1997). *Self-efficacy: The exercise of control.* New York, NY: Freeman.

Bandura, A. (2000). Cultivate self-efficacy for personal and organizational effectiveness. In E. A. Locke (Ed.), *Handbook of principles of organization behavior* (pp. 120–136). Oxford, UK: Blackwell.

Biggs, J. (1979). Individual differences in study processes and the quality of learning outcomes. *Higher Education, 84*, 381–394.

Borman, G. D., & Overman, L. T. (2004). Academic resilience in mathematics among poor and minority students. *Elementary School Journal, 104*(3), 177–195.

Bourdieu, P., & Passeron, J.-C. (1997). *Reproduction.* London: Sage.

Bryant, F. B., & Cvengros, J. A. (2004). Distinguishing hope and optimism: Two sides of a coin, or two separate coins? *Journal of Social and Clinical Psychology, 23*(2), 273–302.

Cousin, G. (2006). Threshold concepts, troublesome knowledge and emotional capital: An exploration into learning about others. In J. H. F. Meyer & R. Land (Eds.), *Overcoming barriers to student understanding: Threshold concepts and troublesome knowledge.* London: RoutledgeFalmer.

Chang, E. C. (1998). Hope, problem-solving ability, and coping in a college student population: Some implications for theory and practice. *Journal of Clinical Psychology, 54*, 953–962.

Cozolino, L. (2014). *Attachment-based teaching: Creating a tribal classroom.* New York, NY: W. W. Norton.

Davidson, O. B., Feldman, D. B., & Margalit, M. (2012). A focused intervention for 1st-year college students: Promoting hope, sense of coherence, and self-efficacy. *The Journal of Psychology, 146*(3), 333–352.

Day, L., Hanson, K., Maltby, J., Proctor, C., & Wood, A. (2010). Hope uniquely predicts objective academic achievement above intelligence, personality, and previous academic achievement. *Journal of Research in Personality, 44*, 550–553.

Fenollar, P., Roman, S., & Cuestas, P. J. (2007). University students' academic performance. An integrative conceptual framework and empirical analysis. *British Journal of Educational Psychology, 77,* 873–891.

Flanagan, M. T. (2015). *Threshold concepts: Undergraduate teaching, postgraduate training and professional development. A short introduction and bibliography.* Retrieved from http://www.ee.ucl.ac.uk/~mflanaga/thresholds.html

Gębka, B. (2014). Psychological determinants of university students' academic performance: An empirical study. *Journal of Further and Higher Education, 38*(6), 813–837.

Hokstad, L. M., Rødne, G., Braaten, B. O., Wellinger, S., & Shetelig, F. (This volume). *Transformative learning in architectural education. Re- thinking architecture and the education of architecture.*

Hoyle, R. (2010). *Handbook of personality and self regulation.* Oxford: Wiley-Blackwell.

Land, R. (2014, July). *Liminality Close-up.* Think piece for 7th Higher Education Close-Up Conference (HECU 7), Lancaster. Retrieved from http://www.lancaster.ac.uk/fass/events/hecu7/docs/ThinkPieces/land.pdf

Land, R., Rattray, J., & Vivian, P. (2014). Learning in the liminal space: A semiotic approach to threshold concepts. *Higher Education, 67,* 199–217.

Land, R., Vivian, P, & Rattray, J. (2014). A closer look at liminality: Incorrigibles and threshold capital. In C. O'Mahony, A. Buchanan, M. O'Rourke, & B. Higgs (Eds.), *Threshold concepts: From personal practice to communities of practice. Proceedings of the National Academy's 6th annual conference and the 4th biennial Threshold Concepts Conference.* Retrieved from http://www.nairtl.ie/documents/EPub_2012Proceedings.pdf

Lopez, S. J., & Snyder, C. R. (2003). *Positive psychological assessment: A handbook of models and measures.* Washington, DC: American Psychological Association.

Luthans, F., & Youssef, C. M. (2004). Human, social, and now positive psychological capital management: Investing in people for competitive advantage. *Organizational Dynamics, 33*(2), 143–160.

Luthans, F., Avolio, B. J., Avey, J. B., & Norman, S. M. (2007). Positive psychological capital: Measurement and relationship with performance and satisfaction. *Personnel Psychology, 60,* 541–572.

Luthans, F., Youssef, C. M., & Avolio, B. J. (2007). *Psychological capital.* New York, NY: Oxford University Press.

Margalit, M. (2010). *Lonely children and adolescents: Self-perceptions, social exclusion, and hope.* New York, NY: Springer.

Meyer, J. H. F., & Land, R. (2005). Threshold concepts and troublesome knowledge: Epistemological considerations and a conceptual framework for teaching and learning. *Higher Education, 49,* 373–388.

Meyer, J. H. F., & Land, R. (Eds.). (2006). *Overcoming barriers to student understanding: Threshold concepts and troublesome knowledge.* Oxford: Routledge.

Pajares, F. (2005). Gender differences in mathematics self-efficacy beliefs. In A. M. Gallagher & J. C. Kaufman (Eds.), *Gender differences in mathematics: An integrative psychological approach.* New York, NY: Cambridge University Press.

Perkins, D. (1999). The many faces of constructivism. *Educational Leadership, 57*(3), 6–11.

Phan, H. P. (2010). Students' academic performance and various cognitive processes of learning: An integrative framework and empirical analysis. *Educational Psychology, 30,* 297–322.

Pintrich, P. R., Marx, R. W., & Boyle, R. A. (1993). Beyond cold conceptual change: The role of motivational beliefs and classroom contextual factors in the process of conceptual change. *Review of Educational Research, 63,* 167–199.

Rattray, J. (2014, July 21–23). *Tools for navigating the liminal tunnel.* Paper presented at the 7th Higher Education Close-Up Conference (HECU 7), Lancaster.

Rutter, M. (2006). The promotion of resilience in the face of adversity. In A. Clarke-Stewart & J. Dunn (Eds.), *Families count: Effects on child and adolescent development.* New York, NY: Cambridge University Press

Scheier, M. F., & Carver, C. S. (1985). Optimism, coping, and health: Assessment and implications of generalized outcome expectancies. *Health Psychology, 4,* 219–247.

Schunk, D. (1991). Self-Efficacy and academic motivation. *Educational Psychologist, 26*(3 & 4), 207–231.

Schunk, D. H., Pintrich, P. R., & Meece, J. L. (2008). *Motivation in education* (3rd ed.). Upper Saddle River, NJ: Pearson Merrill Prentice Hall.

Searle, T. P. (2010). *Psychological capital and performance indicators in educational organizations.* Paper presented at Southwest Academy of Management Southwest Academy of Management 2010. Downloaded 02.02.13

Seligman, M. E. (2006). *Learned optimism: How to change your mind and your life.* New York, NY: Vintage Books.

Seligman, M. E., Ernst, R. M., Gillham, J., Reivich, K., & Linkins, M. (2009). Positive education: Positive psychology and classroom interventions. *Oxford Review of Education, 35*(3), 293–311.

Shogren, K. A., Lopez, S. J., Wehmeyer, M. L., Little, T. D., & Pressgrove, C. L. (2006). The role of positive psychology constructs in predicting life satisfaction in adolescents with and without cognitive disabilities: An exploratory study. *The Journal of Positive Psychology, 1*(1), 37–52.

Snyder, C. R., Shorey, H., Scheier, M. F., & Carver, C. S. (1985). Optimism, coping, and health: Assessment and implications of generalized outcome expectancies. *Health psychology, 4*(3), 219–247.

Snyder, C. R., Harris, C., Anderson, J. R., Holleran, S. A., Irving, L. M., Sigmon, S. T. S., … Wiklund, C. (2002). Hope and academic success in college. *Journal of Educational Psychology, 94*(4), 820–826.

TRANSark. (2015). *Transformative learning in architectural education.* Trondheim: NTNU. Retrieved from http://www.ntnu.edu/transark

Vivian, P. (2012). *A new symbol based writing system for use in illustrating basic dynamics* (Unpublished Ph.D thesis). Coventry University, England.

Weatheral, A. (2012). Discursive psychology and feminism. *British Journal of Social Psychology, 51,* 463–470.

Zimmerman, B. J. (2002). Becoming a self-regulated learner: An overview. *Theory into Practice, 41*(2), 64–70.

Julie Rattray
School of Education
Durham University

AHMAD THAMRINI F. SYED MOHAMED, RAY LAND
AND JULIE RATTRAY

7. AMBIVALENCE, HYBRIDITY AND LIMINALITY

The Case of Military Education

INTRODUCTION

This chapter arises from doctoral research into the threshold concepts required to transform civilians into soldiers, and subsequently into military officers. In addition to identifying the conceptual thresholds involved in a successful transformation, the study also attempts to determine the necessary ontological shifts that such a transformation entails. Drawing on Meyer and Land's (2005) educational application of the anthropological idea of liminality, further notions of 'ambivalence' and 'hybridity' in learning are introduced into our understanding of how particular learners may experience and respond to the liminal state. It will be argued that as learners enter and traverse the liminal space, they clearly do so not in a state of *tabula rasa*, but a state in which their prior experience and knowledge of the world continues to influence any transformative learning experience that they undergo. Analysing findings from the study's in-depth interviews and observations with military personnel, the chapter further employs elements of Bhabha's third space theory, in particular his ideas of *ambivalence* and *hybridity*, to further develop our understanding and discourse of liminality so that it may account for outcomes of transformative learning and subsequent longer-term behaviours which arise from this study.

Meyer and Land's learning thresholds (Meyer & Land, 2003, 2005) – the level or point at which conceptual and ontological transformations begin – have been productively applied to the analysis of learning in many disciplines and professions over the last decade (Flanagan, 2015). The model consequently was adopted to assist the identification and provide greater understanding of the challenges faced in the transformation of civilians into soldiers and, later, into military leaders. Emphasis was placed on the idea that the crossing through the transformative portal requires particular knowledge or capacity from candidates for them to progress and demonstrate capabilities that are desirable or necessary (Abbott, 2013; Kiley, 2009; Loertscher, 2011; Talanquer, 2015; Trafford & Leshem, 2009). Cousin (2006, p. 4) observes that:

R. Land et al. (Eds.), Threshold Concepts in Practice, 77–91.
© 2016 Sense Publishers. All rights reserved.

Grasping a threshold concept is transformative because it involves an ontological as well as a conceptual shift. We are what we know. New understandings are assimilated into our biography, becoming part of who we are, how we see and how we feel.

The understanding gained may entail epistemological transitions (advances in knowledge and knowing) and ontological transformations (development in ways of being) (Meyer & Land, 2003, 2005). Threshold concepts can also be represented as operating as a web within a discipline, emphasising connections between, or clusters of ideas rather than considering single ideas in isolation (Kinchin et al., 2011, p. 211).

LIMINALITY

Meyer and Land (op.cit) borrow the anthropological idea of liminality from van Gennep (1960) and Turner (1967), suggesting that transformative learning can take the character of a rite of passage, marking a person's movement from one status to another in order to enter a specific community.

The transition period may be experienced as exhilarating but also intimidating (Baillie, Bowden, & Meyer, 2012; Osmond & Turner, 2010; Stacey & Stickley, 2012; Wimshurst, 2011). Learners who fail to achieve sufficient necessary understandings may experience the liminal state as a 'stuck' place, obliging them to resort to forms of mimicry (Rodger et al., 2015: 546–547). Kiley (2009) explains the counter-productive effects of being stuck, and potential negative impacts for learners, such as diminished will to continue learning.

In this state students must take time 'to play with the knowledge, experiment with it, apply it, and struggle to resolve conflicts in their understandings' (Higgs & Cronin, 2013: 162). Cousin (2006) further suggests that as this space is unstable, the process of learning may need to be recursive – journeying back and forward across the conceptual terrain. As a result, the period of time spent during the liminal experience might be protracted (Baillie et al., 2012, p. 241) as mastering a threshold concept demands considerable effort (Talanquer, 2015: 4).

THE STUDY

A study of the liminal experience of military personnel undergoing professional training and development was undertaken. It adopted a phenomenographic methodology and was conducted at two European military institutions – Institution A (*Ia*), and Institution B (*Ib*). A total of seven (n = 7) policy makers (*PM*), twenty-four (n = 24) military trainers (*MT*), and twenty-nine (n = 29) cadets (*S*) participated in in-depth semi structured interviews.

It should be noted that the state of liminality experienced by the cadets at Institution A and Institution B took place at a different pace and rhythm. As there is a compulsory conscription period of twelve-months to enter Institution A, the ontological shift and the transformation process from civilian to soldier, and then on to officer, is experienced at a much more gradual and steady pace. In Institution B however, the transformation to soldier is expedited through a prescribed six-weeks Initiation Phase and followed by the institution's officer's training and education. This could be a source for troublesome encounter as the thresholds and ontological shifts confronted by the cadets at Institution B would not be as gradual as those experienced by their counterparts at Institution A. As discussed in Land (2015):

> Insights gained by learners as they cross thresholds can be exhilarating but might also be unsettling, requiring a change of subjectivity and, paradoxically, a sense of loss. The notion of a threshold has always demarcated that which belongs within, the place of familiarity and relative security, from what lies beyond – the unfamiliar, the strange, the potentially threatening. It reminds us that all journeys begin with leaving that familiar space and crossing over into the riskier space beyond the threshold. (p. 20)

THRESHOLD TRANSITIONS IN MILITARY EDUCATION

The findings of the study revealed that military cadets, as part of their development, had to attain important levels of technical skill and proficiency in areas such as shooting, marksmanship, map reading, survival ability and so forth. However the performance of such tasks might also be required of irregulars, or insurgents, or indeed of civilians in other walks of life. Civilians involved in shooting sports would have to learn the same skills for handling, retaining and maintaining their shooting equipment. As one of the military instructors observed, however, knowing 'what and when' to shoot, in action, calls on significantly different judgment from 'how' to shoot. Rescue teams would require similar skills of orienteering and survival. This would not make them a soldier, but an expert in sport or mountain rescue. As one of the policy makers that were interviewed observed:

> For me personally, it is not important for them to know if they can shoot very well. That is not important. They have to know how to handle a weapon, of course. But for me being an officer or a military is more than just being a good shooter. For me it's your whole… inside. Your approach. The way you are as a human being. How you treat the others. Often I say an officer is not just a fighting machine. As a soldier you are a human being. You are a gentleman. You have values. You have a role to play in the society. You should be the example. And people have to be able to rely on you… that they can count on you. (PM2Ib)

The study found that certain distinct forms of transformation were required to enter and be accepted within the military community of practice. The first ontological shift, that concerned with the transformation from civilian to soldier, involves the acceptance of discipline and obedience, recognition of a framework of related ethics and values, loyalty to the unit (putting collective above individual needs) and a sense of obligation. This shift would also prove at a subsequent point, to be the most important stage in becoming an officer also, as failure to negotiate the threshold at this stage would result in the cadet's dismissal from the institution. This shift can be termed *Soldiership*.

The second ontological shift, from soldier to officer, involves assuming the mantle of responsibility and acceptance of a leadership role. What we have termed *Officership* involves a necessary psychological distancing from the troops and a preparedness to impose sanctions and punishment where necessary for mission completion, and to achieve 'the greater good'. This later shift can be seen as the ultimate goal in the institutions under study where cadet officers are given university level education with military training that prepares them as military officers.

We became aware during the study of a third and final ontological shift that is required at the end of military service when both soldiers and officers quit or retire from active service. This transition, which we have termed *Re-civilianisation*, can present many difficulties that are recognisable from other studies of liminal transformation in relation to the letting go of a former identity or status and the psychological and affective adaptation required for a new and altered role and re-entry to civilian life, but this time with past military experience and knowledge. Study in depth of this shift would entail access to a different respondent group, however, and hence was beyond the scope and focus of the current study. However there is substantial extant evidence of the large numbers of former military personnel unable to effect this shift who find themselves subsequently imprisoned or referred to mental hospitals or rehabilitation centres (Whitman, 1995; Iversenet al., 2005; The Howard League, 2011; Jackson, Thoemmes, Jonkmann, Ludtke, & Trautwein, 2012; Samele, 2013; Maringira, Gibson, & Richters, 2014).

Soldiership

Within the broader ontological shift discussed earlier Soldiership was found to present three distinct thresholds which were essential to transformation as a soldier and entry to the military community of practice. These three thresholds are:

1. A preparedness to use legitimised violence
2. A sense of *Esprit de Corps* and unquestioned loyalty to the (collective) before individual need
3. Prompt and unquestioned execution of the line of command

It is important to note that the thresholds are not necessarily sequential. Rather, the thresholds are bonded to one another and the mixture of the experiences has been described by the learners as an 'organised chaos'.

Officership

Within the broader ontological shift of *Officership* discussed earlier there were again found to be three distinct thresholds that candidates had successfully to negotiate to achieve transformation as an officer and entry to the officer class community of practice. These three thresholds are:

1. Personal responsibility for the execution of the mission
2. An obligation to put the needs of one's troops before personal needs
3. The 'power to command'

One of the policy makers interviewed in the study characterised the transformed subjectivity of the officer as follows:

> As an officer you are an example to your soldiers. You have to show that you are able to do the same things, the same detailed, soldier things as they are doing. And then to be respected by them, by the soldiers. By showing professionalism and that comes with the training, with exercise and so on. As I told you, the officer has to understand the broader picture of things like tactical [considerations] for example. And he has to be able to explain the situation for his soldiers. And then he has to be able to give the orders, and maybe he will lose. There will be casualties. But, anyhow, he has to keep the task as number one when he is doing the business. (PM1Ia)

PRIOR AFFINITY

The study's analysis of the liminal state experienced by military cadets, as they progress through education and training to become an officer, is depicted in Figure 1. But before delving further into the discussion at hand, it is important to emphasise, unequivocally, that learners' experiences inevitably differ from one individual to another, making the identification of an unvarying and consistent 'way of experiencing' virtually unattainable. Despite this, the model can serve as a useful interpretive tool for understanding not only the transformation of a civilian into an officer, but also in identifying the 'jewels in the curriculum' (Land et al., 2006, p. 198) of military education.

At the pre-liminal stage, before going through a programme of learning in higher education, learners already hold a 'stock of existing concepts' (Land, 2015, p. 24) that may influence their experience during the liminal state and which inevitably affect its outcome. As the new recruits enter the institution, they encounter new thresholds that may directly result in the transformation of the recruit as a soldier or officer (embodied in path *1*). For example, when asked about their initial opinion of the military, a cadet at Institution A pointed out that:

> S5: 'We knew something beforehand so it was easy... already adjusting to the system. But the first few days, more or less it is a surprise, a good surprise we would say. You will be running, you will get tired. All in all it was the social pressure that is difficult. Not the physical. It was about the new guys coming from all over the country... coming to a single place and suddenly having to making new friends, and that is the core thing basically. Not the

physical stress. Not the 'forced education' and things like that but more like understanding the guys. So instead of sleeping alone when you are with your family, you will have twelve other guys who are sleeping in the same room as you and you start learning about people... very interesting things about people. (Y1Ia) Henceforth, S (Student)1: Y1 (Year 1): Ia (Institution a).

Another cadet explained that;

S1: My experience is very good partially because of previous wars in [*name of his country*], our nationality's a part of that in a sense. We have ancestors who had served during the war; it is nothing new... the military concepts... to protect your own country. And the fact that my dad is in the Army as well. (Y2Ia)

The interview data indicated that having a prior affinity or a degree of background knowledge of *what to expect* helped these cadets to manoeuvre and negotiate thresholds much more effectively than their colleagues who did not possess such knowledge. (Similar prior affinity seems helpful in other professional settings such as medicine or surgery). In addition, those following path *1* exhibited a high level of congruence or conformity with the traditional professional and cultural requirements of becoming a member of military society. Despite these findings, however, it is interesting to note the view of one of the military trainers at Institution A:

As we told you none of my family members was a soldier, so we don't have a very good picture of the military system before we go to my conscript training. Maybe at the beginning we felt that soldiers and officers are 'weapon crazy' people but after we had done my conscript training, we know that we was totally wrong and... we know now that the Defence [Ministry] is the security builder, and they are for independence. (MT5Ia)

As the quotation suggests, this officer's lack of background knowledge of the military could have been a source of trouble for him in navigating the liminal space. And yet the same military trainer appears to have experienced some form of 'epiphany' or ontological shift, in which he came to acknowledge that military life would be the right choice for him. This appears to be, to some extent, a result of his positive outlook and strong motivation to become an officer.

We don't know how much you know about the country's history, but we [have had] war before so we are very proud of our history and independence, and that is one of the reasons why we want to become an officer. (MT5Ia)

This resonates with the findings discussed in Julie Rattray's chapter (this volume) in which hope, optimism and other positive psychological factors seem to be strong affective components in enabling learners to attain the resilience necessary for successful personal management of the liminal state. However, the research found that there are also recruits who, despite having an 'appropriate' or congruent background, experience path *2* and end up withdrawing from the institution. One of the current cadets mentioned that:

S3: There was also this guy whose father is a military but he didn't want to be a military. On the second day, he quits. He started crying and he explained to our Chief what was the situation and he quits. (Y1Ib)

Regardless of arriving with the 'correct and suitable background', a newly admitted cadet will still opt to quit if he or she 'didn't want to be a military'. If the required shift in personal subjectivity appears too daunting, there is a turning away from the threshold and the liminal state will not be entered.

AMBIVALENCE AND HYBRIDITY

Apart from those cadets identified as progressing along pathways *1* and *2* in Figure 1, the research also identified those whose feelings appear more complex and may be the ones caught 'in-between' or stuck, where their inability to understand difficult and troublesome knowledge may result in a 'lack of authenticity'(Land, 2015, p. 18). In her study, Cousin (2003) described the tendency of some learners as 'faking it' – maintaining good results in an examination without making the necessary transformation in subjectivity.

Further insight into, and a possibly fresh perspective on the notions of *mimicry* and liminality may be derived from the work of Homi Bhabha. (1994). His post-colonial discourse employs the notion of mimicry but also those of *ambivalence* and *hybridity*, which may have a relevant bearing on the transformative experience of certain of the military personnel that were interviewed. Whilst a civilian in the pre-liminal phase (Figure 1) might embark on the journey to officership via path *1* and *2*, the same person may, in the liminal phase, occupy a third locus, that of ambivalence. This entails having simultaneous conflicting reactions, beliefs, or feelings towards knowledge deemed troublesome as a result of previously held beliefs. Professional training institutions such as the military academies in this study tend to consider new cadets as the 'other', essentially as *outsiders* (McLeod, 2000, p. 52). In order to abolish their 'otherness', the new cadets are put through a process of domestication to become 'a competent member of the practice' (Wenger, 1999, p. 136). In Bhabha's view the person undergoing transformation occupies a 'discursive space from which "The Real Me" emerges (initially as an assertion of the authenticity of the person) and then lingers on to reverberate – "The Real Me?" – as a question of identity" (Bhabha, 1994, p. 70). This simultaneously puts the person in an ambivalent position – to be *inside* and *outside* – producing an 'other' that does have the required 'knowledge' and can now be seen as a legitimate member of the community (Bhabha, 1994, p. 71) but lacks the self-conviction of being a part of *communitas* (Turner, 1969, p. 96).

Keeping in mind Meyer and Land's notion of 'compensatory mimicry', through which the learner may experience 'oscillation between states, often with temporary regression to an earlier state' (2006, p. 24), we might link this state to that of Bhabha's ambivalent state, which renders those in it 'almost the same but not quite' (Bhabha, 1994, p. 123). Characterised by path *4*, (Figure 1) we might speculate that cadets who mimic may resort to *anxious repetition* of a certain activity or stereotypical behaviour expected within the practice, without properly understanding the reasons they are performing such behaviours. The following account given by a first year cadet from Institution B provides an instance of this:

> S7: What is also difficult was to keep the timing... always be on time which is a problem for us. Because in the Army, it is important for you to be on time and if you are not you will be punished. So it was quite difficult for us. It was not for everyone... because they will give you impossible timing, and they know that it was impossible. And they just make it that way so that they can punish you. But we think that is a part of becoming a soldier. The first week was also a time where they will punish you or yell at you and things like that. We think it is just something that you need to go through to become a soldier. (Y1Ib)

Despite being observant towards the military's culture on time management and 'doing-things-within-a-time frame', the cadet did not fully understand the seemingly arbitrary implementation of time requirements, but concluded that 'it is just something that you need to go through to become a soldier'. And this 'something' refers to a characteristic expectation that the military likes to punish people and hence to become a soldier you must be prepared to be punished. As a result, the cadet may be punctual but not because it is a trait the military highly value, but a compliance to avoid punishment. This lack of conviction may result in a cadet resorting to mimicry; though in time they may come understand the reasoning behind it. A policy maker from Institution B shared his own experience and commented that:

> For us it was not the shouting or the discipline... it was the time management. For us this was my major issue. Getting up in the morning at time... and we got up 10 minutes before my roommates to get ready. And after two days we found it impossible. We got up at 5.45am, they got up at 6.00am... but they are ready and we are not ready. So that was a problem. So I had to learn how to manage my time. And that is very important for an officer... time management. If you are given a task... and you have to give a result to your Chief at the end of the week... well... you have to produce the result at the end of the week. Not on Monday but on Friday. It's time management. But that was my problem. We got up earlier, but my roommates were ready for the 6.15am inspection and not us. But in the end, we got up at 6.00 and we were also ready at 6.15. (PM1Ib)

As these quotes imply, a changed realisation from 'to avoid punishment' to 'the importance of having proper time management' can come about over time. Represented through path *4a* (Figure 1) the cadet may eventually transform and become 'the officer' – either by 'compensatory mimicry' or 'conscious mimicry' (Meyer & Land, 2006, p. 24).

On the other hand, there are those mimics who may not transform and may get themselves 'stuck' over the years of their compulsory service. Depicted as following path *4b* (Figure 1) these officers will, at a point in their service, quit and leaves their profession. One of the policy makers from Institution B commented that:

In our Polytechnic academy for example, we think we have two types of officers. The first one who attends the Polytechnic academy is the one who is much interested in the academic. They want to become civil engineer... they want to go into laboratory... They are interested by military career... but we think for them predominantly it is the academic. Usually when we look at the profile of those who go in for the Social Military Sciences, they are very much military-oriented. And the academic is probably a second place. So you have two different profiles. This is interesting because both of them once they have graduated will go and serve into units, and they will start their career as an officer. (PM5Ib)

Another officer from the same institution provides an interesting standpoint that to become an officer:

is not something you try to do, it is a commitment for life and you have to be convinced that this is your future. If you don't know what you are up against, you will not succeed. As we said, it is a vocation. If you don't have this 'feeling'... especially to become an officer... you won't succeed. Don't try, because you will never succeed. You will leave. A lot of my colleagues have left.

This 'lack of belief' in the profession may leave certain cadets within a troubled liminal state for a much longer period – even after being commissioned as an officer, and long after leaving the military academy. These officers would *act* as an officer, appear to have the outlook of an officer but not really see themselves *as* 'an officer'. Again an instance of Bhabha's 'almost the same but not quite' (1994, p. 123), where 'The Real Me' remains occluded, and the officer operates in a state of silent and hidden ambivalence. In the longer term the ambivalent cadets may eventually accommodate the intended meaning of a certain concept and resolve the ambivalence in a comfortable acceptance of the officer identity and role. Conversely the ambivalence may lead them to quit altogether as a result of poor conviction in the profession.

Bhabha also discusses the idea of *hybridity*. In ontological terms this allows a person's 'subjectivity to be composed from variable sources, different materials, and many locations – demolishing forever the idea of subjectivity as stable, single, or "pure"' (McLeod, 2000, p. 219). We might talk of hybrid cadets who could have followed path *1* (Figure 1) but at the same time feel 'empowered to intervene actively in the transmission of cultural inheritance or "tradition" rather than passively accept its venerable custom and pedagogical wisdom' thus prompting them to 'question, refashion or mobilise received ideas' (McLeod, 2000, pp. 218–219).

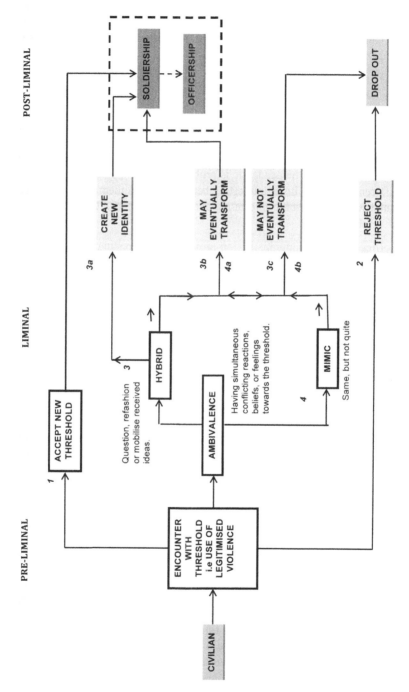

Figure 1. Liminality in officer education

Bringing the lens of hybridity to bear upon our understanding of liminality within the Threshold Concepts Framework helps clarify a number of issues. A learner occupying the liminal space does not necessarily succumb to the *ritual knowledge* that has stood the test of time within the institution (Perkins, 2006, p. 37) but might reinvent and re-envision such knowledge. In the case of the hybrid cadets they might not be sufficiently convinced of existing institutional practice or community belief to confirm and condone it and may consequently be seen as challenging authority. Unlike the cadets who conform to required expectation and accordingly pursue path *1* (Figure 1), these hybrid cadets would more likely follow path *3a* that may lead them to re-define and reconstruct the identity of the officer in some respect. A policy maker from Institution B refers to this changing sensibility:

For instance when I came to the military academy... and they told us 'Jump!', everybody jumps because that is what we were told to do. Right now if you tell a young guy 'Jump!', he will ask you "OK, how high do I have to jump? How long do I have to jump? *Why* do I have to jump?' (PM4Ib)

In many respects this in keeping with Schön's well known account (1983) of the reflective professional and how professionals think in action. The professional:

approaches the practice problem as a unique case. He does not act as though he had no relevant prior experiences; on the contrary. But he attends to the peculiarities of the situation at hand... Rather, each seeks to discover the particular features of his problematic situation, and, from gradual discovery, designs an intervention. (p. 129)

This creates a complex atmosphere within the institution where authority – an asset in military training – comes to be questioned and challenged. Certain practices within military education are seen as no longer valid and effective. One such account is provided by one of the policy makers at Institution B:

We cannot compare my five weeks with the five weeks which is now. It's a different system. We had the Paratroopers... Nowadays, the five weeks is done by the promotion commander [so] there is now less shouting, less running and crying and definitely less punishment. We were punished during my days. When we did something stupid, we had to run on the parade ground with my rifle above my head for five minutes, ten minutes, depending on the mistake we made. Nowadays, that is forbidden. It is not allowed anymore and we are glad it is not allowed. But you see, there is a difference. That was not easy... my time. And we must be honest... two or three times I thought to myself; 'What am I doing here? Perhaps it is better to quit'. (PM1Ib)

This troublesome recognition that some aspect or dimension of the expected transformation cannot, and will not, be accommodated places the cadet into a conflicted state of ambivalence, and this can extend the liminal period for a considerable period. The state of ambivalence gives rise to the disposition, or identity even, of hybridity. This cadet continues his training despite the harsh treatment he is getting. He does not relinquish his opposition to aspects of the training however, but suppresses and occludes this, remaining loyal to the community on the one hand, but conflicted regarding its practice and ontology on the other. The liminal tension, and the hybrid disposition is finally resolved either by quitting the professional role and community altogether (contemplated in the respondent's account above) or by the trainee officer's eventually moving into a position of authority him or herself in which they can reform practice and expectation so that the conflict no longer remains. The former trainee officer and subsequent policy maker reflects further:

> But it was part of the game because it was normal in the early '80's. It was normal for that time. When I was a young cadet, we had already talked about this. 'In twenty, thirty years' time we will stop this. This is not humane'. But it *was* accepted at that period. It was normal so we did it. For the Paratroopers, this was a game. 'How far can we push them with this?' But nowadays, it is the opposite. 'What can we do to keep those guys?' We do not want to lose one. We want to keep all those guys and girls. That is a big difference. One is about 'breaking' while the other is about 'keeping'. (PM1Ib)

He and his colleague had come to a realisation that military education must eventually change to accommodate new ways of thinking. It is interesting to speculate further whether there is a higher likelihood that hybrid cadets will reinvent the military *code of honour* (Janowitz, 1960, p. 217) compared with their colleagues who had dutifully trailed path *1* (Figure 1).

This gives rise to a wider issue regarding the predicament of the *hybrid* cadet. Are these cadets likely, in the general scheme of things, to undergo roughly the same ontological transformation as their non-hybrid counterparts – whose transformation has been more direct and non-conflicted – whilst privately retaining certain ambivalences or reservations? Or do they become 'something else' – and undergo a substantially different ontological transformation which does not become manifest until a much later date? Significantly more data would be required before any definitive conclusion could be offered. Nonetheless, there is evidence within our current data to suggest that there are officers who did not agree with the idea that, as military core business is war, being in the military is consequently concerned with violence and becoming a 'fighting machine'. Instead, certain respondents strongly believe that their presence within the military institution is to prevent violence from happening in the first place. They still subscribe to the necessity for armed force, and the legitimate use of violence, but have come to a different realisation why they need to do so. This would indicate a substantially different military ontology.

We found that there will be those who will follow path *3c* (Figure 1) and leave the institution for reasons very much like those on paths *2* and *4b* (Figure 1). Meyer and Land (2006) comment on the recursive and oscillative nature of the liminal, looping back and forth 'often with temporary regression to earlier status' (p. 24). On this occasion, however, the reflective processes of ambivalence render the cadet to unable to adopt a position of hybridity, leaving them in an 'unhomely' and 'uncanny' environment (McLeod, 2000:220) where experiences of being stuck and unable to effect required ontological shifts become traumatic and full of irresolvable anxiety.

Our study also identified those who reflect and negotiate their situation but who pursue path *3b* (Figure 1). Unlike those who somehow manage to effect a new ontology, these cadets eventually conform to prescribed values and follow path *1* (Figure 1). Initially these cadets present aspects of a *hybrid* cadet, but as a result of collective participation and spending time with their colleagues during training, they in the longer term along orthodox lines. In a focus group with first year cadets from Institution B, we had the chance to pose the question whether the participants felt that they had changed through the initiation process. Reflecting on their experiences, one of them responded that;

> S1: We notice this also... we were in the same platoon with S4. And we think he had changed a lot. He was not really good in keeping time and everything... but at the end of the six weeks, he changed... very fast. (Y1Ib)

S4 himself then responded as follows:

> S4: At first I was not comfortable. People are yelling at us – which we had a lot. For us it was exactly like *Full Metal Jacket*. So some people will get along with I and some will never. Maybe it was because we watched the movie a week before we came here that makes it a little bit harder. You just have this impression that the instructors are just like that, but then you realise that they just want to help you... to make you tougher. (Y1Ib)

CONCLUSION

The Threshold Concepts Framework was found to be a helpful analytic tool in our inquiry into the processes and effects of Military Education. Meyer and Land's (2003) notion of liminality was employed to gain insight into the experience of transformation of civilians to soldier and officer status. This chapter seeks to provide further insight into our understanding of liminality, mimicry and ontological shift by drawing, in complementary fashion, on Homi Bhabha's theoretical constructs of ambivalence and hybridity. Our study indicates that certain learners will not follow a prescribed path of transformation to an established ontology but are capable of conforming to expected communal practices whilst simultaneously feeling 'empowered to intervene actively' by 'questioning and refashioning received ideas'(McLeod, 2000, pp. 218–219). We are of the opinion that experience of ambivalence in liminal states and subsequent adoption of hybrid identities is likely to be found in other processes of professional transformation, and that these lenses may prove fruitful in future inquiry.

REFERENCES

Abbott, R. (2013). Crossing thresholds in academic reading. *Innovations in Education and Teaching International, 50*(2), 191–201.

Baillie, C., Bowden, J. A., & Meyer, J. H. F. (2012). Threshold capabilities: Threshold concepts and knowledge capability linked through variation theory. *Higher Education, 65*(2), 227–246.

Bhabha, H. K. (1994). *The location of culture*. London & New York, NY: Routledge.

Cousin, G. (2006). Section 1: Introduction to threshold concepts An introduction to threshold concepts. *Planet*, (17), 4–5.

Flanagan, M. T. (2014). *Threshold concepts: Undergraduate teaching, postgraduate training and professional development. A short introduction and bibliography*. Retrieved from http://www.ee.ucl.ac.uk/~mflanaga/thresholds.html

Higgs, B., & Cronin, J. (2013). Threshold concepts: Informing the curriculum. In *Emerging issues in higher education III: From capacity building to sustainability* (pp. 161–177). Athlone: Educational Developers in Ireland Network (EDIN). Retrieved from http://www.edin.ie/pubs/ei3-chapters/ei3-ch12.pdf

Iversen, A., Dyson, C., Smith, N., Greenberg, N., Walwyn, R., Unwin, C., … Wessely, S. (2005). 'Goodbye and good luck': The mental health needs and treatment experiences of British ex-service personnel. *British Journal of Psychiatry, 186*, 480–486.

Jackson, J. J., Thoemmes, F., Jonkmann, K., Ludtke, O., & Trautwein, U. (2012). Military training and personality trait development: Does the military make the man, or does the man make the military? *Psychological Science, 23*(3), 270–277. doi:10.1177/0956797611423545

Janowitz, M. (1960). *The professional soldier*. Glencoe, IL: Free Press.

Kiley, M. (2009). Identifying threshold concepts and proposing strategies to support doctoral candidates. *Innovations in Education and Teaching International, 46*(3), 293–304.

Kinchin, I. M., Cabot, L. B., Kobus, M., & Woolford, M. (2011). Threshold concepts in dental education. *European Journal of Dental Education, 15*(4), 210–215.

Land, R. (2015). Facilitating the academy through threshold concepts and troublesome knowledge. In J. Wiewiura & E. Westergaard (Eds.), *On the facilitation of the academy*. Rotterdam, Taipei & Boston: Sense Publishers.

Land, R., Cousin, G., Meyer, J. H. F., & Davies, P. (2005). Threshold concepts and troublesome knowledge (3): Implications for course design and evaluation. In C. Rust (Ed.), *Improving student learning diversity and inclusivity* (pp. 53–64). Oxford: Oxford Centre for Staff and Learning Development.

Land, R., Cousin, G., Meyer, J. H. F., & Davies, P. (2006). Conclusion: Implications of threshold concepts for course design and evaluation. In J. H. F. Meyer & R. Land (Eds.), *Overcoming barriers to student understanding: Threshold concepts and troublesome knowledge* (pp. 195–206). London & New York, NY: Routledge.

Loertscher, J. (2011). Threshold concepts in biochemistry. *Biochemistry and Molecular Biology Education, 39*(1), 56–57.

Maringira, G., Gibson, D., & Richters, A. (2014). "It's in My Blood": The military habitus of former Zimbabwean soldiers in exile in South Africa. *Armed Forces & Society, 41*(1), 23–42. doi:10.1177/0095327X14523001

McLeod, J. (2000). *Beginning postcolonialism*. Manchester: Manchester University Press.

Meyer, J. H. F., & Land, R. (2003). Threshold concepts and troublesome knowledge 1 – Linkages to ways of thinking and practising. In C. Rust (Ed.), *Improving student learning – Ten years on*. Oxford: OCSLD.

Meyer, J. H. F., & Land, R. (2005). Threshold concepts and troublesome knowledge (2): Epistemological considerations and a conceptual framework for teaching and learning. *Higher Education, 49*(3), 373–388.

Meyer, J. H. F., & Land, R. (2006). Threshold concepts and troublesome knowledge: Issues of liminality. In J. H. F. Meyer & R. Land (Eds.), *Overcoming barriers to student understanding: Threshold concepts and troublesome knowledge* (pp. 19–32). London & New York, NY: Routledge.

Meyer, J. H. F., Ward, S. C., & Latreille, P. (2009). Threshold concepts and metalearning capacity. *International Review of Economics Education*, *44*(January). Retrieved from http://www.economicsnetwork.ac.uk/iree/v8n1/

Meyer, J., & Land, R. (2003). *Threshold concepts and troublesome knowledge: Practising within the Disciplines.* Oxford: OCSLD.

Osmond, J., & Turner, A. (2010). The threshold concept journey in design: From identification to application. In J. H. F. Meyer, R. Land, & C. Baillie (Eds.), *Threshold concepts and transformational learning* (pp. 347–364). Rotterdam, The Netherlands: Sense Publishers.

Rodger, S., Turpin, M., & O'Brien, M. (2015). Experiences of academic staff in using threshold concepts within a reformed curriculum. *Studies in Higher Education*, *40*(4), 545–560.

Samele, C. (2013). *The mental health of serving and ex-service personnel. A review of the evidence and perspectives of key stakeholders.* London: Forces in Mind Trust.

Schön, D. A. (1983). *The reflective practitioner: How professionals think in action.* New York, NY: Basic Books.

Stacey, G., & Stickley, T. (2012). Recovery as a threshold concept in mental health nurse education. *Nurse Education Today*, *32*(5), 534–539.

Talanquer, V. (2015). Threshold concepts in chemistry: The critical role of implicit schemas. *Journal of Chemical Education, 92*(1), 3–9.

The Howard League. (2011). *Report of the inquiry into former armed service personnel in prison.* London: The Howard League for Penal Reform.

Trafford, V., & Leshem, S. (2009). Doctorateness as a threshold concept. *Innovations in Education and Teaching International*, *46*(3), 305–316.

Turner, V. (1967). *The ritual process: Structure and anti-structure.* New Brunswick, NJ: Aldine Transaction.

Van Gennep, A. (1960). *The rites of passage.* Chicago, IL: The University of Chicago Press.

Walsham, G. (1995). The emergence of interpretivism in IS research. *Information System Research*, *6*(4), 376–394.

Whitman, J. P. (1995). The soldier as conscientious objector. *Public Affairs Quarterly, 9*(1), 87–100.

Wimshurst, K. (2011). Applying threshold concepts theory to an unsettled field: An exploratory study in criminal justice education. *Studies in Higher Education, 36*(3), 301–314.

Ahmad Thamrini F. Syed Mohamed
National Defence University of Malaysia (NDUM)

Ray Land
Durham University

Julie Rattray
Durham University

VIRGINIA M. TUCKER

8. LEARNING EXPERIENCES AND THE LIMINALITY OF EXPERTISE

INTRODUCTION

This chapter reports on research that explored the space between novice and expert professional knowledge to ascertain whether or not threshold concepts were present in this liminal space. The study explored the learning experiences of highly proficient novices, those who demonstrated expertlike practices and attributes, and discipline experts with more than 30 years professional experience, thus creating a centred study space for the liminality of expertise. The research focus was search expertise, and the study explored knowledge that is independent of both the specific search engine (features, commands, and the like) and the subject domain of the database content. This domain is of significant interest as search expertise has cross-disciplinary relevance; the content of searching can belong to any academic field or subject.

The study identified threshold concepts that exist within the liminal space between novice and expert; it also identified traits and praxes of expert searchers that did not have the characteristics of threshold concepts but which helped fill out the portrait of expertise. This chapter reports these findings which have implications for other disciplinary settings and a deeper understanding of the nature of expertise and the transformative learning involved in novice-to-expert experiences. Tucker, Weedman, Bruce, and Edwards (2014) provide an integrated and multi-dimensional model of this liminal space.

PRACTICE CONTEXT

Expert searchers are rare, just as chess masters, concert pianists, and experts in any discipline are rare, and perhaps particularly so in the most cognitively demanding fields (Simon & Chase, 1973; Gladwell, 2013). We can benefit from studying those who have become experts, along with those who are moving in a trajectory toward expertise or endeavoring to do so. Exploring the transitional—and transformational—space between the highly proficient novice and the expert was the focus of this research, exploring the learning experiences, information experiences, and the conceptual knowledge engaged. *Expert searchers* in today's information environment may include reference librarians, information architects, university faculty who teach advanced search, and other professionals in a variety of

R. Land et al. (Eds.), Threshold Concepts in Practice, 93–106.

information-intensive settings. Their professional experiences are characterised by a profound understanding of both information concepts and content *and* they have an agile ability to apply this knowledge to interacting with and having an impact on the information environment, often including a role in the information experiences of others (Tucker, 2014). The study examined novice-expert literature (Dreyfus, 1980, 2004; Simon & Chase, 1973; Ericsson, 1993) and considered practices relevant to the learning experiences of experts, such as how they: structure knowledge (Bransford, 1999), process ambiguous information (Berliner, 1994), solve problems and use representations (Ericsson, 2000), and use reflection when learning (Schön, 1983).

METHODOLOGY

Methodological challenges when studying threshold concepts have been the subject of research literature and, indeed, the effort to identify threshold concepts is itself a study in troublesomeness. Rowbottom was an early critic, highlighting "serious difficulties that any empirical exploration of threshold concepts is liable to encounter" (2007, p. 268). A variety of methodologies have been used to study threshold concepts (Davies & Mangan, 2005), and the studies have come from a far-reaching range of academic disciplines and subject areas (Tucker et al., 2014). Researchers have combined phenomenography and variation theory in studies involving threshold concepts (Åkerlind, McKenzie, & Lupton, 2014); Quinlan et al. (2013) recently reviewed six research methods and Barradell (2013) discussed various forms of consensus methodologies, to name but a few.

Grounded theory methodology was used for this study, providing a set of rigorous research procedures that can be used in developing—through the process of emergence—conceptual categories and themes. This study takes an original approach in using grounded theory to identify threshold concepts. The methodology has been widely used in other kinds of qualitative studies for discovering anchors that allow the key points of the data to be collected, organised, and for findings to emerge (Charmaz, 2014). Thus, rather than looking from the beginning for threshold concepts, the researcher allows concepts to emerge from the data and examines them to see whether or not they have the characteristics of threshold concepts.

Differentiating categories and themes is a thorny aspect of grounded theory methodology. Although categories and themes are different in nature—and, indeed, in how they "capture different forms of knowledge"—they are sometimes used "almost interchangeably in completed research" (Morse, 2008, p. 927). Morse suggests opera as a fitting and elegant metaphor to clarify the difference between them:

> A category is a collection of similar data sorted into the same place…a theme, on the other hand, is a meaningful 'essence' that runs through the data. Just as a theme in opera occurs over and over again, sometimes in the foreground, sometimes in the background, and sometimes co-occurring with other tunes,

so does the theme in our research. It is the basic topic that the narrative is about, overall. This comparison of categories and themes becomes clearer if we carry our opera metaphor one step further. I heard on the radio a content analysis of an opera. The writer had sorted all the trills and … into categories and the result was ludicrous. But this example makes the difference between a category and a theme immediately obvious. (2008, p. 927)

In this research, categories and themes were used according to Morse's definition: I coded the data according to categories (and into subcategories, called code clusters, within the categories), but the themes that emerged ran like threads, at times woven through multiple categories, and represented the deeper conceptual essence of the data.

Another aspect of grounded theory studies is that researcher and participant may work together toward "meaning making" (Limberg & Alexandersson, 2009) and the method proved effective for eliciting evidence of critical concepts present in learning experiences and, from there, exploring threshold concepts. However, it is important to note that, in grounded theory, the introduction of theoretical frameworks and, indeed, relevant research literature as a whole, comes into play late in the game, with the goal being that it not "stifle creativity or strangle your [own] theory" (Charmaz, 2014, p. 308). However, in the practical sense, it is not possible for grounded theory researchers to wholly "jettison all their prior knowledge of the field" (Dunne, 2011, p. 117). As is typical, I did not begin this study from a vacuum of knowledge about the literature nor without professional experience as a searcher, and it was not possible to entirely 'un-know' this base of knowledge.

Complicating the data collection processes, the ambiguity of liminal experiences presented particularly thorny challenges for study participants. In addition, working with highly experienced professionals meant that they were often recalling long-ago experiences that might have taken on new meaning or might have become foggy altogether for meaning-making or impact. Indeed, identifying a threshold concept is problematic due to the very ambiguity of the liminal state. "Because of the transformative nature of threshold concepts, we may feel that we've always known something or looked at the world in that way. It is very difficult to remember what it looks like from the other side of the threshold" (Townsend & Brunetti, 2009, p. 6). For experts, this is particularly difficult: "an expert's perception may be radically different from a novice's, and a novice may struggle with difficulties that the expert can no longer see" (Kneebone, 2009, p. 955). Expert educators as study participants deal with an additional challenge in this regard because, as described by Cousin (2006), "one of the difficulties teachers have is that of retracing the journey back to their own days of 'innocence', when understandings of threshold concepts escaped them in the early stages of their own learning" (p. 1). For these reasons, when considering research methodologies and data collection, learners as well as educators should be studied in order to fully explore liminal learning experiences;

indeed, student-centredness itself has been put forth as a threshold concept within higher education (Blackie, Case, & Jawitz, 2010).

Participants

The research plan was designed so that insights were gained from learners on edges of the liminal space of expertise and from those who may have been journeying through it. The study's sample of 20 participants drew from two population groups: graduate students pursuing advanced coursework in online searching and highly experienced professional searchers (averaging 32 years relevant experience), such as information science professors and search engine developers, who were recalling their own learning experiences. Using these two groups allowed a nuanced understanding of the experience of learning to search in expertlike ways, with data from those who perform at a very high level as well as those who may be actively developing expertise. The highly experienced participants were both learners (recalling their learning experiences) and [for several] instructors who were reflecting on the learning experiences of their students. (It should be emphasised that the study did not compare the two groups; in fact, in some instances, participants from the highly proficient novice group displayed more expertlike behaviours than some of the very experienced participants.)

Study Protocols

The study used semi-structured interviews, search tasks with think-aloud narratives, and talk-after protocols. Through the search tasks component of the research design, I hoped to elicit—and perhaps even to observe in real time—critical learning experiences of the liminal space among the participants. Particularly for the highly experienced participants, I further hoped, based on established protocols (Branch, 2000; Lewis & Rieman, 1994), that the activity of engagement in the tasks would help to roust memories of learning experiences.

Searches were screen-captured with simultaneous audio-recording of the think-aloud narrative. Data were coded and analyzed using NVivo software and manually. Once theoretical saturation was achieved in accord with grounded theory method, during the final stage of analysis the coded data were viewed through lenses of existing theoretical frameworks, in this case threshold concept framework (TCF), and analysed to discover themes that represented the "meaningful essence that [ran] through the data" (Morse, 2008, p. 927).

LITERATURE CONTEXT

Two areas of research literature were of particular interest for the context of the study: expert practices and novice-expert literature that ranges across multiple disciplines; and the literature investigating the practices of professional searchers, relevant to the study's domain. There is, in addition, a relatively small selection of works that discuss expertise within the context of the threshold concepts theoretical framework.

Novice-Expert Studies

Novice-expert studies extend far back in the research literature and I looked to see how they might inform this study, provide a backdrop to its terrain, and be integrated into exploring learning experiences that take place for the highly experienced novice who is developing expertlike behaviours.

Hubert and Stuart Dreyfus in 1980 outlined five stages of skill acquisition: novice, advanced beginner, competence, proficiency, and expert (Dreyfus & Dreyfus, 1980; Dreyfus, 2004); their model has been fundamental to novice-expert research, though not without its detractors (Eraut, 1994), and continues to be influential (Kinchin & Cabot, 2010; Kinchin, 2012). Ericsson's equally seminal research (1993) focused on how experts approach problem-solving; it showed they are highly selective about what they retrieve from their memories, encoding it in representations that facilitate alternative courses of action. He emphasised that, although experts did indeed have a larger and more complex storehouse of knowledge than non-experts, there were radical and qualitative differences in this knowledge base and in how selective the experts were in retrieving from it.

In his second edited volume on expertise research, Ericsson (2009) looked not only at the development of professional expertise but also the design of learning environments to optimise it. In this collection, Van Lehn and van de Sande reported findings from their research into what constitutes "conceptual expertise" in physics (2009). They identified three stages in expert conceptualisation when understanding a given physics formula: first, a qualitative understanding of domain principles; next, extensive practice to move through stages of superficial and semantic understanding; last, qualitative understanding. They described the level of understanding or "class of knowledge" as *confluences* (p. 360). The novices they studied, by contrast, suffered from misconceptions (about a formula, for example); the researchers explained that the progression from novice to expert occurs as these misconceptions meet up against contradictions with further learning and, from this, confluences develop.

Another study involving physicists was conducted by Chi—cited by Van Lehn and van de Sande—in which she focused on the ways novices and experts categorise and represent problems to be solved (Chi, Feltovich, & Glaser, 1981). The key finding was that experts took a qualitatively different conceptual approach to problems; they began by "perceiving more in a problem statement than do novices" (p. 147). They selected a principle to apply to the problem and also constructed a representation of the problem. Novices, on the other hand, based their approach on the literal aspects of apprehending the problem.

Expert Practices

A key practice among experts is *reflection*, particularly as it affects the process of learning. Schön described a stark contrast between knowledge acquisition—extreme or otherwise—and learning at a level he called *professional artistry*. He explained, "Artistry is an exercise of intelligence, a kind of knowing, though different in crucial respects from our standard model of professional knowledge. It is not inherently mysterious; it is rigorous in its own terms; and we can learn a great deal about it— within what limits, we should treat as an open question—by carefully studying the performance of unusually competent performers" (1987, p. 13). He further stated that this type of learning is accomplished only through *reflection-in-action* (1983), described as:

> The practitioner allows himself to experience surprise, puzzlement, or confusion in a situation which he finds uncertain or unique. He reflects on the phenomenon before him, and on the prior understandings which have been implicit in his behaviour. He carries out an experiment which serves to generate both a new understanding of the phenomenon and a change in the situation. (1983, p. 68)

In his subsequent book (1987), Schön built upon these ideas and developed proposals and curriculum for teaching reflection-in-action practices. Mezirow (2003) likewise considered reflection an essential practice for any adult learning, such that he termed it *critical reflectivity* in his writings on andragogy (Glancy & Isenberg, 2013).

Berliner detailed additional practices and characteristics of experts:

- Experts represent problems in qualitatively different ways than do novices. Their representations are deeper and richer.
- Experts recognise meaningful patterns faster than novices.
- Experts are more flexible, are more opportunistic planners, and can change representations faster when it is appropriate to do so. Novices are more rigid in their conceptions.
- Experts impose meaning on ambiguous stimuli. They are much more "top down processors." Novices are misled by ambiguity and are more likely to be "bottom up" processors.
- Experts may start to solve a problem more slowly than a novice, but overall they are faster problem solvers.
- Experts are usually more constrained by the task requirements and the social constraints of the situation than are novices.
- Experts develop automaticity in their behaviour to allow conscious processing of ongoing information.
- Experts develop self-regulatory processes as they engage in their activities (1994, p. 4).

Relatively little research literature has examined threshold concepts and expertise, and, in some instances, there is not a shared or common definition for what is meant by *expert*. The overview above of foundational work in novice-expert research helps in establishing the difference between 'highly experienced' and 'expert' within a field. Simon and Chase's early work (1973) is often cited for setting the 10-to-50-thousand-hours bar when a person may begin to develop expertise in a given subject or practice area (Gladwell, 2013), however, expertise may never develop, and yet it is the trajectory toward it that may have transformative characteristics.

Identifying threshold concepts for expert educators has been an active area of research. Kinchin, Cabot, and Hay visualised a model of pedagogy expertise in the context of clinical education in which expertise in teaching is conceived as a threshold concept (2010). "Our view of expertise, as being composed of the dynamic links between chains of practice and underlying networks of understanding is a *transformative* notion" (p. 81). They stated that their concept of expertise had the characteristics of irreversibility as well as some degree of boundedness within the professional disciplines.

Professional Searchers

Researchers and professional organisations such as the Medical Library Association (2005) have studied the qualities and practices that define professional searchers, some of whom will develop expertise. Their professional roles continue to evolve and information professionals increasingly fulfill educator and trouble-shooter positions and perform complex searches for others, particularly in corporate or government agencies "where search experts are an important part of research teams, competitive intelligence operations, patent searching, and so forth" (Tenopir, 2010, p. 1). Separating practitioner (or 'operationalist') knowledge from conceptual knowledge was done early on in library and information science research (Fidel, 1984) and the literature has stayed true to this model (Smith & Roseberry, 2013).

Subject domain knowledge is a significant factor for professional searchers who work with specialised clientele, for example, in medicine and the law where understanding the terminology and the practice or profession greatly enhances one's search abilities. However, an expert searcher may or may not have subject domain knowledge or need it for a given situation.

Four prototypical searchers are represented in Figure 1 as defined by their levels of: (1) generic knowledge of searching (x-axis, GK); (2) subject domain knowledge (y-axis, SK).

1. A new library and information science (LIS) student searching in a database where subject knowledge would be important might have average GK (generic knowledge) and average SK (subject knowledge)—in the lower-left quadrant in the figure.

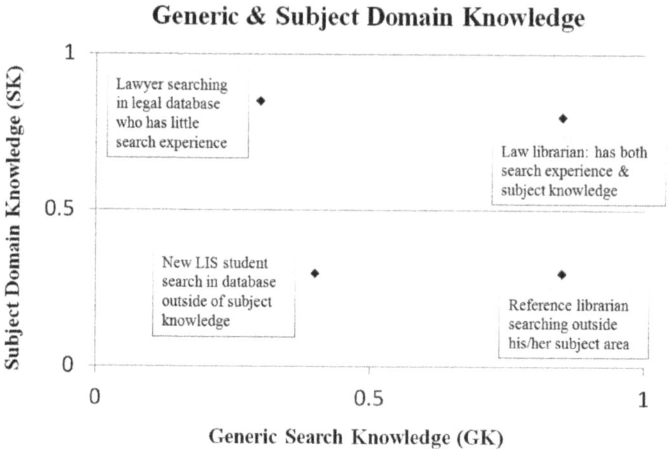

Generic & Subject Domain Knowledge

Figure 1. Model of Subject (SK) and Generic Knowledge (GK) (Tucker, 2012)

2. An attorney with little search experience who is searching in a legal database would have SK-high and GK-low (upper left quadrant).
3. A reference librarian with strong generic searching knowledge working in a database outside his/her subject area would be GK-high and SK-average (lower right quadrant).
4. A competent law librarian would have both SK and GK high (upper right quadrant).

Of the four searchers represented, both #3 and #4 may have expertise, though only #4 has subject knowledge for the domain (law). (As described above, the research design of this study minimised the impact of subject domain knowledge in order to focus on generic knowledge relevant to acquiring expertise.)

FINDINGS & DISCUSSION

The results and findings from the study are briefly described next and then discussed. The data were analyzed and six core categories emerged; each of these included multiple coding clusters (not detailed here), reflecting the specific content and meaning of the participants' actions and statements. The resultant core categories were: A: Broad view, B: Subject domain, C: Nature of learning, D: Qualities/ approaches, E: Tools/search knowledge, and F: Work-related experiences. Next, the data were analyzed for thematic content and for the characteristics of threshold concepts; the categories were then re-examined accordingly. During this stage, the data in categories for nature of learning and work-related experiences (C and F) emerged as indicating practices of expert searchers, but not having characteristics of threshold concepts. The thematic findings are summarised in Table 1.

Table 1. Coding summary extract: Themes & categories

Theme	Core category
threshold concept: information environment	
client or organisation rapport	A: Broad view
concern re. misunderstanding information environment	A: Broad view
knowledge of provider practices	A: Broad view
reference interview from broad view	A: Broad view
search engine rapport	A: Broad view
total environment, sources	A: Broad view
knowing databases generally	B: Subject domain
threshold concept: information structures	
structures of information	A: Broad view
transparency of information retrieval system	A: Broad view
visual way of constructing search	D: Qualities/approaches
cited reference connections	E: Tools & search knowledge
database structure	E: Tools & search knowledge
fields as important, weighted	E: Tools & search knowledge
term weighting, frequency	E: Tools & search knowledge
unpacking the topic, building blocks	E: Tools & search knowledge
threshold concept: information vocabularies	
natural language, keywords	A: Broad view
controlled vocabulary fluency	E: Tools & search knowledge
proximity relationships	E: Tools & search knowledge
using thesaurus	E: Tools & search knowledge
word-term fluency, truncation, synonyms	E: Tools & search knowledge
threshold concept: integration/fusion	
can learn new system easily	A: Broad view
synthesising information	A: Broad view
connection making	A: Broad view
integration, magic factor, light on feet	A: Broad view
styles of search	A: Broad view
combining sources	B: Subject domain
anticipating, visioning, rehearsing	D: Qualities/approaches
combining different tools	E: Tools & search knowledge

As mentioned earlier, there were also coding categories for data that did not have the characteristics of threshold concepts but were related to expert praxes and traits, representing further information the participants had reported as being important to the defining nature of search experts. These data were also analysed and provided additional dimensions for the integrated model of search expertise that was put forth (Tucker et al., 2014). Praxes, for example, included approaches and strategies used during a search, such as 'pearl growing' to retrieve related documents ('more like this') or planning out a strategy before the search; traits included attitudes and qualities, such as open-mindedness, curiosity, and perseverance.

Themes and the Integrated Model

Themes that emerged provided evidence of four concepts having the characteristics of threshold concepts. The initial three are: *Information environment*: the total information environment is perceived and understood; *Information structures*: content, index structures, and retrieval algorithms are understood; *Information vocabularies*: fluency in search behaviours related to language, including natural language, controlled vocabulary, and finesse using proximity, truncation, and other language-based tools.

The fourth threshold concept is *Concept fusion*, the integration of the other three threshold concepts and further defined by additional properties. In addition to the threshold concepts were findings not concept-based, including *praxes* and *traits* of expert searchers; most prominent were the traits of extreme perseverance, being willing to adventure, and knowing when to stop a search. A model of search expertise was put forth with the four threshold concepts at its core that encompassed these traits and praxes. This allowed the study to present an integrated model of the novice-expert space for the domain of search expertise. In addition, melding understandings from novice-expert research and threshold concept theory literature (Meyer & Land, 2003; Cousin, 2010), the study found ontological shift to be a critical component of the model, in addition to critical changes in discourse (Flanagan & Smith, 2008). Concept fusion is further described as:

> [T]he integration of critical concepts that characterize how an expert searcher interacts with information. This holistic information experience was described by research participants as being a 'magical thing', 'almost organic' or having 'synergy'. The ability to fuse concepts was further defined by three attributes: visioning (knowing and anticipating the next moves); dancing (being light on one's '*search feet*', ready to quickly change direction); and profound ontological shift (not just 'I search' but 'I am a searcher'). (Tucker, 2014, p. 247)

CONCLUSION

The research adds to our understanding of the transformative learning experiences involved in the acquisition of expertise. The study has implications for understanding the novice-expert space more broadly and offers an effective methodology in grounded theory for exploring threshold concepts. It puts forth a model for search expertise that may inform other areas of expertise, perhaps particularly for higher education. In addition, the research demonstrated that the methodology of grounded theory is highly effective in eliciting evidence of conceptual knowledge that may have the characteristics of threshold concepts. For data collection, the protocol of having participants actively engage in relevant tasks was effective in surfacing long-ago learning experiences, helping to overcome the obstacles of "retracing the journey" (Cousin, 2006, p. 1), in this case, for the liminality of expertise.

The study suggests areas for further research into the learning that takes place in the novice-expert liminal space, raising questions for exploration, such as:

- Can subject domain knowledge be understood separately from generic knowledge in other areas of learning—and can this further deepen a broad-based understanding of the nature of expertise, using the threshold concept framework (TCF)?
- Are there liminal learning experiences for the novice-expert learner that mark threshold knowledge for a given profession or discipline? Does this connect to the discipline's episteme or "underlying game" (Perkins, 2006, p. 42)?
- Are there concepts in other domains that are similar to the encompassing nature of the threshold concepts of information environment, vocabulary, and structure—as well as the presence of concept fusion, requiring the ability to combine these high-level threshold concepts in addition to agility, visioning, and deeply profound ontological shift?

Implications for curriculum design are also an outcome of the research. This aligns with Cousin's statement, "Broadly, the purpose of threshold concept research is to explore difficulties in the learning and teaching of subjects to support the curriculum design process" (2008, p. 201). Davies and Mangan explored the qualities of the conceptual changes in learning experiences in order to help guide curriculum design efforts (2005). And, more recently, the troublesomeness characteristic has been shown to be critical component in the liminal space of learning experiences if the student is to be capable of ontological shift and reformulating conceptual meanings (Land, Rattray, & Vivian, 2014).

If, as educators, we are working to move students forward in their journeys toward and through troublesome and transformative learning—and perhaps further toward expertise—then we are also and truly "temporary guides" (Higgs & Cronin, 2013, p. 163) in the best sense; indeed, the very transience of an educator's role is one measure of the integrative nature of a threshold experience for the student. My own teaching and curriculum development work has been forever altered since completing this study and viewing the results through the lens of threshold concept theory; as an illustration, there is deliberate creation of opportunities for wrestling with concepts, more making of space for discovery moments and for students to experience—and get to know—unknowing and uncertainty for a time.

Walker (2013) wrote of balancing uncertainty in the liminal state for the learner when discussing the affective and ontological components of threshold concepts, stating, "Too much uncertainty in this liminal state and the learner will not be able to progress beyond a surface understanding. Not enough uncertainty and the learner will not make the required transformation into a full participating member of a community of practice" (p. 250). This also means helping students overcome their habituation with past experiences of having been 'taught to the test'; they tend to look for right-answer recipes, creating barriers to learning experiences that engage threshold knowledge and identity shift, of taking in knowledge as part of self and transformation. Entwistle expressed this clearly too, writing early on in the threshold concepts literature that they are "crucial topics or concepts that affect *how the teaching is carried out* [emphasis added] and how understanding develops within that subject area" (2003, p. 3).

The integrated model put forth by this research provides a structure for further understanding the liminality of expertise in disciplinary settings beyond the domain of search expertise; it is particularly pertinent to cognitively challenging fields and broadly within higher education.

REFERENCES

Åkerlind, G., McKenzie, J., & Lupton, M. (2014). The potential of combining phenomenography, variation theory, and threshold concepts to inform curriculum design in higher education. In J. Huisman & M. Tight (Eds.), *Theory and method in higher education research II* (pp. 227–247). Bingley, UK: Emerald Group Publishing.

Barradell, S. (2013). The identification of threshold concepts: A review of theoretical complexities and methodological challenges. *Higher Education, 65*(2), 265–276.

Berliner, D. (1994). Expertise: The wonder of exemplary performances. In J. N. Mangieri & C. C. Block (Eds.), *Creating powerful thinking in teachers and students: Diverse perspectives* (pp. 141–186). Fort Worth, TX: Harcourt Brace College.

Blackie, M. A., Case, J. M, & Jawitz, J. (2010). Student centredness: The link between transforming students and transforming ourselves. *Teaching in Higher Education, 15*(6), 637–646.

Branch, J. L. (2000). Investigating the information-seeking processes of adolescents: The value of using think alouds and think afters. *Library & Information Science Research, 22*(4), 371–392.

Bransford, J. (1999). *How people learn: Brain, mind, experience, and school.* Washington, DC: National Academies Press.

Charmaz, K. (2014). *Constructing grounded theory* (2nd ed.). Thousand Oaks, CA: Sage Publications.

Chi, M. T. H., Feltovich, P., & Glaser, R. (1981). Categorization and representation of physics problems by experts and novices. *Cognitive Science, 5*(2), 121–152.

Cousin, G. (2006). Introduction to threshold concepts. *Planet, 17,* 4–5.

Cousin, G. (2008). Transactional curriculum inquiry: Researching threshold concepts. In G. Cousin (Ed.), *Researching learning in higher education: An introduction to contemporary methods and approaches* (pp. 201–212). New York, NY: Routledge.

Cousin, G. (2010). Neither teacher-centred nor student-centred: Threshold concepts and research partnerships. *Journal of Learning Development in Higher Education, 2,* 1–9.

Davies, P., & Mangan, J. (2005, August 23–27). *Recognising threshold concepts: An exploration of different methods.* European Association in Learning and Instruction Conference (EARLI), Nicosia, Cyprus.

Dreyfus, S. E., & Dreyfus, H. L. (1980). *A five-stage model of the mental activities involved in directed skill acquisition* (Technical Report ORC-80-2). Berkeley, CA: University of California.

Dreyfus, S. E. (2004). The five-stage model of adult skill acquisition. *Bulletin of Science, Technology, & Society, 24*, 177–181.

Dunne, C. (2011). The place of the literature review in grounded theory research. *International Journal Social Research Methodology, 14*(2), 111–124.

Entwistle, N. (2003). *Concepts and conceptual frameworks underpinning the ETL project* (ETL Project Occasional Report 3). Edinburgh: University of Edinburgh.

Eraut, M. (1994). *Developing professional knowledge and competence.* London: Falmer Press.

Ericsson, K. A. (1993). The role of deliberate practice in the acquisition of expert performance. *Psychological Review, 100*, 363–406.

Ericsson, K. A. (2000). *Expert performance and deliberate practice: An updated excerpt.* Retrieved from http://www.psy.fsu.edu/faculty/ericsson/ericsson.exp.perf.html

Ericsson, K. A. (2006). *The Cambridge handbook of expertise and expert performance.* New York, NY: Cambridge University Press.

Ericsson, K. A. (2009). *Development of professional expertise.* New York, NY: Cambridge University Press.

Fidel, R. (1984). Online searching styles. *Journal of the American Society for Information Science, 35*(4), 211–221.

Flanagan, M. T., & Smith, J. (2008). From playing to understanding: The transformative potential of discourse versus syntax in learning to program. In R. Land, J. H. F. Meyer, & J. Smith (Eds.), *Threshold concepts within the disciplines* (pp. 91–104). Rotterdam, The Netherlands: Sense Publishers.

Gladwell, M. (2013, August 21). Complexity and the ten-thousand-hour rule. *The New Yorker.*

Glancy, F. H., & Isenberg, S. K. (2013). A conceptual learning-centered eLearning framework. *Journal of Higher Education Theory, 13*(3/4), 22–35.

Higgs, B., & Cronin, J. (2013). Threshold concepts: Informing the curriculum. In C. O'Farrell & A. Farrell (Eds.), *Emerging issues in higher education III* (pp. 167–177). Belfast: EDIN.

Kinchin, I. M. (2012, June 28–29). *Threshold concepts and the expert student.* Fourth Biennial Conference on Threshold Concepts: From personal practice to communities of practice, Trinity College, Dublin.

Kinchin, I. M., & Cabot, L. B. (2010). Reconsidering the dimensions of expertise: From linear stages to dual processing. *London Review of Education, 8*(2), 153–166.

Kinchin, I. M., Cabot, L. B., & Hay, D. B. (2010). Visualising expertise: Revealing the nature of a threshold concept in the development of an authentic pedagogy for clinical education. In J. H. F. Meyer, R. Land, & C. Baillie (Eds.), *Threshold concepts and transformational learning* (pp. 81–95). Rotterdam, The Netherlands: Sense Publishers.

Kneebone, R. (2009). Perspective: Simulation and transformation change: The paradox of expertise. *Academic Medicine, 84*(7), 954–957.

Land, R., Rattray, J., & Vivian, P. (2014). Learning in the liminal space. *Higher Education, 67*(2), 199–217.

Lewis, C., & Rieman, J. (1994). The thinking aloud method. In C. Lewis & J. Rieman (Eds.), *Task-centered user interface design: A practical introduction* (section 5.5). Retrieved from http://hcibib.org/tcuid/

Limberg, L., & Alexandersson, M. (2009). Learning and information seeking. In M. J. Bates & M. N. Maack (Eds.), *Encyclopedia of library and information sciences* (3rd ed.). Boca Raton, FL: CRC Press.

Medical Library Association. (2005). Role of expert searching in health science libraries: Policy statement. *Journal of the Medical Library Association, 93*(1), 42–44.

Meyer, J. H. F., & Land, R. (2003). Threshold concepts and troublesome knowledge (1): Linkages to ways of thinking and practising within the disciplines. In C. Rust (Ed.), *Improving student learning: Ten years on* (pp. 1–16). Oxford : Oxford University Press. (Originally published as *ETL Occasional Report 4.*) Retrieved from http://www.etl.tla.ed.ac.uk/publications.html

Mezirow, J. (2003). Transformative learning as discourse. *Journal of Transformative Education, 1*(1), 58–63.

Morse, J. M. (2008). Confusing categories and themes. *Qualitative Health Research, 18*(6), 727–728.

Perkins, D. (2006). Constructivism and troublesome knowledge. In J. H. F. Meyer & R. Land (Eds.), *Overcoming barriers to student understanding: Threshold concepts and troublesome knowledge* (pp. 33–47). New York, NY: Routledge.

Quinlan, K. M., Male, S. A., Baillie, C. A., Stamboulis, A., Fill, J., & Jaffer, Z. (2013). Methodological challenges in researching threshold concepts: A comparative analysis of three projects. *Higher Education, 66*(5), 585–601.

Rowbottom, D. P. (2007). Demystifying threshold concepts. *Journal of Philosophy of Education, 41*(2), 263–270.

Schön, D. A. (1983). *The reflective practitioner: How professionals think in practice.* New York, NY: Basic Books.

Schön, D. A. (1987). *Educating the reflective practitioner.* San Francisco, CA: Jossey-Bass Publishers.

Simon, H. A., & Chase, W. G. (1973). Skill in chess. *American Scientist, 61,* 394–403.

Smith, C., & Roseberry, M. (2013). Professional education in expert search: A content model. *Journal of Education for Library & Information Science, 54*(4), 255–269.

Tenopir, C. (2010, October 1). Swan song and issues unresolved. *Library Journal.*

Townsend, L., & Brunetti, K. (2009). Save a horse, ride a new train of thought: Using threshold concepts to teach information literacy. *37th Annual LOEX Conference Proceedings.*

Tucker, V. M. (2012). *Acquiring search expertise: Learning experiences and threshold concepts* (Ph.D. dissertation). Queensland University of Technology, Brisbane, Australia.

Tucker, V. M. (2014). The expert searcher's experience of information. In C. S. Bruce, K. Davis, H. Hughes, H. Partridge, & I. Stoodley (Eds.), *Information experience: Approaches to theory & practice* (pp. 239–255). Bingley, UK: Emerald Group Publishing.

Tucker, V. M., Weedman, J., Bruce, C. S., & Edwards, S. L. (2014). Learning portals: Analyzing threshold concept theory for LIS education. *Journal of Education for Library & Information Science, 55*(2), 150–165.

Van Lehn, K., & van de Sande, B. (2009). Acquiring conceptual expertise from modeling: The case of elementary physics. In K. A. Ericsson (Ed.), *Development of professional expertise* (pp. 356–378). New York, NY: Cambridge University Press.

Walker, G. (2013). A cognitive approach to threshold concepts. *Higher Education, 65,* 247–263.

Virginia M. Tucker
School of Information
San José State University

TERJE BERG, MORTEN ERICHSEN AND LEIF M. HOKSTAD

9. STUCK AT THE THRESHOLD

*Which Strategies Do Students Choose When Facing Liminality
within Certain Disciplines at a Business School?*

INTRODUCTION

Background and Motivation

This study is motivated by Berg and Erichsen's 2014 paper which for two years
studied the effects of a learning activity among students aiming at deep learning
(Berg & Erichsen's, 2014). The paper suggests four hypotheses that motivate deep
learning students:

1. what have been pupils at the secondary school, must be triggered to immediately
   become students because they are eager to learn,
2. efficient feedback must be timely, personal, specific, give guidance for further
   work (feed forward) and strengthen the sense of achievement,
3. students wants to be seen, and
4. students with a deep approach to learning are primarily motivated by knowledge
   application.

This study also revealed that a substantial number of the students did not have
the stamina to complete the entire learning activity, even though all these criteria
were reported to be present. 90 students participated at the first assignment (out of a
total of seven assignments). The initial questions in the assignments were quite easy
and then the degree of difficulty increased. When facing obstacles mastering the
materials many students dropped out of the learning activity and this was especially
clear from the third assignment. As a result, only 30 students fulfilled the entire
learning activity. But, what happened to the two-third of the students that dropped
out?

Topic, Relevance and Contribution

This led us to the issue of how and why students act as they do when they face
difficulties coping with the challenges at hand. This project thus attempts to
investigate into student experience, their potential strategies, or lack thereof, in

R. Land et al. (Eds.), Threshold Concepts in Practice, 107–118.

this liminal stage of their learning trajectory. We suggest that what seems to be lacking in these students learning trajectory and the course design is to facilitate the development of studenthood, how to become a student, which differs from being a pupil.

Relevance of Topic

In the bigger scheme of things, the fact that the PISA surveys show that Norwegian pupils at primary schools have the lowest perseverance among the Nordic countries, as well as below the average within the OECD region, makes this problem area a more substantial one than the isolated subject at hand might suggest. This common understanding assumes that the student is to blame for whatever ailments of the educational system (Biggs, 1999). When these pupils become students, their reality is substantially more demanding. If we understand more about how students cope with the liminal stage, we have a better foundation to adjust the design of their teaching and learning trajectory accordingly.

Our Contribution

This chapter will build upon findings collected according to the principles of the threshold concepts research framework. The collection of the findings and the following discussion is based on the mixed method approach. We have conducted in-depth interviews among a group of bachelor students, and these findings are supported by quantitative evidence. This chapter will suggest possible ways of incorporating student experience into the design of a teaching and learning trajectory by applying Nolan's methodology of joint enquiry (Nolan, 2005) as a possible means to facilitate the learners' access to the "underlying game" (Perkins, 2006). To the best of our knowledge, this contribution is the first to study stuckness at the threshold among Norwegian business schools students.

Research Question

With this as a backdrop, this chapter will be guided by the following research question:

When confronted with troublesome issues and threshold concepts, which strategies do students choose when facing liminality?

The Article's Structure

In the next section we present the theoretical framework, and describe the chosen method and empirical findings. Then we discuss the empirical findings, and before we close the chapter, we reflect on a principled level, and suggest further research.

THEORETICAL FOUNDATION

The focus of interest in this research is the stage in a learning process where learners either find ways to cope with their difficulties or to withdraw without further efforts. By understanding the characteristics and mechanisms of this highly critical stage, we propose that we may improve the teaching and learning environments.

We frame these issues within notions of liminality and stuckness. In the threshold concept framework, liminality plays an important role, in that it describes the period of possible transition from old to new insights (Meyer and Land, 2006, Land, Cousin, Meyer, & Davies, 2005). The liminal stage is described as a stage where the learner is challenged in several ways. In the liminal stage previous knowledge and insights are challenged, while at the same time there are no immediate or quick fixes readily at hand. The solution, as it were, is that the learner needs to change the way of looking at things. In psychological research, the idea of a fight or flight response to stressful situations is well established (Cannon, 1929). We also draw upon Nolan's ideas of stuckness (Nolan, 2005). In Nolan's perspective, stuckness is not only an individual state, but emerges from a collective practice, "located in the mental models or hidden assumptions driving individual practitioners' behaviour" (Nolan, 2005). We are particularly concerned with stuckness, since this state of mind too frequently leads to the feeling of failure, defeat and loss of self-confidence (Kiley & Wisker, 2009).

METHOD

This study is a case study and data is collected by qualitative and quantitative methods, and is thus informed by a mixed methods approach (Johnson, Onwuegbuzie, & Turner, 2007), as well as the method of exploratory study within the area of qualitative research (Remenyi, Williams, Money, & Swartz, 2002). The quantitative data collection in the mixed method approach will provide both mass and frequency of phenomena to be pursued by qualitative data collection, thereby giving the opportunity to develop a deeper meaning and understanding of a phenomenon we identify as *stuckness in the liminal zone*. The data collection in the shape of in-depth interviews seeks to allow an interpretative analysis, and not statistical generalization. However, this will give a foundation for new theory development. The research questions call for in-depth analysis and such an approach may provide more nuanced data than would be possible with a survey. The method does not limit the respondents with respect to answers. This is important because of the difficulties involved in pre-specifying response categories.

Research Design

Furthermore, the composition of the research design aligns with the threshold concepts research design method. By using subject matter teachers, students and an external researcher from HE research we hopefully avoid the teacher – student binary, and elude the limiting notion of either student-centeredness or teacher-centeredness (Cousin, 2010).

Quantitative Data

Exam statistics from two specific grading regarding two of the applied threshold concepts are as follows:

Table 1. Exam statistics – Opportunity costs

Correct answer	Fairly good answer	Fairly bad answer	No answer/Completely misunderstanding	Total
42	21	30	177	270
16%	8%	11%	66%	100%
	23%		77%	100%

Table 2. Exam statistics – Price elasticity

Correct answer	Fairly good answer	Fairly bad answer	No answer/Completely misunderstanding	Total
24	13	30	33	100
24%	13%	30%	33%	100%
	37%		63%	100%

The statistics are collected among the sample outlined below.

Selection of Respondents for Qualitative Data

Our sample consists of 20 bachelor students from 1st to 3rd grade at BI Norwegian Business School. The interview candidates were chosen by random selection among students attending the school over a two-week period. The interviews lasted from twenty to forty minutes with an average of twenty-five minutes; conducted in April and May 2014. Two of the authors carried out the interviews. Given the fact that the interviewees also are lecturers, we aimed at interviewing students we did not have a lecturer-student relationship with. This was done to avoid internal validity. In order to ensure construct validity, a test interview was carried out with a recent graduate. The pre-test in the questionnaire sought to reduce any ambiguity in the questions (Remenyi, Williams, Money, & Swartz, 2002).

External validity in qualitative research may be a general problem due to the limited number of respondents (Remenyi, Williams, Money, & Swartz, 2002). The selection of interviewees may be biased, but in our context they represent cross section of the students at the school when it comes to gender, age and study programs. Having completed these interviews, we experienced saturation, as no new patterns of knowledge appeared. Furthermore, by comparing three different study levels, i.e. 1st and 3rd grade students, the study should give indications about possible disparities or similarities. As the similarities revealed, this increases validity to a certain extent.

In order to make this study as reliable as possible, all of the interviews were conducted in the students' area at the school. This was done in order to reduce the effect of context. All interviews ended with a summary in order to clarify possible misunderstandings. They were then transcribed and a first material check was done in order to ensure that the interviews were recognizable.

Interview Guide

The study is based on a semi-structured interview with open-ended questions, which allowed amplification of the questions based on the interviewees' answers, as well as spontaneous questions as the interview proceeded (Remenyi, Williams, Money, & Swartz, 2002). By being a guide and not a questionnaire, the questions in the test interview (which allowed for some modifications to be made) proved to open way for further enquiries regarding the fundamental question about the threshold concept in the liminal zone. Applying this approach, we were able to get closer to the underlying research problem. As opposed to a questionnaire, the study could focus on the main topic. The empirical material was not codified, but instead analyzed textually, with each author highlighting emergent themes pertaining to the conceptual elements, and outlining circular and contingent causalities.

EMPIRICAL FINDINGS

The empirical findings are condensed and visualized in Figure 1 below. Before going into details about the matrix we would stress that the process described is not to be seen as a linear process. Rather, it is best seen as an iterative, back and forth process in the course of the learning trajectory.

We see two main strategies for the learners, either a strategy of fight or one of flight, two typical psychological responses to liminality, expressed in stuckness (Cannon, 1929; Meyer & Land, 2006; Nolan, 2005). Although the two strategies may be equally interesting from a teaching and learning perspective, in this chapter we choose to focus on the fight strategies. The reason for this, is the fact that the insight from our study of coping strategies in general, and fight strategies in particular, gives lecturers knowledge about how to conduct these strategies back to new students. In the material some categories of fight strategies became more clearly expressed. At this stage or possible transition, the potential threshold concepts may be identified. The present material suggests a number of potential threshold concepts, to be made subject for further research. The concepts are according to the lecturers' previous experiences as concepts hard to grasp. These are *'opportunity cost'*, *'sunk cost'*, *'internal rate of return'*, *'price-elasticity'*, *'elaboration likelihood model'*.[1] The list of potential threshold concepts is based on a triangulation of the available data sources; interviews, questionnaires and discussions, observations, exam statistics, and an external researcher. The concepts of opportunity cost and sunk cost, are both fundamental for the understanding of a wide area of topics within economics, finance and accounting. Furthermore, these concepts may be considered counter-intuitive; the concepts' meanings are essential to think as an economist and accountant, something which implies the knowledge that the numbers never speak for themselves.

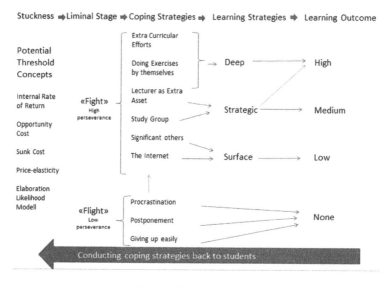

Figure 1. Threshold – Learning – Motivation

In the following the coping strategies of the learners are presented and discussed. Coping strategies are understood as putting effort into solving problems. A small group of learners chose extracurricular efforts, such as being very well prepared for the lectures, as well as working immediately after the lectures. Approximately half of the respondents reported actively studying the concepts, and among other things, doing more exercises on their own. This was particularly the case for quantitative subjects such as accounting and finance. This implies understanding an endurance aspect as a part of their learning process, and a willingness to commit the necessary time on task, or engaged time, as a part of their learning trajectory (Slavin, 2003). There seem to be a pattern that these students also are more intrinsically motivated towards the subjects, and more active setting short-term as well as long-term goals.

Surprisingly, just a small group of learners chooses dialogue with the lecturer as a strategy. In fact, the majority did not take the advantage of asking the lecturer in or after class to explain the concept one more time. On the other hand, almost everyone chose dialogue with their study group in this situation. Moreover, the interviews revealed that many students rely on significant others, such as family and friends. Even more, Google seems to be a significant source for seeking information and explanations for the identified potential threshold concepts, something that at best can be labelled as unqualified search. We suggest that this use of internet resources is under-researched and warrants further research.

Although we emphasis the fight strategies, we will briefly comment on the flight strategies as well: Half of the respondents report giving up easily to some concepts, put off the difficult problems, and never return to them. Some students choose to postpone the concepts until preparing for the exam, while others choose to procrastinate. In other words, they either continue being stuck in the liminal zone, or retract to the "comfort" of the previous position of "pupilhood".

DISCUSSION

Fundamentally, the question is what the learning outcome will be, depending on the different coping strategies chosen by the learners. The bridge between coping strategies and learning outcome is learning strategies, or more specifically: deep, strategic or surface learning.

We suggest that students choosing extra-curricular efforts and doing exercises by themselves are most likely to be deep learners. This is in line with a previous study (Berg & Erichsen, 2014) that shows that doing exercises by themselves bring the students into a deep learning trajectory and higher learning outcome is found in the shape of better grades at the final exam. Deep learning is based on students showing engagement in the subject. They are interested in the subject as such, are motivated by understanding the fundamentals of the topic, and are interacting with the subject. These students are more goal-directed than those choosing surface learning. They focus on the subject as a whole and an integrated totality. Furthermore, their motivation is that what they learn will be important for them and they are also motivated by their sincere interest for the subject (Marton & Säljö, 1976; Biggs, 1987). To achieve their goals they are more willing to increase time on task. As a consequence, our hypothesis is that these students are more likely to have a high learning outcome.

As mentioned previously, a rather small number of students take advantage of dialogue with the lecturer as a coping strategy. One reason may be the large-class syndrome (classes have an average size of 150–200 students). However, we will claim that those taking advantage of the lecturer as an asset, have a strategic learning strategy (Gibbs, 2006), something which may be the first step into the community of practice. Although, strategic learners are mainly motivated by good grades, and adjust their learning towards what the exam is expected to demand. These students do not put extra efforts into activities not relevant for the exam to come. We find these to represent *mimicry*. Notwithstanding this fact, feedback from the lecturer are from several researchers claimed to be the most efficient way of learning (Black & Wiliam, 1998). However, this feedback must be personalized, timely, specific, goal-directed, give guidance, and stimulate further studies (Berg & Erichsen, 2014). Are these necessary conditions present, there is a potential that what started out as strategic learning, actually may turn into deep learning.

In this material, another possible cause is reported to be the transition from high school where classes are at the average size of 25 pupils, and hence there is both a physical and psychological distance between students and learner. On the contrary, peer student consultations are very much applied. This angle may be chosen because these students are in the same situation, and must solve the same problems. On the other hand, there are different levels of knowledge within the group, and they have complementary skills. Thus, the learning strategies may be two-fold within the group: Some may be strategic (Gibbs, 2006), and others, i.e. those aiming at being the group's teacher, may be deep learners. Our hypothesis is that the latter group may achieve a high learning outcome, while the first most likely will achieve a medium learning outcome.

We also suggest that students choosing to depend on significant others and the Internet, are surface learners. This is based on the fact that particularly the Internet may definitely not give correct answers to the threshold concepts the learners experience. More specifically, one of the interviews revealed an example of a concept positively defined incorrectly at a commonly used internet site for Norwegian business school students. Surface learning is based on a fragmented learning approach, and the holistic view is absent (Marton & Säljö, 1976). These surface learners are concerned with quick solutions to comprehensive subjects. At best, they aim at reproducing the threshold concepts' definitions, and they are not able to apply this knowledge. Hence, the learning outcome is low.

On the other hand, if this non-verified or unsubstantiated information acquired from the Internet, does not become the end-state, more an inspiration to return to extracurricular activities, learning outcome will increase. Thus, the learning trajectory is not static, rather, it is dynamic.

Obviously, giving up easily, postponement and procrastination do not have a substantial learning outcome. However, procrastination may be a short-term put-off, and thus there is potential for getting back into the loop of fighting the thresholds concepts. Procrastination is a flight strategy, an escape into doing more pleasant things at the expense of difficult tasks. Most of the interviewees stated that this contributed to building enough self-confidence before revisiting the threshold concepts.

Nevertheless, more fundamentally confidence is built from doing extracurricular efforts, doing exercises, and to some extent using the lecturer or the study group as extra assets. This self-confidence may give the student the necessary belief in how to overcome threshold concepts. Thus, next time the student is facing other threshold concepts, she has increased her ability to cope with these concepts.

CONCLUDING REMARKS AND FURTHER RESEARCH

The point of departure for this chapter was: which coping strategies students choose when confronted with troublesome issues and threshold concepts, something? However, the present material also invites to reflections on a more principled level. In addition to identifying potential threshold concepts and coping strategies on a disciplinary level, the material also raises issues of a more overarching nature. In sum, we observe learners at the very beginning of their learning trajectory, at the intersection between a student and a pupil. The stuckness these learners experience is as much connected to their understanding of what it takes to be a student and its requirements, as to stuckness connected to discipline related issues. Although this study is by far sufficiently comprehensive to be conclusive, we suggest that the notion of "*becoming a student*" or "*studenthood*" emerges as a potential and highly suggestive threshold concept. Drawing upon work by van Gennep and Turner, we may perceive the student coping strategies as the intermediate part of a rite of passage, where a previous stage, being a pupil, is left (van Gennep, 1909; Turner, 1969). The separation from this previous state is still not replaced with re-assimilation, where new perspectives are incorporated. The coping strategies are missing or underdeveloped. To a large degree this is caused by the fact that the students have not yet fully become socialized into a community of practice where the repertoire of "how things are done" is not adopted, and is left in an unclear studenthood, which has its own "underlying game", not yet fully acknowledged by these learners (Perkins, 2006). Within the area of business studies, this can be stated as acknowledging that "the numbers do not speak for themselves", i.e. all calculations are based on (more or less politically laden) assumptions. Parts of the underlying game lacking in many of the students are the realization of endurance, or the need for time on task, i.e. a slower, more meticulous learning process than experienced previously. Or, in Cousin's words; the "messy journeys back, forth and across conceptual terrain" (Cousin, 2006).

The components of such an understanding on the learner's behalf are cultural and as well as ontological. The cultural issues of becoming a student mean entering into a community of practice in an asymmetric master-apprentice relationship. The liminal stage represents a middle position in the transition from being an outsider to becoming an insider. We argue here that such an understanding on the learner's part is a prerequisite for the learning trajectory.

Among the respondents, we experienced a substantial degree of maturation from 1st to 3rd year when it comes to conducting strategies. The mature students are more conscious about which of the strategies are most suitable for understanding different subjects. For instance, regarding quantitative threshold concepts, the application of exercises where the most preferred, and regarding qualitative threshold concepts, most effort where put into understanding key models. Fundamentally, the question is how the lecturers can apply this knowledge. Although this is a qualitative study, we will propose some guidelines for designing learning activities. The essential hub is not surprisingly the lecturer, who must be the facilitator so that students become aware of the possible paths to (high) learning outcome. One key is to stimulate the students to be prepared for class. Furthermore, be aware of the concept threshold concepts as such: We, as lecturers tend to treat all topics within a subject very much the same. Focusing on the challenges threshold concepts within a course represents, may enhance a safe learning *and teaching* environment, and thus reduce the fear of asking questions in class. A consequence of this is that the lecturer must allocate more time to these concepts, including more thorough explanations, and even enhance repetition. This means that both learner and teacher must acknowledge the non-linear nature of the learning trajectory. Our hypothesis is that this awareness and efforts will reduce the application of significant others, as well as surfing the internet for unqualified knowledge. In addition, lecturers focusing on threshold concepts, we will claim, enhance learning processes within the study groups, and/or doing exercises by themselves or within the study groups.

If the assumptions discussed above are correct, we see that a more effort is needed in early stages of higher education courses. To this end we will in future work pursue Nolan's idea of a joint enquiry; "an emergent, conversational, narrative inquiry into the taken-for-granted collective practices through which emerges further forms as practice and practitioner are transformed together" (Nolan, 2005). This implies an approach that addresses changes and transformations in learner and teacher alike. Indeed, the present focus on "student centredness" needs to be balanced to avoid the "mortification of the teacherly self" (McShane, 2006, quoted in Cousin, 2010). Nolan's perspective aligns with Cousin's concern of the student vs teacher centredness binary (Cousin, 2010). By inviting to a joint inquiry including teachers as subject specialists, students and educational researchers' clearer notions of what is means to become a student may be arrived at.

This explorative study has generated hypotheses suitable for a larger survey. The next step might be to carry out this, among the 10,000 students enrolled at the BI Norwegian Business School. Such a study will be based on factor analysis, and thus contribute to accepting or rejecting the hypotheses and regarding coping strategies, as well as explaining possible interactions. Furthermore, our hypotheses can also be the foundation for a survey among lecturers, and how they design learning activities mainly with respect to threshold concepts.

NOTE

[1] 'Opportunity cost' as a threshold concept has also previously been established in the seminal work by Davies and Mangan (2007).

REFERENCES

Berg, T., & Erichsen, M. (2014). Hvordan stimulere de flinkeste studentene? *Uniped – Tidsskrift for universitets- og høgskolepedagogikk, 37*(3), 34–48 [How to stimulate highachieving students? *Uniped Journal of Higher Education Pedagogics.*].

Black, P., & Wiliam, D. (1998). Assessment and classroom learning. *Assessment in Education: Principles, Policy & Practice, 5*(1), 7–74.

Biggs, J. (1987). *Student approaches to learning and studying.* Melbourne: Australian Council for Educational Research.

Biggs, J. (1999). What the student does: Teaching for enhanced learning. *Higher Education Research & Development, 18*(1), 57–75.

Cannon, W. B. (1929). *Body changes in pain, hunger, fear and rag*e. New York, NY: Appleton Century Crofts.

Cousin, C. (2006). Threshold concepts, troublesome knowledge and emotional capital: An exploration into learning about others'. In J. H. F. Meyer & R. Land (Eds.), *Overcoming barriers to student understanding: Threshold concepts and troublesome knowledge.* Abingdon: Routledge.

Cousin, C. (2010, February). Neither teacher–Entered nor student-centered: Threshold concepts and research partnerships. *Journal of Learning Development in Higher Education,* Issue 2.

Davies, P., & Mangan, J. (2007). Threshold concepts and the integration of understanding in economics. *Studies in Higher Education, 32*, 711–726.

Gibbs, G. (2006). Why assessment is changing. In C. Bryan & K. Clegg (Eds.), *Innovative assessment in higher education.* London: Routledge.

Johnson, R. B., Onwuegbuzie, A. J., & Turner, L. A. (2007). Toward a definition of mixed methods research. *Journal of Mixed Methods Research, 1*(2), 112–133.

Kiley, M., & Wisker, G. (2009). Threshold concepts in research education and evidence of threshold crossing. *Higher Education Research and Development, 28*(4), 431–441.

Land, R., Cousin, C., Meyer, J., & Davies, P. (2005). Threshold concepts and troublesome knowledge: Implications for course design and evaluation. In C. Rust (Ed.), *Improving student learning diversity and inclusivity.* Oxford: Oxford Centre for Staff and learning Development.

Marton, F., & Säljö, R. (1976). On qualitative differences in learning: I – Outcome and process. *British Journal of Educational Psychology, 46*(1), 4–11.

McShane, K. (2006). *Technologies transforming academics: Academic identity and online teaching* (Unpublished PhD thesis). University of Technology Sydney, New South Wales.

Meyer, J. H. F., & Land, R. (2006). Threshold concepts and troublesome knowledge: Issues of liminality. In J. H. F. Meyer & R. Land (Eds.), *Overcoming barriers to student understanding.* Abingdon: Routledge.

Modell, S. (2010). Bridging the paradigm divide in management accounting research: The role of mixed methods approaches. *Management Accounting Research, 21*(2), 124–129.

Nolan, M. (2005). The emergence of global stability in local interaction in a consulting practice. In R. Stacey (Ed.), *Experiencing emergence in organizations. Local interaction and the emergence of global pattern.* New York, NY: Routledge.

Perkins, D. (2006). The underlying game: Troublesome knowledge and threshold conceptions. In J. H. F. Meyer & R. Land (Eds.), *Overcoming barriers to student understanding: Threshold concepts and troublesome knowledge.* Abingdon: Routledge.

Remenyi, D., Williams, B., Money, A., & Swartz E. (2002). *Doing research in business and management.* London: Sage.

Slavin, R. (2003). *Educational psychology: Theory and practice.* Boston, MA: Pearson Education.

Turner, V. W. (1969). *The ritual process: Structure and anti-structure.* Chicago, IL: Aldine.

van Gennep, A. (1909/2004). *The rites of passage.* Abingdon: Routledge.

T. BERG ET AL.

Terje Berg
Norwegian University of Science and Technology

Morten Erichsen
BI Norwegian Business School

Leif M. Hokstad
Norwegian University of Science and Technology

PART 3

THRESHOLD CONCEPTS AND INTERDISCIPLINARITY

JASON DAVIES

10. 'THRESHOLD GUARDIANS'

Threshold Concepts as Guardians of the Discipline

SETTING THE INTERDISCIPLINARY SCENE

Writing about co-operation and solidarity means writing at the same time about rejection and mistrust. (Douglas, 1986, p. 1)

Interdisciplinarity

Interdisciplinarity has undoubtedly changed the landscape of academic work in recent years and, increasingly, students are also 'living the dream'; but it can be a dream of interdisciplinary possibilities that do not always come good, and have sometimes 'succeeded' only when we offset a great deal of time and effort that went on in the background. It is the implications of some of those difficulties that will be explored here: there are often 'basic' organisational difficulties but there are also profound difficulties for students facing conflicting epistemological claims and/or threshold concepts. What do you do when your tutors or supervisors are *literally* arguing from different premises, with the implication that meaning-construction and intellectual reference points are as different as the physical buildings?

Threshold concepts are very much the children of an interdisciplinary age: the idea arose (Meyer & Land, 2003) from interdisciplinary collaboration but also gained traction partly because it is a boon to thinking about learning across disciplinary fields. It offers a way to begin the task of understanding why disciplinary differences can run so deep, something which was simply not of interest in a world where academics rarely stepped outside their disciplinary knowledge for long (and, when they did, on their own terms). Considering incommensurability in interdisciplinary work through the lens of threshold concepts ought to enrich both discourses: as Carmichael (2010, p. 60)'s subject 'D' put it '[threshold concepts] help *define the discipline*'.

Interdisciplinarity and Us

Too many claims have been made for interdisciplinary work to rehearse here (e.g., Klein's foundations for the field in Klein, 1990, 1996, 2001, 2004, 2005;

R. Land et al. (Eds.), Threshold Concepts in Practice, 121–134.
© 2016 Sense Publishers. All rights reserved.

Lattuca, 2001; Nowotny, Scott, & Gibbons, 2003). Calls to 'knock down walls' and 'liberate knowledge' from the 'restrictions' of (mono)disciplines have become less strident with the widespread adoption of interdisciplinarity as institutional policy (e.g., Castronovo, 2000, pp. 781–790; Klein, 1996, p. 224). Notable moments in its rise are Roy's (1979, p. 165) much-quoted line that 'the real problems of society do not come in discipline-shaped blocks' and the corollary that universities must move beyond the disciplines to formulate 'real' solutions to 'real' problems': a similar and influential thesis is that of 'Mode 2' knowledge put forward originally by Gibbons, Limoges and Nowotny (1994) and reformulated in Nowotny, Scott and Gibbons (2003). Similarly ambitious (but also similarly vague) claims were put forward for 'superconcepts' by Wilson (2010).

Publicly there is now little doubt expressed that interdisciplinary work will 'change the world' both within and also beyond the academy, though locally the experience is sometimes more fractured (Townsend, Pisapia, & Razzak, 2013). There is a sense (or a claim) that tangible and meaningful effects on 'real life', previously inaccessible to introspective monodisciplinary approaches and interests, can be reached successfully by interdisciplinary collaboration.

Interdisciplinary Ravines

There are difficulties with some of the more ambitious formulations which cannot be addressed fully here for reasons of space: put in brutally simple terms, it may be that even 'real life' does not come in 'real-life shaped chunks', because it is different materials, and the formulation of distinct questions and answers, that tends to give rise to disciplinary expertise in the first place (see, for instance and across different fields, Concerns, 2001; Ziman, 2003; Rowland, 2006; Hunt, 1994; Fish, 1994 & 1995; Davies, 2011). Furthermore, new (inter)disciplines must create their own meanings, and will begin to look suspiciously comparable to 'traditional' disciplines if they are to generate a disciplinary community.

Translated into the discourse of threshold concepts, we are dealing with a claim that reducing concepts' particularity (e.g., making them 'less difficult to understand' or 'reducing their specialism' by 'knocking down walls') makes them somehow easier to combine, and 'better', once combined. This seems less convincing in translation than it did in the original. That is not to say that the effort to combine them and do interdisciplinary work is not worthwhile or productive: but it underlines that all too often, 'thinking outside the box' requires the immediate construction of a new box with a different design and a different set of understandings for what constitutes 'success'.

THRESHOLD CONCEPTS AND INTERDISCIPLINARITY

To put it another way, incommensurability – the supposed bane of interdisciplinary work – is emphatically predicted by threshold concepts: they are 'transformative', 'irreversible', 'integrative', 'bounded', and 'troublesome'. Most of these terms prescribe difference from common or inexpert understanding: an irreversible, learned transformation in perspective can only be part of a shared understanding in a strictly defined context – a 'disciplined' space (in both senses). A group who have distinctive, overlapping and potentially competing threshold concepts will approach the same task and materials very differently. Neither they nor disciplinary methods and values can simply be added to or multiplied by one another.

Threshold concepts have, of course, been invoked to explore (inter)disciplinarity (Trowler, Saunders, & Bamber, 2012, p. 24; Irvine & Carmichael, 2009; Carmichael, 2010) and could be used further in this regard, since they bring a sense of texture to the incommensurability that is so embedded in interdisciplinarity (Rowland, 2006, pp. 87–103; Davies, 2011). Dexterity in interdisciplinarity is *(l)earned*: Land (2012), touching on many issues developed in here, argues that it is itself a threshold concept. Considering incommensurability in interdisciplinary work through the lens of threshold concepts ought to enrich both discourses. This study, in the spirit of the opening quote by the anthropologist Mary Douglas, intends to explore that possibility by focussing on breakdowns, evasions and other opportunistic 'tactics' (de Certeau, 1984, p. 84).

TROUBLE IN PARADISE

In a monodisciplinary research environment, there is shared understanding (describable as 'shared threshold concepts') – enough for people to know how to disagree, for instance. In a teaching environment, the teacher's authority will normally be a proxy for this common ground, with the implied assurance that s/he will decide what is relevant. Thus, when awkward, interesting but tangential questions are asked, they are usually (and legitimately) evaded on the grounds that there is a point 'which we need to stick to'. This commonality is so deep that should an eminent researcher ask 'what is the point of our subject?', the audience will generally expect that the questioner can offer some kind of coherent answer rather than treat it as an invitation to throw in the towel altogether.

Interdisciplinary work brings its own particular frictions: one can more easily find oneself staring into the abyss of what authenticates and characterises the discipline(s) in question, and therefore 'the point we must stick to' is an unknown. More importantly, it is likely to evade any attempts to fix it: what can be drawn on to make judgements is itself subject to contestation. Will the group want a consensus about what is sought or tolerate huge ambiguity and polyvalence? How would a group decide whether it needed a consensus? By consensus?

This kind of scenario is implicitly acknowledged in discussions about interdisciplinary research—'stay clear on focus, extend the benefits of serendipity to more people, and remember that one size does not fit all', recommend Townsend et al. (2013), after noting the calls for 'headspace' by academics attempting to do meaningful interdisciplinary work. In practice this often means respecting each others' expertise while patiently seeking ways to find the new mutual understandings that characterise successful interdisciplinary work. Much time can pass with a truce rather than genuine integration. This kind of situation is, of course, something that can, like anything else, be scrutinised by academic analysis or enquiry. The question is: by which methods?

Disciplines as Tribes

Becher and Trowler (2001) famously dubbed disciplinary communities 'tribes'. Notwithstanding recent reformulations (especially Manathunga, Brew, & Bamber, 2012), 'tribes' has advantages as a metaphor for disciplinary communities.

'Tribes' encountering others must form *some* kind of relationship (usually with the assumption, well-known to anthropologists, that 'we', unlike 'them', do things 'properly'); there may be trading, exclusion, assimilation, defence manoeuvres (such as retreat or fence-building) or outright aggression (colonisation, deprecation, disciplinary imperialism). In such encounters there will be a range of different artefacts and objects put to use, and/or shared 'zones' established, sometimes deliberately, sometimes reluctantly. Notions such as Star and Griesemer (1989)'s 'boundary objects' and Collins, Evans and Gorman (2007)'s 'trading zones' are established motifs in the history of science where distinct groups with different interests must co-operate. Objects may have multiple meanings for different groups and where this polyvalency is permitted and understood, trade and communication is thereby facilitated. Should a particular group attempt to establish a monopoly on an object's meaning, however, then co-operation ceases and conflicts arise. Notwithstanding the frustration, these are interesting opportunities to discover more about the protagonists as they (re-)articulate their values in an attempt to establish that elusive hegemony (Rowland, 2006, pp. 87–103). The logical inference is that if threshold concepts can be 'enabling', they might also be implicated in disciplinary self-defence.

In my experience of interdisciplinary research and teaching, threshold concepts have also been crucial 'objects', but enquiry into, and articulation of, their role has tended to be implicit and inchoate. Through three metaphors, I wish to explore here the deployment of threshold concepts not as enabling 'doorways' but rather as locked doors or 'threshold guardians'.

Methodology and Fieldnotes

The material discussed below generally only appears during free-ranging reflective discussion; it touches on issues that are rarely discussed explicitly, generally to the extent that they are intractable: they are not likely to appear in questionnaires. The following fieldnotes came to light in varied contexts; some during formal study in academic development work as part of teaching on an MA at University College London (UCL), and others within an interdisciplinary programme on *Evidence* that ran at UCL from 2003, culminating in conferences during 2008 and a collected volume (Twining, Dawid, & Vasilaki, 2011). As described in greater detail in Davies (2011, pp. 49–52), we (Stephen Rowland and myself) developed an approach that sought to privilege enquiry over conclusions and evaded the use of particular disciplinary methods that might exclude interesting but exotic pieces of information. We were working ethnographically with partial glimpses of life within disciplines, in situations where tacit knowledge was emphatically *not* common knowledge.

To give an evocative example, we spent several hours discussing the relative status of 'off-hand comments in the corridor' and 'official' communications in wondering what the programme 'actually was' before deciding, essentially, to include anything that either of us thought was interesting or difficult as a starting point for sustained enquiry. Violations of expectations and a sense of being wrongfooted (whether in us or our colleagues), which were often initially attributed by many to 'personal differences' or '(lack of) manners', increasingly looked less like 'personal' quirks or approaches as we explored them; they usually began to resemble the tips of disciplinary knowledge-and-praxis icebergs. Because these responses were so context-sensitive and unpredictable, each encounter was unique (unless it seemed to fall into a pattern). As I extended the habit of compiling such fieldnotes outside the *Evidence* project, certain broad types of interdisciplinary engagements and scenarios seemed to emerge in other contexts.

Needless to say, this is not a quantitative study. It is at the more elusive end of the ethnographic scale and evokes the tradition of anthropological fieldwork rather than large-scale social science questionnaires.

This does not mean that my examples are trivial: what they share is that they arose at moments where the operation of the discipline (and good candidates for threshold concepts) were implicitly challenged. In each case, the disciplinary construct was protected from the implicit challenge, and threshold concepts became 'threshold guardians'. They are enactments of an 'expert pragmatism' that acknowledged and responded to the unexpected emergence of incommensurability.

Limitations of This Enquiry

If we had a table of canonical threshold concepts against which to map these moments of incommensurability, this would be less of an enquiry; it would be possible to indicate which universally-accepted threshold concepts were being violated and move on to building a solid and canonical taxonomy for classifying 'threshold guardian' moments. Fortunately, such instrumentalism has generally been eschewed in the discourse of threshold concepts.

My suggested framework is therefore no more than possible starting points and is deliberately restricted to being evocative metaphors that highlight the distinctiveness of these encounters. Just as the ethnographer is interested in the social *use* of cognitive objects as much as their content, so too we can begin an enquiry into the swampy areas of how a discipline's threshold concepts (or plausible candidates for the title) feature in the building and maintenance of disciplinary integrity by 'tribes' in academia.

THRESHOLD GUARDIANS

Scenario 1. 'Surrender Your Passport'

Students moving from one discipline to another, typically in the transition from undergraduate to postgraduate, may find they cannot take their most cherished threshold concepts with them. A chemical engineer told me of the difficulty she has 'persuading' (perhaps rather than 'teaching') chemistry graduates entering her field precisely what 'balancing an equation' means in applied chemical engineering (industrial plants-based) rather than in pure chemistry (labs). Different margins of error are permitted in the respective disciplines because of their criteria of what is sufficient for explanation and application. Chemical engineers have their eye on such factors as cost and acceptable (material and financial) losses, and therefore cannot disregard minor fluctuations that barely qualify as curiosities in a lab. The loss of a single gram in an experiment involving test-tubes—perhaps attributable to a barely-detectable spillage during the mixing—could translate into thousands of tons on the scale that chemical engineers work at. On the other hand, chemical engineers must allow for *larger* margins of error simply because of the scale of their operations. What is at stake in chemical equations will subtly but profoundly alter as someone moves from one field to the other, even if this seems a good candidate for being a threshold 'skill' (Sanders et al., 2012) rather than a threshold 'concept'.

This disciplinary difference is not initially epistemological (physical chemistry has not changed) but becomes so when we consider 'balancing an equation' as a threshold concept. Considerations arising in the application of 'pure' theory are what make the disciplines distinctive: what is critical is that there are very different consequences when *mistakes* are made and only then do different aspects of 'balancing an equation' become more or less interesting. My fieldnote notes her (the aforementioned chemical engineer) wry comment highlighting one other aspect that would be less inconvenient on a small scale and in a laboratory: 'I just don't want them to blow up the plant: it's messier than blowing up a lab'.

This kind of difference can be counter-intuitive: there is a tendency for complete outsiders to assume that neighbouring disciplines will have *common* understandings but it is often precisely in those apparent overlaps where threshold concepts are most energetically applied, precisely to make disciplinary work distinctive. In other words, 'what counts as balancing an equation', far from constituting some 'pan-chemical' understanding, might be *the* difference between a chemist and a chemical engineer (being neither, I am wary of assuming I can elaborate further on this topic).

These kinds of differences can of course be widely acknowledged and publicly (i.e. within the field) debated: to move to a completely different intellectual corner, historians of religion and anthropologists have grappled for many years with the need to displace and then re-place conceptions of religion (or programmatically dispense with it altogether), precisely because modern assumptions will almost certainly mislead students. Rüpke (2007) spends his first chapter (38 pages) tackling every ancient religionist's lot—the so-called 'negative canon' of what religion was *not* in the Roman world. In anthropology, Saler (1993) is a useful overview of (and pragmatic response to) the same kinds of issues: western conceptions should, for him, be subjected to the same contextualisation as non-western ones, becoming objects of study rather than unproblematised methods. Non-western ideas should similarly be used alongside them as heuristics for comparative purposes. 'Religion' cannot persist in anything remotely like its familiar westernised form.

Boundary crossing is not out of the question in these kinds of situations, but there is no room for compromise: one must 'go native' in the new field by surrendering the irreversible change of perspective that had previously been obtained, and taking on the local threshold concepts on their own terms. If the change in perspective really is irreversible (and I suspect it is), it must be effortfully set aside cognitively in the new context, and existing disciplinary identity 'loosened', as Land (2012, p. 182) puts it. This implies a post-disciplinary stage of academic practice, where one must learn to *evade* the hard-won understanding enshrined in threshold concepts in order to do interdisciplinary work.

Scenario 2. 'Here Be Dragons'

My second scenario is of experts 'locking the doors' to keep the disciplined *in* (or perhaps 'safe') and draws on an example from an interdisciplinary email thread that I have discussed elsewhere (Davies, 2010). Under discussion was the 'Chinese Room' thought experiment, which explores differences (if any) of the intelligence of a 'comprehending being' from a computer programme (or other 'uncomprehending being').

A physiologist wrote:

I don't have patience for arguments from the Chinese Room experiment, because as a physiologist I consider the human brain to be a machine.

A historian responded:

Who makes that judgement ... The brain? How does the brain do so? Automatically, presumably, if we keep to the logic of your position? ... Or are you implicitly distinguishing 'brain' from 'self'?

And a pharmacologist responded privately to that historian:

If the brain is not a machine, then what is it? The only other possibility seems to be start talking about souls or some other form of mysticism. I'd prefer not to do that myself.

This is a rich exchange and I must, for reasons of space, limit my observations. Each practitioner has reached the limits of where their fundamental concepts obtain and will go no further: for the physiologist, this is 'organism as machine'; the historian seeks to preserve the historiographically necessary category of non-mechanical 'human agents'; and for the pharmacologist, we have 'organism as machine' but more explicitly non-deistically.

The final, private, comment makes explicit something that the first, more public, email only implies: an awareness that outside normal disciplinary frameworks, not only do habitual explanatory structures fail to provide useful insight, those concepts might fail to find *any* purchase. Each beats a tactical retreat from the engagement rather than expose their essential concepts to such danger. The historian, on the other hand, cannot produce a meaningful historical account if humanity's actions derive from machine behaviour and must therefore seek *something* with conscious and deliberate agency, though he is nervous of where he is forced to go (and in fact the exchange ended there).

Another example was relayed to me personally, where a professor of history was despairing of Derridean deconstructionism. His (not incorrect) reading was that adopting such an approach meant that 'one can *never* escape from a text'. Given historians' heavy reliance on texts and particularly their need to 'take ideas *out* of the text' with the assumption that they have a reasonable chance of conveying 'factual information', his response was simple: he ignored Derrida, though not without some genuine and persistent misgivings that he was neglecting something potentially important.

Scenario 3. 'Cattle-Raiding'

On the same theme, another historian put things differently: my note of his response paraphrases a more assertive stance.

> *The interesting question is not whether Derrida and his peers were correct but why they backed themselves into a corner where it was almost impossible to say anything about the world.*

The best form of defence is attack; by *historicising* Derrida, he neutralised the threat of the infinite, imagined and imagining textual world with an entrance but no exit: no longer is there a text into which one steps, never to return, but rather a historically real man creating a historically real text. One threshold concept, (the wor(l)d of the text) has lost out to others (chronological and spatial locatedness); and the hegemony of historical knowledge re-established by the sheer act of knowledge-construction.

Deconstructionism can now be referred to without any threat of contagion because all meaning has been assimilated to a historicising discourse: the infinite text-world now stems from a particular agent, the construction of a particular culture, time and location. But then, of course, a textual critic might flip it back by saying 'the author' has now been inscribed as a historical text: the academic game continues. And this is not to say that postmodern textuality is ignored or utterly denatured in history, far from it: Derridean methods are certainly heeded but principally used to sharpen history's sword, as it were (as occurs, for instance, in Jenkins, 1995).

Why 'cattle-raiding' as a metaphor? Indo-European myths of cattle asserted that not only was the tribe granted their cattle at the beginning of time by the deity, they were granted *all* cattle: any found in the possession of neighbouring tribes had therefore been stolen at some point and one was therefore perfectly entitled to go and get them 'back' from the other, alien, tribe (Walcot, 1979). That this game is rigged from the start to justify *any* appropriation is obvious to us in this example, but less obvious is the similarity of the expectation in academia that almost any field of activity or knowledge can legitimately be appropriated into disciplinary discourse. That process often comes about by asserting an account that brings threshold concepts into play. Once seen through a disciplinary gaze, the material has been claimed.

This is perhaps more aggressive as a metaphor than my example invites, but I have known more energetic sallies than these examples to 'assimilate' other disciplines' 'property'. Conversely, there are areas where disciplines politely decline to go: anthropologists, for instance, nowadays virtually never mount raids or even send scouts to classical antiquity, even though the two had strong links in the early 20th century. This is also despite the fact that as the discipline builds up a past for itself, it is increasingly dealing with historical rather than contemporary material. In contrast, the new interdiscipline of cognitive science of religion, has no such qualms and is cheerfully sending out would-be colonists to relevant fields (e.g., Martin & Sørensen, 2011).

COMING CLEAN FOR THE SAKE OF THE STUDENTS

In this initial exploration of these difficulties, I risk going against two grains: both interdisciplinarity and threshold concepts are generally deployed as 'enabling' (see e.g., Cousin, 2010; Kinchin, 2010; Irvine & Carmichael, 2009, esp. 116–117) and to point at 'disabling' practices might easily be understood to be identifying 'areas for improvement' and 'practices that should be deprecated'. That is far from my intention: attempts to 'solve' these issues would lead to an infinite regress as each new and distinctive approach created its own ravines and abysses, border skirmishes and so on. Land (2012)'s succinct echoing of many of the epistemological and institutional difficulties underlines how reflexive one must become to do cross-disciplinary work.

Yet we have a dilemma: to permit or even encourage explicit disciplinary self-defence could be a step *backwards* by acting as a charter for disciplinary imperialism and in appearing to lend legitimacy to refusals to engage with other fields of expertise on a suitably humble and open-minded footing. I do not wish to go in that direction – we are not yet in a position to be complacent about interactive work in the academy but its value seems undeniable (see for instance the range of initiatives and variable outcomes of collaborative work in Walsh & Kahn, 2010).

Suffer the 'Children'

There is more: postgraduates are almost certainly the group who suffer the most in interdisciplinary projects. Firstly, they do not have the luxury of waiting to see if the project bears fruit or not: they will have a viva all too soon.

Secondly, if obtaining a PhD is generally the point at which they internalise the threshold concepts and customs of their discipline (Kiley, 2009), they are unlikely to be dextrous enough to practise threshold guardianship: students may well be expecting their knowledge to fit together more cohesively than I have suggested it will. In practice, when their supervisors in different departments dodge the most incommensurable issues, the student, probably suffering from chronic liminality, is left to traverse the ravines alone in a high-stakes experiment.

Thirdly, they do not have a single group into which they can be assimilated and 'get to know the ropes': they must simultaneously enter more than one community – which makes impossible any persistent sense of immersion and naturalisation. In short, their PhD is almost primarily in interdisciplinarity itself, and in 'subjects', second.

The dynamics of disciplinary boundary work must, it seems, be made more explicit: not to do so simply becalms new members of our community unfairly and, if my argument rings true, rather dishonestly. How then might we do a better job of showing them a fuller picture of what disciplined academic life is like without empowering arrogant 'discipline wars' or the evasion of genuine interdisciplinary enquiry?

Distinction Over Definition

One possibility is a promoting a culture of disciplinary *distinction* (identifying characteristic aspects) rather than definition (identifying dividing lines and borders). 'Walls' seem increasingly unhelpful as a metaphor. This could be done in academic practice or academic development circles. This in turn would make heuristics such as threshold concepts increasingly nuanced as we articulated 'the way we do things'. And how might it end? It ends just the way it began and was then conducted: pragmatically, and in response to a contextual sense of 'whether we have reasonably answered the question for our current purposes'. Given that there is no realistic possibility of mastering every discipline one encounters, there is no other option than this kind of 'immediate-need' pragmatism, which is itself typical of 'Mode 2' knowledge: the conversation itself cannot be anything but an enactment of interdisciplinarity.

The potential role of (articulating) threshold concepts will be obvious, indeed almost unavoidable, if this approach is taken. If thinking about threshold concepts is useful pedagogically, the time is well spent just for that: but it might also provide a basis for more harmonious and humble interdisciplinary work. The evasions and defensive tactics that disciplinary tribes deploy to retain their integrity inevitably become more obvious in an interdisciplinary context because of the variety of immediately available vantage points and values: what one discipline wishes to sidestep may be of great interest to another. In a disciplinary setting, those values are (and must be) taken for granted but not so in interdisciplinary contexts where *no* value is self-evident. Nor can they be persuasively articulated because to do so requires a position that must itself assume values (Fish, 1994, 1995): these values are just as contestable. Once again, we face infinite regress.

Threshold Concepts as Our Common Ground

Put differently, the interdisciplinary group does not have shared threshold concepts: even experts on rational decision-making (e.g., anthropologists and economists, or economists and epidemiologists) may immediately find themselves at loggerheads (see e.g., Douglas & Ney, 1998; Joffe, 2011), This is entirely harmonious with the notion of threshold concepts providing initiates with a distinctive gaze, but can easily become disruptive as academics move to defend or extend their disciplinary base. But, in the framework being outlined here, what they have in common is that, for our heuristic purposes, they *all operate with threshold concepts.* These do not compete or invite competition, but are discrete: they are the site of incommensurability. Framed thus as an inquiry into one's disciplinary framework, we are less likely to encounter bald statements such as 'history's not a proper discipline then' (as a chemistry PhD student once bluntly responded to me after I explained that interpretation can profoundly shape evidence in history). Threshold concepts are thus potentially a great leveller, and their articulation at some point, whether deliberately or piecemeal, is usually a necessary part of collaboration.

To some academics, of course, this might be unacceptably close to relativism, and indeed exposure to this kind of epistemic pluralism might well appear to complicate the transmission of 'true' disciplinary knowledge. For many students, also, it will be a challenge to encounter avowedly pluralistic regimes of truth, since, as every teacher knows, the cult of the 'right answer' is alive and well: claims to truth are *so* seductive (and the elucidation of 'claim' is harder even than the deconstruction of 'truth' much of the time). But such a move is hardly out of step with the rest of the university: in so many subjects, we are increasingly teaching students to deal with *not*-knowing (e.g., Barnett, 2000; Land 2012). There is, however, also the practical difficulty that so few academics can make authentic claims to expertise in more than one field or, to put it differently, the fact that successful interdisciplinarians typically struggle to get and/or retain employment (Lattuca, 2001, pp. 178–184).

Nonetheless, all kinds of possibilities for more reflexive and outward-facing disciplinary work beckon, with all the possibilities, challenges and difficulties that shared endeavours guarantee and what is often needed is ways for different 'tribes' to retain their integrity without impinging on others'. We would have to accept that knowledge *changes* in different contexts: as Fish (1995, pp. viii–x) puts it, '[social constructivist] accounts of how disciplines come into being are correct, but ... such accounts, rather than telling us that disciplines are unreal tell us just how disciplines came to be as real and as productive as they are'.

More urgently, and to bring the focus back to students, it may bring enormous relief to students who are trying to synthesise incompatible knowledge systems, not yet realising they are beyond the reach of 'right answers', to have this aspect of interdisciplinary work *deliberately* presented to them: incommensurability can then become an intriguing puzzle and a mystery that can be put aside or picked up as they need or choose rather than a set of dilemmas they must resolve (but never can).

Bringing 'threshold guardianship' out of the shadows could allow students to avoid being dominated by the conflicting demands put upon them by interdisciplinary work: it could create a much more level playing field for interdisciplinary work; and, if we place any stock in their pedagogic value, it would unlock all kinds of doors for teaching and learning.

ACKNOWLEDGEMENTS

I learned much from presenting these ideas at the NAIRTL/Threshold Concepts Conference of June 2012 in Dublin; Professor Stephen Rowland and Dr. Nick Grindle both commented on early versions, Professor Eva Sorensen saved me from specific errors, and Sophie Harris helped me untangle many of them, insofar as they became untangled.

REFERENCES

Barnett, R. (2000). *Realising the university in an age of supercomplexity.* Buckingham: Society for Research into Higher Education & Open University Press.

Becher, T., & Trowler, P. (2001). *Academic tribes and territories: Intellectual enquiry and the culture of disciplines* (2nd ed.). Philadelphia, PA: Open University Press.

Carmichael, P. (2010). Threshold concepts, disciplinary differences and cross-disciplinary discourse. *Learning and Teaching in Higher Education: Gulf Perspectives, 7*(2), 53–72.

Castronovo, R. (2000). Within the veil of interdisciplinary knowledge?: Jefferson, du Bois, and the negation of politics. *New Literary History, 31*(4), 781–804.

Collins, H., Evans, R., & Gorman, M. (2007). Trading zones and interactional expertise. *Studies in History and Philosophy of Science Part A, 38*(4), 657–666.

Concerns, T. (2001). Interdisciplinarity and nursing: "Everything is everything," or is it? *Nursing Science Quarterly, 14*(4), 274–280.

Cousin, G. (2010). Neither teacher-centred nor student-centred: Threshold concepts and research partnerships. *Journal of Learning Development in Higher Education,* (2).

Davies, J. P. (2010). The messiness of academics speaking across the disciplines. In L. Walsh & P. E. Kahn (Eds.), *Collaborative working in higher education: The social academy.* London: Taylor & Francis.

Davies, J. P. (2011). Disciplining the disciplines. In P. Dawid, W. Twining, & M. Vasilaki (Eds.), *Evidence, inference and inquiry* (pp. 37–72). Oxford: Oxford University Press.

de Certeau, M. (1984). *The practice of everyday life.* Berkeley, CA: University of California Press.

Douglas, M. (1986). *How institutions think* (1st ed.). Syracuse, NY: Syracuse University Press.

Douglas, M., & Ney, S. (1998). *Missing persons: A critique of the social sciences.* Berkeley, CA: University of California Press.

Fish, S. E. (1994). *There's no such thing as free speech: And it's a good thing, too.* New York, NY: Oxford University Press.

Fish, S. E. (1995). *Professional correctness: Literary studies and political change.* Cambridge, MA: Harvard University Press.

Gibbons, M., Limoges, C., & Nowotny, H. (1994). *The new production of knowledge: The dynamics of science and research in contemporary societies.* London: Sage Publications.

Hunt, L. (1994). The virtues of disciplinarity. *Eighteenth-Century Studies, 28*(1), 1–7.

Irvine, N., & Carmichael, P. (2009). Threshold concepts: A point of focus for practitioner research. *Active Learning in Higher Education, 10*(2), 103–119.

Jenkins, K. (1995). *On what is history?: From Carr and Elton to Rorty and White.* London: Routledge.

Joffe, M. (2011). What would a scientific economics look like? In P. Dawid, W. Twining, & M. Vasilaki (Eds.), *Evidence, inference and inquiry* (pp. 435–464). Oxford: Oxford University Press.

Kinchin, I. M. (2010). Solving Cordelia's dilemma: Threshold concepts within a punctuated model of learning. *Journal of Biological Education, 44*(2), 53–57.

Klein, J. T. (1990). *Interdisciplinarity: History, theory, and practice.* Detroit, MI: Wayne State University Press.

Klein, J. T. (1996). *Crossing boundaries: Knowledge, disciplinarities, and interdisciplinarities.* Charlottesville, VA: University Press of Virginia.

Klein, J. T. (Ed.). (2001). *Transdisciplinarity: Joint problem solving among science, technology, and society: An effective way for managing complexity.* Basel: Birkhauser.

Klein, J. T. (2004). Prospects for transdisciplinarity. *Futures, 36*(4), 515–526.

Klein, J. T. (2005). *Humanities, culture, and interdisciplinarity: The changing American academy.* Albany, NY: State University of New York Press.

Kiley, M. (2009). Identifying threshold concepts and proposing strategies to support doctoral candidates. *Innovations in Education and Teaching International, 46*(3), 293–304.

Land, R. (2012). Interdisciplinarity as a threshold concept. In *Tribes and territories in the 21st-century: Rethinking the significance of disciplines in higher education* (pp. 175–185). London: Routledge.

Lattuca, L. R. (2001). *Creating interdisciplinarity: Interdisciplinary research and teaching among college and university faculty.* Nashvile, TN: Vanderbilt University Press.

Manathunga, C., & Brew, A. (2012). Beyond tribes and territories: New metaphors for new times. In P. Trowler & M. Saunders (Eds.), *Tribes and territories in the 21st century: Rethinking the significance of disciplines in higher education* (pp. 44–56). Abingdon, UK: Routledge.

Martin, L. H., & Sørensen, J. (2011). *Past minds: Studies in cognitive historiography.* London: Equinox Publishing Limited.

Meyer, J. H. F., & Land, R. (2003). Threshold concepts and troublesome knowledge: Linkages to ways of thinking and practising within the disciplines. *ETL Project Occasional Report, 4.*

Nowotny, H., Scott, P., & Gibbons, M. (2003). Introduction: 'Mode 2' revisited: The new production of knowledge. *Minerva, 41*(3), 179–194.

Rorty, R. (1989). *Contingency, irony, and solidarity.* Cambridge: Cambridge University Press.

Rowland, S. (2006). *The enquiring university: Compliance and contestation in higher education.* Maidenhead: Open University Press.

Roy, R. (1979). Interdisciplinary science on campus: The elusive dream. In J. J. Kockelmans (Ed.), *Interdisciplinarity in higher education* (pp. 161–196). University Park, PA: Pennsylvania State University Press.

Rüpke, J. (2007). *Religion of the Romans.* Cambridge: Polity Press.

Saler, B. (1993). *Conceptualizing religion: Immanent anthropologists, transcendent natives, and unbounded categories.* Leiden: Brill.

Sanders, K., Boustedt, J., Eckerdal, A., McCartney, R., Moström, J. E., Thomas, L., & Zander, C. (2012). Threshold concepts and threshold skills in computing. In *Proceedings of the ninth annual international conference on international computing education research* (pp. 23–30), New York, NY.

Star, S. L., & Griesemer, J. R. (1989). Institutional ecology, 'translations' and boundary objects: Amateurs and professionals in Berkeley's Museum of Vertebrate Zoology, 1907–39. *Social Studies of Science,* 387–420.

Townsend, T., Pisapia, J., & Razzaq, J. (2013). Fostering interdisciplinary research in universities: A case study of leadership, alignment and support. *Studies in Higher Education,* 1–18.

Trowler, P., Saunders, M., & Bamber, V. (2012). *Tribes and territories in the 21st century: Rethinking the significance of disciplines in higher education. International studies in higher education.* London: Routledge.

Twining W., Dawid P., & Vasilaki D. (Eds.). (2011). *Evidence, inference and enquiry.* New York, NY: Oxford University Press.

Walcot, P. (1979). Cattle raiding, heroic tradition, and ritual: The Greek evidence. *History of Religions, 18*(4), 326–351.

Walsh, L., & Kahn, P. E. (2010). *Collaborative working in higher education: The social academy.* New York, NY: Taylor & Francis.

Wilson, A. G. (2010). *Knowledge power: Interdisciplinary education for a complex world.* London: Routledge.

Ziman, J. (2003). Emerging out of nature into history: The plurality of the sciences. *Philosophical Transactions: Mathematical, Physical and Engineering Sciences, 361*(1809), 1617–1633.

Jason Davies
University College London

AMINUL HUQ, MARCIA D. NICHOLS AND BIJAYA ARYAL

11. BUILDING BLOCKS

Threshold Concepts and Interdisciplinary Structures of Learning

INTRODUCTION

Ray Land and colleagues have recently proposed that the semiotic concept of signification could be used to elucidate liminality by suggesting that, when faced with a new concept, students "journey" through a liminal tunnel in which the new concept or sign becomes incorporated into their worldview or knowledge (Land et al., 2014). Although Land et al. use Signification as a metaphor for understanding liminality, this chapter will suggest that we should look at Signification itself–and the underlying concepts of ambiguity and context (Wisker et al., 2008; Higgs & Cronin, 2013) as threshold concepts. Because words are unstable signs that continually aggregate new connotations, meanings and references – i.e. signification – then this has profound implications for every discipline (Carmichael, 2010; Brearey, 2014), perhaps especially for STEM subjects that rely on language to be precise, transparent signs. In part, this chapter will explore ambiguity and context as threshold concepts in literature as well as in two STEM disciplines, mathematics and physics.

In literature, ambiguity is a key concept with which novice students often struggle, yet one they must master if they are to succeed in analysing literary texts. Words themselves are inherently ambiguous: words are referential signs with multiple meanings and multiple connotations, which continually accrete to them like barnacles on a ship. Thus, ambiguity is troublesome (Meyer & Land, 2003; Cousin, 2006; Meyer et al., 2010): Recognizing and appreciating the ambiguity of literary texts means leaving the comfortable shallows of surface meaning and diving deep into the possibilities of language and meaning that can be disturbing, uncomfortable, unfamiliar. Ambiguity is irreversible: The realization that words are multivocal, multivalent and unstable signs that are often deployed in ways that deliberately play with instability can't be unrealized without also engaging in cognitive dissonance. Ambiguity is integrative: Once one recognizes words as unstable signs, one realizes that, on the one hand, authors play with these instabilities, deliberately manipulating the context of words – their connotations, their referential natures. On the other, ambiguities of language also always escape authorial intentions, with new connotations and references accreting seemingly on their own. Ambiguity is transformative: The recognition of the instability and multiplicity of language opens up new worlds of possibility and nuance, not just in literary texts, but in

R. Land et al. (Eds.), Threshold Concepts in Practice, 135–151.

all verbal and written communication, including scientific discourses. Ambiguity is discursive: One must articulate ambiguity in order to work through the liminal tunnel of signification (Land et al., 2014).

In mathematics and physics, there are four basic types of ambiguity: content, language, context and symbolic. Thus, ambiguity is an important concept for problem solving in mathematics and physics – when students are asked to move away from formulaic problems to consider more complex, 'real world' problems, all sorts of ambiguities slip in, and students must learn to use context to navigate the uncertain terrain (Garber, 1999; Barwell, 2003; Feferman, 2004; Byers, 2007; Ganesalingam, 2013). In mathematics or physics, the symbolic language of math plays an important role in abstraction and application; it is through signification that the complex behaviour of the physical world can be formulated as ideal or theoretical. To wit, translating a concept from everyday language into symbolic language and back again necessarily introduces ambiguities. In the mathematics and physics courses discussed in this chapter, the instructors focused on a related threshold concept – context – rather than on ambiguity directly since content ambiguity tends not be encountered at the introductory level. Ambiguity and context are related concepts because students must learn to use context clues as the signposts with which to navigate ambiguity.

Context is a threshold concept because it is troublesome. Students often find it difficult and frustrating to pick out relevant bits of context to help them solve a problem. It is irreversible. Once one learns how to look for context clues, one can use that skill to solve complex problems or apply relevant theory. It is integrative. Learning about context means learning to look for the relationships among facts, situations, peoples, environments, etc. It is transformative. Recognizing the importance of context shows students how interrelated their environments are. It is discursive: Identifying pertinent contextual clues is always at least in part an examination of discourse.

We suggest that ambiguity and context are Interdependent threshold concepts. We define Interdependent threshold concepts as those that are not only salient in multiple disciplines but that also can but taught across disciplinary lines. In contrast, Independent threshold concepts are discrete concepts at a specific learning stage within a discipline that do not require the previous mastery of another threshold concept, such as the concept of Function in Calculus (Pettersson, 2012; Pettersson et al., 2013), or Genre in Literature (Adler-Kessner et al., 2012; Clark & Hernandez, 2011) or measurement uncertainty in Physics (Wilson et al., 2010). Independent threshold concepts can be applied to other concepts, but the concept itself does not depend upon learning other threshold concepts in near simultaneity. Intradependent concepts are those that are still at a particular learning stage within a single discipline, but that are dependent upon other concepts within that same discipline, like Symbolism in Literature or Limit, which depends on the concept of Function in Calculus or Entropy depending on the concept of Energy in Physics.

This chapter is a retrospective, descriptive examination of how a group of students approached and grappled with ambiguity and context in three courses: Introduction to Literature, Introduction to Physics, and Calculus I. This chapter emerges from pedagogical conversations of the instructor/researchers, who, through discussion, came to the realization that ambiguity and context could be considered important TCs for each discipline. Thus, the student coursework under consideration is not experimental – we did not design these courses to deliberately integrate TCs across disciplinary lines. Only in Introduction to Literature is either of these TCs explicitly taught. In the two STEM disciplines, ambiguity and context are largely present as implicit TCs. This situation piqued our curiosity, leading us to examine a small sample of shared students to determine if student performance with these threshold concepts (1) correlated with one another within one course and (2) correlated among the different courses. This type of retrospective, descriptive study would allow us to determine if learning transfer is occurring across disciplinary lines and to provide a foundation for us to more deliberately imbed curricular points of integration that would better promote the transfer of learning and understanding on the TCs.

METHOD

Our sample size consists of students from a small, public Midwestern US university, and data was collected with IRB approval. Our university is unique because it has only one major, Health Sciences, that is housed within an interdisciplinary department. Except for 4 students in Physics, all the students' data can be compared among at least two of the courses, and in most cases across 3 or all of the courses. The data presented was gathered from 24 students (14 male and 11 female), enrolled in Physics in either Fall 2012, Spring 2013, Fall 2013 or Spring 2014 semester. Out of the 24 students, 20 students (12 male and 8 female) enrolled in Literature, from Spring 2013, Fall 2013 and Spring 2014 semester; and 15 students (8 male and 7 female) enrolled in Calculus from Fall 2011 or Fall 2012 semester.

These students were randomly picked from the pool of students who took at least two of the three courses, Calculus I, Literature, and Introductory Physics. The ACT (MATH, ENG, SCI) scores of this group of students are representative of the first year cohort (either 2010, 2011, or 2012) to which they belong. Additionally, there was no significant difference between the ACT scores of male and female students in the group. All students took the mathematics courses before either Physics or Literature, but students took Physics or Literature in any order or in some cases simultaneously.

Data from Physics was collected from (1) response to survey questions (Adams et al., 2006) that asked students to rank their comfort with ambiguity and context on a five scale Likert scale, (2) scores from exam questions that ask about context-related tasks, and (3) total scores on exams. Data from Literature include (1) course grade, (2) student performance with ambiguity and context on the first and final drafts of two critical analysis papers by looking at the categories of Content (ambiguity) and Evidence (context) from the course rubric, and (3) Instructor ranked comfort/ willingness to engage with ambiguity in course reading journals kept over the entire semester. Data from Calculus include (1) student performance with Independent, Intradependent and Interdependent threshold concepts in quizzes in Calculus as classified by the instructor. (2) student performance on exams in Calculus. All analysis was done using R statistical software version 3.1.2 (R 2013).

Data from all courses was compiled and analysed for

1. correlation between exam grade and ambiguity or context for students within physics
2. correlation between exam grade and different TC performance including ambiguity or context from quiz for students within calculus
3. correlation between exam grade and ambiguity or context for students within literature
4. correlation between summative assessment and ambiguity or context for students common in calculus-physics, physics-literature and calculus-literature.

RESULTS

Within Calculus

To explore student performance on TCs in the Calculus courses, we classified quiz questions as asking about or utilizing either Independent, Intradependent or Interdependent TCs, focusing primarily on contextual and non-contextual problems that depend on student understanding of previously-identified TCs (Petterson, 2011; Pettersson, 2012; Pettersson et al., 2014; Scheja & Petterson, 2009; Easdown & Wood, 2012; Lloyd & Vera, 2013). Scores were averaged from each category for comparison. The Calculus I course was designed to include more context based problems that the traditional courses in calculus because of the health science focus of the degree program. Figure 1 shows the comparison of student performance on quiz questions involving Interdependent, Intradependent and Independent threshold concepts verses their exam average in Calculus I. The quiz questions were used for this study for mainly two reasons. First, quiz scores are good indicators of exam/ course performance (with r value of more than 0.85 for the courses these students were enrolled). Secondly, many quizzes over the semester provides a strong representative sample for each TC classification. We classified questions like

'Find the derivative of the function $f(x)$ using the limit definition at $x = 1$'

as intradependent because it relies on other TCs, limit and function. Questions like

'Suppose we know the following facts about the dynamics of a medication for a horse. Each day, a patient uses up two thirds of the medication in his bloodstream per liter. However he is given a new dose sufficient to raise the concentration in the blood stream by 0.025 mg per liter. If $m(t)$ denote the concentration of the medication in the blood stream. Write down the model that describes this situation'

were classified as interdependent because it requires not only mathematical knowledge, but also context awareness. Questions related to concepts like finding properties of a function were treated as independent.

A multiple linear regression was calculated to predict average exam performance based on performance on Independent TCs, Intradependent TCs and Interdependent TCs. A significant regression equation was found ($F(3,11) = 11.85$, $p < .001$), with an R^2 of .7637. Students predicted average exam score in percentage is equal to 30.622 + 0.21369 (*Independent TCs*) + 0.33339 (*Intradependent TCs*) + 0.11147 (*Interdependent TCs*). Interestingly the students performance on the Intradependent TCs were a significant predictor ($r(13) = 0.80$, $p < .000$) for the average exam scores than Interdependent TCs ($r(13) = 0.68$, $p < .005$) and Independent TCs had the lowest correlation ($r(13) = 0.51$, $p < .05$) with the average exam score. It would be interesting to find out if such differences exist using a larger sample. Instructors do not focus on ambiguity while teaching introductory level mathematics but they do creep in as part of learning a new disciplinary language. There is also a push toward using context heavy or application oriented problems while introducing troublesome concepts in mathematics and it would be interesting to see whether the performance on the Interdependent TCs are influenced by the ambiguity involved in dealing with them.

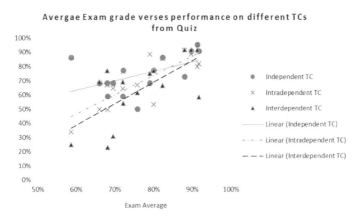

Figure 1. Student performance on average exam grade vs Interdependent, Intradependent and Independent Mathematical Threshold Concepts in Calculus I

Within Physics

As a discipline, Physics doesn't identify ambiguity and context as important content knowledge; however, the physics education research community has recognized that knowing the nature or epistemology of physics is very important for physics learning. In order to be successful in physics learning, students must know the nature of physics content and know what physics learning means (Elby, 2001). We consider context and ambiguity as two interdependent threshold concepts in relation to physics epistemology. Thus, students must recognize that physics requires the navigation and understanding of ambiguities in context to help them resolve ambiguities in the physical realm.

To explore students' attitude towards relevance of context and ambiguity in physics, we used the Colorado Learning Attitudes of Science Survey (CLASS) (Adams et al., 2006). It is a Likert scale test of five ranks. Students received positive scores (+2 or +1) for favourable, negative (−2 or −1) for unfavourable and zero for neutral responses. We categorized some items as focused on ambiguity or context. Context items measure students' perceptions about physics being a contextual discipline, whereas, ambiguity items measure students' comfort level with ambiguity in physics content. Depending on the degree of agreement or disagreement with the survey items when compared to expert physicists' responses, students receive +1 or +2 for favourable responses, −1 and −2 for unfavourable responses and 0 for neutral response. The average response was calculated from similar context or ambiguity items for each students. One typical example of a survey item in the ambiguity category is as follows 'There is usually only one correct approach to solving a physics problem'. Likewise here is an example of context item in the survey, 'I find that reading the text in detail is a good way for me to learn physics'. Scores were averaged for various questions in each category.

A simple linear regression was calculated to predict the comfort level with ambiguity in physics based on their perception of physics as a contextual discipline. A significant regression equation was found ($F(1,22) = 27.26$, $p < .000$), with an R^2 of .5534. Students predicted comfort level with ambiguity is equal to perception of physics as a contextual discipline. Figure 2 shows a positive correlation ($r(22 = 0.775$, $p < .001$ with the regression line shown) that a majority of students

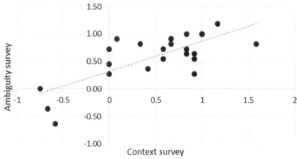

Figure 2. Correlation between students' comfort level in ambiguity vs context survey

receiving positive scores indicating that they agreed to the experts in the field of physics regarding the ambiguity and relevance of contexts in physics. Interestingly, we found that, in general, students who recognize that physics deals with contexts are more comfortable with ambiguous scenario in physics learning.

We also used data on students' performance in physics that was based on exam performances. Exam questions contained contextual problem solving, conceptual questions and applications in contextual questions. The study used the same or isomorphic problems or questions for all the participant students. The exams were graded by the same graders for all participant students. Contextual questions were used in regular class as a form of formative assessment. Those questions required students application of conceptual and algorithmic (procedural knowledge) when a real world context is presented. Whereas, most of the exam questions typically assess students' conceptual (factual) knowledge and procedural (algorithmic) knowledge.

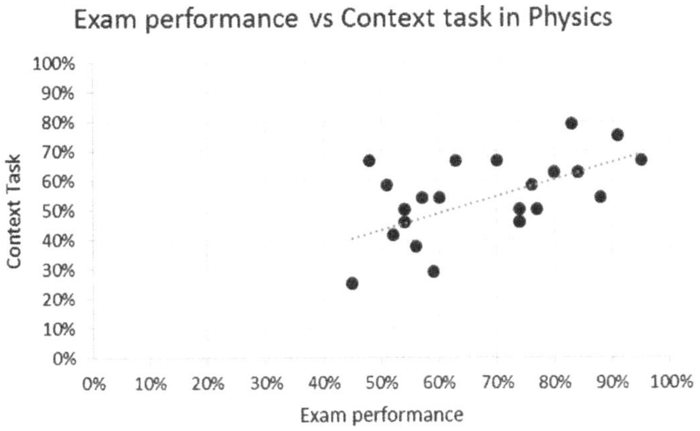

Exam performance vs Context task in Physics

Figure 3. Relation between students performance on context task and exam in Physics

A simple linear regression was calculated to predict the exam performance in physics based on performance on the context tasks. A regression equation was found ($F(1,22) = 12.35$, $p < .002$), with an R^2 of .5596. Students predicted exam performance is equal to 33.709 + .63027 (performance on context task). Figure 3 shows that students performance in the context tasks had lower correlation with their exam performance ($r(22) = 0.2984$, $p < .001$). One might expect a much higher correlation between students exam performance with the contextual tasks as both involve the similar physics principles. However, based on the data from the study we suggest that real world scenario might sometimes prevent students from identifying relevant physics concepts imbedded within the context. Such 'context blockage' could cause students to fail to use their conceptual and procedural knowledge successfully.

Within Literature

In Introduction to Literature, ambiguity is explicitly taught as a key intradependent TC. Belletristic language is marked by its deliberate play with the inherent ambiguities of language, and meaning is made as a reader attempts to reconcile or deconstruct a literary work. Either analytical move requires a careful attention to contextual evidence, an independent TC in literature, to construct an interpretation. Both ambiguity and context are introduced in the beginning of the semester and a significant amount of class time is spent modelling how to use contextual evidence to navigate through literary ambiguity.

To explore student attitudes toward ambiguity in Literature, the reading journal assignment was utilized since no attitudinal surveys were given. It is our opinion that the reading journal could be thought of as similar to a survey because it is a loosely structured assignment in which students are asked to respond in virtually any way to the literary texts that they read for the course. Reading journals are informal writing situations in which students are instructed to respond in any way other than summary to class readings, including sharing thoughts, observations, and/or reactions to the reading, any questions, and/or any connections between the text and other readings or experiences. Thus, students could ignore, complain about, question or attempt to grapple with the ambiguity of these texts. We used the scale given in Table 1 to rank student willingness to engage with ambiguity in each of 13 journal entries, which were then averaged for a composite score. The scale is meant to mimic a Likert scale to better enable comparison with survey data. The scale assumes that the degree of engagement with ambiguity would roughly correspond with comfort, i.e. a 1 ranking assumes that avoiding mentioning ambiguity indicates high discomfort with it, whereas a ranking of 4, in which ambiguity is questioned indicates a marked level of comfort. An obvious pitfall to this method is that it substitutes a researcher's judgement for the personal response and self-reflection of students.

To explore student performance in context and ambiguity, performance on two critical analysis essays was examined. In Literature, students wrote two essays in which they analyse or interpret a literary text. Students were required to submit at least two drafts of each paper, and papers were evaluated using a rubric with the following categories: Introduction, Conclusion, Documentation, Content (weighted

Table 1. Ranking of student willingness to engage with ambiguity

1	2	3	4	5
avoids ambiguity or much beyond plot summary	expresses dislike or little more than frustration and confusion	uses personal or intertextual connections to discuss ambiguity	asks questions about ambiguous areas	makes an analysis/draws solid conclusions about what ambiguity may be doing

Table 2. Rubric for papers analysed in literature

	Content	Evidence
Excellent (5)	There is a central idea that meets the paper requirements and that is discussed, analyzed and explored with insight. The student's sophisticated comprehension of the topic is demonstrated.	Sufficient and varied evidence is incorporated accurately and seamlessly into paper for all major points.
Good (4)	There is a central idea that meets the paper requirements. The discussion is mostly insightful, but may include some gaps in logic.	Sufficient evidence for most points that is incorporated accurately but not always seamlessly into paper.
Satisfactory (3)	The central idea meets the paper requirement, but the discussion is shallow and lacking in insight and sophistication.	Evidence to support some, but not all points. Some evidence may not be fully discussed or integrated into paper.
Poor (2)	The paper attempts to meet the paper requirements, but ultimately fails to contain a thesis and therefore fails to develop a central idea.	The paper offers random details of support, and/or fails to provide sufficient appropriate evidence. Evidence is not incorporated into paper.
Unacceptable (1)	The paper fails to contain a thesis, and therefore fails to develop a central idea. All or part of paper may be plagiarized.	Provides no appropriate evidence.

double), Evidence, Organization, Flow, Language and Grammar/Mechanics. Student performance in two categories, Content and Evidence were considered, as well as the final grades on the essays. Content and Evidence were chosen as best correlating to ambiguity and context, respectively.

Content refers to the development of a coherent interpretation or argument about a literary text; therefore, Content corresponds to ambiguity because developing an interpretation requires students to grapple with and work through the ambiguities of a literary text. Evidence refers to the deployment of textual evidence from the literary work to support the argument developed in Content. The evidence correlates to context or context clues that one might find in math or physics 'word problems'. Student papers were assigned a score using the rubric given in Table 2.

A multiple linear regression was calculated to predict course grade based performance on *ambiguity* and *context* tasks within writing assignments. After identifying one outlier using the residuals vs. leverage plot and Cook's distance a significant regression equation was found ($F(2,16) = 45.57$, $p < .000$), with an R^2 of .8507. Students predicted course grade in percentage is equal to 74.052 + .2557 (*Ambiguity tasks*) – 0.0590 (*Context tasks*). Figure 4 shows that student performance

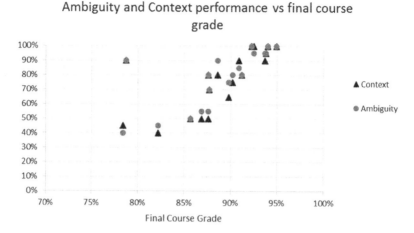

Figure 4. Ambiguity and context evidence vs final paper grade in the papers

on *ambiguity* and *context* tasks within writing assignments has a good positive correlation (ambiguity $r(17) = 0.920$, $p < .000$ and context $r(17) = 0.887$, $p < .000$) with final grades in the class, suggesting that high performers also tend to perform very well with navigating ambiguity using context evidence.

Calculus and Physics

We collected students' exam scores in physics and calculus and compared student performance. Physics and calculus are quantitative sciences; thus, one should expect a high correlation of students' performances in these disciplines. The

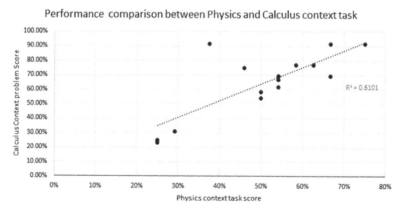

Figure 5. Graph showing the plot of students' scores in physics contextual tasks vs. scores in calculus contextual tasks

expected correlation between physics and calculus exam performance is evident ($r(14) = 0.689$, $p < .004$) among our sample students; thus, we would expect to find a similar correlation between specific context-tasks as well. A simple linear regression was calculated to predict the performance in physics context tasks based on performance on calculus context tasks (Interdependent TCs). A significant regression equation was found ($F(1,13) = 20.34$, $p < .000$), with an R^2 of .6101. Students predicted performance on physics context tasks is equal to 16.4315 + .5280 (performance on calculus context tasks). It is interesting that the correlation between physics context tasks and calculus context tasks (Interdependent TCs) is even higher than the correlation between respective exam scores. Figure 5 shows the positive correlation ($r(13) = 0.78$, $p < .000$) with physics and calculus context tasks.

It is worthwhile to revisit Figure 3 in which we presented a comparison of students' performance in exam and contextual task within physics. One may expect a high correlation between contextual task score and exam score because both of them relate to physics understanding. Surprisingly, we observed that students' performance correlated more strongly between contextual tasks in physics and calculus than their performances between physics exam and physics contextual tasks. This result suggests that students' ability to apply their understanding in contextual tasks is transferable from one disciplinary area to another. Practice journeying through the liminal tunnel in one discipline can perhaps make similar journeys in another discipline easier.

Calculus and Literature

From Figure 6, we also see somewhat good correlation ($r(12) = 0.62$, $p < .017$) between student performance in literature and calculus context task (Interdependent TCs). At first blush, this finding may appear surprising or even counterintuitive – we

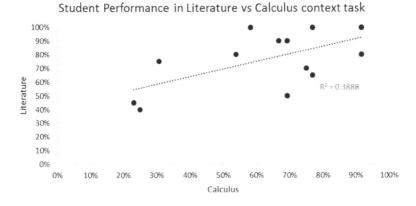

Figure 6. Student performance in literature verses calculus context task

tend to believe that there are 'math people' and 'word people' and ne'er the twain shall meet. However, our findings suggest otherwise. Students who perform well in calculus develop good analytical skills, which would seem to transfer to their ability to perform well in literature. Good analytical ability enables students to navigate ambiguity with context evidence in both mathematical and literary problems. Students total course grade in Calculus and Literature also had the same correlation. A simple linear regression was calculated to predict the performance in literature context tasks based on performance on calculus context tasks (Interdependent TCs). A regression equation was found ($F(1,12) = 7.635$, $p < 0.17$), with an R^2 of .3888. Students predicted performance on literature context tasks is equal to $41.68 + .5573$ (performance on calculus context tasks).

Physics and Literature

Figure 7 shows that there is almost no correlation ($r(18) = 0.26$, $p < .2$) between the comfort with ambiguity expressed by students in physics with their apparent comfort with ambiguity as gathered from reading journals in literature. However, the graph does reveal some interesting information. For instance, although no students are very comfortable with ambiguity in physics, none express high levels of discomfort, either, with most students falling just above the neutral range. In contrast, in literature, students generally fall just below the neutral range. Moreover, the student that scored highest in comfort with ambiguity in literature was on the lower end of comfort with ambiguity in physics, while several students that exhibit more discomfort with ambiguity in literature express greater comfort with it in physics. Surprisingly, this would seem to indicate that most students are more comfortable

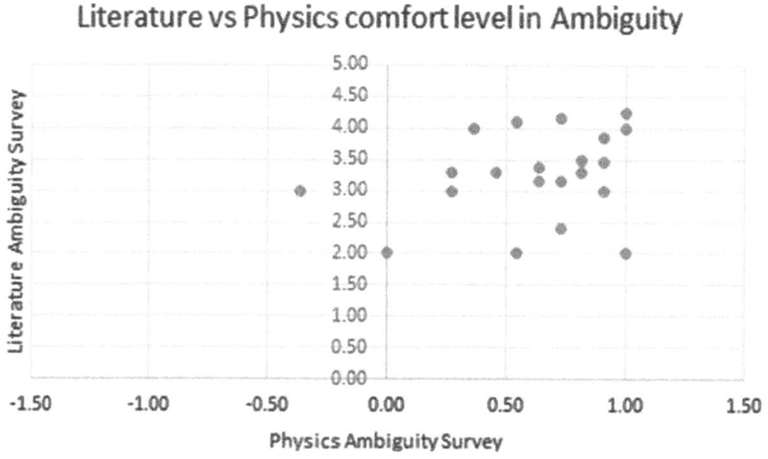

Figure 7. Comfort with ambiguity in physics and literature

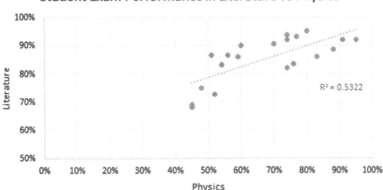

Figure 8. Graph showing the plot of student average exam grade in
physics with average paper grades in literature

with physical rather than lexical ambiguity. However, there are potentially many problems with these conclusions.

First, data from the physics course was gathered from self-reported student responses using a Likert scale, whereas in Literature, student comfort with ambiguity was determined by the researcher who ranked reading journal entries using scale described above. In any case, whether self-reported or ranked by the researcher, few students exhibit high levels of comfort – or discomfort – with ambiguity, with most students falling somewhere in the neutral to somewhat comfortable range for both courses. Moreover, the small correlation between Physics exam performance

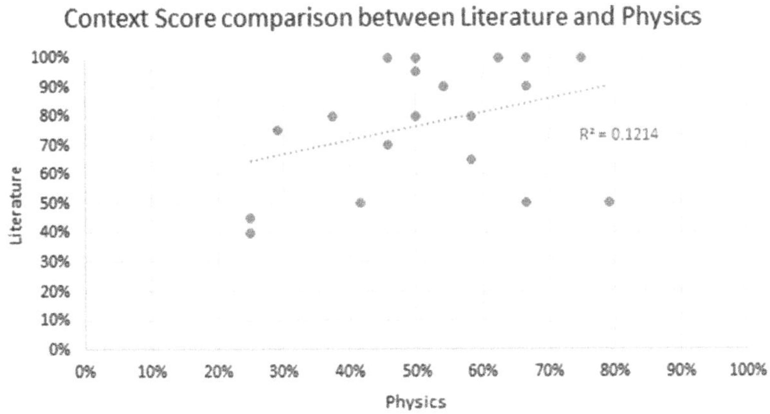

Context Score comparison between Literature and Physics

Figure 9. Graph showing the plot of student average score on
context task in Literature vs Physics

147

and performance on critical analysis essays in literature, as seen in the figure below, suggests a Likert-scale survey of literature students might produce more correlative findings.

Figure 8 suggests that there may be a correlation ($r(18) = 0.729, p < .000$) between how students perform on physics exams with how successfully they write a critical analysis paper for literature. In both situations, students have to use context in order to solve a problem (in physics) or to create a plausible argument of the meaning of a literary (and therefore ambiguous) text (in literature). A simple linear regression was calculated to predict the performance in literature paper grade based on performance on physics exam. A significant regression equation was found ($F(1,18) = 20.48$, $p < .000$), with an R^2 of .5322. Students predicted performance on literature papers is equal to 59.747 + .37689 (performance on physics exam).

As the plot in Figure 9 indicates, we found a negligent, small, positive correlation ($r = 0.348, p < .095$) between students' performance in physics contextual tasks and literature contextual task. On the other hand, the correlation that we observed in between calculus and physics contextual task is much higher. We speculate that the way students' frame contexts depends on nature of disciplines. Students share the common physical elements in quantitative disciplines like physics and calculus while approaching tasks. Whereas, more abstractness of literature does not permit them to identify common elements inherent within tasks. Moreover, because students have to gather appropriate context from lengthy literary works, the ability to winnow the fruit from the chaff can be much more challenging than word problems in calculus and physics. This finding is interesting and we hope to pursue it more purposefully in the future.

CONCLUSION AND DISCUSSION

This retrospective study reveals some surprising correlations and raises many important questions. Although our study is limited by our decision to examine only past student performance with performance in the Interdependent Threshold Concepts of ambiguity and context using a small sample size, we think that it has implications for not only the design of our future courses, but also for instruction with the Humanities and STEM disciplines as a whole.

Our study reveals some surprising, even counterintuitive, correlations between Literature, Physics and Calculus. Most surprising is the finding that students may be more comfortable with ambiguity in physics rather than in literature, since we tend to think of the physical realm as an objective and solid reality, whereas wordplay is common almost from the moment humans learn to talk. But perhaps because students expect to have some of their preconceptions about the physical world challenged in an Introduction to Physics course, they are prepared for ambiguity. With literature, however, perhaps they seek the opacity of signs to relieve the uncertainties of the human condition that literature explores and questions.

Less surprising perhaps, is the finding that high performers perform well across all three disciplinary boundaries, suggesting that, despite the popular idea that people who are good at Math and Science are not good with words and vice versa, this is simply not true. In fact, good analytical skills are not only necessary for success in all disciplines, but also can transfer from STEM to Humanities and back again. High performers are more comfortable with ambiguity, perhaps because they are also good at picking up on relevant context. High performers not only navigate the liminal tunnels of threshold concepts, they also grasp the connections among TCs and build upon each journey. In fact, a thorough understanding of context is crucial for success in all three courses.

So, how do we raise low performers up? In what ways can we help them become more comfortable with ambiguity, to recognize pertinent contextual information, to utilize and build upon Independent TCs to master complex Intradependent ones? Could explicit interdisciplinary instruction in Interdependent TCs help? How can we change our instructional approaches of these concepts in our individual courses so that they are structured to reinforce one another? Moreover, even though they are often treated as though they are from different planets, there are shared interdependent Threshold Concepts between STEM and Humanities disciplines. Recognition of these shared concepts can not only help people to see the importance of the Humanities, but also help students contextualize what might otherwise seem like esoteric questions in physics and mathematics. Making manifest such interdisciplinary, interdependent Threshold Concepts like ambiguity and context can only heighten their already integrative and transformative qualities. If the liminal tunnel is the process of signification, how much more effective and useful is that journey when one is not only prepared for the ambiguity, the uncertainty, that inevitably lurks there, but also knows that the way out is through the recognition and mastery of relevant context clues?

REFERENCES

Abelson, R. P. (1985). A variance explanation paradox: When a little is a lot. *Psychological Bulletin, 97*(1), 129–133.

Adams, W. K., Perkins, K. K., Podolefsky, N. S., Dubson, M., Finkelstein, N. D., & Wiemann C. E. (2006). New instrument for measuring student beliefs about physics and learning physics: The Colorado Learning Attitudes about Science Survey. *Physical Review Special Topics.* Retrieved from http://journals.aps.org/prstper/abstract/10.1103/PhysRevSTPER.2.010101

Adler-Kassner, L., Majewski, J., & Koshnick, D. (2012). The value of troublesome knowledge: Transfer and threshold concepts in writing and history. *Composition Forum, 26.* Retrieved from http://compositionforum.com/issue/26/troublesome-knowledge-threshold.php

Barwell, R. (2003). Ambiguity in mathematics classroom discourse. In *Proceedings of the British Society for Research into Learning Mathematics, 23*(3). Retrieved from http://www.bsrlm.org.uk/IPs/ip23-3/BSRLM-IP-23-3-1.pdf

Brearey, O. (2014, March 19–22). *Advancing the discussion of threshold concepts: Decoding the disciplines, critical junctures, and students' attainment of rhetorical awareness.* CCCC (Conference on College Composition and Communication), Indianapolis, IN. Retrieved from http://www.oliverbrearey.com/Advancing%20the%20Discussion%20of%20Threshold%20Concepts.pdf

Byers, W. (2007). *How mathematicians think: Using ambiguity, contradiction, and paradox to create mathematics.* Princeton, NJ: Princeton University Press.

Carmichael, P. (2010). Threshold concepts, disciplinary differences and cross-disciplinary discourse. *Learning and Teaching in Higher Education: Gulf Perspectives, 7*(2). Retrieved from http://lthe.zu.ac.ae/index.php/lthehome/article/viewArticle/43

Clark, I. L., & Hernandez, A. (2011). Genre awareness, academic argument, and transferability. *The WAC Journal, 22*, 65–78.

Cousin, G. (2006). An introduction to Threshold Concepts. *Planet, 17*, 4–5.

Easdown, D., & Wood, L. (2012). *Novel threshold concepts in the mathematical sciences.* In C. O'Mahony, A. Buchanan, M. O'Rourke & B. Higgs (Eds.), Threshold Concepts: From Personal Practice to Communities of Practice, Proceedings of the National Academy's Sixth Annual Conference and the Fourth Biennial Threshold Concepts Conference [e-publication] (pp. 44–50), NAIRTL, Ireland, January 2014. ISBN: 978-1-906642-59-4, Retrieved from http://www.nairtl.ie/documents/EPub_2012Proceedings.pdf#page=54

Elby, A. (2001). Helping physics students learn how to learn. *American Journal of Physics, Physics Education Research Supplement, 69*, S54–S64.

Feferman, S. (2004). Typical ambiguity: Trying to have your cake and eat it too. In G. Link (Ed.), *100 years of Russell's Paradox* (pp. 131–151). Berlin: Walter de Gruyter.

Ganesalingam, M. (2013). *The language of mathematics: A linguistic and philosophical investigation.* Berlin: Springer-Verlag.

Garber, E. (1999). *The language of physics: The calculus and development of theoretical physics in Europe, 1750–1914.* Boston, MA: Springer.

Higgs, B., & Cronin, J. (2013). Threshold concepts: Informing the curriculum. *Emerging Issues in Higher Education III, 167*–177. Retrieved from http://www.edin.ie/pubs/ei3-chapters/ei3-ch12.pdf

Land, R., Rattray, J., & Vivian, P. (2014). Learning in the liminal space: A semiotic approach to threshold concepts. *Higher Education, 67*, 199–217.

Lloyd, P., & Frith, V. (2013). Proportional reasoning as a threshold to numeracy at university: A framework for analysis. *Pythagoras, 34*. doi:10.4102/pythagoras.v34i2.234

Meyer, J. H. F., & Land, R. (2003). Threshold concepts and troublesome knowledge: Linkages to ways of thinking and practising within the disciplines. In C. Rust (Ed.), *Improving student learning – Ten years on.* Oxford: OCSLD. Retrieved from https://www.dkit.ie/ga/system/files/Threshold_Concepts__and__Troublesome_Knowledge_by_Professor_Ray_Land.pdf

Meyer, J. H. F., Land, R., & Baillie, C. (2010). *Threshold concepts and transformational learning.* Rotterdam, The Netherlands & Boston, MA: Sense Publishers.

Pettersson, K. (2011). Threshold concepts: A framework for research in university mathematics education. In *Proceedings of the Seventh Congress of the European Society for Research in Mathematics Education* (pp. 2063–2072). Retrieved from https://www.cerme7.univ.rzeszow.pl/WG/14/CERME7-WG14-Paper---Petterson-REVISED-Dec2010.pdf

Pettersson, K. (2012). The threshold concept of a function–A case study of a student's development of her understanding. *Eighth Swedish Mathematics Education Research Seminar.* Retrieved from http://www.mai.liu.se/SMDF/madif8/Pettersson.pdf

Pettersson, K., Stadler, E., & Tambour, T. (2013). Development of students' understanding of the threshold concept of function. *Eighth Congress of European Research in Mathematics Education.* Retrieved from http://cerme8.metu.edu.tr/wgpapers/WG14/WG14_Pettersson.pdf

R Core Team. (2013). *R: A language and environment for statistical computing.* Vienna, Austria: R Foundation for Statistical Computing. Retrieved from http://www.R-project.org/

Scheja, M., & Pettersson, K. (2009). Transformation and contextualisation: Conceptualising students' conceptual understandings of threshold concepts in calculus. *Higher Education, 59*, 221–241. doi:10.1007/s10734-009-9244-7

Wilson, A., Akerlind, G., Francis, P., Kirkup, L., McKenzie, J., Pearce, D., & Sharma, M. D. (2010). Measurement uncertainty as a threshold concept in physics. In *Proceedings of The Australian Conference on Science and Mathematics Education* (formerly UniServe Science Conference), 16. Retrieved from http://ojs-prod.library.usyd.edu.au/index.php/IISME/article/view/4686

Wisker, G., Cameron, S., & Antoniou, M. (2008). *Connotations and conjunctions: Threshold Concepts, curriculum development, and the cohesion of English studies.* Retrieved from http://www.english.heacademy.ac.uk/explore/projects/archive/general/documents/ConnotationsandConjunctions-UBrightonProjectFinalReport08.doc

Aminul Huq
Centre for Learning Innovation
University of Minnesota Rochester

Marcia D. Nichols
Centre for Learning Innovation
University of Minnesota Rochester

Bijaya Aryal
Centre for Learning Innovation
University of Minnesota Rochester

PART 4

THE DOCTORAL JOURNEY

MICHELLE SALMONA, DAN KACZYNSKI AND LEIGH N. WOOD

12. THE IMPORTANCE OF LIMINAL SPACE FOR DOCTORAL SUCCESS

Exploring Methodological Threshold Concepts

OVERVIEW

Mastering social science research methodology is a daunting challenge for doctoral candidates. This chapter explores these challenges by considering what comprises the essential threshold concepts of social science methodology. Particular attention is given in this discussion to the doctoral dissertation phase of learning and the critical role of supervision. Underlying this research are the ongoing efforts to improve instruction in research methodology and to increase successful completion rates for doctoral candidates. The study draws upon the importance of instructional scaffolding designed to support autonomous student learning. Such an approach offers a means to explore the mastery of threshold concepts as the learner experiences liminal space. Conclusions examine strategies which promote the modeling of dichotomies in methodological concepts which may facilitate student entry into liminal space.

INTRODUCTION

Doctoral degree completion rates have remained consistently low for over 50 years. Only 50% of humanities candidates and 56% of social sciences candidates successfully complete their doctoral degree in the United States (Grasso, Barry, & Valentine, 2009). In Australia completion rates have recently improved ahead of the United States yet remain unacceptably low (Group of Eight, 2013; Bourke, Holbrook, Lovat, & Farley, 2004). Solutions to increase these low rates of doctoral program completion remain elusive for higher education.

Many requirements and milestones confront the candidate as they progress in their doctoral studies, concluding with the completion of the dissertation. Deegan and Hill (1991) describe the doctoral dissertation process as "a liminal journey, a passage characterized by ambiguity, uncertainty and crisis" (p. 322) in which the candidate must overcome internal barriers for success. The final milestone is recognized as the culmination point for becoming an independent scholar and researcher (Golde, Bueschel, Jones, & Walker, 2006; Lovitts, 2008; Walker, Golde, Jones, Bueschel, & Hutchings, 2008). Unfortunately, there is no one right delivery model to meet the diverse needs of graduate students exhibiting differences which vary by times or

R. Land et al. (Eds.), Threshold Concepts in Practice, 155–164.
© *2016 Sense Publishers. All rights reserved.*

phases of the graduate experience (Gardner, 2010). Doctoral education programs, however, must continue to incorporate proven strategies such as the delivery of structured coursework designed to assist the learner toward independence and successful completion (Melles, 2009). Clearly, building competency in research methodology is recognized as an essential part of completing the dissertation for the candidate as they strive to become an independent scholar and researcher.

Threshold concepts are embedded in the teaching and learning of research methodology concepts for doctoral candidates. Understanding more about the role threshold concepts hold in the doctoral experience offers a means to deconstruct and restructure teaching and learning. As Meyer (2012) contends, the process of exploring threshold concepts is "… energising and provoking discussion by faculty about their own courses in their own disciplines, and often leading to the discovery of transformational concepts that occasion epistemic and ontological shifts in their students" (p. 8). By approaching advanced research in social science as a knowledge domain of shared characteristics, our capacity to recognize and identify threshold concepts may increase. As a result, improvements in the teaching and learning of research methodology during the doctoral dissertation phase can occur. In addition, improvements in doctoral education can further advance practices in doctoral candidate supervision.

Irvine and Carmichael (2009) state that "… the idea of threshold concepts can provide a point of focus for reflection-as-action by both teachers and students. Such focused enquiry, set in a non-directive framework which encourages participants to reflect on and elucidate notions of 'value', may provide an alternative to approaches which encourage de-contextualized ideas of 'reflection' or overly generalized commitments to discover 'what works'" (p. 116). For the doctoral student, the effects of intelligence on academic performance are commonly recognized as an essential indicator of potential success. A hungry mind with intellectual curiosity, however, may be considered a core determinant of academic achievement (von Strumm, Hell, & Chamorro-Premuzie, 2011). When combined, intellectual curiosity and intelligence stimulate reflections on discovery. Our contention is that candidates seek to enter a professional community of scholars engaged in high quality social science research. Such recognition draws upon a curiosity to explore the research process as a dynamic web of inquiry from which to achieve success.

Kiley and Wisker (2009) shifted the discussion of threshold concepts to what doctoral-level researchers encounter and the perceptions of supervisors in judging when student threshold crossing may occur. Their work identified six major conceptual challenges which could possibly be classified as threshold concepts:

- "Argument
- Theorising
- Framework
- Knowledge creation
- Analysis and interpretation
- Research paradigm" (p. 439).

Our study explores the underlying elements of key methodological concepts in order to enhance understandings beyond a checklist of established research skills in methods. A checklist of components may be useful to ensure inclusion of all essential steps in research methods, however, each social science path of inquiry represents a unique conceptual framework from which to reflect upon and visualize alternative design decisions (Moss, Phillips, Erickson, Floden, Lather, & Schneider, 2009). From this perspective each social science researcher must extend their methodological thinking beyond mimicry and bring their own voice to a unique inquiry. This process places considerable demands upon the doctoral candidate as they engage in complex considerations when designing and conducting a dissertation study.

Thinking about research methodology offers a path into the complex challenges candidates encounter. Developing a social science study design can be potentially over simplified into a linear sequence of selecting a topic, then framing the problem statement, purpose, focus, and research questions. The doctoral candidate must also apply the appropriate research paradigm and theoretical perspective to their construction of a credible research design. As straight forward as this sequence appears, the doctoral candidate is confronted with an overwhelming number of methodological decisions prior to implementing their research study which geometrically expand with each step taken (Salmona, Kaczynski, & Smith, 2015).

Doctoral education has adopted a wide range of phrases and metaphors to describe the bounded space doctoral candidates enter. Some of these descriptors portray the candidate as a student traveler on a journey, undergoing a rite of passage, or other rituals in which the doctoral student experiences a transformation of self (Keefer, 2015; Kiley, 2009; Kamler & Thomson, 2008). Such labels position doctoral education as a daunting process in which many graduate students feel unprepared to transition forward and are impeded from successful completion (Lovitts, 2008). For this study the notion of liminality as a metaphor for bounded space (Land, Rattray, & Vivian, 2014) provides a means to illuminate such a setting in which to explore doctoral candidate relationships with methodological threshold concepts and the challenges of overcoming impediments.

STUDY DESIGN

The following is a list of generic desirable competencies which the authors identified by drawing upon a combined total of over 35 years' experience as doctoral supervisors. This stage of the inquiry was purposely taken to provide a starting point of potential methodological challenges from which to clarify the scope of the study. Each competency represents a skill which supervisors and external examiners would likely seek from doctoral candidates.

- Building a logical cohesive scholarly argument
- Recognizing when to bring theory into the study
- Gaining critical value from the literature to the study

- Progressing from description to analysis
- Credible evidence-based analysis and interpretation
- Contributing trustworthy high quality research

Competencies such as these represent abstract constructs which doctoral candidates find challenging to master due to the inherent ambiguity in subjectively determining success. For example, at what point, or how, does a candidate know when their dissertation is convincing, of critical value, credible and trustworthy? Given these uncertainties, our study set out to explore what is considered to comprise essential threshold concepts of doctoral education in social science methodology. Such an investigation raised the issue of identifying the space where threshold concepts may be found. Threshold concepts exhibit the characteristics of being transformative, irreversible, bounded, and comprised of troublesome knowledge (Meyer & Land, 2003). Methodological competencies are recognized to be bounded within the structure of doctoral studies. The study therefore was positioned to explore a bounded space where doctoral candidates pursue troublesome methodological irreversible knowledge which promotes their scholarly transformation.

A survey instrument was developed to explore potential threshold concepts in research methodology from the perspective of doctoral faculty, supervisors, candidates, and examiners. The survey was delivered online using the Qualtrics software program. All members of the International Doctoral Education Research Network (IDERN) were invited by email to complete the survey. IDERN was formed in 2007 as a global forum for researchers to explore and promote a collaborative international research agenda into doctoral education. The listserve is maintained by the University of Wisconsin. In addition, an open invitation to participate in the survey was posted on the QUALRS-L, an international qualitative interest group listserve which is maintained by the University of Georgia.

FINDINGS

A total of 41 respondents completed the online survey. Of this sample, 14 respondents were doctoral candidates and the remaining 27 respondents self-identified in multiple roles as doctoral faculty, supervisors, and examiners (see Table 1).

Table 1. Respondent categories

Self-identified categories	
Doctoral Candidates:	14
Doctoral Supervisors:	15
Doctoral Panel or Committee Members:	12
Doctoral Examiners:	12
Other (exit survey)	5

The intent of the study design was to gather initial reactions and discussions by drawing from a mix of roles. As this sample represents responses from two global researcher forums, the data provided an internationally diverse exploration of what the participants considered as comprising essential threshold concepts of social science methodology from both novice and experienced academics engaged in social science doctoral education.

Question two of the survey involved an open response identification of the "5 most important concepts in the research process". The intent of this question was to encourage respondents to reflect upon their own views of social science inquiry. Responses were open coded to promote the construction of multiple meanings from a qualitative research paradigm. Patterns were then coded and grouped based upon commonality. Through this approach the following 10 categories were identified representing what respondents considered as important concepts in the research process. Identifying these concepts was important as it then allowed the authors to return to the literature and compare the findings from this study to previous work. Each of the bullets represents a respondent theme grounded in the literature which informed this study. Table 2 is then provided as an overview of these key points grounding the study in the literature.

- Framing a Social Science Argument (Melles, 2009)
- Literature Review (Wisker, 2015)
- Theoretical Framework (Salmona et al., 2015)
- Methods Competency in Data Collection (Kaczynski, Salmona, & Smith, 2014)
- Analysis (Kiley & Wisker, 2009)
- Ethical Conduct, Protection of Human Subjects (Ward, 2013)
- Write, Write, Write (Humphrey & Simpson, 2012)
- Independence – Persistence – Creativity – Confidence (von Strumm et al., 2011)
- Academic Integrity – Respecting the Discipline (Trafford & Leshem, 2009)
- Issues of Quality (Moss et al., 2009)

Question three of the survey provided a table in which respondents were asked to translate what they considered to be important concepts in the research process into four characteristics of threshold concepts; transformative, integrative, irreversible, and troublesome (Meyer & Land, 2005). A few of the respondents, expressed uncertainty in completing the table and difficulty in drawing distinctions between their role as supervisor and their practices in research.

Respondents indicated the degree of fit they considered their important concepts in the research process identified in question two shared characteristics with threshold concepts. The degrees of fit choices were either positive, negative, or unsure. On average, 70% to 85% indicated a positive response with the remaining responses as unsure or negative. This disconnect may suggest a perceived difficulty in applying a general discussion of the challenges involving the doctoral research process to a threshold concepts framework.

Table 2. Comparing study findings to previous work

Conceptual challenges (Kiley and Wisker, 2009)	Desirable competencies	Important concepts from study	Proposed threshold concepts from survey
Argument	Building a logical cohesive scholarly argument	Framing a Social Science Argument	Conceptualising framing the argument from purpose through study focus to research questions
Theorising	Recognizing when to bring theory into the study	Theoretical Framework	Show how theory underpins the study design with strong connections
Framework	Gaining critical value from the literature to the study	Literature Review	Demonstrating a coherent and in-depth understanding through a well-organised review of literature
Knowledge creation	Progressing from description to analysis	Methods competency in data collection	Design a robust study that will produce trustworthy outcomes regardless of philosophical paradigm
Analysis and interpretation	Credible evidence-based analysis and interpretation	Analysis	Conceptualise the difference between inductive and deductive thinking and how to grapple with multiple meanings
Research paradigm	Contributing trustworthy high quality research	Writing, Characteristics, Integrity and Ethics	Develop a strong plan to complete the work with deadlines. Be persistent, ethically aware, creative and confident about producing trustworthy and valid research. Respect the discipline. Write, write, write

The final question of the survey allowed respondents to provide open ended comments regarding their research studies. Responses reinforced perceptions that were categorized earlier in question two. In addition, several comments reflected upon the transformational nature of experiencing the research process. This is of particular interest in this study as the purpose sets out to explore what is considered to comprise essential threshold concepts of social science methodology. What we found was something different. Insights into transformational shifts may illuminate a deeper understanding of the research process. In this study the research process was described by respondents as a journey where the researcher is moving beyond accepted theory, exploring more levels of nuance to knowledge and acknowledging the uniqueness of the experience and challenges for each social science researcher.

CONCLUSIONS

Findings from this study are intended to stimulate further inquiry into the transformational journey which social science doctoral candidates experience. The actual process of accessing the liminal space (Keefer, 2015; Land et al., 2014; Ward, 2013) in which doctoral candidates enter is of particular interest in this discussion. As earlier found in a series of teaching and learning in higher education projects, we found in this study that both candidates and faculty view methodological threshold concepts as "ways of thinking and practicing" (Entwistle, 2005, p. 5). As Trafford and Leshem (2009) suggest, perhaps demonstrating an awareness of being in liminality and the difficulties of contending with troublesome knowledge associated with the doing and achieving of a doctorate, in itself, is a threshold concept. In this sense the resulting ontological shifts which the doctoral candidate experiences may represent a threshold concept gateway which provides a framework to explore advances in the mastery of social science research.

Consider the notion of a liminal space in which doctoral candidates must enter to complete their dissertation. In this space the candidate is confronted with many dichotomies. Dichotomies are viewed in this discussion to represent two contrasting perspectives to a shared concept. By its nature, such a contrast creates a troublesome tension which the doctoral candidate confronts. In this sense each dichotomy represents an entry point into liminal space. Exits from this liminal space require the candidate to reach resolution with each dichotomy.

From the survey results of this study we have identified potential dichotomies of troublesome knowledge which may offer entry points into liminal space. The list includes:

- Inductive reasoning / Deductive reasoning
- Methods / Theory
- Discipline Theory / Research Theory
- Trustworthiness / Validity
- Truth / Multiple Meanings
- My Research / My Student's Research

Such a listing of dichotomies is helpful in the identification of potential troublesome tensions. Although recognition of difficult concepts can aid in instructional delivery and curriculum reform, these dichotomies are intended to represent insights into threshold concepts beyond procedural aspects of identifying research methodology. Of greater value is the consideration that dichotomies may be used as portals into liminal space and that entry may be beneficial for the doctoral student.

As discussed earlier, the actual entry process into liminal space is an intriguing notion for doctoral faculty and supervisors to consider. If our instructional objectives include the stimulation of creative insights by doctoral candidates then we should carefully consider that student entry into liminal space is a desirable outcome. What then can we do to promote this process? Findings from this study are intended to draw attention to the potential value and importance of student entry into liminal space as a transition or threshold crossing (Kiley & Wisker, 2009) which should be encouraged in a positive way. Keefer (2015) found in his study that doctoral candidates reported that "liminality was often hidden from discussion" (p. 25). His conclusion calls for "future research to explore whether active supervisory discussion of doctoral liminality could alleviate potential despair and positively affect postgraduate attrition and retention" (p. 26). The critical importance of support mechanisms for the doctoral candidate can be drawn from this discussion. Scaffolding represents a related, if not directly spoken, concept of building sociocultural connections for the student to form relationships with troublesome knowledge. Given appropriate scaffolding, learners can externalize their thinking by building connections to their immediate environment (Bogard, Liu, & Chiang, 2013). Our findings suggest that we must learn to approach liminal space as a positive experience from which to investigate troublesome knowledge in a setting that promotes creativity, inductive insights, and the generation of new knowledge.

Both supervisors and students are urged to appreciate that the tensions discovered when unpacking these dichotomies may provide an important path into liminal space. Dealing with these tensions will involve the deconstruction and restructuring of research methodology concepts. As doctoral candidates struggle, supervisors must ensure that teaching and learning strategies are in place to help candidates overcome resistance to engaging with troublesome knowledge. We, as supervisors and teachers, must learn how to help students to better identify when they are stuck and to appreciate stuckness as a first step to an enjoyable journey. In this discussion we envision the exit from liminal space to occur as the doctoral candidate successfully completes and defends their dissertation study. Gaining the most knowledge while in liminal space may ultimately represent the most important instructional objective.

REFERENCES

Bogard, T., Liu, M., & Chiang, Y. V. (2013). Thresholds of knowledge development in complex problem solving: A multiple-case study of advanced learners' cognitive processes. *Educational Technology Research and Development, 61*(3), 465–503.

Bourke, S., Holbrook, A., Lovat, T., & Farley, P. (2004). *Attrition, completion and completion times of PhD candidates.* Paper presented at the meeting of the Australian Association for Research in Education, Melbourne, AU.

Deegan, M. J., & Hill, M. R. (1991). Doctoral dissertations as liminal journeys of the self: Betwixt and between in graduate sociology programs. *Teaching Sociology, 19*(3), 322–332.

Entwistle, N. (2005). Learning outcomes and ways of thinking across contrasting disciplines and settings in higher education. *Curriculum Journal, 16*(1), 67–82.

Gardner, S. (2010). Contrasting the socialization experience of doctoral students in high- and low-completing departments: A qualitative analysis of disciplinary contexts at one institution. *The Journal of Higher Education, 81*(1), 61–81.

Golde, C. M., Bueschel, A. C., Jones, L., & Walker, G. E. (2006). Apprenticeship and intellectual community: Lessons from the Carnegie Initiative on the Doctorate. In *Conference proceedings of the National Conference on Doctoral Education and the Faculty of the Future.* Cornell University, Ithaca, NY: The Carnegie Foundation for the Advancement of Teaching.

Grasso, M., Barry, M., & Valentine, T. (2009). *A data-driven approach to improving doctoral completion* (Occasional Paper). Washington, DC: Council of Graduate Schools.

Group of Eight. (2013, March). *The changing PhD* (Discussion Paper). Turner, ACT, Australia: Author.

Humphrey, R., & Simpson, B. (2012). Writes of passage: Writing up qualitative data as a threshold concept in doctoral research. *Teaching in Higher Education, 17*(6), 735–746.

Irvine, N., & Carmichael, P. (2009). Threshold concepts: A point of focus for practitioner research. *Active Learning in Higher Education, 10*(2), 103–119.

Kaczynski, D., Salmona, M., & Smith, T. (2014). Qualitative research in finance. *Australian Journal of Management, 39*(1), 127–135.

Kamler, B., & Thomson, P. (2008). The failure of dissertation advice books: Toward alternative pedagogies for doctoral writing. *Educational Researcher, 37*(8), 507–514.

Keefer, J. M. (2015). Experiencing doctoral liminality as a conceptual threshold and how supervisors can use it. *Innovations in Education and Teaching International, 52*(1), 17–28.

Kiley, M. (2009). Identifying threshold concepts and proposing strategies to support doctoral candidates. *Innovations in Education and Teaching International, 46*(3), 293–304.

Kiley, M., & Wisker, G. (2009). Threshold concepts in research education and evidence of threshold crossing. *Higher Education Research & Development, 28*(4), 431–441.

Land, R., Rattray, J., & Vivian, P. (2014). *A closer look at liminality: Incorrigibles and threshold capital.* Proceedings of the National Academy's Sixth Annual Conference and the Fourth Biennial Threshold Concepts Conference, Ireland.

Lovitts, B. (2008). The transition to independent research: Who makes it, who doesn't, and why. *The Journal of Higher Education, 79*(3), 296–325.

Melles, G. (2009). Global perspectives on structured research training in doctorates of design – what do we value? *Design Studies, 30*(3), 255–271.

Meyer, J. H. F. (2012). Variation in student learning as a threshold concept. *Journal of Faculty Development, 26*(3), 8–13.

Meyer, J. H. F., & Land, R. (2003). Threshold concepts and troublesome knowledge: Linkages to ways of thinking and practising within the disciplines. In C. Rust (Ed.), *Improving student learning: Improving student learning theory and practice – Ten years on.* Oxford: Oxford Centre for Staff and Learning Development.

Meyer, J. H. F., & Land, R. (2005). Threshold concepts and troublesome knowledge (2): Epistemological considerations and a conceptual framework for teaching and learning. *Higher Education, 49*(3), 373–388.

Moss, P. A., Phillips, D. C., Erickson, F. D., Floden, R. E., Lather, P. A., & Schneider, B. L. (2009). Learning from our differences: A dialogue across perspectives on quality in education research. *Educational Researcher, 38*(7), 501–517.

Salmona, M., Kaczynski, D., & Smith, T. (2015). Qualitative theory in finance: Theory into practice. *Australian Journal of Management, 40*(3), 403–413.

Trafford, V., & Leshem, S. (2009). Doctorateness as a threshold concept. *Innovations in Education and Teaching International, 46*(3), 305–316.

von Strumm, S., Hell, B., & Chamorro-Premuzic, T. (2011). The hungry mind: Intellectual curiosity is the third pillar of academic performance. *Perspectives on Psychological Science, 6*(6), 574–588.

Walker, G. E., Golde, C. M., Jones, L., Bueschel, A. C., & Hutchings, P. (2008). *The formation of scholars: Rethinking doctoral education for the twenty-first century.* San Francisco, CA: Jossey-Bass.

Ward, M. H. (2013). *Living in liminal space: The PhD as accidental pedagogy* (Doctoral Thesis). University of Sydney, Australia. Retrieved from http://ses.library.usyd.edu.au/handle/2123/9397

Wisker, G. (2015). Developing doctoral authors: Engaging with theoretical perspectives through the literature review. *Innovations in Education and Teaching International, 52*(1), 64–74.

Michelle Salmona
Institute for Mixed Methods Research

Dan Kaczynski
Central Michigan University & University of Canberra

Leigh N. Wood
Macquarie University

GINA WISKER

13. BEYOND BLOCKAGES TO OWNERSHIP, AGENCY AND ARTICULATION

Liminal Spaces and Conceptual Threshold Crossing in Doctoral Learning

OVERVIEW

Research into doctoral student learning has focused on stages of the learning journey (Wisker et al., 2010), communities (Wisker et al., 2003; Vekkaila, Pyhältö, & Lonka, 2013; Wisker & Morris, 2010; Holbrook et al., 2003) and doctoral 'orphans' (Wisker & Robinson, 2012). Building on that earlier work, this research is concerned with how doctoral students identify and deal with two kinds of blockage in their research learning journey: problems with the supervisor, and a struggle with writing or articulation. Students report silencing, loss of confidence and paralysis in their work with each of these blockages, but offer evidence of strategies which can overcome the problems so that they move on in their research and writing. Identifying and tackling the issues with changed behaviours and ownership of their work are, I argue, often evidence of conceptual threshold crossings (Wisker & Kiley, 2009).

Re-scrutiny of the data from three earlier projects and new data gathered for this project involving face-to-face and email interviews offers insights into the ways in which doctoral students identify blockages and meet and cross conceptual thresholds in their work. It indicates how they evidence and articulate their awareness of moving forward to the achievement of their doctoral learning journeys and identities as researchers and writers, through ownership, agency and articulation.

INTRODUCTION

If only I'd known that I was just in a stuck place it would have made it so much easier. (Kiley, 2014)

Research reported here considers how, in their work, doctoral students identify and deal with the two kinds of stuck places and liminal spaces which have emerged from the data:

- Relationship (problems) with supervisor,
- Writing (a struggle with articulation).

R. Land et al. (Eds.), Threshold Concepts in Practice, 165–176.
© *2016 Sense Publishers. All rights reserved.*

Students report silencing, loss of confidence and paralysis in their work with each of these blockages. Successful strategies are suggested in the data leading to breakthroughs – conceptual threshold crossings – for some.

Research into doctoral student learning tends to concentrate on three broad areas: the functional issues – strategies of research, and supervisory practices to support those strategies; issues to do with learning and the metacognition that engages with that learning; and more recently there have been links made between issues and practices of wellbeing more broadly concerned with success in learning.

In any of the areas of relationships with the supervisor and with writing, among others, there can be problems during the learning journey, and there are also findings about practices which support the journey. Our own research (Wisker et al., 2007–2010; Report 2010) linked all the elements of the journey together. This and other research has focused on stages of the learning journey built on theories of meta-learning (Flavell, 1977), threshold concepts (Meyer & Land, 2003, 2005; Land, Cousin, Meyer, & Davies, 2005, 2006), and our own earlier work, particularly doctoral learning journeys (2007–2010). There has also been a focus on communities (Wisker et al., 2003), troublesome encounters (Vekkaila, Pyhältö, & Lonka, 2013; Wisker & Morris, 2010; Holbrook et al., 2003), and doctoral 'orphans' (Wisker & Robinson, 2012, 2013), respecting the links between the personal, a sense of wellbeing and ontological security, and the learning process during the doctorate. Research and theorising considers transition and transformation in learning processes and learners' identity (Vygotsky, 1978); liminality and 'not knowing' in learning; reflective learning (Schön, 1983, 1987; Mezirow et al., 1990); fostering transformative and emancipatory learning amongst adults; academic disciplines and communities (Becher & Trowler, 1989); and the various blocks to learning and the transitions which enable it to be clarified and embedded. The latter is a situation and process defined by Lather (1998) as moving through liminal spaces, and 'praxis', taking the transformational change into practice.

Developing supportive academic communities of practice (Lave & Wenger, 1991) has been shown to provide ongoing sharing, support and mutual learning among communities of doctoral learners. Power and authority emerge as issues in student supervisor relations (Manathunga, 2007; Grant, 2008) and in the right to write and contribute to new knowledge, and the research and writer identity. Research on writing and overcoming writing blocks indicates issues wrapped up with doctoral learner identity as well as managing the writing energy (Wisker & Savin Baden, 2009). Recently, Lucia Thesen identifies the 'deep structure of postgraduate research and its central function, to make new knowledge. This will always involve profound issues of power and authority which are experienced as dilemmas' (2013). This work looks at such issues as dilemmas with the supervisor, power, authority, and issues with writing blocks, breakthroughs, and ways of supporting and enabling the kind of self-awareness, perseverance and autonomy which lead to doctoral student success.

Research into student success at undergraduate and postgraduate level identifies mind states and behaviours as playing a big part. David Wilkinson mentions the negative and then positive stories a student might tell themselves, of success or failure in the viva, for example (Wilkinson, 2011) and when considering undergraduates, Horstmanshof and Zimitat (2007) talk about persistence. Our own earlier work on doctoral wellbeing and the part that supervisors can play in this (Morris & Wisker, 2011) also identifies characteristics of perseverance, imagining forward a positive way of working and succeeding, and strategies for wellbeing and support.

Learner disposition (Perkins et al., 2000) could begin to explain some of the positive strategies doctoral students can use to maintain their research and writing and to make 'learning leaps' and cross conceptual thresholds to produce conceptual, critical and creative work. In considering learner disposition, Ray Land asks about dispositions which might help students get through the liminal state more effectively and uses work from 'PsyCap' (Luthans, Youssef, & Avolio, 2007) as 'an individual's positive psychological state of development' to identify those dispositions, characterised by:

1. Self-efficacy – having confidence to take on and put in the necessary effort to succeed at challenging tasks (Bandura, 1997, 2002; Schunk, 2011);
2. Optimism – making a positive attribution about succeeding now and in the future;
3. Hope – persevering toward goals and, when necessary, redirecting paths to goals in order to succeed; and
4. Resilience – when beset by problems and adversity, sustaining and bouncing back and even beyond to attain success (Luthans et al., 2007, p. 3).

Land notes: 'Thus a learner who believes they are capable of making sense of troublesome and initially just-out-of reach knowledge is more likely to expend effort on trying to understand the new idea and more likely to cross the threshold than one with no such belief' (Land, 2014). These characteristics could offer insight into the strategies for continuation and success noted by respondents in the research.

Conceptual threshold crossings or 'learning leaps' emerged in our early work as a term to identify stages of breakthroughs in the kinds and quality of learning during the research learning journeys of doctoral students. While threshold concepts are seen as key concepts to unlock the ways in which disciplines perceive how knowledge is constructed and understood, and were initially identified at the undergraduate level, they characterise the moments in research learning when students have breakthroughs in their thinking and understanding and start to work in more conceptual, critical and creative ways.

Conceptual threshold crossings resemble threshold concepts, described as 'akin to a portal, opening up a new and previously inaccessible way of thinking about something. It represents a transformed way of understanding, or interpreting, or viewing something without which the learner cannot progress…' (Meyer & Land,

2003). They are each transformative, irreversible, integrative and show engagement with troublesome knowledge.

Conceptual threshold crossings refer to *stages* in research learning when students make breakthroughs in their thinking, understanding, researching and writing. At postgraduate level, they evidence *ontological change*: change in the way you see yourself in the world and changes in learner identity, and *epistemological contribution*: change in the way you construct knowledge and see yourself as a creator-owner and user of knowledge. Students who cross conceptual thresholds in their work show that they are (more) confident, assured, clear, and their work is (more) conceptual, critical and creative.

LEARNING MOMENTS/CROSSING CONCEPTUAL THRESHOLDS

Research students gain threshold concepts in their discipline or the inter-disciplines which often form doctoral work, and they also, it is hoped, cross conceptual thresholds in their work and contribute to knowledge during the course of their doctorate (and possibly also their master's). Some of our research has identified supervisors and examiners who realise that doctorates have been gained while few if any thresholds have been crossed, producing work which is just 'good enough', but in terms of the good or mediocre thesis (Kiley & Mullins, 2002) this would probably lack challenge, risk-taking, coherence and a clear sense of contribution.

Doctorates which enable breakthroughs in thinking, crossing conceptual thresholds and being aware of the contribution to knowledge at conceptual critical and creative levels are not always a straightforward journey of course. There are blockages and hurdles as well as opportunities, nudges and revelations. Students often perceive blockages as major issues which they need the strength to overcome, as the role of subcultural gossip about doctoral learning journeys reveals. One of our respondents commented at the start of their learning journey that:

> OK. That's reassuring. I'm hearing horror stories of failed marriages and the sky falling on one's head. I'm not coming under any of it. My conviction of self and purpose is strong; this is the chance of a lifetime. It would be great to explore and push some boundaries too. That I'll not be able to help... Can't help myself... (2, C)

Stuck places before breakthroughs take place can be seen in terms of what Patti Lather (1998) and others talk of as 'liminal spaces', particularly with regard to learning development moments, those related to writing clarity and the breakthroughs in thinking which suddenly precede it. These liminal spaces are good descriptions of moments before realizing the main dialogue in a literature review, what main theories help you address your research question, and what methodological approach you should take to approach that research. They also precede understandings about what the data tells us, and what overall knowledge the research findings are making, so that liminal space moments are understandable as transformational. That is the positive reading; for some they might well be dead ends, from which no revelation or movement forwards takes place, a kind of unpleasant, unbreakable research silo. It is possible that students freeze up at these points, when they cannot make headway with their supervisor, their methodology and methods, contribution to the literature, research activities, or writing.

Specifically focusing on liminality and breakthroughs, positive thoughts from the literature engage with moments related to understanding, conceptual threshold crossing, and to articulation.

Liminality can be defined as when students are on the threshold of deeper conceptual understandings, often becoming frustrated, losing confidence or dropping out (Land, Cousin, Meyer, & Davies, 2005).

> Gaining clearer insights into why some students find it troublesome both to understand and to express particular threshold concepts, and into why certain students undergo a transformational or even creative experience in what we have termed the liminal space of learning, whilst others clearly get 'stuck', is…a quest well worth pursuing. (Meyer & Land, 2005)

Lather (1998) seeking a 'praxis of stuck places', offers a narrative located within feminist and poststructural problematics, 'contrasting the rhetorical position of the "the one who knows" with a thinking within Derrida's "ordeal of the undecidable"'. She argues for 'a praxis of not being so sure', and advocates the practices of feminist pedagogy:

> where the effort is to speak from discontinuities, the failures of language, self deception, guilty pleasures, and vested interests: what Ellsworth calls 'a speech which comes from elsewhere' to provoke something else into happening – something other than the return of the same. (Lather, 1998, p. 492)

A praxis of stuck places might tolerate 'discrepancies, repetitions, hesitations, and uncertainties, always beginning again' (ibid, p. 491). What it refuses is:

> the privileging of containment over excess, thought over affect, structure over speed, linear causality over complexity, and intention over aggregate capacities. Ontological changes and category slippages mark the exhaustion of received categories of mind/body, nature/culture, base/superstructure, and spiritual/secular. (ibid, p. 497)

The last quotation from Lather suggests that the clarity of view and understanding which comes from moving through the liminal space leads to different ways of considering learning and its achievements and expression. In our discussion here, this refers to research learning. The features of crossing liminal spaces also remind us of the alternatives: containment through over theorizing, over structuring (at the expense of quick thinking? conceptual work?), and a reductive reliance on linear causality, so missing the challenge, risk-taking, complex thought and findings. Lather's understanding of praxis, thinking and practice coming together as we move on through liminal spaces involves new energies and a rejection of binary oppositions between mind and body, nature and culture. She locates this thinking in feminist theory, with which I align my own work, however/and I would argue that such generosity, challenge, riskiness and new conceptual, creative thinking is possible in much research. I haven't found a discipline which prevents it, even though the expectations of processes and the characteristics of what might be seen as only 'good enough' could well indicate limits in such breakthroughs in thinking and practice on the research journey.

Liminal spaces can be considered as opportunities for stalling, but also for movement through to conceptual threshold crossing in terms of several categories of development two of which are considered here: writing, and working with supervisors.

METHODOLOGY AND METHODS

This research is concerned with how doctoral students identify and deal with two kinds of blockage and breakthroughs – stuck places and liminal spaces – in their work:

- Relationship (problems) with supervisor,
- Writing (a struggle with articulation)

Students report silencing, loss of confidence and paralysis in their work with each of these blockages. Successful strategies are suggested in the data leading to breakthroughs – conceptual threshold crossings – for some.

An interpretivist constructivist approach was taken using a two-part structure in order to maximise the usefulness of established data which had emerged from earlier projects, but had not been considered fully in terms of these issues, and to build on this with a small new research project focusing directly on these issues. The work is in two related parts:

1. Re-scrutiny of the data from two earlier projects (2007–2010, (1a); 2009 (1b)) and
2. New data gathered from face-to-face and email interviews with doctoral students and supervisors internationally in a range of disciplines (2013–2014 (2)). Each focuses specifically on conceptual threshold crossing in doctoral students' research learning journeys, and the identification of blockages to and breakthroughs in relation to relations with supervisors and writing.

The earlier projects 1a and 1b were carefully re-read through and re-scrutinised, and themes which had earlier emerged but not been focused on were brought to the fore and data analysed and interpreted to enable their discussion. Several themes emerged, of which working with the supervisor and articulation emerged from this rescrutiny and from the focus of this piece. Following this rescrutinising and identification of themes, new research was undertaken asking students and supervisors in the UK and international contexts about their stuck places, liminal spaces and ways of moving through these to successful completion. There are several other themes which have emerged which will inform further work and reports.

The projects offer insights into the ways in which doctoral students experience blockages, deal with stuck places, transitional and troublesome moments in their learning journeys and how they identify, meet and cross conceptual thresholds in their work. The data indicates how they evidence and articulate their awareness of engaging with transformational knowledge, moving forward to achievement of their doctoral learning journeys and identities as researchers and writers, through ownership, agency and articulation.

DATA AND DISCUSSION

The themes of stuck places, breakdowns and breakthroughs in the two areas, work with supervisor, and writing development, emerged from my re-reading the data from the Doctoral Learning Journeys (and parallel project) (Wisker et al., 2010) (1a) and writing research (Wisker & Savin-Baden, 2009) (1b).

Defamiliarisation, uncertainty and new disorder can lead to breakthroughs and interception, which then has to be turned into work, structuring, articulation.

Doctoral students identify being stuck and in a liminal space:

> ... you see in one sense I want to say hitting a blank wall but in another sense it isn't because it, it's only a very momentary experience, when I'm thinking 'oh where am I going with this, what's happening' because I just keep going and doing something until it makes sense. (1a, J)

> And 'I hit a brick wall'; 'I stopped moving'; or 'I reached a plateau'. (1a, J)

Reported conceptual threshold crossings are described with metaphors and in relation to the senses – using auditory, kinaesthetic and visual imagery:

> 'ding goes the bell'; 'it clicked into place'; 'a light went on'; 'the fog cleared'; 'a jigsaw piece coming together'; 'a good feeling, like an adrenaline rush creating feelings of pride that you are going to write a good PhD'; 'a peeling away of layers of arrogance'; 'getting through a mountain'; 'ideas coming together and learning to think more realistically'; and 'a narrative weaving a pattern'. (1b, K)

Problem Area (A) Identifying and Dealing Positively with Challenges in the Supervisory Relationship

Problems with supervisors were many. Usually these centred round lack of guidance, accessibility, broken relationships, not understanding the guidance and finding the feedback damaging, even paralysing. For one student, the breakdown with the

171

supervisor caused a breakdown in their work, followed by using the institutional process to change supervisor, with a more positive result.

> ... I reached a stone wall. I thought I would have to drop the entire Ph.D. idea.

> 'I not only changed advisors, but I totally changed programs'; 'I not only changed programs but countries – there were different demands made on me. (1b, B)

At which point in relation to their thesis: 'Parts had to be researched and much of it re-written'. They had a feeling of anxiety 'from having different perspectives and making new demands'. However, the new advisor 'knew the field I was working in extremely well, thus being able to give me the necessary direction' (1b, B). They built bridges with the new supervisor and were closely in touch. What worked for another with supervisor issues was 'the well-built program, an interested supervisor, my own drive and compulsion' (1b, N). One suffered an initial loss of self esteem but 'after that I pulled myself together and said it's my work, I will manage... I became calm' (1b H). What helped was 'the drive to finish' – 'I decided to finish the Ph.D. no matter what', plus family support (1b H).

In these tales of loss of supervisor and breakdown in relationships due to lack of communication and misunderstandings, the resilience, perseverance, optimism and hope of the students helped their development (Luthans et al., 2007, p. 3).

Supervisors were also aware of demands of taking on new students and suggested strategies for 'nudging' their work to continue and to achieve conceptual, critical and creative levels. One noted:

> we touched on the importance of deconstructing the construct and that was quite a big discussion between us, that it's not always about building up but actually about pulling apart.

> ... one thing I think is very important and powerful question that we need to ask all of ourselves, is that we don't place our own map of coherency onto our students...to the point that it suffocates their own different ways of thinking. (2, A)

They offered further reading on conflicting ideas to move their thinking on and enable the students to complete:

> I had to provoke them to think in another way. ...are you sure this is right, read this book then, it says another thing. You have to just wake them. (2, A)

Driven, autonomous learners who work with the new supervisory practice and supervisors who challenge help the student to move on; each enable progress and success. Supervisor flexibility, challenge and support augment the work of supportive communities (families, critical friends and academic others, communities of practice).

Problem Area (B) Stuck Places, Liminal Space and Breakthrough – Writing

Students were aware of getting stuck in their writing and using a variety of strategies to release their thinking, such as exercise, cooking, doing something different, and they commented on the enhanced quality of their writing once they had stepped back and seen the full picture of their work, presented to peers, and written an abstract. Persistence and clarity were important:

> Yeah even when I've felt more confident latterly, I've still had to sit there because all of a sudden I'll get absolutely overwhelmed with 'what am I saying again, you know I've lost it again?' and it's that, trying to keep, keep a hold of it you know what it is I'm trying to say. (1b, J)

Redrafting helps focus:

> I think well that doesn't make sense and you know I might need to do some editing and so then it gets tricky and you might have to get yourself into a 'loop' where you can't see how you are going to get out of this, you know you maybe need to write your way out of it or whatever, so that is to do with getting stuck I suppose. (1b, K)

They experience breakthroughs in their writing which take over even from ambient noise and are often enabled by reflection:

> Most of the time I 'feel' little breakthrough, but then…ping…a knowing leap. I have encountered more of these in the last two years than ever before. Often it is through the processes of writing back, drawing back to myself (2, C)

Students are aware of the delicacy of writing moments, which they have to seize:

> If I recognise a writing interlude in there, I try to make sure everything is in place to accommodate it. But the process of doing that can often destroy it. I have to wait for another. I can't manufacture writing moments. (2, A)

They are aware of moving through a liminal space to breakthrough, multitasking to release creativity, and articulate (Wisker & Savin-Baden, 2009), and persistence as an important characteristic, alongside reflection and really using the right moments to write.

> anything that actually isn't writing that shifts it. (1b, J)

> it's like looking at a kaleidoscope you know and things go out of focus and suddenly they come back in again…and you can see the pattern. (1b, L)

Asked how they moved on, through blocks to writing:

> through persistence I think, through – and the guidance of other people, people telling me that it you know, it's, trying to make sense, I need to make sense of what's being written, what's out there. (1b, J)

They are aware of positive practices to shift stuck places and articulate their thoughts and work. Multitasking, mimicry, reflection, abstracting and standing back to see patterns, sharing in groups, all help, as does realising their own rhythms of writing and right to write. Supervisors also offered insight, support and structured practice to enable students. The main positive developments were empowerment, a sense of ownership resulting from perseverance and the insights into their own achievements and strategies. Reflection enabled them to be aware of their achievements, move through stuck places and produce conceptual, critical and creative work at the right level for a PhD.

CONCLUSIONS

This research focuses specifically on ways in which doctoral students deal with transitional and troublesome moments, stuck places and liminal spaces in their learning journeys, considering their awareness of how and when they identify and engage with transformational knowledge, challenges with supervisor relationships and writing blocks, and success in the development and use of positive supervisory relationships and successful self aware writing strategies. It focuses on their recognition of troublesome, transitional moments, and the ways in which they take ownership and agency, cross conceptual thresholds, articulate their research projects and the contribution of their findings, through a range of strategies, including supportive work with supervisors, engagement with the research literature, developing community support, and above all their own perseverance.

REFERENCES

Bandura, A. (1997). *Self-efficacy: The exercise of control*. New York, NY: Freeman.
Bandura, A. (2002). Social cognitive theory in cultural context. *Applied Psychology: An International Review, 51*, 269–290.
Becher, T., & Trowler P. R. (1989/2001, 2nd ed.). *Academic tribes and territories*. London: McGraw-Hill Education.
Flavell, J. H. (1977). *Cognitive development*. Englewood Cliffs, NJ: Prentice Hall.
Grant, B. M. (2008). Agonistic struggle. Master-slave dialogues in humanities supervision. *Art & Humanities in Higher Education, 7*(1), 9–27.
Holbrook, A., Dally, K., Cantwell, R., Scevak, J., Bourke, S., & Lovat, T. (2003, June). *Doctoral examiners as supervisors*. HERDSA Conference, Christchurch, New Zealand.
Horstmanshof, L., & Zimitat, C. (2007). Future time orientation predicts academic engagement among first-year university students. *British Journal of Educational Psychology, 77*(3), 703–718.
Johansson, T., Wisker, G., Claesson, S., Strandler, O., & Saalman, S. (2014). PhD. supervision as an emotional process – Critical situations and emotional boundary work. *Pertanika: Journal of Social Science and Humanities, 22*, 21.
Kiley, M. (2014, January). *'Now I know why I have been knocking my head against a brick wall': Doctoral candidates and stuck places*. NAIRTL proceedings, Ireland.
Kiley, M., & Mullins, G. (2002). 'It's a PhD, not a Nobel Prize': How experienced examiners assess research theses. *Studies in Higher Education, 27*(4), 369–386.
Kiley, M., & Wisker, G. (2009, November). Threshold concepts in research education and evidence of threshold crossing. *Higher Education Research and Development, 28*(4), 431–441.

Land, R. (2014, January). A closer look at liminality: Incorrigibles and threshold capital in threshold concepts: From personal practice to communities of practice. In C. O'Mahony, A. Buchanan, M. O'Rourke, & B. Higgs (Eds.), *Proceedings of the national academy's sixth annual conference and the fourth biennial threshold concepts conference* [e-publication].

Land, R., Cousin, G., Meyer, J. H. F., & Davies, P. (2005). Threshold concepts and troublesome knowledge (3): Implications for course design and evaluation. In C. Rust (Ed.), *Improving student learning – Diversity and inclusivity. Proceedings of the 12th Improving Student Learning Conference* (pp. 53–64). Oxford: Oxford Centre for Staff and Learning Development (OCSLD). Retrieved from http://www.brookes.ac.uk/services/ocsld/isl/isl2004/abstracts/conceptual_papers/ISL04-pp53-64-Land-et-al.pdf

Land, R., Cousin, G., Meyer, J. H. F., & Davies, P. (2006). Conclusion: Implications of threshold concepts for course design and evaluation. In J. H. F. Meyer & R. Land (Eds.), *Overcoming barriers to student understanding: Threshold concepts and troublesome knowledge* (pp. 195–206). London: Routledge.

Lather, P. (1998). Critical pedagogy and its complicities: A praxis of stuck places. *Educational Theory, 48*(4), 487–497.

Lave, J., & Wenger, E. (1991). *Situated learning: Legitimate peripheral participation.* Cambridge: Cambridge University Press.

Lee, A. (2008). How are doctoral students supervised? Concepts of doctoral research supervision. *Studies in Higher Education, 33*(3), 267–281.

Luthans, F., Youssef, C. M., & Avolio, B. J. (2007). *Psychological capital* (p. 3). New York, NY: Oxford University Press.

Manathunga, C. (2007). Intercultural postgraduate supervision: Ethnographic journeys of identity and power. In D. Palfreyman & D. L. McBride (Eds.), *Learning and teaching across cultures in higher education* (pp. 93, 95). Basingstoke: Palgrave Macmillan.

Meyer, J. H. F., & Land, R. (Eds.). (2003). *Overcoming barriers to student understanding: Threshold concepts and troublesome knowledge.* London/New York, NY: Routledge.

Meyer, J. H. F., & Land, R. (2005). Threshold concepts and troublesome knowledge (2): Epistemological considerations and a conceptual framework for teaching and learning. *Higher Education, 49,* 373–388.

Mezirow, J. (1990). *Fostering critical reflection on adulthood: A guide to transformative and emancipatory learning.* San Francisco, CA: Jossey-Bass.

Morris, C., & Wisker, G. (2011). *Troublesome encounters: Strategies for managing the wellbeing of masters and doctoral education students during their learning processes.* HEA ESCalate Subject Centre Report. Retrieved from http://escalate.ac.uk/6828

Perkins, D., Tishman, S., Richart, R., Donis, K., & Andrade, A. (2000). Intelligence in the wild: A dispositional view of intellectual traits. *Educational Psychology Review, 12*(3), 269–293.

Schön, D. A. (1983). *The reflective practitioner: How professionals think in action.* New York, NY: Basic Books.

Schön, D. A. (1987). *Educating the reflective practitioner.* San Francisco, CA: Jossey-Bass.

Schunk, D. H. (2011). *Learning theories: An educational perspective* (6th ed.). London: Pearson.

Strandler, O., Johansson, T., Wisker, G., & Claesson, S. (2014). Supervisor or counsellor? – Emotional boundary work in supervision. *International Journal of Researcher Development, 5,* 70–82.

Thesen, L. (2013). Risk in postgraduate writing: Voice, discourse and edgework. *Cristal, 1*(1), 105.

Trowler, P., Saunders, M., & Bamber, V. (2012). *Tribes and territories in the 21st-century: Rethinking the significance of disciplines in higher education.* Abingdon & New York, NY: Routledge.

Usher, R., Bryant, I., & Johnson, R. (2002). Self and experience in adult learning. In R. Harrison (Ed.), *Supporting lifelong learning: Perspectives on learning* (pp. 78–90). London: Routledge Falmer.

Vekkaila, J., Pyhältö, K., & Lonka, K. (2013). Experiences of disengagement – A study of doctoral students in the behavioral sciences. *International Journal of Doctoral Studies, 8,* 61–81.

Vygotsky, L., Cole, M., John-Steiner, V., Scribner, S., & Souberman, S. (1978). *Mind in society: Development of higher psychological processes.* Cambridge, MA: Harvard University Press.

Wilkinson, D. (2011). *Email communication to author.*

Wisker, G., Robinson, G., Trafford, V., Warnes, M., & Creighton, E. (2003). From supervisory dialogues to successful PhDs: Strategies supporting and enabling the learning conversations of staff and students at postgraduate level. *Teaching in Higher Education, 8*(3), 383–397.

Wisker, G., Morris, C., Cheng, M., Masika, R., Warnes, M., Trafford,V., ... Lilly, J. (2010). *Doctoral learning journeys–Final report of the NTFS-funded project.* Retrieved from http://www.heacademy.ac.uk/resources/detail/ntfs/Projects/Doctoral_Learning_Journeys

Wisker, G., & Robinson, G. (2012). Doctoral 'orphans': Nurturing and supporting the success of postgraduates who have lost their supervisors. *Higher Education Research and Development, 32*(2), 300–313.

Wisker, G., & Robinson G. (2013). Picking up the pieces: Supervisor and doctoral 'orphans'. *International Journal for Researcher Development, 3*(2), 139–153.

Wisker, G., & Savin-Baden, M. (2009). Priceless conceptual thresholds: Beyond the 'stuck place' in writing. *London Review of Education, 7*(3), 235–247.

Gina Wisker

University of Brighton & University of Johannesburg

PART 5

THRESHOLD CONCEPTS IN PROFESSIONAL PRACTICE

ANTHONY PARKER AND DANIEL MCGILL

14. MODULAR APPROACH AND INNOVATIONS IN AN ENGINEERING PROGRAM DESIGN

INTRODUCTION

The review and restructure of the undergraduate Engineering program at Macquarie University created an opportunity to consider the basic structures and intentions of the degree program. The opportunity to move away from the traditional standard approach of large, disconnected units with little overlap or continuity and the potential for redundancy and duplication within the curriculum, was informed by an increasing awareness of and exposure to the principles of *threshold concepts* in contemporary education theory. In this restructure, each standard twelve-week teaching unit is partitioned into three modules of four-week duration.

This chapter further develops the idea of implementing a modularised Engineering curriculum in an undergraduate program as has been proposed by the authors, Parker and McGill (2014). The implementation of *threshold concepts* in the design of this modular format is described as a singularly important influence in the actual implementation. The innovation of *concept modules* that develop *transformative* and *associative concepts* is reviewed and the application of a *threshold concepts* approach to Engineering pedagogy is demonstrated through case studies presented here.

BACKGROUND REVIEW

The idea of *Threshold Concepts* has been developing since the seminal work of Meyer and Land (2003). There is a growing body of work that is informing innovative curriculum design and practice in undergraduate teaching, postgraduate training, and professional development, Flanagan (2013). While this work is informing teaching practices and emphasis in the classroom, the topic of program wide design remains a subject for ongoing investigation.

Because threshold concepts can be universally applied to all disciplines we have identified this as strategy that can applied to all areas of engineering education. In the early phase of our own program re-development significant challenges were presented by growth in student numbers, the need to orient teaching staff, and the requirement for flexibility. The opportunity was taken to implement an alternative delivery mode based on threshold concepts. The threshold concept approach was

R. Land et al. (Eds.), Threshold Concepts in Practice, 179–193.
© *2016 Sense Publishers. All rights reserved.*

therefore proposed as an elegant means to address the issues associated with curriculum design in our rapidly growing integrated Engineering program, Parker and McGill (2014).

The insight gained from early work related to threshold concepts is that a concept becomes more complex when more than one concept is in focal awareness at one time, Carstensen and Bernhard (2013). From the perspective of threshold concepts, the corollary is that one should be addressed at any one time, Scott and Harlow (2012). Extending this fundamental idea to the design of an entire program of study, each individual teaching unit should address only one troublesome concept, Meyer and Land (2005, 2006). This is the central idea behind the design methodology of an integrated program that is presented here.

Integration

The objectives for the new program were integration of mechanical and electronic fundamentals, identification and provision of flexible student pathways, and accommodation of increased class sizes.

Integrating disciplines into one program of study is at odds with the desire to deliver discipline specific Bodies of Knowledge (BoK). Integration implies a fair portion of common teaching units, so specialisation in terms of the BoK must be limited. However, delivering four-fifths of the program as an integrated offering is consistent with Engineers Australia's recommendation that only one fifth of the program is specialisation specific. The integration can be envisaged in terms four-fifths commonality that share the same threshold concepts while still accommodating streaming of the relevant BoK.

To provide more specialisation specific treatment, common outcomes are typically streamed, so as to be treated in the context of a specific discipline. There is a significant portion of clearly common outcomes, such as those related to professional practice and a component of obviously shared science background, the remaining can be presented in discipline specific contexts. An example would be second-order systems in the context of springs versus tuned circuits. Thus, the BoK delivered for the Electronic specialisation differs from that for Mechanical specialisations by far more than one-fifth of the program.

In terms of threshold concepts, however, the Electronics and Mechanical specialisations have far more in common. For example, whether treated with springs or circuits, the concept of 'second-order systems' is clearly common to both specialisations. Indeed the requirement for an understanding of second-order systems applies to all engineers, so that a Mechanical Engineering graduate would be able to easily appreciate an Electrical equivalent of a second-order mechanical system, or vice versa. Thus, in terms of themes and learning outcomes defined by threshold concepts, diverse specialisations will easily require four-fifths commonality.

Flexibility

A well designed Engineering program should enable students to enter the program with various levels of prior learning, such as trade qualifications, transfers from alternative degrees, or international qualifications. Achieving flexible student pathways requires close matching of future and previous studies. A one-size-fits-all approach is not able to achieve this, so some flexibility in choice is required.

Traditional first year programs comprise eight to a dozen foundation. Recognition of prior learning normally is accommodated on a per unit basis. When these units were modularised, exemptions can be accommodated on the basis of twenty to thirty modules. To achieve this, the nature and definition of each module needs provide room for choice of options within teaching units.

Threshold concepts provide a natural basis for defining modules, Land, Cousin et al. (2005). Teaching units designed in terms of threshold concepts modules enables easier mapping of prior knowledge.

OPPORTUNITY

As the new program is evolving, there is an opportunity to embrace a fresh approach to curriculum design. A modular approach to curriculum design has been identified as one that could enable fundamental notions within the curriculum to be developed in an explicitly coherent manner. In this approach, the core issues are mapped to each other in order to achieve a comprehensive structure where each element is informed by and informs the modules that precede or follow. There is an opportunity to structure a curriculum that allows for the development of deep understanding of the key underpinnings of the program and related disciplinary features. These key outcomes can be more easily interspersed at key points in a modular structure by organising modules into packages that develop threshold concepts.

The new approach that we propose is to set threshold concepts as the theme for a package of modules. Each module in a package is called a *concept module*. In our implementation the sequence of modules respectively introduces, develops and then applies the threshold concept. Thus a typical package would be made up of three modules. Within each module, concepts that we call *associative* are presented to support the development of the *transformative threshold concept*.

ENGINEERING PROGRAM

Australian Engineering programs consider the level of qualification relative to duration of study. A typical four-year Engineering program is packaged into a set of teaching units over eight semesters. Under the Australian Qualification Framework, AQF Council (2013), the last year is a graduate (AQF8) level of study, so the first three years can be considered as an undergraduate program (AQF7). Two levels of qualification are achievable at different time periods.

As an accredited program the learning outcomes and objectives must conform to Engineers Australia's Stage 1 Competencies, Engineers Australia (2011). This imposes a coarse structure to the implementation of learning outcomes and teaching praxis in terms of required competencies and BoK, Bradley (2008).

The program structure ensures that the required units are delivered to meet the overall learning outcomes, Parker and McGill (2009).

The aims of the program are to teach technical skills and knowledge and to develop critical understanding and conceptual approaches to Engineering. The former is typically articulated in a BoK specification while the latter is considered to be an experiential outcome.

Traditional Approach

Learning outcomes for teaching units might well be defined by a required set, or list, of knowledge concepts and technical competencies, in terms of the BoK. This is called this the *Body of Knowledge* (BoK) *approach*. The aim of the unit is merely the presentation of knowledge, and assessment relies on ability to recall the information. Success is measured by coverage of topics rather than student understanding of concepts.

This approach conflates cognate topics from the BoK in to each teaching unit. Traditionally, these are developed sequentially along with, possibly several, relevant threshold concepts. A lesson that comes from the idea of threshold concepts, however, is that it is better to develop only one at a time, Scott and Harlow (2012).

The BoK approach is a distraction from the function of the unit within the overall engineering program, Parker and McGill, (2014). Program design needs to ensure that the integrity of the program objectives is guaranteed, which can be achieved through a measured development of threshold concepts.

Threshold Concepts Approach

The alternative is that the learning outcomes for individual teaching units are defined by a required set, or list, of threshold concepts. That is, the outcome is defined in terms of a required critical understanding and conceptual approaches. The aim of the unit becomes the development of concepts at the required level, underpinned by associated knowledge and skills. This is a *threshold concept approach*.

The implication of this approach is that the top-down design of an Engineering program should be carried out in terms of clearly articulated threshold concepts. This approach addresses the issues of program integrity of delivery, integration, flexibility, and student experience.

The principle is to structure all aspects of program design and teaching around threshold concepts. The basic teaching package should consider only one main threshold concept. In this way, the program should be considered as a coherent development of threshold concepts. This places the emphasis on understanding each concept and mandates the clear articulation, to teachers and students, of the concepts required in the whole of the program, Parker and McGill (2014).

At each point in the curriculum, a threshold concept is precisely specified, developed, and assessed within the teaching package. The technical skills and knowledge topics that are taught at any position in the program should only be those that are appropriate to the concepts that have or are being developed. In this manner topics are incorporated from the BoK at positions in the program taking into consideration the position of the package in the program relative to its own and previously developed concepts. A consequence of this is that certain topics in the BoK will be identified and unreachable in the undergraduate program because the required concepts are yet to be developed.

MODULARISATION

Given that the learning outcomes for an Engineering Program are predicated on a set of *transformative threshold concepts*, the program can be designed in terms of these concepts. Thus the critical understanding and conceptual approaches form a scaffold on which the technical skills and knowledge for the program is supported.

The number of genuine threshold concepts, that is those that are *transformative* in nature, is relatively small, so an Engineering program will have a corresponding small number of *threshold concept packages.*

Concept Hierarchy

There are other difficult concepts that are important for the programs but are not necessarily transformative. These require time and experience to understand, so should be the theme of a distinct teaching module.

These difficult concepts should be developed at a position in the program that is appropriate to the transformative concepts that have or are being developed. Hence there are non-transformative concepts that can be associated with threshold concepts. These *associative concepts* become the learning outcome for modules within the *threshold concept package.*

These ideas come together to form a hierarchical framework for the design of the Engineering Program. At the top level, the program is a set of *threshold concept packages* that develop *transformative threshold concepts*. Each *threshold concept package* is made up of *concept modules* that develop the related *associative concepts*. In the development of its concept, each *concept module* builds skills and knowledge drawn from the BoK. Thus the elements of the BoK are grouped as a customized package within the *associative concepts* that develop the *transformative threshold concepts.*

Threshold Concept Package

The two important characteristics of student's processing of *transformative threshold concepts* are that it is a protracted process that takes time and that only a few such concepts can be simultaneously considered. The implication is that each threshold concepts need to be delivered in a process that is protracted over time and that no more than a few of these should be presented in parallel. To achieve these characteristics in an the design of an integrated program of study, we

- define a *threshold concept package* as a block of teaching activity that extends over a period of time, at least a few weeks or more, and deals with only one *transformative threshold concept*, and
- mandate that no more than a few of these packages will be being presented at any one time.

The innovation presented here is that program is made up of discrete packages that focus on only one threshold concept. The creation of a *threshold concept package* is intended to allocate space within a program of study to provide a focused and staged development of the specific threshold concept.

Concept Modules

The delivery of a specific threshold concept should follow stages of introduction, development, and application. The teaching and learning of the *transformative threshold concept* requires interaction and challenged thinking about difficult ideas. At each stage, an *associative concept* is the means by which learning of the *transformative threshold concept* is scaffolded.

To achieve this, each *threshold concept package* comprises a themed sequence of clearly defined *concept modules*. We define a *concept module* as a sub-block of teaching activity that

- supports the package's *transformative threshold concept*, and
- engages with only one or two *associative concepts*, and
- is presented sequentially within a package

This extends the idea of dealing with only one difficult concept at a time down to discrete teaching modules.

Skills and Knowledge

The curriculum for each concept module comprise specific skills and knowledge topics drawn from the disciplinary BoK that

- develop and engage with the module's concept, and
- are accessible to the student in terms of their pre-requisite understanding, and
- are coherent in terms of the student's development through the program.

The program comprises sequences of *threshold concept packages* that are each formulated in terms of the concept hierarchy. The packages develop each *transformative threshold concept* sequentially through the program. *Associative concepts* inform the teaching activity that delivers relevant BoK topics as well as scaffolding the *transformative threshold concept*. It is likely that the same concepts, albeit at maturing levels, recur as the program progresses. In a similar manner BoK topics are expected to recur at increasing depth inside subsequent packages. This gives a progressive and continuous development where skills and knowledge are incrementally introduced in synch with development of the underpinning threshold concepts. The hierarchy and overlap of sequential *threshold concept packages* is illustrated in Figure 1.

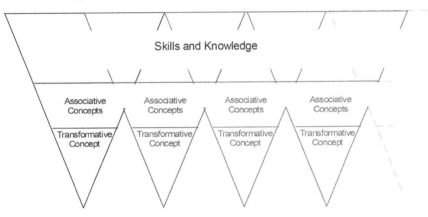

Figure 1. Illustration of the underpinning of the incremental development of skills and knowledge through sequential threshold concept packages

MODULE STRUCTURE

Within each *concept module* there are teaching activities that include, Parker and McGill (2014):

- Weekly lectures of equivalent unilateral delivery of information, such as, reading list, or online media.
- Weekly tutorials or small-group interaction sessions to develop the *associative concept*.
- Regular laboratory or workshops to develop practical skills.

The teaching should place an emphasis on interactive sessions within the module, as these provide the best forum for engaging with difficult concepts. A communication channel from students to teachers is fundamental to ensure the continuity of information throughout the module. Key to the success of this process is the interaction of teaching assistants with the teachers, and the responsiveness of teachers to feedback.

Once a teacher is assigned to a module they become responsible for development and presentation of that module's single precisely defined concept. This implies that the teacher must assess each student's level of prior knowledge at the start and the level of outcome achieved at completion. There needs to be a formal handover process to facilitate an evaluation of each student's understanding of the concepts that should have been developed in prerequisite modules. This protocol allows the success or otherwise of individual modules to be accommodated throughout the delivery of the overall program. Thus, as illustrated in Figure 2, the module begins with an evaluation phase informed by a handover process and concludes with assessments that inform a subsequent handover process. The evaluation phase considers previous work and assessments anticipate subsequent work. The handover implies involvement of both the teaching teams from sequential modules.

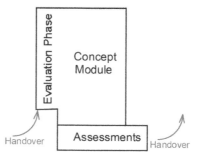

Figure 2. Idealised concept module *structure, which starts with an evaluation of prior knowledge*

The focus on teaching in the module is precisely framed by the *associative concept*, which in turn is supporting the transformative concept of the package. These concepts inform the teaching and assessment activities. Success is measured by the demonstration of the understanding of the concept. Assessment is designed such that familiarity with the BoK is necessarily explicit in the ability to demonstrate understanding of that concept.

For our implementation, there is a thirteen-week semester in which a three credit point teaching unit is delivered. Four such units in parallel constitute a full-time load. This provides for a natural division of a three-credit point teaching unit into three modules each corresponding to one third of the unit. The convenient shape of each module is therefore a four teaching block with a student load of fifty hours. The four-week module involves stages of

- Evaluation during the first week in which understanding of prerequisite concepts is determined,
- Skills and knowledge development and praxis in the body of the module, and
- Reporting and assessment in the last stages of the module.

All of these focus on the development of relevant topics from the BoK.

CONCEPT PACKAGE STRUCTURE

As previously discussed, a *threshold concept package* is a sequence of modules that introduce, develop, and implement a *transformative threshold concept* through the development of *associative concepts*. Provided the primary *transformative threshold concept* remains the focus of teaching, and the package is assessed as a whole, there is a degree of flexibility in the treatment and discipline for the *associative concepts*. Figure 3 illustrates a structure of a package of modules that flexibly develop a *transformative threshold concept*.

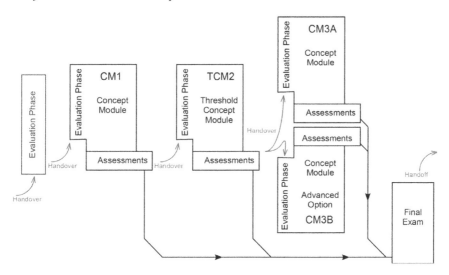

Figure 3. Idealised threshold concept package *structure*

The package structure provides both pedagogical and administrative convenience. Modules are packaged into a single administrative teaching unit with one convenor, formal examination, study guide, and academic result. The modules may have different teachers and continuous assessment activities.

The may also be alternative modules covering the same *associative concept* in different disciplinary contexts. This facilitates flexibility in disciplinary choice, particularly in the foundation years, within the three module grouping. For example, one of the concept outcomes can be delivered in two disciplinary contexts, Mechanical versus Electronics, using parallel modules that students choose between. Coherence of the integration of the disciplines is achieved by maintaining common modules for the other concepts. In addition, specific modules can be repeated throughout the year to assemble bridging units to effectively dovetail with the prior learning background as determined in the evaluation phase in each concept module.

In our implementation, the unit is delivered over thirteen weeks with the first week set aside for evaluation and streaming of students through their choice of modules, which correspond to each student's disciplinary focus. This achieves the required specified outcome while enabling the allocation of specific topics from the BoK to each student.

PROGRAM IMPLEMENTATION

Figure 4 illustrates our structure for the four-year Engineering Program divided into the components that satisfy the accreditation requirements of Engineers Australia. The structure apportions these components of Engineering Competency in accordance with the recommendation of Engineers Australia. That is, one quarter of the program is background that comprises the induction, background, launch pad and foundation components. This is followed by specialisation stream that comprises discipline specific concepts and technical development. Approximately one-third of the program forms a common spine that comprises professional practice, and design and project streams which span the entire program. The remaining one-quarter of the program is allocated to electives and Engineering options where students can develop breadth and depth. A feature that has been applauded in the recent accreditation review is that the development of engineering competencies is integrated contiguously throughout the program.

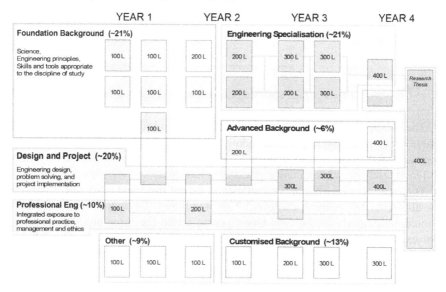

Figure 4. Overall program from 100–400 Level illustrating common and specialisation streaming

In the Foundation Background section, the student deals with the fundamental and intermediate concepts required for the advanced Engineering Specialisation stream.

In the Professional Engineering and the Design and Project streams, the concepts essential for a professional Engineering qualification are delivered. These are common to all disciplines. The first of these modules is an induction package, ENGG100, which is described below.

The Engineering Specialisation stream focuses on a specific discipline leading to a 400-Level capstone package that provides an in-depth treatment. The learning is broadened with a cognate Advanced Background stream. The modular structure allows a refinement of focus towards a specific discipline as the student progresses through the foundation sequence. This prepares the student for the specialisation foundation component, which develops and consolidates concepts in a specific Engineering discipline, culminating in an in-depth treatment in a technical context.

The program includes streams for Customised Background and Other electives, so that a student can pursue other engineering disciplines or accommodate approved double degree combinations.

At the program level, the student is presented with a significantly more accessible statement of their learning outcomes, so their understanding of the structure and direction of their program is more clearly articulated. The emphasis on threshold concepts equips the students for lifelong learning, which enables them to independently fill gaps and further develop the BoK.

IMPLEMENTATION CASE STUDY

Against the background of a introducing the Bachelor of Engineering program the challenge of rapid growth required a program design that was scalable in both load and breadth. A top-down program proposal in 2009, Parker and McGill (2009), was followed by the development of a modular approach to implementation. The decision was made to roll out an entirely modularized program, with the first few teaching units converted in 2013. This roll-out is continuing on the back of the initial success with broad support of the academic staff and Faculty.

Two of six converted units are described below as diverse examples of the implementation of modularization and concepts. These two units are a first-year induction unit (ENGG100) and a third-year technical unit in Electronics Engineering (ELEC376). The concepts addressed in each are 'Transition to University' and 'Weak Nonlinearity' respectively. These concepts transcend the specific topics of professional engineering and electronic systems covered the body of knowledge developed in these units. The concept that moving to a new situation involves a transition is fundamental to a change of setting, job, or culture. Similarly, the concept of weak linearity is fundamental to any discipline where analysis of a complicated interaction is involved.

189

Introduction to Engineering – ENGG100

Designed as the first unit that students engage with when they enrol into the undergraduate Engineering program, the broad purpose of ENGG100 is to induct the student into the expectations and practices of University life, the Department, and Professional Engineering.

Following the model we have proposed here, ENGG100 is designed around the core *transformative threshold concept* of the Transition to University. The issue addressed is that the transition 'gap' experienced by students varies considerably, which is consistent with its threshold nature, Bolsius and Williams (2013), McConnell and Carden (2010). Within the transformative concept of transition, a first year pedagogy can be seen to comprise the concepts associated with it; diversity, design, engagement, assessment, and evaluation and monitoring, Kift (2009).

We identify that this transition is a profound shift of culture for students and as such recognise that it needs mediation. The unit presents this transition in a staged and structured manner. This is significant as the students will be encountering a similarly staged process in all their subsequent Engineering units and we expect that the skills and expectations that are instilled into the student cohort through this unit will be reflected throughout their undergraduate program.

The sequence of modules in the unit provides a staged progression through *Introduction, Complication,* and *Application* of the *transformative threshold concept.*

Module 1, as the first element of their unit and program of study is focussed on the *Introduction* of students to their new environment. Accordingly, the *associative concepts* scaffolded through this Module relate to teaching modes, notebooks and recording, Occupational Health and Safety (OH&S) and the question of 'What is Engineering?'

Building on this base, Module 2 adds a *Complication* to logically expand on the introductory elements with an extension of the concepts into more problematic content. The *Complication* developed in Module 2 is *Independent learning* and the *associative concepts* expand the understanding of the students' programs of study and options, self-management, accountability and study principles.

Module 3 acts as the *Application* of the themes being developed within the unit: as such, the theme of the Module is *Skills and Practices.* The *associative concepts* developed in this Module are, approach to assessments, learning styles, study habits and rules.

It is notable here that this unit needs to incorporate an elaborate suite of themes and practices in order to achieve its pedagogical goals: students must be introduced to these new cultural settings; the University, the Department, Laboratories, the Library, lectures and workshops, group work, their own learning practices and management skills while also engaged in three other units.

The learning and integration by the students of this extensive range of activities within such a novel setting requires that a closely structured and multi-focussed approach must be taken with the preparation and presentation of this unit. The

Module structure with its closely woven sets of *transformative threshold concepts* scaffolded by focussed *associative concepts* allows these aims to be achieved.

Nonlinear Electronic Devices and Systems – ELEC376

The third year unit for the Electronics specialisation is ELEC376. Students come into the unit with an understanding of the concepts of linear networks, circuit equivalence, impedance and trans-dependence. The core transformative threshold concept for ELEC376 was set to be Weak Nonlinearity, which involves the application of superposition of nonlinear signals. The difficulty with this idea is apparent paradox that a sum of linear results generates nonlinearity. This concept builds on the identified concepts of circuit equivalence and modelling, of dynamic resistance and linear approximation and of trans-dependence, Scott, Peter and Harlow (2012)

Module 1, as the *Introduction* to the process of linearization, is focussed on the first-order approximation of a nonlinear system. The associative concepts of amplifier models, transistor bias, and small-signal approximations scaffold the common problem of linearization.

The *Complication* added in Module 2 is to extend the approximation to high-order. The students observe that the same systems dealt with in Module 1 are revisited with the new *associative concepts* of Volterra analysis, distortion generation, and intermodulation. The perspective is shifted slightly from a simple ratio of output and input to that of ratio of signals and signal generation.

Module 3 develops the theme of large-signal *Application*, which is the ultimate reason for dealing with the concept of superposition of nonlinear signals. The *associative concepts* developed are, power amplifiers, mixing, and feedback.

In each module students complete a full lecture, tutorial, laboratory and assignment cycle. Each module focuses on the clearly defined associative concept and elements of the BoK and technical competencies related to electronic devices and circuits.

The teaching activities for the unit deal with the catalogue of transistor circuit topologies and functional blocks that appear in the standard text books. The array and combinations of circuits can easily be analysed in terms of the concept of superposition of nonlinear signals. Thus, the complexity of the circuit that a student can deal with correlates with their understanding of the concept.

An important element of the teaching activity is close interaction between tutors and the students. This is supported by weekly review meetings between the tutors and the unit convener to define the single concept to be developed for each activity. Through this mechanism, the teaching praxis is adapted to track the staged development of student understanding.

In practice activities are staged, starting with very basic circuits and followed by more complex additions and scenarios. Because the aim is to develop the concept behind the operation of the circuit, that is set as the assessment criteria for student success even if only in the context of a simple circuit. From the student learning perspective, the more complex scenarios consolidate the understanding of the learning outcomes.

CONCLUSION

The innovation presented here is the idea of a *concept module* as a specifically focussed teaching space for the teaching of *associative concepts* that develop the comprehension of a precisely defined and articulated *transformative threshold concept*. The latter is treated within a *threshold concept package* that focuses on a common threshold concept. The package comprises a sequence of *concept modules* to provide a focused and staged development of its specific threshold concept.

The advantage of this approach is clarity in the statement of the overall outcomes and particularly the significant threshold themes of the unit. The *concept module* requires that the development of the relevant concept is covered appropriately and comprehended by all participants. It is significant to emphasise that this clarity and comprehension refers as much to the students in the unit as it does for the academics engaged in the program of study.

The *concept module* structure further ensures that all key BoK elements in a unit and program of study are not only covered within the curriculum but are dealt with when the prerequisite *transformative threshold concepts* have been developed. The overall progression of the program will be more easily understood by both staff and students because the learning outcomes are presented with a clear focus on the process with minimum distractions.

The *concept modules* provide the opportunity for students to gain exposure and experience with a threshold concept by engaging with it from multiple perspectives thereby having greater opportunity to recognise the implicit threshold nature of the associated concept.

REFERENCES

AQF Council. (2013). *Australian qualifications framework* (2nd ed.). Retrieved from http://www.aqf.edu.au/

Bolsius, J., & Williams, B. (2013). *'Bridging that Gap' between foundation degrees and top-up to honours level: The transition experiences of students entering level 6 at the University of Worcester.* University of Worcester Academic Development and Practice Unit Research Document. Retrieved from http://www.worc.ac.uk/adpu/documents/Briony_Williams_Bridging_the_Gap.pdf

Bradley, A. (2008). *Engineers Australia Accreditation Criteria Guidelines* (Document G02 30/8/08). Engineers Australia, (2011) *Stage 1 Competency Standard for Professional Engineer.* Retrieved from https://www.engineersaustralia.org.au/about-us/program-accreditation

Carstensen, A-K., & Bernhard, J. (2013, September 16–20). *To learn a complex concept is to keep more than one concept in focal awareness simultaneously – An example from electrical engineering.* 41st SEFI Conference, Leuven, Belgium. Retrieved from http://www.sefi.be/conference-2013/images/179.pdf

Flanagan, M. (2013). *Threshold concepts: Undergraduate teaching, postgraduate training and professional development a short introduction and bibliography.* Retrieved from http://www.ee.ucl.ac.uk/~mflanaga/thresholds.html

Kift, S. (2009). *Articulating a transition pedagogy to scaffold and to enhance the first year student learning experience in Australian higher education.* Final Report, ALTC Senior Fellowship Program. Retrieved from http://fyhe.com.au/wp-content/uploads/2012/10/Kift-Sally-ALTC-Senior-Fellowship-Report-Sep-092.pdf

Land, R., Cousin, G., Meyer, J. H. F., & Davies, P. (2005). *Threshold concepts and troublesome knowledge (3): Implications for course design and evaluation. Improving Student Learning – equality and diversity.* Oxford: OCSLD

McConnell, C., & Carden, R. (2010). *Learning leaps: Making the transition from foundation degree to BA/BSc Top-Up in HLST subjects.* Higher Education Academy Network for Hospitality, Leisure, Sport and Tourism Project Report.

Meyer, J. H. F., & Land, R. (2003). Threshold concepts and troublesome knowledge – Linkages to ways of thinking and practising. In C. Rust (Ed.), *Improving student learning – Ten years on.* Oxford: OCSLD.

Meyer J. H. F., & Land R. (2005). *Threshold concepts and troublesome knowledge* (2): Epistemological considerations and a conceptual framework for teaching and learning. *Higher Education, 49*(3), 373–388.

Meyer, J. H. F., & Land, R. (2006). Threshold concepts and troublesome knowledge: Issues of liminality. In J. H. F. Meyer & R. Land (Eds.), *Overcoming barriers to student understanding: Threshold concepts and troublesome knowledge* (pp. 19–32). London & New York, NY: Routledge.

Parker, A., & McGill, D. (2009). Top-down synthesis of an engineering program of study. *Proceedings of AaeE, Adelaide* (pp. 1063–1068).

Parker, A., & McGill, D. (2014). Modularisation of learning outcomes in terms of threshold. *Waikato Journal of Education, Faculty of Education, The University of Waikato, 19*(2), 105–114. Retrieved from http://wje.org.nz

Scott, J., & Harlow, A. (2012). Identification of threshold concepts involved in early electronics: Some new methods and results. *Australasian Journal of Engineering Education (AJEE), 18*(1), 1–8.

Scott, J., Harlow, A., Peter, M., & Cowie, B. (2010). Threshold concepts and introductory electronics. *Proceedings of AaeE, Sydney, 1–8.*

Scott, J., Peter, M., & Harlow, A. (2012, August 20–23). *An electronics threshold-concept inventory: Assessment in the face of the dependency of concepts.* Proceedings of IEEE International Conference on Teaching, Assessment and Learning for Engineering (TALE) 2012, Hong Kong.

Anthony Parker
Department of Engineering
Macquarie University, Sydney

Daniel McGill
Department of Engineering
Macquarie University, Sydney

JAN H. F. MEYER, DAVID B. KNIGHT, TOM E. BALDOCK,
DAVID P. CALLAGHAN, JULIE MCCREDDEN
AND LIZA O'MOORE

15. WHAT TO DO WITH A THRESHOLD CONCEPT

A Case Study

INTRODUCTION

At a general level we would argue that programmes [of study] should be designed and systematically reviewed according to ... the processes through which learners are made ready for, approach, recognise, and internalise threshold concepts. [An] *excursive* account of the learning experience would see these processes as *a framework of engagements*, designed to assist students. (Land, Cousin, Meyer, & Davies, 2006, p. 198, emphasis added)

This chapter introduces a study carried out at the University of Queensland as part of a strategically funded 2011–2014 research project ('the project') on 'Enabling visible and effective learning in engineering'. Initial exploratory discussions with colleagues took place in a number of course contexts in the first three years of the undergraduate curriculum. A third-year Civil Engineering course on 'Open catchment hydraulics' ('the course') invited attention as one known – from years of prior teaching experience, student feedback, and the marking of answers to examination questions – to present some challenging and troublesome concepts for students. This course forms the context of the present case study.

Presented here is a narrative that essentially reports on, and references, a framework of engagements – each generating a particular 'type of knowledge' focussed, in this case, on the learning of a threshold concept, and other concepts associated with it. The narrative begins with an account of the analytical methodology used to isolate a threshold concept in the course. There follows a summary of how a consideration of subsequent data – various other 'types of knowledge' including empirical evidence of contextualised variation in student learning, and metalearning, of the concept – led to a teaching 'representation' of the concept as embedded in a novel form of sustainable pedagogy expressed as a 'metacognitive assessment activity' (MaA). This activity focused students' metacognitive attention on variation in levels of structural complexity in answers (including their own) to an examination-level question requiring application of the threshold concept, and associated concepts that it integrates.

R. Land et al. (Eds.), Threshold Concepts in Practice, 195–209.
© *2016 Sense Publishers. All rights reserved.*

THRESHOLD CONCEPTS ANALYSES

Two interlaced activities contributed to this phase of the project. In general, and stated here in content-free terms: An analysis *for* threshold concepts sought answers to exploratory questions such as: do they exist, what makes us think so, how many are there, and how are they distributed within the course? An analysis *of* threshold concepts sought answers to a deeper consideration of attendant questions regarding epistemological and epistemic status; specifically an articulation of their *critical features*. That is, those features that are critical to students' understanding of them; features that are essential for developing a new, previously unknown, way of understanding, that define critical differences in departing from an existing way of understanding, and that might also represent 'stuck places' inhibiting progression to what Baillie, Bowden and Meyer (2013) have described as *threshold capabilities*.

The Threshold Concept

Critical flow[1] is the threshold concept, the portal, that leads to the understanding of hydraulic controls – the *threshold capability* – the consequence of which leads, in turn, to what we actually need, which is our students' capability to analyse gradually varied flow[2] in any circumstances (Baldock, project leader, quoted from project notes).

Many hours of discussion and independent concept mapping led the two subject experts in the present authorship (Baldock and Callaghan, both Civil Engineers with relevant industry experience in the practical application of the course content) to provisionally conclude that there was only one likely candidate threshold concept: that of *critical flow*. The threshold status of 'critical flow' – a concept that is transformative, integrative, and troublesome – was duly confirmed in a subsequent triangulation of three sources of evidence, each representing a 'type of knowledge': (a) further conceptual analysis by the two subject experts, (b) variation in students' experiences of learning, and developing metalearning capacity in relation to, this concept and, (c) statistical analyses of students' answers to past examination questions involving the concept (Knight, Callaghan, Baldock, & Meyer, 2013).

VARIATION IN STUDENT LEARNING

Acknowledged at this stage of the project was that, in general, the threshold status of a concept is of limited use in the absence of 'responses' to it that may respectively emanate from a student learning engagement, assessment, pedagogical, or curriculum, perspective. In particular, pedagogic responses that proceed from knowledge of how students vary in their learning, and metalearning, engagement with it (Meyer, 2010).

Contextualised threshold-concept based 'variation in student learning' is thus emphasised, and is important for three reasons: First, when exhibited in an educational development context (informally and collegially so in the spirit of the project) such variation represents a troublesome focus of attention in its own right and, in doing so, it may serve as a threshold concept in its capacity to transform the conceptualisation of existing or developing, teaching practice (Meyer, 2012). Second, conceptually discrete patterns of learning within such variation represent finer grained particular 'types of knowledge' that each establish a theoretical basis for pedagogical responses, including mechanisms for developing students' metalearning capacity in relation to that concept (Meyer, Ward, & Latreille, 2009; Ward & Meyer, 2010). Third, these same patterns – and also those exhibited in the dynamics of changed or changing metalearning capacity (another 'type of knowledge') – partially explain why a particular threshold concept will be apprehended and experienced by students in varying degrees attributable to individual differences. And in doing so a basic proposition is reinforced: the epistemic and ontological[3] shifts associated with threshold concepts constitute dimensions of inter-individual *variation*, not conformity.

METALEARNING ACTIVITY

The next phase of the project accordingly adapted the methodology of Meyer et al. (2009) as a scoping exercise for identifying metalearning opportunities in the first three undergraduate years and, in particular, 'made visible' how students' varied in their learning of 'critical flow' (Meyer, Knight, Baldock, Kizil, O'Moore, & Callaghan, 2012; Meyer, Knight, Callaghan, & Baldock, 2012a,b). This particular 'type of knowledge' was explicitly visible in dimensions of variation in student learning at a discrete concept level; factor pattern solutions that clearly contrasted patterns of deep-level integrative, versus pathological, forms of contextualised learning behaviour. The former and latter forms of learning are respectively theoretically associated with high and low quality learning outcomes. Conceptually reflected in these patterns was an *opportunity to help individual students* to develop their metalearning capacity in relation to 'critical flow'. And especially so given the argument that embedding learning experiences to help students to develop their metalearning capacity – to become aware of, and to take control of, themselves as learners in some designated concept-context – is one of the most important, and also one of the most neglected, aspects of curriculum design (Meyer, 2010).

Having established a theoretically clear empirical basis from which to proceed, metalearning activities were accordingly trialled in the course and evaluated in terms of students' written comments (Meyer, Knight, Callaghan, & Baldock, 2014). Findings were reassuringly consistent with other reported studies that focussed on threshold concepts using a similar implementation methodology, and underpinned by the same conceptual model in the instrumentation – The Reflections on Learning Inventory (RoLI) discussed in Meyer (2004) – but carried out in the context of first-year economics courses (Meyer et al., 2009; Ward & Meyer, 2010).

There was also an implicit focus in these activities on another 'type of knowledge'; namely, students' conceptions of 'learning' in relation to 'critical flow'. Students were enabled to interpret, and reflect on, their self-declared conceptions of what 'learning' meant in this specific context, and in relation to achieving 'quality' learning outcomes. And as a consequence of this reflection there was an expectation that students would be empowered – as deemed necessary on the basis of personal judgement – to self-initiate *change* to their learning behaviour. That students were generally able to do so was clear from their reflective comments (Meyer et al., 2015).

That metalearning activity can be successfully focussed on a particular threshold concept and that this activity clearly benefits a substantial majority of students in a variety of intended ways was reaffirmed. Reported benefits expressed by individual students in the present study (and in the earlier studies referred to) included a positive reinforcement of self, a change in conception of what 'learning' is, to self-initiated and theoretically desirable forms of change. Also clear was that, despite best intentions, a few individuals apparently misunderstood the purpose of the activity and misappropriated it to justify their self-reported conceptually problematic forms of learning behaviour. Students' reported descriptions of their experiences, and analysis of complementary quantitative data, enabled another particular 'type of knowledge' acquisition; knowledge of variation in content-specific metalearning activity at discrete concept level and an understanding of how and why this activity could contribute to a pedagogic, and further curriculum 'response' in its own right, to variation in the learning of 'critical flow'.

THEORETICAL INTERLUDE

Having established metalearning as a precursor activity focussed on 'critical flow', attention in the project shifted to the question of additional theoretically underpinned, 'responses' likely to positively influence students' learning behaviour and the quality of associated learning outcomes. And, importantly, 'quality' in observed learning outcomes (answers to examination-level questions) was interpreted as evidence of 'structural complexity' (after Biggs & Collis, 1982) in the manner in which students structured, in relation to 'critical flow', and in the integration of other concepts associated with it, their understandings in the analysis and solution of gradually varied flow problems.

The theoretical basis for using metalearning to model learning outcomes is primarily grounded in the proposition that (variation in) the quality of cognitive learning outcomes is fundamentally a function of (variation in) contrasting forms of 'mechanisms of production'; that is, *learning processes*. Learning processes have a direct (first-order) effect on learning outcomes (as does one specific aspect[4] of prior knowledge not further considered here). A student learning 'response' to 'variation in student learning', conceptually located within this general aspect of explanatory models of student learning, was thus in place.

However, at a generic level, 'process' refers here to one family of *contrasting* learning processes and, at this level of abstraction, the explanatory model is essentially univariate.[5] At this same level of abstraction other sources of explanatory variation were considered. Two propositional extensions, again common to multivariate models of student learning, were clearly relevant:

- Conceptions of learning influence learning processes either directly, or via regulatory activity including the 'control' aspect of metalearning. Basically what students believe 'learning' to be is reflected in varying degrees *in what they do* when they 'learn'; specifically how they engage subject content in process terms.
- Perceptions of assessment requirements also influence learning processes either directly, or indirectly via regulatory activity; basically 'reading the signals' of assessment requirements – what level of 'learning' is perceived to be required to satisfy them – will be reflected, again in varying degrees, in how 'learning' is engaged in process terms.

The thus elaborated multivariate model offered an opportunity for a 'response' in that part of the theoretical model emphasising assessment and perceptions of its learning requirements. The project team accordingly determined to design a 'response' that focussed explicitly on 'structural complexity'.

METACOGNITIVE ASSESSMENT ACTIVITY

A single prototype 'metacognitive assessment activity' (MaA) based on 'critical flow' was duly developed for the course and trialled. This activity is a novel one, and its theoretical basis and framing literature review is fully discussed in Meyer, Knight, Callaghan and Baldock (2014). A concise summary of this activity is presented here in content-free terms, together with the observation that at first sight the real purpose of the activity will be unclear to students. Also emphasised (in italics) are four sources of resultant (qualitative) metacognitive data that are discussed further on.

- The first step in the methodology – a short written answer to an examination-level question related to a threshold concept – lies well within familiar student experience.
- The next two steps place students in relatively unfamiliar terrain. By means of a self-referencing process internal to themselves, they are now required to record, *and justify*, the assignment of a mark (scored out of ten) to each answer within a range of previously unseen 'alternative answers' to the same question – answers specifically constructed by experts at varying levels of exhibited structural complexity. Examples of questions and some corresponding 'alternative answers' are presented in the Appendix.
- The fourth step exposes students to the expert judgement and marking logic of the subject experts who: (a) explain how each of the 'alternative answers' would have been marked (out of ten) in a real examination, based on a consideration

of the level of structural complexity contained within each, (b) provide their own short answer to the original question, thus reinforcing the rationale for the metacognitive assessment activity as well as creating further opportunity for questions on how the presence of different levels of complexity affect the quality of the answer to the question.

- In light of this 'expert judgement' experience students are next, in the fifth and crucial step, required to assign a mark (out of ten) to their own original answer and *explain the reason* for that level of mark using an accompanying guide that reflects the five levels of the SOLO taxonomy developed by Biggs and Collis (1982).
- Students are then referred back to the alternative answers and asked to identify which of them made them think the most about the original question, *and for what reasons*.
- Students are finally asked to answer the following question: *How can this exercise be valuable as you continue to learn in this course?*

This prototype MaA was trialled (Meyer et al., 2014) with outcomes consistent with theoretical expectations as evidenced in demonstrably improved student engagement, satisfaction, and performance (Knight, Meyer, Baldock, Callaghan, & McCredden, 2013). The prototype has also subsequently undergone several stages of refinement in the manner in which the alternative answers are constructed and presented.[6]

Positive student feedback, and further qualitative assessment of student engagement, supported a decision to embed three additional metacognitive activities[7] – all conceptually interlinked with the concept of 'critical flow' – within the conceptual structure of the course as illustrated in Figure 1. The pedagogic rationale for this embedment decision was that while 'critical flow' enjoys a fundamental enhanced status in the structure of the course, it is not in itself a terminal end point in the learning journey; it is in fact 'the portal' leading to the development of capability which comes in two forms – course-level capability (content or subject matter) and discipline-level capability (characteristic capability).

In course-level capability the threshold concept of 'critical flow' leads to a threshold capability which is the application of the principle of hydraulic control, which leads in turn to content capability – the capability in the course to solve any gradually varied flow problem. This capability, emphasised in the first lecture, integrates every aspect of the course, including the fundamental principles of energy, momentum and uniform flows and their application to engineering practice for the design of waterways. At a higher level, the integration of threshold capabilities leads to discipline-level capability, which encapsulates elements of both cognitive and ontological shift; that is, complete mastery of subject matter and the ability 'to think like an engineer'.

In the course it is emphasised from the outset that success in assessment, particularly for a grade of 6 and above, is not based on topics, but on integration

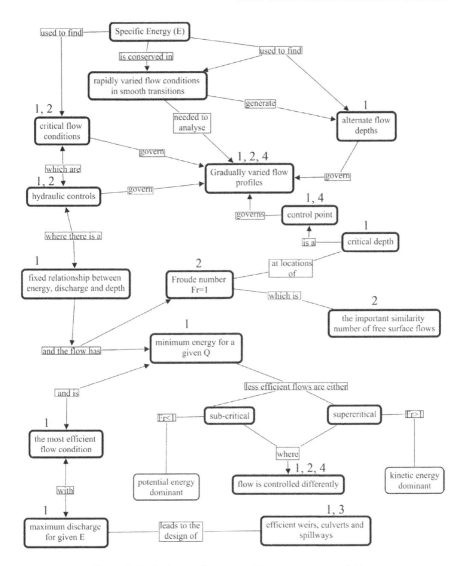

Figure 1. Embedment of metacognitive assessment activities.
Numerals identify the embedment context; 1–critical flow,
2–Froude similarity; 3–hydraulic control, 4–gradually varied flow

of those topics. Analyses of metacognitive data (another 'type of knowledge') were accordingly articulated with a focus on the examination performance of students who participated in more than one MaA session. An initial exploratory analysis supported a conservative and encouraging interpretation that *frequency of participation* in MaA activity was probabilistically associated with higher examination marks. To control for between-subgroup GPA variation (those who did not participate in any MaA, those who participated in only one MaA, and so on), the probability of a *test group* having greater final examination marks than a *control group* was estimated.

Table 1. The probability that the final examination mark for each test group is higher than that for the control group

Test groups	Probability estimates
1 or more MaA	0.54 ± 0.01*
2 or more MaA	0.58 ± 0.01
3 or more MaA	0.58 −0.01/+0.02
any single MaA	0.48 −0.01/+0.02
any 2 MaAs	0.57 −0.02/+0.01
any 3 MaAs	0.54 ± 0.02
those who did MaA 1	0.54 ± 0.01
those who did MaA 2	0.58 −0.02/+0.01
those who did MaA 3	0.58 −0.02/+0.01
those who did MaA 4	0.59 −0.00/+0.02
those who did MaA 1, 2	0.58 −0.02/+0.01
those who did MaA 1, 2, 3	0.58 ± 0.02
those who did MaA 1, 2, 3, 4	0.63 −0.03/+0.02

* ± *values are the 95% confidence limits for each estimate*

Control groups were randomly selected from those students who did not participate in any MaA and with near identical GPA distribution as the test group. The iterative procedure of bootstrapping, which generated some 1000 randomly selected control groups before convergence, determined the mean and 95% confidence limits of this probability. It is clear from the analysis presented in Table 1 that the highest probability was evidenced for the test group that participated in all four MaA activities. Nevertheless, there was a beneficial impact for *this population* for all test groups except the one-off MaA participation one. A general trend also appears in these estimations leading to the conservative interpretation that the greatest benefit is attenuated by decreasing frequency of MaA participation.

An analysis of the captured metacognitive qualitative data referred to earlier on confirmed the presence of variation in the meaningful expenditure of effort in responding to the open-ended questions. There was, in particular, a contrast between those students exhibiting minimal engagement, and those attempting to articulate – and process, in terms of their own answer to the original question – reasons for deficiencies in their understanding. There were two underlying themes in students' comments that were subsequently operationalised for modelling purposes:

- The extent to which they grappled with the idea that relevant concepts need to be explicitly interrelated in answers to examination-level questions. Accordingly coded was the degree of effort expended in grasping the 'how' of answering; in basically requiring an understanding of the conceptual distinctions between the levels of the SOLO taxonomy, and using this understanding to reflect on the structure of their own answers.
- The varying ability of some students to apply the newfound awareness of the above need in describing how they would improve the content of their own answers (even though this step was not asked for). Accordingly coded was the degree of effort in applying their metacognitive awareness to improve the content of their answers (the 'how' to answer being used to regulate the 'what' to answer).

Further resultant quantitative analyses (McCredden, Baldock, Callaghan, Meyer, Knight, & O'Moore, 2015) provided a deeper interpretation of the data in Table 1 in indicating that it was the *amount of effort* expended in the need to explain how concepts are interrelated (structural complexity), rather than simple frequency of participation, that contributed significantly to examination marks on top of GPA effect. That is, participating students improved their examination mark by investing effort and reflection into MaA's and this observation applies to both high and low achieving students. And in the particular context of 'critical flow' the available evidence supported the conclusion that MaA's benefitted students in improving their structural understanding of how concepts fit together in this challenging knowledge domain. This benefit however is not simply a function of multiple exposure to related metacognitive activities; it is a function of expended, and largely self-directed, effort in that exposure.

CONCLUDING DISCUSION

There is nothing as practical as a good theory. With some project members initially sceptical of the Threshold Concepts Framework, it nevertheless provided a focus for immediate activity. Such activity is good, especially if it persuades others (outside the project) to do something new. Our approach has always been bottom up, so any spin off activities that develop from a focus on threshold concepts are beneficial. (Baldock project leader, quoted from 2014 project notes)

The work reported here proceeded from the simple argument that there is no point in pursuing the threshold status of a concept in the absence of 'responses' that are designed to impact on the quality of student learning and its outcomes. 'Responses' that are informed in particular by the theoretical interpretation of an amalgam of different 'types of knowledge' in context – Integrated Threshold Concept Knowledge as proposed by Meyer and Timmermans (this volume) – that has a bearing on the learning of that concept, and other concepts associated with it, that establish the basis for threshold capability.

'Responses', as illustrated in the present study, originate from student learning, metalearning, metacognitive, pedagogic, and curriculum perspectives, with 'types of knowledge' represented by qualitative and quantitative data essentially:

- Generated from analyses *for,* and *of,* threshold concepts.
- Representing (variation in) learning, metalearning, and metacognitive assessment, activity and succinctly captured by a relevant subset of process observables – representing 'the mechanisms of production' of learning outcomes – that also theoretically underpin the 'responses'.

The work reported has had a positive impact on student learning with 'responses' sustainably embedded. In short, participating students positively evaluate their metacognitive experiences, and generally exhibit higher levels of comprehension achievement in the final examination compared to non-participants.

Repeated exposure to the metacognitive assessment activity is furthermore also seen as a positive response to an important issue facing many academics; namely, a persistent student focus on 'just in time' learning. The development of activities that can be performed in large, tiered lecture theatres to counter the other issue of suitable teaching space is an important complementary benefit. The next step in future work will be to persuade students to invest time and meaningful effort in such activities when there is 'no new material' on offer. There is a need to progress students from an understanding of a threshold concept towards a threshold capability, to 'think like an engineer' involving that concept, and other related concepts; a capability that requires an order of magnitude increase in conceptual integration.

The project has also served as a vehicle for nurturing and developing the notion of Integrated Threshold Concept Knowledge. That the individuals in the present authorship were able to contribute to the social construction of such knowledge is a given. It is also a given that it is possible to explain and provide theoretical justification for the methodology of its construction, such methodology being adaptable to other contexts. Equally adaptable to other contexts is the methodology of the various 'responses'. The basic methodology of the MaA is in fact content free and has been adapted to concepts to other disciplinary contexts, while the pedagogy targeting 'structural complexity' in student understanding is adaptable as appropriate to other threshold and their associated concepts.

NOTES

[1] In simple non-technical terms: The interest here is in the behaviour of flowing water in what are referred to as natural or engineered 'open channels' such as rivers, streams, sluices, and drainage systems. 'Critical flow' refers to a specific state of flowing water between what is referred to as

(a) 'subcritical flow' (deep and slow moving water) and, (b) 'supercritical flow' (shallow and fast moving water), with both these latter two states having the same energy and total mass flow rate (discharge). Critical flow occurs specifically when the flow velocity equals the wave speed; a state in which the controlling relationships between energy, depth, and discharge are fixed. The phenomenon of critical flow may be visually observable for some, but it is difficult to explain, and it is troublesome for students because it cannot be interpreted by simply watching flowing water. There is furthermore no obvious physical visualisation to assist in this interpretation. Critical flow is a transformative concept in explaining how and why flowing water in different states *behaves differently* within constrictions caused by, for example, weirs, culverts, and the submerged supporting structures of bridges; in particular in explaining why flowing water switches between sub- and super- critical flow states causing counterintuitive opposite behaviour such as in changes in depth or velocity. Critical flow and associated concepts also play a role in the design considerations of engineered constrictions.

[2] What is referred to as a 'normal flow' condition occurs in an open channel when gravity and friction are in equilibrium. In contrast, 'gradually varied flow' is a term that refers to the flow of water in an open channel in situations where small changes in flow depth along the channel occur because gravity and friction are in disequilibrium. These small changes in flow depth are usually not visually observable. So, for example, when the channel slope increases, it takes some distance and gradual depth changes for friction to once more reach equilibrium with gravity. 'Critical flow' usually occurs at some location in the channel, with the flow at such a location then controlling the behaviour of gradually varied flow upstream or downstream from it. And it is here, when students are required to draw extensively on the role that critical flow plays in hydraulic control in predicting gradually varied flow, that the troublesome nature of critical flow is compounded. Civil Engineers have a particular interest in gradually varied flow in regions of water catchment runoff, and they use statistical modelling to estimate the probability of flood risk (for example 1 in 100 years) for neighbouring property and dwellings.

[3] Ontological shifts were not explicitly modelled in the project. Ontological aspects of 'thinking like an engineer' are however implicit in the progression towards threshold capability and, as indicated in the concluding discussion, are a focus for future work.

[4] Prior knowledge can also directly produce a learning outcome as 'declarative knowledge' without any additional cognitive activity other than recall. Simply put there is no need to learn what you already know and can declare.

[5] And as an aside it is acknowledged that, within the domain of such a specific learning process model, the affective and ontological experiences (and associated outcomes) that are emphasised within the Threshold Concepts Framework cannot be adequately modelled or inferred. To do so requires modelling that focuses on how students feel, rather than what they do, when they are learning.

[6] It is possible for example to construct alternative answers for 'critical flow' that contain either (a) mathematics and text, (b) diagrams, mathematics, and text, (c) plain text only. 'Critical flow' is also a phenomenon amenable to either a physical or mathematical representation which opens up further possibilities of engagement with phenomenographic variation theory. It has been demonstrated for example that it is possible to simultaneously vary the representation of the critical features of 'critical flow' in the repertoire of answers in the metacognitive assessment activity. For a theoretical discussion on threshold concepts and variation theory see Meyer, Land and Davies (2008).

[7] The logic being that the initial metacognitive assessment activity (MaA) for 'critical flow' and the second one for the 'Froude number' have conceptual links, with the second MaA returning to a fundamental principle of Fluid mechanics, that of *similarity*. The third MaA links 'critical flow' with a practical application (that of culvert design), while the fourth MaA for 'gradually varied flow' links hydraulic controls and friction, the latter being fundamental to uniform flows. Along the way, it might be expected that students evaluate where they can improve their own learning and recognise the importance of extending and generalising their 'answers' to link all the course concepts together, and not just 'answer the question'. The opportunity to practice this four times instead of once is clearly more likely to change student behaviour.

REFERENCES

Baillie, C., Bowden, J. A., & Meyer, J. H. F. (2013). Threshold capabilities: Threshold concepts and knowledge capability linked through variation theory. *Higher Education, 65*(2), 227–246. doi:10.1007/s10734-012-9540-5

Biggs, J. B., & Collis, K. F. (1982). *Evaluating the quality of learning: The SOLO taxonomy.* New York, NY: Academic press.

Knight, D. B., Callaghan, D. C., Baldock, T., & Meyer, J. H. F. (2013a). Identifying threshold concepts: Case study of an open catchment hydraulics course. *European Journal of Engineering Education, 39*(2), 125–142. Retrieved from http://dx.doi.org/10.1080/03043797.2013.833175

Knight, D. B., Meyer, J. H. F., Baldock, T. E., Callaghan, D. P., & McCredden, J. (2013b, December 8–11). *Embedding metacognitive exercises in the curriculum to boost students' conceptual understanding.* AAEE Conference Proceeding, Gold Coast, Australia. Retrieved from http://www.engineersaustralia.org.au/australasian-association-engineering-education/2013-annual-conference

Land, R., Cousin, G., Meyer, J. H. F., & Davies, P. (2006). Implications of threshold concepts for course design and evaluation. In J. H. F. Meyer & R. Land (Eds.), *Overcoming barriers to student understanding. Threshold concepts and troublesome knowledge.* Abingdon & New York, NY: Routledge.

McCredden, J., Baldock, T., Callaghan, D., Meyer, J., Knight D., & O'Moore, L. (2015). *Impact of a metacognitive reflective exercise on exam performance in a high level engineering course.* Occasional paper, School of Civil Engineering, The University of Queensland.

Meyer, J. H. F. (2004). An introduction to the RoLI. *Innovations in Education and Teaching International, 41*(4), 491–497.

Meyer, J. H. F. (2010). Helping our students: Learning, metalearning, and threshold concepts. In J. Christensen Hughes & J. Mighty (Eds.), *Taking stock: Research on teaching and learning in higher education* (pp. 191–213). Montreal & Kingston: McGill-Queen's University Press.

Meyer, J. H. F. (2012). 'Variation in student learning' as a threshold concept. *The Journal of Faculty Development, 26*(3), 8–13.

Meyer, J. H. F., & Timmermans, J. (2014, July 10–11, this volume). *Integrated threshold concept knowledge.* Plenary paper, 5th Biennial Threshold Concepts Conference, Durham University, Durham.

Meyer, J. H. F., Land, R., & Davies, P. (2008). Threshold concepts and troublesome knowledge (4): Issues of variation and variability. In R. Land, J. H. F. Meyer, & J. Smith (Eds.), *Threshold concepts within the disciplines* (pp. 59–74). Rotterdam, The Netherlands: Sense publishers.

Meyer, J. H. F., Ward, S. C., & Latreille, P. (2009). Threshold concepts and metalearning capacity. *International Review of Economics Education, 8*(1), 132–154. Retrieved from http://www.economicsnetwork.ac.uk/iree/v8n1/meyer.pdf

Meyer, J., Knight, D., Baldock, T., Kizil, M., O'Moore, L., & Callaghan, D. (2012). *Scoping metalearning opportunity in the first three years of engineering.* Proceedings of the 23rd annual conference of the Australasian association of engineering education, Melbourne. Retrieved April 2, 2013, from http://www.aaee.com.au/conferences/2012/documents/AAEE-Conference-proceedings-2012.pdf

Meyer, J. H. F., Knight, D. B., Callaghan, D. P., & Baldock, T. E. (2014). An empirical exploration of metacognitive assessment activities in a third-year civil engineering hydraulics course. *European Journal of Engineering Education, 40*(3), 309–327. Retrieved from http://dx.doi.org/10.1080/03043797.2014.960367

Meyer, J. H. F., Knight, D. B., Callaghan, D. P., & Baldock, T. E. (2015). Threshold concepts as a focus for metalearning activity. Application of a research-developed mechanism in undergraduate engineering. *Innovations in Education and Teaching International, 52*(3), 277–289. Retrieved from http://dx.doi.org/10.1080/14703297.2015.1017515. doi: 10.1080/14703297.2015.1017515

Ward, S. C., & Meyer, J. H. F. (2010). Metalearning capacity and threshold concept engagement. *Innovations in Education and Teaching International, 47*(4), 369–378.

Jan H. F. Meyer
School of Civil Engineering
The University of Queensland

David B. Knight
Department of Engineering Education
Virginia Tech

Tom E. Baldock
School of Civil Engineering
The University of Queensland

David P. Callaghan
School of Civil Engineering
The University of Queensland

Julie McCredden
School of Civil Engineering
The University of Queensland

Liza O'Moore
School of Civil Engineering
The University of Queensland

APPENDIX

a.	*Explain why flow depth can in some instances increase, and in other instances decrease, in open channel contractions*
1a.	Assuming $f = 0$ then $H = d + \dfrac{V^2}{2g} =$ constant. If supercritical then depth goes up as velocity head goes down to keep H constant. In an opposite way, subcritical flow keeps H constant by decrease flow depth. In both cases, H is constant throughout the contraction.
2a.	For steady flow, total energy is $E = \rho g d + \rho \dfrac{q^2}{2d^2} =$ constant, with the first term being potential ($E_p \sim \rho g h$) and second being kinetic ($E_k \sim \dfrac{1}{2}\rho V^2 \sim \rho \dfrac{q^2}{2d^2}$) energy. As flow depth approaches zero, any increases in q sees energy transfers from kinetic to potential, i.e., depth increase. If at critical depth, no energy transfers occurs. As flow depth approaches energy height, any increases in q sees energy transfers potential from to kinetic, i.e., depth decreases.
3a.	Comes from keeping energy constant through the horizontal bed contraction. Using $E = h + \dfrac{q^2}{2gh^2}$, specific energy of a rectangular section as an example, $\dfrac{q^2}{2gh^2}$ (kinetic energy) includes d (potential energy), hence $q \sim h^3$, and plotting dimensionless:

	This illustrates a significant difference between scenarios where the geometry does not vary with flow properties (e.g., pipe flow) and where it does (variable geometry flow such as open channel flow). $\dfrac{dq}{dd} = 0$ gives $d_c = \sqrt[3]{\dfrac{q^2}{g}}$ and from small wave amplitude assumption, the fluid velocity at this depth equals the wave celerity. Now $W \downarrow$ gives $q \uparrow$ $(Q = VA)$ and hence supercritical flow depths increase, while subcritical flow depths decrease (see plot). The reason for the opposite behaviour comes from changes in q combined with conserving both mass and energy. There are other inferences on flow behaviour, e.g. supercritical flow is controlled from upstream, and supercritical flows can flow off a cliff with no apparent impact on upstream flow.
4a.	The energy diagram representing the cubic energy equation in d or h, is 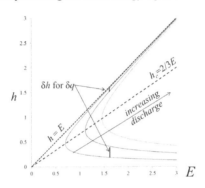 A change in q leads to a reduction in depth for subcritical flow and an increase in depth for supercritical flow. The influence of bed level change (change in E) is similarly different for the different flow regimes, giving a reduction in depth in subcritical flow and an increase in supercritical flow.
b.	*Why are culverts sometimes inlet controlled and sometimes outlet controlled?*
1b.	Because critical flow can occur at either the inlet or outlet. This depends on if the culvert is flowing full or not. The head loss is different if the culvert flows full or with a free surface. The head loss controls if it is inlet or outlet controlled. If the head loss is too large, afflux occurs and you don't want this because it leads to a flood.
2b.	It depends on whether the inlet is a free surface flow or is submerged, the slope of the culvert, and the downstream water level. The head loss is different in each case. If the head loss is too large the upstream water level rises, causing afflux, i.e. a flood. Generally, inlet control is more efficient and minimises afflux.

ANNA-KARIN CARSTENSEN AND JONTE BERNHARD

16. MAKE LINKS

Overcoming the Threshold and Entering the Portal of Understanding

INTRODUCTION

In engineering the student is often 'faced with contrasting representations or models' (Entwistle et al., 2005, p. 9), which Entwistle explores as 'ways of thinking and practising' (ibid). These contrasting representations are in electric circuits for example: graphs, mathematical models, drawings of circuits and the real circuits. In our research we have found that exploring the relationships – links – between these different representations, as well in the theory/model domain as in the object/ event domain (Tiberghien, Vince, & Gaidioz, 2009) is of uttermost importance. We have developed a tool for investigation of 'the learning of a complex concept' (Carstensen & Bernhard, 2008a) which we have used in order to find critical aspects, which we call "key concepts" (Carstensen & Bernhard, 2008b), which open up the portal of understanding threshold concepts.

In this chapter we will explore these links further. As we have continued our work on how students make links between the different islands of single concepts, in order to make a whole of the complex concept, we have noted that the links between these islands are of different kinds. We will here discuss what kinds of relationships these links consist of, and how they differ in ways of coping with them for students, and how the teachers may notice and highlight these relationships in their instructions.

We have video recorded students interactions during lab-work and analysed these tapes according to the Theory of Variation (Marton & Tsui, 2004). Now we are taking this further, and make a more detailed analysis of what the links are, and by that we contribute to the understanding of the nature of a threshold concept.

LINKS EXPLORED

Already when we formed the model of a complex concept (see figure below and Carstensen & Bernhard, 2004) it was obvious that the *links between the islands* were not just there to learn, but that the students had to *make links*, create ways to pass from one island to another. One of the links is to calculate the transfer function for a given circuit. This could be considered as "just something to learn", but what does it mean to learn this? Molander (1993) gives a similar example: "mass is energy", and claims for this and similar statements that "it is obvious that there is no *knowledge*

R. Land et al. (Eds.), Threshold Concepts in Practice, 211–222.

in *the statements themselves*, there is something to know only if one *understands* the included *concepts* and the *activity context* where they belong" (p. 61, my translation, italics in original). The learning process is in the action.

To create links is also to be aware of more than one island at the same time; to make links is to keep more than one island in focal awareness simultaneously, which according to variation theory is a necessary condition for learning. The model became a way to see what students had in focal awareness, while working with the tasks. But the model also became a way to see what students did not do, what concepts they worked with in isolation, i.e. what links they did not make. When they made links it was possible for the students "to go on" (Wittgenstein, 1953, §154) with the task, while when they did not make links, but focused on only one, single island, at a time, the students were hindered both in the task itself and in the learning process.

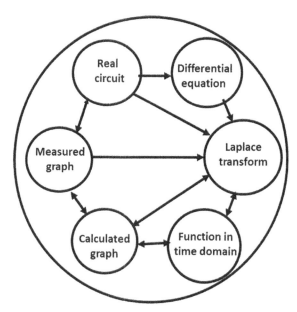

Figure 1. The model of the learning of the complex concept transient response, showing the intended object of learning, i.e. with all intended links marked as arrows and concepts to learn drawn as nodes or islands

Following the circumference of the circle, the links are the following. One link is from the real circuit to the differential equation. This link consists of the mathematical modeling of the physical properties. The next one consists of deriving the Laplace transform from the differential equation, which gives the transfer function. The next one is to do the inverse transform in order to get the time function (which in the first versions of the model was named "inverse transform" although it ought to be called "time function"). From that to the calculated graph the link is to draw the graph. The next link is to associate the measured and calculated graphs by means of expressions like frequency, amplitude, damping. The link from the circuit to the measured graph, is to do the measurements using a connected computer interface. In order to extend the parts-whole-relationship to include more islands in focal awareness simultaneously, the student might establish links across the circuit, e.g., directly from the circuit to the transfer function, and in the new course also a direct link from the transfer function to the calculated graph is made possible through simulations.

The links are thus different, but all of them consists of an action, something to do, or make. Something that also gives the relation between two islands of knowledge – or concepts. There is something for the students to do, to grasp, to make, more than just to associate, learn about or relate to.

The model was initially a result of an analysis of the video-recordings. Listening to the students' conversations gave us both the islands, i.e. the concepts they were dealing with, and the routes they took going from one task to another, i.e. the arrows in the model. We found that this tool was useful in analyzing what students were doing. It showed how the parts-whole-relationship was enacted, whether or not students were working with one or more concepts at a time. But when writing about the model and the learning the model was aiming at describing, the arrows, the relationships, the links seemed to be more than just a route of actions.

This chapter will explore each of the links in terms of what learning each arrow, each link represents. The method used is earlier described in several papers, among them Carstensen and Bernhard (2008a), and will not be described here.

THE LINK FROM REAL CIRCUIT TO DIFFERENTIAL EQUATION AND ONTO THE TRANSFER FUNCTION

The link from the real circuit to the differential equation is a modelling procedure, making a mathematical model from physical experience, which in this laboratory class is not very much elaborated. In the course 2002 this modelling procedure is only carried out in lectures and problem-solving sessions, and not a specific task in the laboratory class, and thus such data could not be obtained. However, it is presented in the recommended text book (Nilsson & Riedel, 2001). It is also introduced in another lab, where the steps to go from the circuit onto the differential equation and further to the transformation of the expression by means of the Laplace Transform, a series of mathematical manipulations.

THE LINK FROM THE TRANSFER FUNCTION TO THE TIME DOMAIN

In our very first description of the *circle* representing *the object of learning* in the transient lab *the island* between *the transfer function* and *the calculated graph* was called *inverse transform*, since it was the time function that the calculated graph should show, and the route from the transfer function to the graph is to do the inverse transform to obtain the time function. This reveals two questions: (1) If it was just a route, a link between the transfer function and the calculated graph, why would it be *an island* of its own? Or put in another way: If it is *an island* why is it not expressing a result? (2) Why was it not obvious to the researchers that *the islands* had to be *results* and *the arrows* had to be something *to do*.

Reflecting on the first question, it is only possible to go directly from the transfer function to the calculated graph in the time domain by means of computer simulations. By hand the inverse transform renders a time function as its result, and thereafter, the calculated graph can be drawn. In the computer program that the students use, Datastudio, they have the possibility to draw their own curves in the same graph window as they get the measured graph, they make a *curve fit*, where they choose a user defined graph, which is the time function. So the short answer to the first question is that the island was necessary, and it is just a matter of choosing the right label, to name the *island time function* instead of *inverse transform*.

Noting that the island now has a noun as the name, the time function, which is the result of an action rather than the action itself, makes it possible to notice that all islands have nouns as their names, and that all links represent something *to do*. The answer to the second question is thus, that the choice of a faulty label made it possible to notice, to become aware that *all islands are nouns and all links are activities*.

Seeing that the transformed function (the transfer function) and the inversely transformed function (the time function) are nouns and thus islands, while the transformations are links is thus an important learning for the teachers and researchers. However, this also makes it possible to notice that the links are not just to manipulate mathematical routines, rather it is to keep these two concepts (nodes or islands) in *focal awareness* (Marton & Booth, 1997, p. 143) whilst both comparing results in the Laplace domain and in the time domain, and going between them. If it were just to learn the links, the manipulations would be enough to learn, but since it implies keeping both domains *and their relation* in focal awareness simultaneously, it is a link that has to be worked out by the students themselves. Talking in terms of *Threshold concepts* to just do the manipulations would be a type of mimicry, whereas keeping the relationship in focal awareness simultaneously, while studying the time functions, the transfer functions or carrying out the transformations is to have passed through the portal. In phenomenographical terms it would be considered as seeing the object of learning in a new way, having reached a deeper understanding, and to be able to give a more *complex* explanation.

COMPARING THE MEASURED GRAPH TO THE CALCULATED
GRAPH – A TRIANGULAR ROUTE – MEASURED GRAPH,
TIME FUNCTION AND CALCULATED GRAPH

This route is the main purpose of the "Transient response" laboratory class. The students are asked to compare a measured graph to a calculated graph, which in the computer program DataStudio, is called make a *curve fit*. The computer interface measures the voltages and currents chosen, here the input voltage, the output voltage and the current through the circuit. The time function can principally be one of two different functions: a damped sine wave or a sum of two exponential functions. Only one of the functions (the damped sine wave) is given in the lab-instruction, and the students are asked to start with that one, but are also told that they may need another function.

Although the Laplace transform, and its inverse transform, have been derived during the lectures (both courses) and in classroom-sessions (in the old course), only two groups start doing calculations in order to see what types of functions they may come up with, before they try to make a curve fit. The students are not used to having to do calculations in the lab room, but the teacher claims that it is necessary for them to do the calculations, and that they have enough time to do them. Still most students hesitate, and do not even look in their notes from problem-solving sessions or lectures spontaneously (some don't even bring their materials to the lab sessions at all).

One group, group 13 repeat the sentence the teacher has told them:

2002_Group_13 _Tape_2 13:03

A: We are supposed to do some tiny adjustments and make them fit, and doing that you use the Laplace transform and find the poles

This repeated citation, shows that the student has understood that it may be necessary to do calculations in order to know what to do, still he does not start calculating until about an hour later, and when doing calculations he doesn't want to be disturbed, until he has reached the result.

All groups 2002 except G22, need help with the third curve fitting as well the first curve fitting. Although they get the function in the first one, they do not know how to start choosing parameters. They have difficulties predicting how the graph will change with the change in parameters. Often in mathematics courses the drawing of graphs has been to draw a simple function, e.g., a sine wave or an exponential function, but combined is seen as "just to apply". The second and fourth curve fits are similar to the first and third respectively, so no one asks for help doing those.

The link between the measured graph and the calculated graph is not possible to make until the link between the time function and the calculated graph is made. On the other hand the link between the time function and the calculated graph has to be made in both directions – it is not sufficient to have drawn curves from functions in a math class, it is also necessary to be able to analyze what function a graph represents, to go from graph to formula.

Thus to make the link from measured graph to calculated graph requires to have both graphs and the time function in focal awareness simultaneously, still there seems to be no direct link between the measured graph and the time function, which the title of this section (triangular route) suggested. Possibly this link is emerging, but as far as the video recordings show, the link between the measured graph and the time function always goes through the calculated graph. Those students who refuse to accept that calculations are necessary never show the link between the mathematical expressions, the formulae and the graphs. All students who finish their measurements before they take on the mathematical work, ask after each curve fit: "Is this good enough for the report". One group actually leaves the lab room in frustration without finishing even one of the tasks.

THE LINKS ACROSS THE CIRCLE – FROM TRANSFER FUNCTION TO CALCULATED GRAPH AND FROM MEASURED GRAPH TO TRANSFER FUNCTION

This link was not found in 2002. While studying the video recordings from 2002 the researchers suggested that a link between the transfer function and the calculated graph should be introduced. The reason was that following the circumference of the circle would make it possible to transcend the two worlds (theory/model and object/ event worlds) only by two links and given the possibility, of transcending the worlds on more occasions it facilitates more feely the students traverse between the worlds. Therefore simulations were introduced that would allow this. Students were asked to use Simulink (Matlab™) to show the graphs in the time domain using six different but similar transfer functions, the same as those for which they also were asked to calculate the inverse transform in the new course. The examples were chosen so that only one parameter was altered at a time, but so that all three different kinds of poles were rendered (two real, two identical real or two complex conjugated roots to the characteristic polynomials and two different relationships between the numerator and denominator polynomials were explored.

Also in 2003 there are groups who hesitate doing the mathematics, even when there are explicit tasks to calculate, and one group sits for as long as two hours trying other types of functions, e.g., $a \times e^{bx} \times \ln(cx)$ before they finally accept that they need to do the calculations. Since they in 2003 are forced to do calculations – there are explicit tasks – all students do calculations and after they have done so, the question "is this good enough for the report" never occurs in 2003. Without the mathematics the gap was a lingering gap, whereas with mathematics the gap was filled.

The simulations helped the students to know what kind of answers to expect from the tedious calculation, and although they hesitated to do the maths, they kept working until they got the results. In terms of threshold concepts this would be to be in the liminal space that is necessary for passing the threshold to enter through the portal.

THE LINK FROM CIRCUIT TO MEASURED GRAPH

The link from the circuit to the measured graph is about doing the measurements, i.e. how to connect the circuit, and to choose what to measure. The link in the other direction, from graph to circuit is about analyzing the measured graph in terms of what it physically means.

Two different questions occur, one is "What does 'connect over the whole circuit' mean?" and "What is the step response?" The first one concerns confusing semantics. The output voltage from the computer interface is the input voltage to the circuit and the output voltage from the circuit is measured by a "voltage sensor". The teacher shows how to do it and the problem is solved.

The other one is a matter of how to retrieve a step response. In theory classes a step is easily taken for granted as a theoretical construct, but in laboratory classes you need a repeated step in order to see it, which means that a square wave of low frequency is required. One group actually uses a square wave with too high frequency and asks why the step does not reach zero, a matter that the teacher does not notice. Later the group uses an appropriate frequency, and get the step right.

As soon as the students recognize the rising edge of the square wave as a step this issue is resolved.

LINKS AS FACILITATION FOR ENTERING INTO THE LIMINAL SPACE

To facilitate learning is not just to teach each island, each concept, but also to make the students do what is needed in order to make links. As noted above, when a gap is noticed, students enter what in terms of Threshold concepts is called *the liminal space*. As noted by the founders of threshold concepts this liminality is required, when learning threshold concepts, but we have noticed that it is possible to help students enter into, as well as pass the liminal space through highlighting critical aspects of the links as well as the two (or more) islands that need to be kept in focal awareness simultaneously. One example is the combination of calculations and simulations, where very systematically varied examples, varying the critical aspect that is to be focused (here the different kinds of graphs that are possible), makes the students enter the liminal space but also gives them an opportunity to see the way out. To find these critical aspects is to find the keys to learning, which we have called *key concepts*. In this laboratory class the key concept is the palette of possible solutions.

ACKNOWLEDGEMENT

Support from the Swedish Research Council (grant *VR 721-2011-5570*) is gratefully acknowledged.

REFERENCES

Carstensen, A.-K., & Bernhard, J. (2004, August 18–21). *Laplace transforms – too difficult to teach, learn and apply, or just matter of how to do it.* Paper presented at the EARLI sig#9 Conference, Gothenburg.
Carstensen, A.-K., & Bernhard, J. (2008a, July 2–5). *Keys to learning in specific subject areas of engineering education – an example from electrical engineering.* Paper presented at the SEFI 36th Annual Conference, Aalborg.

Carstensen, A.-K., & Bernhard, J. (2008b). Threshold concepts and keys to the portal of understanding: Some examples from electrical engineering. In R. Land, J. H. F. Meyer, & J. Smith (Eds.), *Threshold concepts within the disciplines* (pp. 143–154). Rotterdam, The Netherlands: Sense Publishers.

Entwistle, N., Hamilton, A., Kelly, R., Nisbet, J., Chapman, R., Hayward, G., & Gachagan, T. (2005). Teaching and learning analogue electronics in undergraduate courses: Preliminary findings from the ETL project. *International Journal of Electrical Engineering Education, 42*(1), 8–20.

Marton, F., & Booth, S. (1997). *Learning and awareness.* Mahwah, NJ: Erlbaum.

Marton, F., & Tsui, A. B. M. (Eds.). (2004). *Classroom discourse and the space of learning.* Mahwah, NJ: Lawrence Erlbaum.

Molander, B. (1993). *Kunskap i handling.* Göteborg: Daidalos.

Nilsson, J. W., & Riedel, S. A. (2001). *Electric circuits.* Upper Saddle River, NJ: Prentice-Hall.

Tiberghien, A., Vince, J., & Gaidioz, P. (2009). Design-based research: Case of a teaching sequence on mechanics. *International Journal of Science Education, 31*(17), 2275–2314.

Wittgenstein, L. (1953). *Philosophical investigations.* Oxford: Blackwell.

Anna-Karin Carstensen
Engineering Education Research group
Linköping University, Norrköping
and
School of Engineering
Jönköping University

Jonte Bernhard
Engineering Education Research group
Linköping University, Norrköping

APPENDIX: EXAMPLES OF SYSTEMATICALLY VARIED LAPLACE-FUNCTIONS TO ANALYSE, MATHEMATICALLY AND GRAPHICALLY

$$G(s) = \frac{2s + 5}{s^2 + 2s + 5}$$

$$G(s) = \frac{2s + 5}{s^2 + 2s + 1}$$

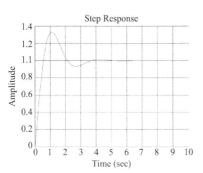

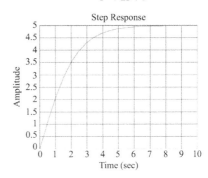

$$G(s) = \frac{2s + 5}{s^2 + 2s + 0.51}$$

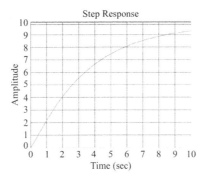

$$G(s) = \frac{3}{s^2 + 2s + 5}$$

$$G(s) = \frac{3}{s^2 + 2s + 1}$$

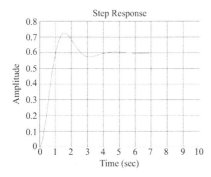

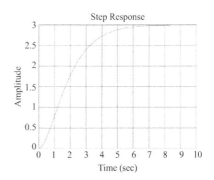

219

$$G(s) = \frac{3}{s^2 + 2s + 0.51}$$

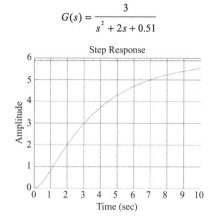

Important characteristics:

1. Solutions to the characteristic polynomial, i.e. the poles to the transfer function give different shapes to the curves:

$$s = -1 \pm \sqrt{1-5}$$

$$s_1 = -1 + 2j$$

$$s_2 = -1 - 2j$$

$$s = -1 \pm \sqrt{1-1}$$

$$s_{1,2} = -1$$

$$s = -1 \pm \sqrt{1-0.51}$$

$$s_1 = -1 + 0.7 = -0.3$$

$$s_2 = -1 - 0.7 = -1.7$$

gives under-critically damped behavior

gives critically damped behavior

gives overcritically damped behavior

2. Note the different start behavior that depends on the difference in degree of powers in the nominator and denominator polynomials
3. The Steady-State value depends on the transfer-function's limit-value when s approaches zero.

VARIATION THEORY

Part of paper presented at SEFI annual conference in Aalborg 2008. (Bernhard, 2008)

Variation theory, developed by Marton and co-workers (Bowden & Marton, 1998; Marton & Booth, 1997; Marton & Tsui, 2004), provides an explanatory framework describing the conditions required for learning. Central to this theory is that we learn through the experience of difference, rather than the recognition of similarity. To open up for learning should be understood in terms of *discernment*, *simultaneity* and *variation*. Learning is seen as developing certain capabilities and values that enable the learner to handle novel situations in powerful ways.

Powerful ways of acting emerge from powerful ways of seeing, and our previous experiences affect the way in which we experience a new situation. Our perception also affects the experiences we see as relevant, and the powerfulness of one's act is relative to one's aims in a given situation. Seeing something in a particular way can be defined by the aspects discerned by a person at a certain point in time. The difference between 'discerning' and 'being told' should be noted. People discern certain aspects of their environment by experiencing variation. When one aspect of a phenomenon or an event varies, while another aspect or other aspects remain the same, the varying aspect will be discerned. One of the main themes of variation theory is that the pattern of variation inherent in the learning situation is fundamental to the development of certain capabilities. In the words of Marton, Runesson, and Tsui (2004):

> What we believe is that variation enables learners to experience the features that are critical for a particular learning as well as for the development of certain capabilities. In other words, these features must be experienced as dimensions of variation.

Experiencing variation amounts to experiencing different instances simultaneously. This simultaneity can be either *diachronic* (experiencing instances that we have encountered at different points in time, *at the same time*) or *synchronic* (experiencing different co-existing aspects of the same thing at the same time). Marton et al. (2004) also introduce the concept of a learning space:

> The space of learning tells us what it is possible to learn in a certain situation [from the point of a particular object of learning]. ... The space of learning ... is ... an experiential space. ...

Marton and co-workers (Marton et al., 2004; Marton & Tsui, 2004; Runesson & Marton, 2002) distinguish between the *intended object of learning*, the *enacted object of learning* and the *lived object of learning*. The intended object of learning is the subject matter and the skills that the teacher or curriculum planner is expecting the students to learn. The enacted object of learning is the space of learning constituted in a learning environment, i.e. what is actually made possible for the student to learn.

The lived object of learning is the way students see, understand, and make sense of the object of learning and the relevant capabilities the students develop.

REFERENCES

Bernhard, J. (2008, July 2–5). *Conceptual labs as an arena for learning: Experiences from a decennium of design and implementation.* Paper presented at the SEFI 36th Annual Conference, Aalborg.

Bowden, J., & Marton, F. (1998). *The university of learning. Beyond quality and competence in higher education.* Sterling, VA: Stylus Publishing.

Marton, F., & Booth, S. (1997). *Learning and awareness.* Mahwah, NJ: Erlbaum.

Marton, F., & Tsui, A. B. M. (Eds.). (2004). *Classroom discourse and the space of learning.* Mahwah, NJ: Lawrence Erlbaum.

Marton, F., Runesson, U., & Tsui, A. B. M. (2004). The space of learning. In F. Marton & A. B. M. Tsui (Eds.), *Classroom discourse and the space of learning* (pp. 3–42). Mahwah, NJ: Lawrence Erlbaum.

Runesson, U., & Marton, F. (2002). The object of learning and the space variation. In F. Marton & P. Morris (Eds.), *What matters? Discovering critical conditions of classroom learning* (pp. 19–38). Göteborg: Acta Universitatis Gothoburgensis.

ANDY WEARN, ANNE O'CALLAGHAN AND MARK BARROW

17. BECOMING A DIFFERENT DOCTOR

Identifying Threshold Concepts When Doctors in Training Spend Six Months with a Hospital Palliative Care Team

You matter because you are you, and you matter to the end of your life. We will do all we can not only to help you die peacefully, but also to live until you die.
– Dame Cicely Saunders, founder of the hospice movement (1918–2005)

BEGINNINGS

This work arose from some early conversations around a related PhD thesis and a sharing of some concurrent interest in Meyer and Land's theoretical framework of threshold concepts (Meyer & Land, 2006; Meyer & Land, 2005). We talked widely about clinical communication skills, the processes of change in learning, and the clinical setting of palliative care where Anne worked. In many ways this was the perfect storm of serendipity, a clearly transformative learning setting and a desire to explore Threshold Concepts in a practice context.

Anne recounted informal conversations with junior doctors that had taken place during and after their six-month placement with a hospital palliative care team. These doctors talk about a learning experience that was different to any other in their training, resulting in a transformed idea of what it means to be a doctor and a sense of being unable to go back to being the 'type of doctor' that they were beforehand. These doctors, three to eight years out from graduation, appeared to be describing the crossing of some sort of threshold.

INTRODUCTION

Learning in the health professions is profoundly ontological – it is about 'becoming' a practitioner. In this process of 'becoming', students and trainees can often recall significant moments when they felt stuck, challenged or enlightened. At these times they may be compelled to think differently about their practice and themselves as practitioners. These experiences clearly resonate with the Threshold Concepts (TCs) theoretical framework (Meyer & Land, 2003). Threshold concepts capture the key transformative processes that learners have to navigate. Little research on threshold

R. Land et al. (Eds.), Threshold Concepts in Practice, 223–238.

concepts has been conducted within medicine, although the framework has had been applied in other health professional contexts.

In our setting, we were particularly interested in the troublesome nature of TCs, where the learning is in some way cognitively, physically or emotionally challenging (Cousin, 2009; Meyer & Land, 2006; Meyer & Land, 2005; Perkins, 2006). That third affective challenge is something that our learners are likely to encounter due to the nature of practice where they will confront illness, death and dying, workload, ethical dilemmas, decision-making and advocacy. There is perhaps an 'ideal' cognitive/affective mix to create liminality.

BACKGROUND TO THIS STUDY

There is a small literature exploring TCs in medical education, much of it being discussion pieces rather than reports of empirical research. The role of TCs in surgical and anaesthetic simulation training has gained some attention (Evgeniou & Loizou, 2012; Kneebone, 2009; Littlewood, 2011). Kneebone (2009) notes that the use of oversimplified simulations hinders learner transformation. In considering the process of developing e-learning, TCs have been identified as a useful potential framework for building content (Evgeniou & Loizou, 2012). More recently, the difficulty often experienced by students in moving from conventional secondary school learning to a problem-based learning medical school environment has been described as a threshold concept, albeit at a macro level (Bate & Taylor, 2013). All of these papers are conceptual, descriptive and discursive.

With this study, we aimed to provide some theory-based empirical evidence to assist in moving TC research in medical education from conceptual to exploratory and applied. Our primary hypothesis was that formal focussed exploration of the learning experiences of doctors in training who were undertaking six months of palliative medicine would identify TCs for that setting.

The participants in our study were junior doctors who elected to undertake a palliative medicine attachment during their training to become either a specialist (*other* than in palliative medicine) or a general practitioner. These doctors work as registrars for six months alongside a specialist palliative care team of doctors and nurses in a hospital setting. They are supported as they learn to assess and manage the needs of patients with life-threatening or life-limiting illness who are referred by their primary hospital team. In addition they provide support for the primary team itself. The aims of our research in relation to these doctors were to:

- identify and explore their transformative and/or troublesome learning experiences
- propose a series of TCs for doctors undertaking an attachment in palliative medicine, derived from their experience

We hoped to use the findings to inform and improve the curriculum, learning experience and supervision of doctors undertaking six months palliative medicine training. Taking into account our secondary aim, it was also possible that the

224

identified TCs in this context would represent concepts that might be relevant to the 'good doctor' in other contexts.

DEVELOPING A METHOD

Research around TCs often draws on the content experts; commonly teachers, practitioners or faculty. Evgeniou and Loizou suggest that experts might not be best-placed to identify TCs as they may be less aware of the concepts that were once troublesome to them as novices (Evgeniou & Loizou, 2012). In our study we weighed up the players in our setting and chose to collect data from the learners. After all, this is where we began our discussion and had speculated that we might be seeing possible TCs.

Studies exploring TCs have largely used qualitative methodologies and have examined a range of data sources: some of these you will encounter in other chapters of this book. In our setting, we needed to capture our learners' narrative and their reflections, but were aware of the small numbers in our potential population. Each year, two or three registrars opt to take six months in palliative care in our teaching hospital as part of their training. We wanted these doctors to be able to recall their experiences, so a retrospective four year period was chosen from which to draw our participants. Given the small numbers and the potential benefits of participants triggering recollections in each other, we opted for focus groups and maintained a TC framework as our underlying theoretical model.

Meyer and Land were deliberately inclusive and non-prescriptive about the characteristics of TCs in their initial writing (Meyer & Land, 2006); and still hold to that view. It is not a requirement of a TC that it fulfils all of the characteristics that have been proposed. However, this provides some difficulties for the researcher where the goal is to identify TCs rather than simpler concepts within a discipline. Our planned approach was to look for evidence of eight characteristics of TCs (transformative, irreversible, integrative, bounded, troublesome, discursive, reconstitutive, liminal), to code text against them and then to seek potential TCs by looking for common conceptual themes across these coded sections.

STUDY METHOD

Ethical approval was obtained from our local Human Participants Ethics Committee.

We conducted semi-structured focus groups with registrars who had included a palliative medicine attachment as a part of their training programme. Potential participants were identified by one of the authors (AO'C) and approached by a research assistant to ascertain their willingness to participate in the research. Participants were given some introductory information about the focus of the study.

Each focus group was facilitated by two people drawn from two of the authors (MB and AW) and a research assistant. To ensure consistency, the facilitators designed and used a written guide. The focus groups were audio recorded using a digital recorder. Groups began with a scripted explanation of the research, including an explanation of TCs. Participants were provided with an opportunity to ask questions before considering some questions about their overall experience of the palliative medicine attachment. They were asked to consider the challenges and surprises of the experience, the learning issues encountered, and how they processed their learning. In particular we explored experiences that they believed were fundamentally different to those they had in other attachments. We also explored the ways in which the palliative care attachment influenced their understanding of the role of the doctor and how it may have influenced their view of themselves as a medical practitioner. Focus group recordings were transcribed verbatim by a contracted transcriber and the transcriptions checked for accuracy by the research team.

The analytical process had both deductive and inductive phases and was carried out in three rounds. Constant comparison and researcher consensus were central to the whole process. In a first round of analysis we coded statements from the participants against a coding framework of our chosen eight characteristics of TCs (schematic analysis, deductive phase). This was done independently by each author, who having become familiar with the transcripts, coded data from the first focus group. We met to compare our coding and to reach a consensus where we had coded differently. One author (AO'C) then coded the data from the second focus group transcript.

Having considered the results of the first round of analysis we met to generate a list of potential TCs in the setting of palliative medicine (inductive phase); second round analysis. This was then followed by a third round which used a thematic analysis drawing upon framework method (Ritchie, Lewis, Nicholls, & Ormston, 2013). Participant statements, coded with the threshold characteristic that they exemplified, were allocated (by AO'C) to one or more of the identified TCs that they appeared to illustrate (deductive phase). In this final round of analysis there was likely to be variation in the quantity and clustering of characteristic-coded statements and identified TCs.

RESULTS

From a potential population of 11 registrars, nine agreed to participate in a focus group and eight attended. We conducted two focus groups. Five registrars attended the first focus group (facilitated by MB and AW), while three attended the second (conducted by MB and a research assistant). The focus groups lasted 80 and 60 minutes respectively. One participant was in the final stages of the palliative care attachment, the others had completed the attachment within the preceding four years and were in the process of completing training in a range of careers from general practice to intensive care. During their interactions, participants discussed areas where they had common views and also areas where they had differences of opinion.

In the first round of analysis, coding of statements to TC characteristics resulted in some statements being coded to more than one characteristic. By consensus we agreed 'best-fit' single codes for the majority of statements, but accepted multiple codes for a few. Seven potential TCs were generated in the second round of analysis. At this stage it was clear that some of the identified TCs were well supported by the participants' comments, whereas others were supported by less 'evidence'. To a degree, we found ourselves caught between qualitative and quantitative paradigms. We sought to reach some balance between Meyer and Land's stance on the presence or absence of characteristics, along with considerations of credibility and confirmability. It was difficult to avoid some of the discourse of quantitative research, so we devised the following scheme:

- Strong evidence – eight characteristics of a TC were present
- Some evidence – at least four characteristics of a TC were present
- Weak evidence – three or fewer characteristics were present

This scheme allowed us to classify the potential TCs according to the strength of the evidence for them in the data. In the process of applying this scheme to our potential TCs, it became clear that there was a strong overlap between two of them. These were combined into a new TC which then displayed four characteristics (some evidence). One which would have sat in the weak evidence category was discarded; we did not feel that there was sufficient evidence in the data to support our initial TC identification.

From this process we propose five TCs in the setting of palliative medicine learning, from the perspective of our participants:

1. Emotional Engagement (Strong evidence)
2. Communication Management (Strong evidence)
3. Embodied Shared Care (Some evidence)
4. Active Inaction (Some evidence)
5. Uncertainty Embraced (Some evidence)

It is worth raising another methodological issue at this stage, that of defining a concept. There has been some debate in the TCs literature about what constitutes a concept (Rowbottom, 2007). Arguments have been framed around cognition, abstraction and action. The names that we gave to our identified TCs went through a number of iterations, aiming for a description that was operational and described a process.

In the following sections we discuss the two TCs for which there was strong evidence in detail. We then outline some of the findings for the three TCs for which some evidence was found.

After each quotation, we identify the TC characteristic in parenthesis.

Two TCs Supported by Strong Evidence

Emotional engagement. Discussion of emotions featured heavily in the interviews. Prior to their attachment, registrars had rightly anticipated that they would be seeing many patients with incurable illnesses, with some close to death. Their previous experience was mainly in making diagnoses and treatment plans, rather than dealing with the emotional responses of patients. They feared that their interactions would result in triggering of emotions in patients or family members that they would not be able to address and were also worried about their own emotional responses to distressing events or situations:

> You're there to hold all that emotion alongside the patient, where[as] a lot of what we do in our own specialties is drop the bomb and then potentially pass it on for someone else. (Bounded)

> I think that it's like Pandora's Box, you always assume that when you open it everything is going to be catastrophic afterwards. (Troublesome)

> It was a little bit terrifying … you aren't practiced at difficult questions, difficult emotion, the feeling of wanting to run away but not being able to because you are there to do a job for the person and the family. It was quite scary. (Troublesome)

The difference between the palliative medicine attachment and others, however, was that they had the opportunity to develop a fresh approach to dealing with strong emotions. With support they consciously encouraged emotions to be expressed and attempted to respond empathically. This was very different to their previous experience of imparting information and avoiding emotional responses. The daily practice of palliative care allowed them frequent opportunities to engage with this liminal space in a recursive and transformative manner which was new for them. As they did this, they noticed that they were better able to manage distress in themselves and others; the emotional engagement that they had been feared had become part of their practice.

> I think the big thing that I got out of it is being able to sit in someone else's intense emotion and not feel frightened and want to run away, like to be there surrounded by it and just let them let it out, which is very different to the rest of the medicine that I had done before. (Transformative)

> In palliative care you come back and see a patient every day, work through the issues where you left off yesterday and dealing with those humanistic qualities that you appreciated in your practice previously, but … weren't able to deliver on. (Liminality)

As a result of being able to cross the threshold of emotional engagement, they began to see themselves as having new roles to play; there were new ways of thinking and acting beyond the threshold. Their altered response to emotion was seen to be both therapeutic for the patient and manageable for the doctor. Previously they had feared that their response would make the situation worse. They reflected that they had become, to some extent, a different kind of doctor and continued to use their new approach despite moving onto other areas in their training.

> And by the end of it … I felt that I could sit there and I could say useful things or not say anything to allow them to express whatever it was they needed to express, in order hopefully, the patient or family or whoever I was talking to, to move through what they were experiencing. (Reconstitutive)

> I think one of the things as well that stops you going backwards, once you stepped over the threshold … is that there's that little bit of fear before you do palliative care about broaching these things, and once you've lost that fear you can't really regain it… that's one of the things that takes you over the threshold is losing that fear. (Irreversible)

> You end up sort of changing, changing your focus from where you have previously come, and you take it with you. You apply it to every little consult that you do. (Irreversible)

Communication management.   The registrars were challenged as they thought about the way that their communication behaviours had been modified by their previous experience. During undergraduate and postgraduate training, they had learnt and practiced communication skills. However, the imperatives of the workplace and the pressure of work practices and cultures had caused them to discard and take short-cuts with skills. Palliative care provided a context where they could re-find, explore and discover value in their unused communication skills. They were able to see communication theory in practice, in a way that was practical and achievable. Once they had a new framework for clinical communication skills they realised that they had been unconsciously avoiding skills or using skills to stop patients from talking, in order to cope with the pressures of their workload.

> Because going from, in GP-land, having 15 minute blocks and a room full of patients…I didn't realise how much over the last years I'd learnt all these techniques to block everyone… to find what they needed and get them out in 15 minutes. (Troublesome)

> In fact they [communication skills] get worse as you go through medicine because you just get busier and busier, you are more focused on other things… I think it's probably worsened my communication skills over time. (Troublesome)

The palliative medicine attachment gave them time to enter repeatedly into a liminal space where they could try new ways of communicating, without the previous time pressure. Although they were slow to start with, the consequence of the learning was that they came to understood clinical communication in a new way in terms of focusing back on the patient. Importantly, they also became aware and able to use these skills in a time-efficient manner.

So you do learn those skills, and I feel now I don't need the two hours that I needed at the beginning, but in sort of 15 or 20 minutes I can sometimes get where that patient needs to be. (Reconstitutive)

But probably the only time ever in your training when you are solely focused, and you've got the opportunities to go into all these difficult situations all the time, and take as long as you want. And if you get it wrong, come back and go back and try again. (Liminality)

And then you... think of a strategy or you talk to somebody and say look this is what I've done, I don't know how to untangle it, and then you learn about it and then you untangle it and then you learn more. (Liminality)

We spend all this time being taught to... work out quickly what's going on and then tell the person what they should do, and then all of a sudden you have to re-learn, you have to listen to what their issues are. (Reconstitutive)

I think it made me a much better listener which I think is one of the keys to getting there faster. (Integrative)

...and actually you are just seeing it on their face, actually finally someone has asked what the real problem is. (Integrative)

The process changed the ways that the registrars viewed their practice and their role as doctors. They were unable to go back to seeing the world in the old way. They felt empowered as doctors and noticed a difference between themselves and others who had not had the palliative medicine training experience. Interestingly, they viewed the transformation as liberating and spoke passionately about the change.

It's sort of about empowering in a way... asking 'what is important to you?' Instead of ... focussing on how impossible the situation is, because it is and nobody can change that, but talking to them about what is important, 'what are your goals, what matters to you'? (Integrative)

And once you are there, you can't go back because you could never stop attending to those things that are just so apparent to you in any clinical contact that you have, even if it's collegial contacts. So you can't turn it off. (Irreversible)

You don't stop being the palliative care doctor that you were for six months, that you actually do this in 'Vivid'[1], that you still continue to do it. You just can't understand how other ... you look at them and go, how can you not see this? So you all of a sudden you feel like you belong to this secret club... (Irreversible)

Three TCs Supported by Some Evidence

Embodied shared care. The palliative care attachment caused the registrar's to change their view of the roles of patients and families. They may have previously paid lip-service to partnership or patient-centeredness, but through this experience they came to see them as genuine partners in care provision. We found evidence of four TC features in this area; of transformation, integration, boundedness and irreversibility. Evidence of the other features was not apparent.

Although familiar with the concept of shared decision-making, in which the doctor and patient (plus important others) bring their mutual expertise and knowledge to the process of making decisions, the registrars had not previously embodied this in their practice. They learnt that in the setting of palliative care, they could align medical expertise with the uniqueness of their patient to get the best possible outcome in the circumstance.

> Someone is coming to you … within their own context, with their own goals of treatment, within a whole different context … all of a sudden you realise … you're here to be able to discuss what is going on, and what they want to do. (Transformative)

> [in] palliative care …you are not just looking at physical symptoms… the patient tends to take the lead and you kind of work with them… 'what is their agenda what do they want addressing first, what is bothering them the most, how can I help with that?' It's a different approach I think. (Bounded)

> I feel much more able to work with the person, to work out whether what my treatment has to offer is worth the trade-off of what they are going to lose, their time or the side effects … (Transformative)

> Palliative care broadens your focus again… putting the…medical aspect of it into a small… part of that… you are looking at …their well-being, their family, where they are at in their disease, what does all of this mean to them… (Integrative)

The change continued as they embarked on new roles so that they understood their medical care in a broader context of the patient's life and how this might impact on decision making:

> Having gone back to my regular day job afterwards, I found it made me much more focused on how whatever was happening was impacting on the person's life, … it gave me a much better insight into … how well they were and what might be important to them, in helping them make decisions about what to do treatment wise. (Irreversible)

Active inaction. The registrars were confronted with situations in which their usual approach to patients did not work. Their previous paradigm was about fixing problems and suddenly they had to engage with finding ways of dealing with situations in which they were unable to provide an answer or solution to an illness or problem. They realised that the very act of remaining present, despite an uncomfortable feeling of having nothing to offer, was in itself a helpful behaviour.

> Yeah, I find that quite hard, sitting there when there's nothing I can do to make it better, and having someone tell me that they've got pre-school children and they are dying. (Troublesome)

> It's a complete attitudinal change really, because we are brought up ... [to be a] problem solver, find an answer, if possible a black and white answer and do it. ... all of a sudden you have an impossible diagnosis, an impossible situation that you can never solve and nobody can, and you have to be able to accept that (Transformative)

> ... it's not about ... you saying something that is going to make everything better, it's not about that at all. It's about listening to fears and helping, just sitting alongside them... (Integrative)

This reframing gave them a new understanding of how a doctor could be in situations they had previously perceived as 'hopeless' and then experienced satisfaction at being able to make a difference after all:

> You still care for the patient, but nothing is still something. (Reconstitutive)

> I do feel like I actually made a difference most days, even if you are just letting someone talk or working with a family around what's going on ... but you do feel like you are actually doing something that is quite positive for people. (Reconstitutive)

Often, this was simply by acknowledging their own and their patient's humanity and journeying alongside them. The process of becoming a doctor in their previous training had focussed strongly on being a competent technician, but now they were re-connecting with values that they may have had when they first entered the profession:

> It's almost coming back to those things that you knew were important before you were a doctor. (Transformative)

Uncertainty embraced. The challenge of dealing with uncertainty was apparent in much of the data, but had considerable overlap with the other identified TCs. The prominence of uncertainty reflected care of a group of patients who were very sick, but with considerable uncertainty as to exactly how their illness would unfold or how long they had left to live. Only some of the features of TCs were evident when uncertainty was explored on its own.

The doctors felt they had little previous assistance in dealing with their clinical response to uncertainty. They had experienced the reaction of patients who had been given prognostic information by others, as if it were certain, when actually the prognosis remained very uncertain.

... people have been given a prognosis, 'you are only going to live two weeks' or 'you are going to die of a catastrophic bleed in a short period of time', and you end up ... having to unpick all that, 'well actually we don't know what is going to happen, there is lots of uncertainty'. (Troublesome)

... that's one thing you don't get taught as a doctor, is to sort of embrace uncertainty and have no idea [several – yes, yes], and say 'I'm absolutely as helpless as you'. (Troublesome)

To address this they developed new strategies, particularly articulating the uncertainty and responding empathically to the difficulties this created for people. They learnt that hope could be adjusted despite uncertainty and that admitting to uncertainty did not undermine their relationship with the patient.

... as well as acknowledging that uncertainty with the patient ... [I] probably became better at acknowledging it and dealing with it. Actually acknowledging how difficult that is to live with. Whether this cancer is going to come back one day or you know whatever. I found that like is a very useful thing to acknowledge with the patients. (Reconstitutive)

... and finding things to hope for within that uncertainty. (Transformative)

... all of a sudden, that angst that [is] there and that anger that came out from the patient because of what had happened or leading to their diagnosis, it just sort of melted away, because ... there was no great knowledge holder ... in the room, that sort of set up a differential of 'I'm up here' and 'you're down there'. (Integrative)

DISCUSSION

Principal Findings

This is a small exploratory study using the experience of eight registrars who have spent six months in one hospital palliative care team. There is currently little understanding about what aspects of learning during a palliative care registrar attachment might be both important and difficult. This study provides some empirical evidence for this learning by identifying TCs, which are by definition both transformative and troublesome. We identified five TCs from the data that encapsulate their significant learning. Two of these, 'Emotional engagement' and 'Communication Management', are supported with strong evidence. There is also some evidential support for the threshold status of 'Embodied Shared Care', 'Active Inaction' and 'Embraced Uncertainty'.

One application of these findings is to trial the use of these TCs in the palliative care curriculum; guiding trainees as to their intended learning and encouraging clinical tutors to use them explicitly in dialogue with trainees.

Another potential significance of the findings is that these TCs may not only be of importance for those undertaking palliative care attachments, but may also be relevant for all doctors. The potential for these TCs to be relevant for doctors in other contexts needs further exploration.

Taken at face value and out of the palliative care context, all five would seem to describe attributes that would be useful for doctor-patient encounters. This was supported in our data by registrar comments:

I think a good physician does exactly what we all do in palliative care... actually to care for people with our ability to cure and treat and everything else, the whole package, you don't just do one or the other.

You sort of wonder how difficult medicine must be for them [doctors in other disciplines] and how stressed their life must be to go through it without recognising all of the things that you've seen

If this is the case, then exploring what is required in a learning environment that facilitates crossing the thresholds represented by these concepts is important, especially given that our participants identified that the opportunity for this learning had been unique to their palliative care attachment. How might we reconstruct other postgraduate learning environments so that these TCs are visible and available for engagement?

Further exploration is needed to confirm these TCs as authentic in the palliative care setting, and to assess their role in wider medical education.

Reflection on the Literature

There is a small literature investigating the effects of experience and training in palliative and end-of-life care, predominantly for undergraduate medical students. Hospice experience, for example, has been found to be an important component of undergraduate medical training in order to develop a number of desirable competencies (Jacoby, Beehler, & Balint, 2011). Studies analysing the benefit of such experiences from reflective writing by students, demonstrate learning in cognitive, emotional and identity domains (Corcoran, True, Charles, & Margo, 2013; Jacoby et al., 2011). The student learning experience is usually brief, however, and it is not known whether this learning persists.

A 2007 study identified that aspects of palliative care practice provided lessons for health care delivery and for medical education (Yedidia, 2007). These included authenticity as a central aspect of trust; modifying the approach for each patient based on a good understanding of the meaning of the illness in the broad context of his/her life; the development of self-awareness and explicit mechanisms for dealing with emotions. Yedidia and others have identified that the capacity of physicians to acknowledge and address emotional responses in palliative care is important for both preserving clinical judgement and for reducing stress (Sofia Carolina Zambrano, Chur-Hansen, & Crawford, 2012; Sofia C. Zambrano, Chur-Hansen, & Crawford, 2013).

The findings of our exploratory study are thus congruent with the qualitative findings of others looking at the palliative care learning environment.

Looking at the medical education literature more broadly, our speculation that our TCs might be valuable across medicine are also in keeping with a number of concerns about the postgraduate learning environment that have been highlighted recently. Two areas are briefly discussed, corresponding to our first two threshold concepts.

The first is the ongoing concern that the role of emotion in healthcare is devalued with negative consequences for both patients and doctors (Shapiro, 2011). It has been suggested that this devaluing comes about through the process of socialisation into the cultural norms of medicine which can result in emotional detachment and clinical neutrality (Coulehan, 2005). If the learning environment of postgraduate medicine actually serves to undermine learning emotional engagement then understanding more about the learning environment that supports crossing this threshold, as our participants experienced, may be of value for medicine as a whole.

Second is that despite the significant increase in the teaching of communication skills in the undergraduate curriculum, complaints about the standard of communication in hospitals remain high and there are concerns that transfer of these skills from the undergraduate learning environment into the postgraduate hospital environment is not effective (van den Eertwegh, van Dulmen, van Dalen, Scherpbier, & van der Vleuten, 2012). Research examining why transfer is poor is at the exploratory stage but there is some evidence that factors that are important include a lack of emphasis on feedback in relation to communication skills compared with other clinical skills, the use of summative assessments that assess communication skills with behavioural checklists and a lack of effective role models. Factors that improve transfer include an environment in which the skills are specifically valued and where feedback from role-models is available. Thus again understanding more about how our learning environment promoted communication management may have wider application.

Limitations and Strengths

This study has a number of limitations and strengths. First, the study is based on interviews with registrars in one hospital palliative care service. It is therefore not certain whether these findings would be the same for registrars working in other palliative care settings. On the other hand it is the first study that we know of to use

TCs within medicine to develop an understanding of complex learning that changes the way doctors practice medicine and how they view themselves as clinicians.

A further limitation of the study is the small number of participants. We were limited by the setting; only two or three registrars per year go through the service and we wanted participants to be able to recall their experiences. Small numbers may explain our inability to confirm or reject the three TCs with only 'some evidence'. Further studies will be helpful in clarifying these TCs in the context of palliative medicine and in other medical settings.

Finally, it is possible that the focus groups' facilitators influenced the direction of the discussion. We attempted to reduce this potential bias by using facilitators who were not palliative care clinicians.

Reflection

This study arose out of observations of highly engaged learners who appeared to be enjoying their learning experience, despite facing difficulties. It could be that vigilance by teachers in noticing when learners appear at their most engaged may provide a context to examine whether TCs are being addressed in these moments. If so, it is important to examine the features of the environment that appear to be acting so that this learning can be used to improve other environments in relation to those TCs.

CONCLUSION

The registrars in this study identified the palliative care attachment as providing a unique learning opportunity. Only a few doctors in training, however, will ever have this palliative care experience. If confronting these TCs were to benefit doctors and patients in all areas of medicine, then fully understanding the concepts, and also the learning environment needed for them to be traversed successfully, may have important implications for medical education.

NOTE

[1]   A brand of highlighting pen.

REFERENCES

Bate, E., & Taylor, D. (2013). Twelve tips on how to survive PBL as a medical student. *Medical Teacher, 35*(2), 95–100.

Corcoran, A. M., True, G., Charles, N., & Margo, K. L. (2013). Geriatric palliative care: Do medical students' narrative reflections after a hospice clinical experience link to geriatric competencies? *Gerontology & Geriatrics Education, 34*(4), 329–341. doi:10.1080/02701960.2013.815180

Coulehan, J. (2005). Viewpoint: Today's professionalism: Engaging the mind but not the heart. *Academic Medicine, 80*(10), 892–898.

Cousin, G. (2009). *Researching learning in higher education: An introduction to contemporary methods and approaches.* New York, NY: Routledge.

Evgeniou, E., & Loizou, P. (2012). The theoretical base of e-learning and its role in surgical education. *Journal of surgical education, 69*(5), 665–669.

Jacoby, L. H., Beehler, C. J., & Balint, J. A. (2011). The impact of a clinical rotation in hospice: Medical students' perspectives. *Journal of Palliative Medicine, 14*(1), 59–64. doi:10.1089/jpm.2010.0281

Kneebone, R. (2009). Perspective: Simulation and transformational change: The paradox of expertise. *Academic Medicine, 84*(7), 954–957.

Littlewood, K. E. (2011). High fidelity simulation as a research tool. *Best Practice & Research Clinical Anaesthesiology, 25*(4), 473–487.

Meyer, J. H. F., & Land, R. (2003). *Threshold concepts and troublesome knowledge: Linkages to ways of thinking and practising within the disciplines.* Scotland: University of Edinburgh UK.

Meyer, J. H. F., & Land, R. (2006). Threshold concepts and troublesome knowledge: An introduction. In J. Meyer & R. Land (Eds.), *Overcoming barriers to student understanding: Threshold concepts and troublesome knowledge.* London: Routledge.

Meyer, J. H. F., & Land, R. (2005). Threshold concepts and troublesome knowledge (2): Epistemological considerations and a conceptual framework for teaching and learning. *Higher Education, 49*(3), 373–388.

Perkins, D. (2006). Constructivism and troublesome knowledge. In J. H. F. Meyer & R. Land (Eds.), *Overcoming barriers to student understanding: Threshold concepts and troublesome knowledge* (pp. 33–47). London & New York, NY: Routledge.

Ritchie, J., Lewis, J., Nicholls, C. M., & Ormston, R. (2013). *Qualitative research practice: A guide for social science students and researchers.* London: Sage.

Rowbottom, D. P. (2007). Demystifying threshold concepts. *Journal of Philosophy of Education, 41*(2), 263–270. doi:10.1111/j.1467-9752.2007.00554.x

Shapiro, J. (2011). Perspective: Does medical education promote professional alexithymia? A call for attending to the emotions of patients and self in medical training. *Academic Medicine, 86*(3), 326–332.

van den Eertwegh, V., van Dulmen, S., van Dalen, J., Scherpbier, A. J., & van der Vleuten, C. P. (2012). Learning in context: Identifying gaps in research on the transfer of medical communication skills to the clinical workplace. *Patient Education and Counseling.*

Yedidia, M. J. (2007). Transforming doctor-patient relationships to promote patient-centered care: Lessons from palliative care. *Journal of Pain and Symptom Management, 33*(1), 40–57. doi:http://dx.doi.org/10.1016/j.jpainsymman.2006.06.007

Zambrano, S. C., Chur-Hansen, A., & Crawford, B. (2012). On the emotional connection of medical specialists dealing with death and dying: A qualitative study of oncologists, surgeons, intensive care specialists and palliative medicine specialists. *BMJ Supportive & Palliative Care, 2*(3), 270–275. doi:10.1136/bmjspcare-2012-000208

Zambrano, S. C., Chur-Hansen, A., & Crawford, G. B. (2013). The experiences, coping mechanisms and impact of death and dying on palliative medicine specialists. *Palliative & Supportive Care, FirstView,* 1–8. doi:10.1017/S1478951513000138

Andy Wearn
Director, Clinical Skills Centre
Faculty of Medical and Health Sciences
The University of Auckland

Anne O'Callaghan
Clinical Director, Palliative Care Service
Auckland City Hospital

237

Mark Barrow
Associate Dean (Academic)
Faculty of Medical and Health Sciences
The University of Auckland

LINDA MARTINDALE, RAY LAND, JULIE RATTRAY
AND LORRAINE ANDERSON

18. EXPLORING SOURCES OF TROUBLE
IN RESEARCH LEARNING FOR
UNDERGRADUATE NURSES

INTRODUCTION AND BACKGROUND

This chapter explores the nature of trouble in professional learning, using the case of research learning in the undergraduate nursing curriculum. It draws on the results of a study that identified threshold concepts in research education for undergraduate nursing students and explored the nature of trouble within these threshold concepts. We will examine the different sources of trouble that were found for undergraduate students, when learning about nursing research and will consider the possibility that these sources may be inherent in any threshold concepts or practices encountered in professional disciplines.

Research skills and methods are commonly included in undergraduate nursing programmes, in common with other disciplines in higher education (Christie, Hamill, & Power, 2012) and research teaching in nursing is primarily linked to the development of evidence-based practice (EBP), which combines current research evidence, clinical judgement and the needs and values of patients, to try to ensure best patient care (Barker, 2010). Research is included in undergraduate nursing education to prepare students for EBP, teaching them how to find, appraise and synthesise published research evidence (Gray, 2010). The EBP approach is widely accepted across nursing and other healthcare professions, with many regulatory bodies, such as the Nursing and Midwifery Council in the UK, mandating that students should be able to use evidence in the care of patients by the point of registration (Nursing and Midwifery Council, 2015). Some educators have suggested that students also need to learn how to carry out research (Niven, Roy, Schaefer, Gasquoine, & Ward, 2013) and certainly, teaching of nursing research predates the EBP movement, with evidence of research teaching going back almost 50 years (Wax, 1966). Whatever the aim, there is general agreement that nursing students need to learn about research skills and methods, as a core component of degree-level nursing study (Bloom, Olinzock, Radjenovic, & Trice, 2013; Halcomb & Peters, 2009).

There is some limited evidence from nursing education literature that learning about research is troublesome, though at times this is stated as if it is a generally accepted fact, rather than being evidence based. This trouble appears to be linked

R. Land et al. (Eds.), Threshold Concepts in Practice, 239–251.
© *2016 Sense Publishers. All rights reserved.*

to both cognitive and affective facets of learning, though these conclusions need to be treated cautiously, as there is relatively little discussion in this literature about difficulty or what might cause it. Traditionally, in the threshold concepts literature, trouble in learning has been associated with troublesome knowledge and focuses primarily on the troublesome nature of what is to be learnt (Meyer & Land, 2006). More recently, in thresholds papers associated with professional learning, other perspectives of trouble have been presented, such as Blackburn and Nestel (2014), but trouble in threshold concepts is still predominantly associated with knowledge.

In nursing education literature troublesome knowledge has been associated with discourse and concepts associated with research. In a small qualitative study Ax and Kincade (2001) found that the term "research" was what might be referred to as foreign knowledge (Perkins, 2007), with students believing that this referred to doing a literature search. Examples of conceptually difficult knowledge were also found in research learning, particularly in relation to terminology and statistics (Ax & Kincade, 2001; Dobratz, 2003; Niven et al., 2013). Alongside this sparse evidence from undergraduate nursing education, other examples of troublesome research knowledge have been identified in thresholds literature. These vary in topic and educational level, but include hypothesis development for undergraduate biology students (Taylor, 2006), and quantitative literacy in science learning (Quinnell, Thompson, & LeBard, 2013). Doctoral research education also provides examples of conceptually difficult areas of research for learners and Kiley (2009) has identified (among others) research paradigm and theory as thresholds for doctoral researchers.

Others have identified negative attitudes to research that may contribute to nursing students finding research difficult to learn (Dyson, 1997). Ax and Kincade (2001) identified negative perceptions of research among students, expressed in the study as "resistance" (p. 161), partly because they did not expect to study research during their undergraduate education. Others support this view (Gray, 2010; MacVicar, 1998) and a similar finding of educators "desensitizing negative perceptions about research" suggests that teachers are aware of such attitudes (Porter & Mansour, 2003). These negative attitudes may be linked to a perceived lack of relevance of research to nursing practice. Ax and Kincade (2001) also found that students did not feel that what they had learnt about research was transferable to clinical practice and Halcomb and Peters (2009) also identified challenges related to relevance of research to practice. To address this, some researchers have used practice settings for learning, to investigate whether student attitudes may become more positive. Duggleby (1998) found improved awareness of the importance of research for practice in a group that collected interview data, but Gray (2010) reported more negative attitudes and Florin, Ehrenberg, Wallin, and Gustavsson (2012) found that the relevance of research was better conveyed through classroom based teaching, rather than clinical education.

Despite the general expert consensus that research is challenging for undergraduate nursing students, there remains relatively little evidence about specific aspects of research that students find challenging. Studies about research teaching in nursing education usually look for positive outcomes and improvements following a teaching intervention, so difficulties have not been investigated in depth to establish their nature or how they impact on learning. However the general notion of research learning being troublesome is convincing by the frequency with which those teaching nursing research refer to it and it is supported by thresholds work carried out in other professional and academic disciplines.

THEORY AND METHOD

A narrative research study was carried out to explore how undergraduate nursing students learn about research, particularly the ways in which they experienced trouble. Threshold concepts theory was able to provide a context for investigating how student learning occurs in this professional context, that combines both practice-based and classroom learning. Specifically, using threshold concepts enabled an exploration of how these students encountered and journeyed through a landscape of difficult and challenging learning (Meyer & Land, 2006). It was therefore particularly apt because it specifically addresses obstacles to learning, whereas most theories related to learning and teaching tend to focus on processes and methods to guide learning (Perkins, 2007).

Narrative research or inquiry commonly uses unstructured, in depth interviews to gather stories of events and experiences and it was chosen for its potential to demonstrate the range and complexity of learning, by analysing not just what the participants described, but also how experiences were retold, their choice of language and other aspects of their discourse (Riessman, 2008). Narrative research aligns well with threshold concepts theory, as narratives offer the potential describe in detail the process of learning, from the initial encounter with a threshold, through subsequent negotiation of the liminal space and then beyond the threshold. The spectrum of experience and diverse perspectives on learning that are possible in narrative interviews lend themselves well to exploring the range of ways in which students experience research learning, particularly troublesome aspects.

The study was carried out on two sites of a UK university and the target population was undergraduate students undertaking a module in research and EBP during their third year of nursing study. A cross-section of students was recruited by using email and 17 students agreed to take part in two recorded interviews. The interviews took place on campus and all students took part in an initial interview at the start of the module, with 13 subsequently giving a second interview after the end of the module. The first interview focused on feelings about research and experiences both before entering nursing and during practice placements. Understandings of research were also explored. The second interview centred around the module, including experiences of learning and teaching, difficulties or challenges and perceived changes to understanding and attitudes.

A thematic narrative analysis was undertaken, similar to a traditional thematic analysis, but different in that the themes are derived from the narratives, which remain intact, rather than from coding and categorising phrases or short excerpts of text (Riessman, 2008). Supplementing this, a dialogic analysis was used. This approach to analysing narrative is based in the work of Bakhtin (1981) and focuses on the voice or voices in narratives and the effects on the story (Frank, 2010). Dialogic analysis brings out contextual aspects of the narratives and was threaded through the thematic analysis by studying aspects of the context, the way students expressed themselves and the voices in the narratives. A working definition of narrative in the study was any discrete event or experience about an aspect of difficulty in research learning and from these narratives emerged a threefold theme of trouble.

FINDINGS

Trouble emerged as a complicated and pervasive element in the students' learning and was initially treated synonymously with troublesome knowledge, as defined by Perkins (2006). However many of the troublesome elements in the narratives could not be described as troublesome knowledge and three sources of trouble were identified as themes, classified as follows:

- *Troublesome knowledge*: inherent to the subjects of research and EBP
- *Troublesome selves*: internal to the students set of beliefs, attitudes and perceptions of research and EBP
- *Troublesome environments*: external to the student but related to the places where they learn

Research discourse, including research terminology, was repeatedly found to be the key source of troublesome knowledge. The students identified some specific terms as problematic, including rigour, as well as statistical terms, such as 'p' values, confidence intervals and 'n' to denote number of subjects. In the second interview most student recalled difficulties with some aspect of terminology, related to the research articles they were asked to critique, as well as in module reading materials. This manifested itself in the interviews by students questioning research terms and using research language quite hesitantly, sometimes mispronouncing terms or using them after long pauses.

Mandy[1]: I still don't really, like yeah, like rigour I still don't like, I kind of know what it is and all that stuff, but like rigour, like really why that word? Why not credible? You know what I mean? …but it's [the module] definitely helped for that, cos I had to define, like I know what qualitative is now. Know what qualitative is.

LM: do you think you would have struggled with that before the module?

Mandy: oh yeah I wouldn't have had a clue. It would have been like qualitative, what? That's good quality. I knew what quantitative, like I knew that was numbers and qualitative was quality, but that was it, so it was definitely helpful.

Mandy's narrative appears to reflect confusion, not just about what terms mean, but about differences between terms that to her seem obscure. She refers elsewhere in this narrative to 'buzzwords' suggesting that research language may be deliberately exclusive and inaccessible. The tentative and confused use of terminology was also apparent in the students' conceptions of research, including using research to mean searching for information.

Even going online that's research, that's me looking it up...I'm bringing in other papers and I'm meant to just go research this one... (Ruth)

The volume of terms and time were both suggested as possible reasons for the troublesome nature of the terminology and some students felt that the research terms or concepts were not necessarily difficult in themselves, but were made difficult by the time constraint imposed by a twelve week module. This led on to comparisons of research terminology with that of nursing. The students agreed that, like research, nursing is full of nursing-specific and medical terminology, but felt that they were able to build up their nursing vocabulary over time and were also receptive to healthcare terminology because this relates directly to their chosen discipline, as well as hearing nursing language used in practice settings.

The terms that we use of the wards, I think they're things that you can associate with body processes and people and, and they mean more because of that. Whereas the terms associated with research they're drier, drier, the whole thing is drier. (Sarah)

These facets of troublesome knowledge provide some insight into the specific challenges that students encounter when learning about research, but troublesome knowledge did not explain all the difficulties expressed by the students. A second component of troublesomeness can be referred to as troublesome selves. This refers to any source of trouble that is affective and internal to the individual student, as opposed to the cognitive trouble associated with troublesome knowledge. The notion of troublesome selves arose from narratives in which students expressed negative or ambivalent beliefs, feelings and perceptions about research. Most of the students did not recognise that negative feelings or perceptions could have the potential to cause trouble in their research learning, but some students did appear to make this link.

I think that for me the area's just too big for me to try and learn about on my own... I don't know if it's a bit about confidence as well because I still, well I am still a student so I feel like I need to be taught a lot of stuff... But yeah, I do get really lost in the research world. (Abby)

Despite most of the students not recognising their perceptions and attitudes as potentially troublesome, these may have the potential to interfere with learning, because of the ways in which they may predispose students to thinking of their own learning about research in negative ways. Another example from Sam illustrates how his view of himself with respect to research and researchers, could interfere with his learning.

> I'm just a wee student, so don't want to criticise this woman's hard work that she's done. (Sam)

Sam's use of 'wee' to diminish his status compared to the researcher, who has written the paper, is similar to a comment he made in his first interview, when he referred to a researcher being "in a laboratory with a white coat on, somebody who's very clever with numbers". These examples of students' views of their capabilities in relation to studying research illustrate this type of trouble that seems to originate in the students' views of themselves and which they need to be able to overcome, if this is not to interfere with their learning.

Students expressed a range of negative feelings towards research. For some this negativity was quite mild and reflected apprehension or anxiety about the module; this type of feeling was common when talking about embarking on the module, or when describing experiences of the module. Other negative attitudes were stronger, and words such as 'overwhelming', 'daunting', 'struggling', 'tedious' or 'boring' were not uncommon.

> ...at the beginning because it was like a big, like staring up a big mountain. I mean you couldn't really see the end and it was, it was difficult to begin with, to get into it and everything, again because it was so different to anything that's been, we've done before. (Sally)

Sally's use of a mountain image to reflect her apprehension at the start of the module was quite typical and alongside this general negativity, students identified other specific concerns, which led to negative attitudes. This included scepticism about the value of research or about the module itself, with some expressing a dislike for it. One student, Stuart, opened his interview with 'I hated it...' in response to being asked how he found the module. Other facets of these negative attitudes related to the lack of relevance to practice or future studies.

> ... you're never really going to use it again. When do you ever hear like a nurse critically analysing a guideline on the ward? They don't have time and I feel like to me, three months was long enough to learn a module that may never come up again in my life. (Ruth)

These examples identify negativity towards different aspects of research, but troublesome selves may also reflect uncertainly and liminality that could lead to negative feelings or perceptions of research. Such liminality is clear in the example below.

> ...but I didn't really take on board their points, 'cos I thought this is my plan. This is the way I'm going to make my essay go. And if it's wrong, it's wrong, at least at the end of the day I know it's all my work... And I didn't, I noticed

that a few folk had asked questions and people would answer it but I didn't even refer to them, if I was stuck on that question, because that could have confused me even further, so I just thought, no, I'm just going to stick to my own work. (Sam)

Sam's way of managing a liminal state was to try to avoid any further confusion that might have been caused by listening to other students' comments. This was quite an unusual approach and other students adopted strategies like peer support to manage liminality. However, Sam's feelings of uncertainty were mirrored by other students and narratives of liminal states were quite common when students talked about their experiences of research learning.

The third source of trouble relates to environmental factors, including the interplay between different learning environments. The first difficulty associated with the learning environment emerged in students' narratives about an absence of research teaching prior to the module. Most students reported that they had no research teaching or very little in the first two years of their studies and all those who described this felt that it would have been helpful to have some teaching in these earlier years.

I feel I would have wanted more, like even just like, even maybe like a lecture on it [research]. Not even each semester, but even like once a year something... (Jess)

Subsequent feelings of the module being overwhelming were then partly related to a lack of previous exposure to research teaching. Other elements of the university learning environment were also identified as troublesome. One student raised a concern about the credibility and currency of university teaching staff, because they are not active in clinical practice. Although this concern was only identified by a single student, it reflects the norm in nursing education, i.e. that most academic staff are not in clinical practice, and this could be trouble-making because of its potential to undermine students' trust in university teaching staff.

By contrast, students identified with nurses they met in practice settings, as their future peers and colleagues. Yet, in the practice setting there was a noticeable lack of information and involvement in research. Ten of the 17 students reported some type of research being carried out during a practice placement, but they had not usually been told about the research going on. The message to students appeared to be that the research was not relevant to them and even when students were involved, the experience was not necessarily positive.

And it did kind of put you off a wee bit trying to do stuff, if you were trying to do a dressing or catheters or something like that, you, it was quite off-putting being part of it [the research study]. (Sandy)

Another student, Caitlin, was very positive and confident about both research and EBP, through most of her narratives and in her second interview she expresses a strong desire to do research in the future. However when talking about a research study that she was peripherally involved in during a placement, she becomes atypically less sure about the experience.

> It was one of the psychologists actually was doing some research into relaxation techniques for palliative patients and she used the staff as, I don't know whether we were like the control group, or something... So I remember her using us as I suppose her control group... but I never saw where that went... (Caitlin)

The trouble in learning environments appears to be further compounded by tensions between the university and practice settings, with an undesirable position where the academic learning environment promotes research, but may lack credibility, whereas the practice environment can demonstrate ambiguity towards research, yet is a more real setting for students, given that it is where their future work will be based. The tension and trouble seem to arise from the very different messages from the two environments, relating to the importance of research. These tensions between the two settings are likely to be troublesome because they result in the messages given in university teaching not being substantiated in practice.

Some of the students directly expressed this trouble as a concern with a theory practice gap for research, related to what was being taught.

> ... the lecturers... tell us, this is like when you're doing this, this applies to when you'll see this. So you look, yeah, whereas this [the module] just seems to be theory doubled on theory doubled on theory. (Abby)

In this group of students, these environmental facets of trouble were linked to the requirements of healthcare learning that combine classroom-based learning with practice experience. This source of trouble was described by all the students who were interviewed, but, consistent with troublesome selves, the students did not always recognise that this might negatively impact on their learning.

The students involved in the study came from a range of backgrounds and some had experienced research or been exposed to others doing research in their "pre-nursing" lives. Although this sometimes meant that these students were more familiar with research terms and concepts, their narratives that were still permeated with trouble, often related to troublesome selves or environments. One mature student, Sarah, entered her nursing studies with quite a lot of experience of research, but she talked about trouble related to knowledge, selves and environments, which seemed to link to her emerging nursing identity and the different perspective of research associated with an applied and professional discipline.

> Everything I did before was very, very quantitative... And so, nursing is a much more qualitative discipline... I don't know anything about qualitative research at all. And everything was so black and white, it worked or it didn't, it was positive or negative. The numbers were significant or they weren't, and that's all there was to it. (Sarah)

This experience of trouble appears to be situated in the learning environment of a nursing programme, as well as being influenced by Sarah's previous knowledge, perceptions and attitudes towards research. For all students interviewed, research presented trouble in the learning process, but the conventional label of troublesome knowledge that is usually associated with threshold concepts, did not adequately represent the trouble described in the narratives, and identifying different sources of trouble was a useful way of describing the multi-faceted nature of the trouble that the students encountered.

DISCUSSION

As already discussed, threshold concepts typically characterises difficulty as troublesome knowledge (Perkins, 2006). However, in this study trouble was found to be more complex and pervasive, affecting different aspects of learning. This may relate to the professional nature of nursing education, which means that students are exposed to different learning environments and attitudes among peers, colleagues, other professionals and teachers. For nursing students in particular, unlike many other professions, exposure to practice begins very early in their nursing studies (often in the first semester of study) and, by law, is at least 50% of their study time (European Parliament & Council of the European Union, 2005). The practice environment requires students to learn in a space that is not primarily for learning and where cultures and attitudes may be very different to university learning (Gerrish, Ashworth, Lacey, & Bailey, 2008). It seems likely that exposure to this environment at such an early and formative stage will affect students' learning.

Trouble also seems to compounded for students by negative attitudes and perceptions that may link to nursing identity. Research may not be viewed as part of "being a nurse", by students and / or practising nurses, so learning about research becomes troublesome. This issue was identified as an issue by Ax and Kincade (2001), who found that the students they interviewed had not expected research to be part of the nursing curriculum. MacVicar (1998) also found students had negative attitudes towards research in the early part of their nursing studies, linked to fear and anxiety about research.

The link to nursing identity may be further complicated by the interaction with troublesome learning environments, in which practising nurses' negative or ambiguous attitudes to research may be expressed overtly or implicitly. Such interplay between different types of trouble suggests that, for nursing students learning about research, there may be a complex web of factors impacting on their learning, some of which they may not even be aware of. In this study the students appeared to accept variable experiences of research and EBP in the practice setting as quite normal. However from a learning perspective, the mixed messages such variation sends out can hamper or even prevent development of positive attitudes and learning.

In thresholds literature others have identified different aspects of trouble related to professional learning. Blackburn and Nestel (2014) found a range of troublesome aspects of surgical education, including issues related to roles and the impact of bad experiences, as well as troublesome knowledge. Looking at early childhood education and care, (Taylor, 2013) found workplace culture to be a source of trouble, as was students' ability to participate actively in placements. These examples echo the different sources of trouble found in this study and suggest that trouble is a multi-faceted aspect of professional learning. It may be useful to acknowledge these sources and classify them, to help to unpick the different ways that they may affect students' learning, just as Perkin's original work in troublesome knowledge identified different types of such knowledge (Perkins, 1999). Unlike students following traditional academic pathways, students in professional degrees are subject to a range of external influences, including regulation of professional bodies, projections of their professional identity and ethical and professional norms, as well as being exposed to practice. Not only might these factors create trouble, but there may be interaction between these and identification of the sources of trouble could help to show how different types of trouble interact.

Trouble in learning is inextricably linked to the liminal space in which students encounter new threshold concepts and the experience of liminality has been identified as an aspect of threshold concepts that is well recognised but not very well understood (Land, Rattray, & Vivian, 2014). Separating out the different sources of trouble, as well as defining the factors that are particular to these sources, may offer a way of better understanding the liminal state. It may also help with recognising the different forces that can hold students back from letting go of previous ways of thinking and being able to cross the new threshold.

In the case of research learning in the study described here, some students described liminality in a juxtaposition of the relative absence of research or research-based practice in what they witnessed in practice, compared to being taught that this should be integral to practice. This led them to perceive research as not relevant to nursing practice – the "theory doubled on theory" described by Abby earlier. When trouble like this is linked to the student's attitudes or to their experiences in learning environments, troublesome knowledge may become less of a priority for teachers, because the troublesome selves and environments need to be addressed, if knowledge is to become relevant and meaningful. This was identified by Waite, Schutz, Lansdown, Goodman-Brown, and Higgins (2010) in relation to EBP learning among postgraduate nursing students, who found that when students perceived that they could positively impact practice, through using evidence, this helped them through the liminal state to a transformed understanding.

Overtly classifying trouble by these different sources, or by others that may apply in different disciplines or contexts, has the potential to influence the curriculum, by enabling teachers to identify and address affective and external barriers to learning, as well as the difficulties associated with troublesome knowledge. Given the strong links of trouble to the liminal state, this may also be an approach that can help to develop understanding of what liminality is like for students in professional disciplines, where they need to learn about academic threshold concepts that are also integral to their future practice.

CONCLUSION

These findings point to troublesome areas in threshold concepts which are not necessarily inherent in the subject or concept itself, but which are linked to the culture and environments in which the students are learning and to their perceptions of the topic. In nursing this seems to be particularly problematic because of the need to learn within a higher education institution as well as in a range of healthcare settings.

Understanding the range of factors that may make a threshold concept troublesome, particularly in professional learning, can help to explain students' challenges in learning. This understanding may have the potential to influence curriculum design to address these problems more overtly.

NOTE

[1]   All student names have been anonymised.

REFERENCES

Ax, S., & Kincade, E. (2001). Nursing students' perceptions of research: Usefulness, implementation and training. *Journal of Advanced Nursing, 35*(2), 161–170.

Bakhtin, M. M. (1981). *The dialogic imagination* (C. Emerson & M. Holquist, Trans., M. Holquist Ed.). Austin, TX: University of Texas Press.

Barker, J. (2010). *Evidence-based practice for nurses*. London: Sage.

Blackburn, S., & Nestel, D. (2014). Troublesome knowledge in pediatric surgical trainees: A qualitative study. *Journal of Surgical Education, 71*(5), 756–761.

Bloom, K. C., Olinzock, B. J., Radjenovic, D., & Trice, L. B. (2013). Leveling EBP content for undergraduate nursing students. *Journal of Professional Nursing, 29*(4), 217–224.

Christie, J., Hamill, C., & Power, J. (2012) How can we maximize nursing students- learning about research evidence and utilization in undergraduate, preregistration programmes? A discussion paper. *Journal of Advanced Nursing, 68*(12), 2789–2801.

Dobratz, M. C. (2003). Putting the pieces together: Teaching undergraduate research from a theoretical perspective. *Journal of Advanced Nursing, 41*(4), 383–392.

Duggleby, W. (1998). Improving undergraduate nursing research education: The effectiveness of collecting and analyzing oral histories. *Journal of Nursing Education, 37*(6), 247–252.

Dyson, J. (1997). Research: Promoting positive attitudes through education. *Journal of Advanced Nursing, 26*(3), 608–612.

European Parliament & Council of the European Union. (2005). Directive 2005/36/ec *Official Journal of the European Union.*

Florin, J., Ehrenberg, A., Wallin, L., & Gustavsson, P. (2012). Educational support for research utilization and capability beliefs regarding evidence-based practice skills: A national survey of senior nursing students. *Journal of Advanced Nursing, 68*(4), 888–897.

Frank, A.W. (2010). *Letting stories breathe*. Chicago, IL: University of Chicago Press.

Gerrish, K., Ashworth, P., Lacey, A., & Bailey, J. (2008). Developing evidence-based practice: Experiences of senior and junior clinical nurses. *Journal of Advanced Nursing, 62*(1), 62–73.

Gray, M. T. (2010). Research odyssey : The evolution of a research partnership between baccalaureate nursing students and practicing nurses. *Nurse Education Today, 30*(4), 376–382.

Halcomb, E. J., & Peters, K. (2009). Nursing student feedback on undergraduate research education: Implications for teaching and learning. *Contemporary Nurse, 33*(1), 59–68.

Kiley, M. (2009). Identifying threshold concepts and proposing strategies to support doctoral candidates. *Innovations in Education and Teaching International, 46*(3), 293–304.

Land, R., Rattray, J., & Vivian, P. (2014). Learning in the liminal space: A semiotic approach to threshold concepts. *Higher Education, 67*, 199–217.

MacVicar, M. H. (1998). Intellectual development and research: Student nurses' and student midwives' accounts. *Journal of Advanced Nursing, 27*(6), 1305–1316.

Meyer, J. H. F., & Land, R. (2006). Threshold concepts and troublesome knowledge: An introduction. In J. H. F. Meyer & R. Land (Eds.), *Overcoming barriers to students understanding: Threshold concepts and troublesome knowledge*. Abingdon & New York, NY: Routledge.

Niven, E., Roy, D. E., Schaefer, B. A., Gasquoine, S. E., & Ward, F. A. (2013). Making research real: Embedding a longitudinal study in a taught research course for undergraduate nursing students. *Nurse Education Today, 33*(1), 64–68.

Nursing and Midwifery Council. (2015). *The code: Professional standards of practice and behaviour for nurses and midwives*. London: Nursing and Midwifery Council.

Perkins, D. (1999). The many faces of constructivism. *Educational Leadership, 57*, 6–11.

Perkins, D. (2006). Constructivism and troublesome knowledge. In J. H. F. Meyer & R. Land (Eds.), *Overcoming barriers to student understanding: Threshold concepts and troublesome knowledge* (pp. 33–47). Abingdon: Routledge.

Perkins, D. (2007). Theories of difficulty. *British Journal of Educational Psychology Mongraph, 2*(4), 31–48.

Porter, E. J., & Mansour, T. B. (2003). Teaching nursing research to undergraduates: A text analysis of instructors intentions. *Research in Nursing & Health, 26*, 128–142.

Quinnell, R., Thompson, R., & LeBard, R. J. (2013). It's not maths; it's science: Exploring thinking dispositions, learning thresholds and mindfulness in science learning. *International Journal of Mathematical Education in Science and Technology, 44*(6), 808–816.

Riessman, C. K. (2008). *Narrative methods for the human sciences*. Thousand Oaks, CA: Sage.

Taylor, C. (2006). Threshold concepts in biology: Do they fit the definition? In J. H. F. Meyer & R. Land (Eds.), *Overcoming barriers to student understanding: Threshold concepts and troublesome knowledge*. Abingdon: Routledge.

Taylor, M. (2013). *What early childcare students find 'troublesome' during practice placements*. Paper presented at the International Conference on Engaging Pedagogy (ICEP), The Voice of Educators, Sligo, Ireland.

Waite, M., Schutz, S., Lansdown, G., Goodman-Brown, J., & Higgins, C. (2010). *Evidence based practice, threshold concepts and troublesome knowledge: The perspectives and experiences of postgraduate nursing students in the uk and hong kong*. Paper presented at the Evidence 2010 – Transforming Healthcare, London.

Wax, J. (1966). Attitudes of nursing students toward research. *Nursing Outlook, 14*, 70–72.

Linda Martindale
Durham University/University of Dundee

Ray Land
Durham University

Julie Rattray
Durham University

Lorraine Anderson
University of Dundee

DERMOT SHINNERS-KENNEDY

19. HOW *NOT* TO IDENTIFY THRESHOLD CONCEPTS

INTRODUCTION

Devising a methodology for identifying threshold concepts would represent an important milestone in the evolution of threshold concept scholarship. For the most part the strategies deployed by researchers to-date have yielded tentative proposals only and the uncertain nature of the outcomes has been a frustrating experience for investigators. It is sometimes asserted that perceived difficulties with the threshold concept definition impede the accumulation of empirical evidence that can be used for identification purposes. However, we believe many of the problems experienced thus far are associated with the approaches used to gather the empirical data. In this chapter we identify some of the shortcomings inherent in the commonly-used approaches.

The shortcomings identified represent a small but significant collection of issues that highlight the difficulties associated with acquiring the necessary empirical data for identification. The collection includes the effects of basic level concepts, expert blind spot, hindsight bias and the curse of knowledge, the illusion of memory, the influence of language and the effects of emotion. The analysis shows how these issues actually mitigate against the discovery of the type of data that is sought by investigators.

ASKING LEARNERS

The acquisition of a threshold concept causes knowledge integration and transforms the learner's view of their discipline and possibly even their world. This would appear to qualify it as a 'stand out' experience of profound learning and one that a learner would be able to remember and identify as a critical learning incident. However, this is not the picture of learning that has been painted in many of the empirical studies that have sought to elicit details that would support the identification of a particular concept as a threshold concept. Regardless of whether the method used was interviews, structured tasks or questionnaires almost every study that has asked learners to look back and recall a time when they had a conceptual difficulty that had been resolved, and to recount how it had been resolved, has been unable to accumulate empirical evidence that supports the identification of a particular concept as a threshold concept.

R. Land et al. (Eds.), Threshold Concepts in Practice, 253–267.

Learners are unable to recall a 'critical' moment in their learning. Even when they are aware of the general case, that they had learned something they previously did not understand, they are frequently unable to recall details of the situation – the time or place, what actually caused it to happen, and so on. Some learners may recall revelatory moments, but they are rarely unique and are often reported simply as part of an ongoing experience. In cases where the learners are novices in a discipline (e.g., first years) it might be prudent to discount their difficulties on the basis that their knowledge structures could be fragile (Perkins & Martin, 1986) and their ability to command the language required to articulate their experiences might be suspect. However, the knowledge structures and meta-learning skills of postgraduates should be sufficiently well advanced to support review and examination. Likewise, the learning maturity of undergraduates in the final or penultimate year of their programmes should at least facilitate insightful review of their learning processes.

For the most part the outcomes have been unproductive and raise questions about the methods that were used and what they are capable of illuminating.

The Illusion of Memory

The New York Times[1] edition of 6 January 2009 included a story about the American spiritual writer Neale Donald Walsch who was accused of plagiarising a story he claimed was about a pageant at his son's kindergarten. At one point in the pageant the children participating held up letters spelling the title of a song called Christmas Love. The child with the letter *m* inadvertently held the letter upside down which had the effect of changing the text to 'Christ was love'. Recalling the story Walsch found it so endearing that he used it for a personal message posted on a spiritual website around Christmas 2008. Unfortunately, the story wasn't his and didn't involve his son. It had been written by another writer and published in a magazine ten years earlier. The original author had copyrighted the story with the US Copyright Office in 2003. Coincidentally, both authors happened to have a son with the same name. As part of their reporting of the story the New York Times quoted Walsch as saying

All I can say now—because I am truly mystified and taken aback by this—is that someone must have sent it to me over the Internet ten years or so ago… Finding it utterly charming and its message indelible, I must have clipped and pasted it into my file of 'stories to tell that have a message I want to share'. I have told the story verbally so many times over the years that I had it memorized … and then, somewhere along the way, internalized it as my own experience.

The term *illusion of memory* attempts to capture 'the disconnect between how we think memory works and how it actually works' (Chabris & Simons, 2010, p. 45). Sir Fredrick Bartlett's classic work on remembering is usually credited with distinguishing between the reproductive and reconstructive properties of memory (Bartlett, 1932). Most people believe memory is reproductive and that when we remember something we retrieve an accurate, video-style version of the material from memory. For example, a survey in the US in 2009 revealed that 63% of respondents supported this view and nearly half of the respondents (47%) believed that once we have formed a memory of an event it doesn't change (Chabris & Simons, 2010, p. 45).

Bartlett's work showed that memory recall was a process of construction and not reproduction. He had subjects read an Indian folktale and recall it repeatedly. He noted

> The first notion to get rid of is that memory is primarily or literally reduplicative, or reproductive...In the many thousands of cases of remembering which I collected, a considerable number of which I have recorded here, literal recall was very rare. (Bartlett, 1932, p. 204)

Bartlett developed a theory of remembering to provide a coherent explanation of how 'the past operates as an organised mass rather than as a group of elements each of which retains its specific character'. His theory emphasises the constructive style of remembering which is an active process, frequently error-prone because remembered components are distorted during construction and missing components are filled in. Bartlett describes it thus

> when a subject is being asked to remember, very often the first thing that emerges is something of the nature of attitude. The recall is then a construction, made largely on the basis of this attitude, and its general effect is that of a justification of the attitude. (Bartlett, 1932, p. 207)

Deese (1959) provides an interesting example of how a particular disposition or attitude can evoke recollections that are consistent or justified by the disposition but that are in fact erroneous. Deese chose a theme or critical word and created a word list containing twelve words closely associated with the critical word but that did not include the critical word. For example, the list for the critical word *needle* contained *thread, pin, eye, sewing, sharp, point, pricked, thimble, haystack, pain, hurt,* and *injection*. Subjects were read the word list and then immediately asked to recall it. Deese reported a high incidence of 'extralist intrusions' (i.e. recall of the critical word) induced by the words appearing in the list (Deese, 1959, p. 21) concluded that 'in the process of recollection, words and concepts associated with the remembered items will be added' (Roediger & McDermott, 1995) replicated and extended Deese's work and report that their 'subjects confidently recalled and recognised words that were not present and also reported that they remembered the occurrence of these events'. What Roediger and McDermott describe as 'false memories' are a consequence of the constructive characteristics of remembering.

Using a different approach (Brewer & Treyens, 1981) showed the effects of false memories in an immediate but purely visual context. They recruited subjects for an experiment without specifying the task involved. The subjects were brought to a graduate student's office and asked to wait while the experimenter checked if the previous group had finished the activity. This was a ruse used by the experimenters. In fact, the time spent by the subjects 'waiting' in the office was the experiment. After approximately thirty seconds the subjects were taken to another room and asked to write a list all of the things they had seen in the office. In addition to listing objects that were in the office about 30% of the subjects listed books and around 10% included a filing cabinet. Unusually, there were no books or filing cabinets in the office. The subjects' lists included things they had actually seen as well as things they would normally associate with an office of that type. Their false memories of the presence of some objects emerged from the context they associated with the location.

In a legal context Loftus and Palmer undertook a series of experiments that showed our memories of a variety of complex occurrences contain two kinds of information.

> The first is information gleaned during the perception of the original event; the second is external information supplied after the fact. Over time, information from these two sources may be integrated in such a way that we are unable to tell from which source some specific detail is recalled. (Loftus & Palmer, 1974, p. 588)

As we acquire information it does not just accumulate and lie passively in our cognitive system waiting to be recalled from memory. As time passes new information adds to it, or alters it, and when we recall it we recall the morphed version and not the original, individual components of the recollection (Loftus & Palmer, 1974; Bartlett, 1932).

We might be lured to a degree of scepticism by the fact that in all of the forgoing cases the subjects were, to a certain degree, just casually involved in the studies with no personal commitment to the activities being investigated. But the findings have been replicated in cases where the benefits of reliable recall are crucially important to the participants as well as the investigators.

Consider the work of Kevin Dunbar who reported on a series of in-vivo studies undertaken at a number of renowned research laboratories (Dunbar, 1997). The studies were specifically interested in investigating the processes associated with conceptual change and how it occurred in serious research situations. All of the laboratories were staffed by highly trained and skilled researchers who were experts in their respective disciplines and deeply committed to the work of the laboratories. Thus, all of the people participating in the study had a vested interest in identifying and reflecting on the actions and events that guided their work and how they contributed to the success of the group. Every one of them was acutely conscious of the importance of knowledge integration and its transformative effects on learning.

Dunbar spent a year immersed in the work of the laboratories with the goal of specifically identifying the points in time at which innovative scientific thinking occurred. His observations led him to the conclusion that one of the central places in which new ideas and concepts were generated was the regular meetings of all the laboratory researchers. At these meetings the researchers externalised much of their thinking by talking through the questions, proposals, hypotheses and interpretations that were generated by the group discussion. This made it possible for Dunbar to gain access to what he describes as their 'online' thinking and reasoning.

Dunbar reported his findings in relation to the use of analogy and the reasoning mechanisms used by the research teams but he also reports that 'the scientists had little memory' of how the various thinking and reasoning elements contributed to the conceptual change experienced by the research group. He documents the exchanges at one of the meetings where a significant discovery was made and records the various ideas and reasoning lines that evolved during the discussion. He then describes the crucial point at which it became clear to the group that they had made a breakthrough.

It was at this point that everyone in the lab realized that a conceptual change had occurred and all shouted in excitement. This was followed by some further analogies in which other post-docs suggested other experiments. Finally a post-doc made an analogy to the methods that other researchers have used and the methods that the post-doc had used, explaining why their rival's lab had not made the discovery that they had just made. (Dunbar, 1997, p. 486–487)

One week later, one month later, three months later, and nine months later Dunbar asked the post-doc who had conducted the research how the 'discovery' was made. Dunbar reports

On none of these occasions did he [the post-doc] recall the spontaneous analogies used, nor that distributed reasoning was involved. Thus, much of the online cognitive processes that went into the conceptual change would have disappeared without a record if I had not taped the original meeting. (Dunbar, 1997, p. 488)

Emotion

Acquisition of a threshold concept is described as an emotionally laden event that can have the effect of altering the learner's view of themselves, their chosen discipline and even the world. However, the affective consequences of events can be hard to determine because evidence documenting emotional experiences can be resistant to recall, even in cases where the accuracy of the recalled material is paramount.

For example, since 2006 most European countries have based primary health care planning and configuration decisions on data derived from national health surveys. In the surveys interviewees are asked to report their doctor visits during a *four-week* period because longer periods have been found to be subject to massive degradation of recollection (EHIS, 2008).

Similarly, a number of medical studies investigating lifestyle choices have found that recall associated with choosing to start or give up smoking is markedly different from the recall of choices such as whether a baby was breastfed or vaccinated. An important issue that emerged from the studies was the nature of the material recalled and its relationship to the significance of the original incident. Comparing remembered incidents to documentary sources, or, in some cases, to earlier accounts from the same participant (Berney & Blane, 2003), medical researchers discovered that the *type* of information recalled made a difference (Seldon, 1983). Somewhat counter-intuitively they found that 'hum-drum events which carry little emotional charge and the barely noticed background routines of life appear to be recalled most accurately' and the emotionally laden events 'are least likely to be recalled accurately' (Blane, 1996).

Summary

Asking learners to remember the circumstances surrounding a transformative learning experience is fraught with problems because the learner's memory of the experience is almost guaranteed to be distorted and erroneous, despite their best efforts to provide, and their belief that it is, an accurate account of the experience.

ASKING EXPERTS

An alternative approach to asking learners is to ask experts to identify concepts they believe qualify as threshold concepts. Experts have the advantage of intimate knowledge of a discipline and the conceptual structure of its body of knowledge. However, experts have their own foibles and though we might to think that all experts are equal, in fact, some experts are more equal than others.

For example, the methodologies used by researchers investigating the pedagogical aspects of a discipline are not the same as those used by researchers developing the body of knowledge in a discipline. The two researchers have different epistemological stances and different ways of demonstrating that something is 'true'. (Garfinkel, 1984) notes that what the two researchers do share is a 'vulgar competence' – both are (ordinarily) competent in relation to the discipline under scrutiny and have an understanding of the investigated phenomena and the site of the research, but they don't view it through the same research lens.

Expert Blind Spot

Researchers in many disciplines have attempted to identify threshold concepts using discipline-research approaches. (Davies, 2003) argues that this approach, which has been used in his own discipline of Economics, is unlikely to be successful because of its focus on discipline structure and its indifference to the learner's acquisition of understanding. He suggests that discipline-oriented categorisations like *fundamental* or *core* concepts, and their equivalents, conflate understanding and structure, and divorce understanding from the learner's previous experiences.

Davies' use of language is revealing in the context of the properties of a threshold concept. Conflation is not transformation and divorce is an antonym for integration. The purpose of a core or fundamental concept is significantly different from that of a threshold concept. A core or fundamental concept is agreed within a discipline as an identifiable, important component of the discipline's body of knowledge. Labelling a concept as core or fundamental is the outcome of decisions that are immune to the active learning process. In contrast, a threshold concept is viewed as an identifiable, important concept that acts on the learner's (partially) acquired body of knowledge as a restructuring tool during the learning process.

Consistent with Davies' observations, Nathan and Petrosino invoke the blind spot metaphor of visual perception to highlight some difficulties experienced by educators with advanced subject-matter knowledge. Students' conceptual development and instruction should be guided by the tutor's knowledge of the learning needs and developmental profiles of the students. However, tutors tend to be guided by 'powerful organizing principles, formalisms, and methods of analysis' that serve as the foundations of the discipline and are embodied in the concepts identified as core or fundamental. The tutor then falls victim of expert blind spot because they 'tend toward views of student development that align more closely with the organization of the discipline than with the learning processes of students' and are often 'entirely unaware of having such a blind spot' (Nathan & Petrosino, 2003, p. 906).

This view resonates with the conclusions drawn by Goldman et al. about the incompleteness of tutors' understanding of student learning. Goldman and his colleagues greeted the results of the *Delphi process* (Clayton, 1997) style study they had undertaken with caution because they felt 'teachers have an incomplete (at best) understanding of student learning'. That conclusion persuaded them to interview their students 'to validate the difficulty ratings asserted by our experts' in the expectation that 'some topics that our experts ranked as easy will, in fact, be rife with student misconceptions' (Goldman et al., 2008).

The view is also consistent with the distinction drawn by Gal-Ezer and Harel between the knowledge requirements of an educator and those of a practitioner or discipline-focused researcher. Their description of a 'scientific intellectual' whose knowledge base needs to be far more nuanced than the other two emphasises the need for educators to be actively alert to the dynamics of student learning and the nature of knowledge acquisition (Gal-Ezer & Harel, 1998). This requirement is completely absent from the workbench toolset of a practitioner or discipline-focused researcher.

Basic Level Concepts

All concept categorisations, regardless of whether they are labelled core or fundamental or threshold or something else, are motivated by the desire to facilitate comprehension and use. They are also subconsciously influenced by subtle cognitive goals that privilege and distinguish particular categorisations. Our cognitive system privileges some categorisations because they are the most cognitively efficient. These categorisations are distinguished because they have two important properties – they are informative and distinctive (Murphy, 2002).

For example, when we see a bird we do not identify it specifically by its ornithological classification (say a spotted flycatcher) or more generally as an animal. One provides too much information and the other too little. We simply identify it as a bird because that is informative and distinctive. Similarly, we tend to identify things as chairs because identifying them as furniture reduces the information provided and would be considered too abstract whereas identifying them as dining-room or classroom chairs may provide too much information and would be considered too specific.

Eleanor Rosch and her colleagues discovered the properties of these privileged concepts and used the term 'basic level concepts' to describe them (Rosch et al., 1976). Basic level concepts tend to be associated with the 'functional structure' of a domain (Brown, 1958) or 'the natural partitioning of objects' in the domain (Komatsu, 1992). The empirical findings in relation to basic level concepts show that they are easier to learn, are the first acquired by children, are more informative, pictures of them are identified faster and they are more frequently used in text (Murphy, 2002).

When experts attempt to partition the concepts of a discipline into category classifications they can be lured by the cognitive attractions of the basic level concepts that are part of the conceptual milieu of the discipline. For example, consider the outcomes of three unrelated studies that attempted to formulate categorisations of computer science concepts for pedagogic purposes.

In the first case the investigators were interested in identifying fundamental concepts (Zendler & Spannagel, 2008); in the second a Delphi process was used to identify concepts that are important and difficult for students to learn (Goldman et al., 2008); and in the third a variety of research instruments were used in a five year study to identify threshold concepts (Eckerdal et al., 2006; Boustedt et al., 2007; Eckerdal et al., 2007; McCartney et al., 2007; Moström et al., 2008; Zander et al., 2008; Thomas et al., 2010).

Table 1. Studies yielding basic level concepts

	Zender & Spannagel	Goldman et al	TC group
1	Algorithm	Procedure Design	Pointers
2	Computer	Problem Conceptualisation/ Solution Design	Object-Orientation
3	Data	Abstraction/Pattern use	Data Abstraction
4	Problem	Test Design	Complexity
5	Information	Debugging/Exception Handling	Modularity

Despite the diversity of approaches used the outcomes are characterised by the fact that they all yielded basic level concepts. Table 1 above lists the top five concepts resulting from each study. With the possible exception of *pointers* all of the concepts fall into what computer scientists would view as basic level concepts. One could argue that in Zendler and Spannagel's study the use of the concepts in the ACM classification list predetermined the results because the classifications used in that list are general anyway. Notwithstanding this, the pervasive presence of basic level concepts across all three approaches is significant.

The approaches have not facilitated any sort of fine-grained consideration of the conceptual space and the features that distinguish concepts and allow them to be classified in a purposeful way. Despite taking different routes the authors' destinations have been the same, in fact, almost identical. In all three cases the outcome is an enumerated list with no accompanying insight into the anatomy of the conceptual space or the physiology of the conceptual elements identified. In the context of threshold concept identification the anatomical and physiological issues are pivotal for realising the integrative and transformational properties.

Hindsight Bias and the Curse of Knowledge

Ironically, the possession of expert knowledge can introduce additional difficulties because our view of events in hindsight is not the same as our view in foresight. Fischhoff described *hindsight bias* as the difficulties we experience when, knowing a particular outcome, we try to assess or 'judge' the likelihood of that outcome in a foresightful manner (i.e. as if we didn't know the outcome). Hindsight bias affects our judgements, including the judgements of experts (Fischhoff, 1975). In a series of experiments subjects overestimated their ability to predict the outcome of an event when they knew the outcome. The subjects also overestimated what uninformed others (e.g., novices) would have known. This general finding has been replicated in a variety of settings (Hoch & Loewenstein, 1989; Guilbault et al., 2004).

Fischhoff coined the term *creeping determinism* to describe our tendency to view as inevitable the outcomes we have knowledge of, especially because we can rely on the certitude of that outcome as a viable possibility. He cites the succinct description of the effect provided by (Florovsky, 1969, p. 369) as follows

> In retrospect, we seem to perceive the logic of the events which unfold themselves in a regular or linear fashion according to a recognizable pattern with an alleged inner necessity. So that we get the impression that it really could not have happened otherwise. (Fischhoff, 1975, p. 288)

Providing a rationale for the effect (Fischhoff, 1975, p. 295) suggests subjects

> fail to properly reconstruct foresightful (before) judgments because they are 'anchored' in the hindsightful state of mind created by possession of outcome knowledge.

The anchoring effect occurs because once the subjects have received the outcome knowledge they

> immediately assimilate it with what they already know about the event in question. In other words, the retrospective judge attempts to make sense, or a coherent whole, out of all that he knows about the event… Assimilation of this type would tend to induce creeping determinism. (ibid., p.297)

Fishhoff also showed that even when instructed to do so subjects were unable to ignore their knowledge of the outcome and denied their judgements were influenced by that knowledge.

In the context of economic analyses (Camerer et al., 1989) investigate what they describe as 'violations of normative theories of judgement' which are aberrations of the idea that better-informed people make better decisions. Hogarth called it the *curse of knowledge* because the better-informed agents are unable to ignore their informational advantage even when it is in their best interests to do so. For example, the buyer of a house may pay more simply because they know they can afford it. The seller of a house may reduce the price because of their knowledge of some of its flaws, even if the flaws are unobservable to the buyer. The better-informed person is cursed because their judgements of the less-informed person are biased by their own knowledge and they cannot ignore it. As a consequence the better-informed agent may suffer losses (Camerer et al., 1989) argue.

This exaggeration interferes with the evaluation of decision quality. Outcomes are an imperfect indicator of decision quality; good decisions can lead to bad outcomes and vice versa. But principals must often judge decisions of agents on the basis of outcomes because actions or decision criteria are unobservable. Camerer et al. concluded

> The curse of knowledge suggests that informed subjects will be unable to ignore the information that they have that the uninformed subjects lack, causing bias in their predictions.

Hawkins and Hastie (1990) note that thinking backwards with knowledge of the outcome 'sharply inhibits thinking' and results in 'narrow-minded thinking' because only one outcome requires explanation whereas several possible outcomes must be considered when foresight is involved. Thus, the projection of acquired knowledge into the past can affect the selection of evidence, the evaluation of that evidence and the way in which the evidence is integrated into decisions about the knowledge. For example, when considering possibilities in hindsight 'outcome-congruent information becomes more accessible' and once a piece of information is chosen it may need to be further refined or calibrated (e.g. estimates of speed, time, distance, strength) but always with the implications for the final outcome available. (Henriksen & Kaplan, 2003, p. 46) argue that possession of outcome knowledge changes the way we consider 'a bewildering array of non-convergent events' because they have now become 'a coherent causal framework for making sense out of what happened'.

One interesting feature of hindsight judgements is that whilst the outcome is known with certainty it is rarely possible to identify a well-defined starting point for the combination of actions and events which caused the outcome. (Rasmussen, 1987) discusses the difficulties associated with deciding when to stop an 'explanatory search after the fact'. Ideally the search should continue until the root cause is identified but 'generally the search will stop when one or more changes are found which are familiar and therefore applicable as explanations'. However, such a decision may be based on pragmatic or arbitrary constraints (e.g. time, money or accessibility and availability of the participants) and not informational or causal requirements. In many cases the outcome of the search 'depends entirely on the stop rule applied' and this can have serious implications for the conclusions which are or can be drawn.

The Influence of Language

In a series of experiments (Loftus & Palmer, 1974) demonstrated how the language used in a question can evoke false memories and cause a change in our recollection of an event.

In one experiment, subjects who had viewed film-footage of a car accident were divided into groups. The groups were asked the same questions about the accident but different words were used in the questions. For example, the groups were asked to estimate the speed the cars were travelling when they *contacted, hit, bumped, collided* or *smashed* into each other. Questions using smashed elicited higher speed estimates than the other verbs.

A week later the same subjects were recalled and again questioned about the accident, this time without being shown the film footage. They were specifically asked about the presence of broken glass. There was no broken glass visible in the film they had been shown the previous week. The subjects who were asked questions using the word *smashed* were more likely to report seeing broken glass than the others.

In the first scenario when the subjects had actually seen the film-footage an actual feature of the event (i.e. the speed of the car) was distorted by the use of language. In the second scenario even though only a week had elapsed a fictitious feature was introduced by the use of language.

Troublesome knowledge has been cast as an 'instigative' feature because it triggers or instigates the whole threshold concept 'journey' and marks the beginning of the learner's efforts to deal with the troublesomeness. Despite its centrality to the experience and identification of threshold concepts it is the feature that attracts the least amount of exploration in the literature and, conversely, appears to invite the most restrictive interpretation of all the features.

Several forms of troublesome knowledge have been identified including knowledge characterised as *inert; ritual; tacit; counter-intuitive; alien; conceptually difficult*; as well as *troublesome language*. Despite the multitude of entries in this list only one, *conceptually difficult knowledge*, has tended to appear in the literature and troublesome has become a euphemism for conceptually difficult. For example, Schwartzman talks of 'deeply challenging knowledge'; Stokes et al. refer to threshold concepts as being 'entwined with entrenched or difficult-to-change misconceptions'; Boustedt et al. report that in their instructor interviews 'it was quite apparent that instructors focus on *difficult to learn* more than any other aspects of the concepts they discuss' (Schwartzman, 2010; Stokes et al., 2007; Boustedt et al., 2007).

Other forms of defined troublesomeness (e.g. ritual, inert, tacit) share the characteristic that they are associated with knowledge that has already been acquired – the learner possesses the knowledge but fails to retrieve it appropriately. For example, learners often use existing knowledge in a 'misplaced' fashion (i.e. using knowledge where it does not belong) or in a 'conglomerated' fashion (i.e. several disparate pieces of knowledge are just jammed together erroneously). In these contexts the trouble is associated with deployment and not acquisition (Perkins & Martin, 1986, p. 215).

This type of trouble is far more prevalent than the trouble associated with an inability to comprehend or acquire knowledge in the first place. Despite this consideration an examination of these forms of troublesome knowledge is noticeably absent from the threshold concept literature.

Summary

Simply canvassing experts and asking them to classify concepts as threshold concepts is an unreliable approach to identification. An expert's evaluation of the outcome of an exercise or the material gathered as part of a study may be erroneously based on the knowledge they possess but which the subject lacked. It is difficult for the expert to ignore their knowledge of the outcome even when they consciously try to do so in the interests of making an impartial evaluation. More importantly, identifying the actual or root cause factors and circumstances of an integrative, transformational learning experience can be impeded by the effects of creeping determinism and the apparent coherence of events in hindsight. Often an explanatory search for the source of a transformational trigger is terminated prematurely because what is considered a familiar or explainable source or cause is reached. The disposition of the expert in terms of the type of research lens they view the material through and the language they are disposed to can significantly influence their interpretations and conclusions.

CONCLUSION

Our ability to recall with hindsight the cognitive transitions that constitute learning episodes is an unreliable source of evidence because it actually impedes the discovery of the type of information we seek.

It is almost impossible for individuals to look back with hindsight and accurately recall critical cognitive events which, because they occurred spontaneously, could not be consciously monitored for the circumstances enabling their occurrence (i.e. the pre-event state) or the effect and consequences of their occurrence (i.e. specific identification of the post-event state). Memory is constructive and not reproductive and our memory of something is not recalled with a clinical ability to identify the individual components which provide the specific character of the recollection. Those individual components have been transformed into a compound by the mental chemistry that operates on our cognitive processes and subsumes them.

Interpretations of questions that are phrased using particular language can encourage the recall of events in a particular way or associate properties with an event that may not be factually correct or justified. In the threshold concept literature the word 'troublesome' is invariably associated with difficulty, typically conceptual difficulty, and the literature is dominated by a perspective of troublesomeness that is almost uniquely characterised by that association. However, difficulty is but one of the many sources of troublesomeness originally identified in the formative writings of Meyer and Land.

It is somewhat ironic that attempts to elicit the remembered responses of subjects based on their past experience is actually biased against the identification of the information we are seeking. Investigations based on asking experts or would-be experts to articulate their own experience of acquiring a threshold concept are completely open to the combined effect of the exigencies associated with expert blind spot, hindsight bias, the curse of knowledge, the illusion of memory, the nuances of language and the influence of emotion. The 'betwixt and between' state of liminality and it's rhizomatic properties, that are induced by the emergent nature of the learning process, can act to inhibit the detailed cataloguing of the transformation.

NOTE

[1] http://www.nytimes.com/2009/01/09/books/07book.html?_r=1 (last accessed 4 May 2015).

REFERENCES

Bartlett, F. C. (1932). *Remembering: A study in experimental and social psychology.* London: Cambridge Univeristy Press.

Berney, L., & Blane, D. B. (2003). The lifegrid method of collecting retrospective information from people at older ages. *Research Policy and Planning, 21*(2), 13–22.

Blane, D. B. (1996). Collecting retrospective data: Development of a reliable method and a pilot study of. *Social Science and Medicine, 42*(5), 751–757.

Boustedt, J., Eckerdal, A., McCartney, R., Moström, J. E., Ratcliffe, M., Sanders, K., & Zander, C. (2007). Threshold concepts in computer science: do they exist and are they useful? *SIGCSE Bulletin, 39*(1), 504–508.

Brewer, W. F., & Treyens, J. C. (1981). Role of schemata in memory for places. *Cognitive Psychology, 13*, 207–230.

Camerer, C., Loewenstein, G., & Weber, M. (1989). The curse of knowledge in economic settings: An experimental analysis. *The Journal of Political Economy, 97*(5), 1232–1254.

Chabris, C., & Simons, D. (2010). *The invisible Gorilla: And other ways out intuition deceives us.* London: Harper Collins Publishers.

Clayton, M. J. (1997). Delphi: A technique to harness expert opinion for critical decision-making task in education. *Educational Psychology, 17,* 373–386.

Davies, P. (2003). *Threshold Concepts: how can we recognise them?* EARLI Conference, Padova.

Deese, J. (1959). On the prediction of occurrence of particular verbal intrusions in immediate recall. *Journal of Experimental Psychology, 58,* 17–22.

Dunbar, K. (1997). How scientists think: Online creativity and conceptual change in science. In T. B. Ward, S. M. Smith, & S. Vaid (Eds.), *Conceptual structures and processes: Emergence, discovery and Change* (pp. 461–493). Washington, DC: APA Press.

Eckerdal, A., McCartney, R., Mostrom, J. E., Ratcliffe, M., Sanders, K., & Zander, C. (2006). *Putting threshold concepts into context in computer science education, ITiCSE 06* (pp. 103–107). Bologna, Italy: ACM.

Eckerdal, A., McCartney, R., Mostrom, J. E., Sanders, K., Thomas, L., & Zander, C. (2007). *From Limen to Lumen: Computing students in liminal spaces, ICER 07* (pp. 123–132). New York, NY: ACM.

EHIS European Health Interview Survey. (2008). Eurostat, The Statistical Office Of The European Union.

Fischhoff, B. (1975). Hindsight is not equal to Foresight: The effect of outcome knowledge on judgment under uncertainty. *Journal of Experimental Psychology: Human Perception and Performance, 1*(3), 288–299.

Flanagan, J. C. (1954). The critical incident technique. *Psychological Bulletin, 51*(4), 335.

Gal-Ezer, J., & Harel, D. (1998). What (Else) should CS educators know. *Communications of the ACM, 41*(9), 77–84.

Garfinkel, H. (1984). *Studies in ethnomethodology,* Malden, MA: Polity Press/Blackwell Publishing.

Goldman, K., Gross, P., Heeren, C., Herman, G., Kaczmarczyk, L., Loui, M.C., & Zilles, C. (2008). *Identifying important and difficult concepts in introductory computing courses using a delphi process, SIGCSE 08* (pp. 256–260). New York, NY: ACM.

Gremler, D. D. (2004). The CIT in service research. *Journal of Service Research, 7*(1), 65–89.

Guilbault, R. L., Bryant, F. B., Brockway, J. H., & Posavac, E. J. (2004). A meta-analysis of research on hindsight bias. *Basic and Applied Psychology, 26*(2 & 3), 103–117.

Hawkins, S. A., & Hastie, R. (1990). Hindsight: Biased judgments of past events after the outcomes are known. *Psychological Bulletin, 107*(3), 311–327.

Henriksen, K., & Kaplan, H. (2003). Hindsight bias, outcome knowledge and adaptive learning. *Quality and Safety in Health Care, 12*(2), 46–50.

Hoch, S. J., & Loewenstein, G. F. (1989). Outcome feedback: Hindsight and information. *Journal of Experimenal Psychology: Learning, Memory and Cognition, 15*(4), 605–619.

Lambrecht, J. J. (1999). *Developing employment-related office technology skills, MDS-1199.* Berkeley, CA: National Center for Research in Vocational Education.

Lambrecht, J. J. (2000). Developing end-user technology skills. *Information Technology, Learning, and Performance Journal, 18*(1), 7–19.

Loftus, E. F., & Palmer, J. C. (1974). Reconstruction of automobile destruction: An example of the interaction between language and memory. *Journal of Verbal Learning and Verbal Behavior, 13,* 585–589.

McCartney, R., Eckerdal, A., Mostrom, J. E., Sanders, K., & Zander, C. (2007). Successful students' strategies for getting unstuck. *SIGCSE Bulletin, 39*(3), 156–160.

Mostrŏm, J. E., Boustedt, J., Eckerdal, A., NcCartney, R., Sanders, K., Thomas, L., & Zander, C. (2008). *Concrete examples of abstraction as manifested in students' transformative experiences ICER 08* (pp. 125–135). Sydney, Australia: ACM.

Murphy, G. (2002). *The big book of concepts.* Massachusetts, MA: MIT Press.

Nathan, M. J., & Petrosino, A. (2003). Expert blind spot among preservice teachers. *American Educational Research Journal, 40*(4), 905–928.

Perkins, D. N., & Martin, F. (1986). Fragile knowledge and neglected strategies in novice programmers. In E. Soloway & S. Iyengar (Eds.), *Empirical studies of programmers* (pp. 213–229). Norwood, NJ: Ablex Publishing Co.

Rasmussen, J. (1987). The defintion of human error and a taxonomy for technical system design. In J. Rasmussen, K. Duncan, & J. Lwplat (Eds.), *New technology and human error* (pp. 23–30) Chichester: Wiley.

Roediger, H. L., & McDermott, K. B. (1995). Creating false memories: Remembering words not presented in lists. *Journal of Experimental Psychology: Learning, Memory, and Cognition, 21*(4), 803–814.

Rosch, E., Mervis, C. B., Gray, W. D., Johnson, D. M., & Boyes-Braem, P. (1976). Basic objects in natural categories. *Cognitive Psychology, 8*, 382–439.

Sanders, K., Boustedt, J., Eckerdal, A., Mostrom, J. E., Thomas, L., & Zander, C. (2008). *Student understanding of object-oriented programming as expressed in concept maps, SIGCSE 08* (pp. 332–336). Portland, Oregon: ACM.

Schwartzman, L. (2010). Transending disciplinary boundaries: A proposed theoretical foundation for threshold concepts. In J. H. F. Meyer, R. Land, & C. Baillie (Eds.), *Threshold concepts and transformational learning* (pp. 21–44). Rotterdam, The Netherlands: Sense Publications.

Schwill, A. (1994). Fundamental ideas of computer science. *European Association for Theoretical Computer Science, 53*, 274–295.

Seldon, A. (1983). *By world of mouth: Elite oral history.* London: Methuen.

Stokes, A., King, H., & Libarkin, J. C. (2007). Research in science education: Threshold Concepts. *Journal of Geoscience Education, 55*(5), 434–438.

Thomas, L., Boustedt, J., Eckerdal, A., McCartney, R., Mostrom, J. E., Sanders, K., & Zander, C. (2010). Threshold concepts in computer science: An ongoing empirical investigation. In J. H. F. Meyer, R. Land, & C. Baillie, (Eds.), *Threshold concepts and transformational learning.* Rotterdam, The Netherlands: Sense Publishers.

Zander, C., Boustedt, J., Eckerdal, A., McCartney, R., Mostrom, J. E., Ratcliffe, M., & Sanders, K. (2008). Threshold concepts in computer science: A multi-national investigation. In R. Land, J. H. F. Meyer, & J. Smith (Eds.), *Threshold concepts within the disciplines.* Rotterdam, The Netherlands: Sense Publishers.

Zendler, A., & Spannagel, C. (2008). Empitical foundation of central concepts for computer science education. *ACM Journal on Educational Resources in Computing, 8*(2).

Dermot Shinners-Kennedy
Department of Computer Science and Information Systems
University of Limerick

BERT ZWANEVELD, JACOB PERRENET AND ROEL BLOO

20. DISCUSSION OF METHODS FOR THRESHOLD RESEARCH AND AN APPLICATION IN COMPUTER SCIENCE

INTRODUCTION

Computer Science (CS) is a young discipline and research regarding the teaching of CS is in its infancy. Fincher and Petre's book on CS education research (2004) was an early landmark.

The first Dutch dissertation concerning CS education was by Saeli (2012), built on publications with Perrenet, Jochems, and Zwaneveld (2011, 2102a, 2012b). Saeli et al. studied secondary CS education, specifically programming, from the perspective of Pedagogical Content Knowledge (PCK). Gathering PCK of a subject means looking for answers to the questions 'what to teach?', 'how to teach?', 'with which reasons to teach?', and 'with what students' difficulties to cope with?'. PCK is defined by Shulman (1986) as that expertise that allows experienced teachers to effectively represent the subject to their students; it is the special amalgam between general and specific pedagogical knowledge and content knowledge. Investigating PCK mostly involves a specific methodology based on interviewing groups of teachers using the aforementioned questions . The construct as well as its methodology has been used in educational research in various disciplines.

Threshold concept research is another prominent approach to investigate and improve education. It has been used in many disciplines including CS and mainly in higher education. Shinners-Kennedy and Fincher (2013) summarize the results within CS. Although many threshold concepts have been found, they argue that this kind of research has come to a dead end. They criticize the retrospective methods. Asking students to look back to what they did not previously know, would be an unreliable activity (hindsight bias) and emotionally laden events would be least likely to be recalled accurately (emotional load). They plea for investigating PCK with the use of individual teacher interviews as an alternative for threshold research.

Their arguments against the use of retrospective methods did not convince us, nor their arguments favouring the use of individual PCK interviews. In this chapter we present their argumentation concerning the methodology, followed by our counter argumentation. Next, we report a study of our own. Contrary to Shinners-Kennedy and Fincher's advice we did use the retrospective method;

R. Land et al. (Eds.), Threshold Concepts in Practice, 269–284.

our instrument is a questionnaire presented to CS students concluding their BSc programme. The questionnaire asks for threshold concepts as well as for the applicability of the characteristics ascribed to these concepts (*transformative, irreversible, integrative, alien or counter-intuitive,* and *bounded,* according to Meyer and Land, 2006). Also we questioned teachers; we asked them for *what they think their students would mention* as threshold concepts. In the following, we report the threshold concepts mentioned by the students, compare this set of threshold concepts with those reported by Shinners-Kennedy and Fincher as mentioned by students, and we describe the results of characteristics applicability according to the students. Next, we report the thresholds mentioned by their teachers, and we compare the two sets of responses. Additionally we elaborate on the possibility of using threshold concepts in the educational process.

ARGUMENTS AGAINST THRESHOLD CONCEPTS RETROSPECTION METHODOLOGY

Shinners-Kennedy and Fincher establish that the standard methodology consists of asking students to look back and recall a time when they had a conceptual difficulty, or problem. Whether the elicitive method used was interviews, structured tasks, questionnaires or recollection, the basis of the method is retrospection. They used the retrospection variant of the so-called critical incident method (Flanagan, 1954). This technique was designed to elicit the cause, description and outcome of a self-identified *critical incident*, including the users' feelings and perceptions, any actions taken during the incident, and any changes that the incident precipitated. However, due to lack of useful results – students rarely reported critical incidents with a threshold character – they turned away from their interview data. After reviewing the literature concerning retrospective methods, they "considered that the inbuilt limitations of hindsight bias and emotional recall meant that the methods [...] delivered unreliable evidence" (p. 15).

Hindsight bias (Henriksen & Kaplan, 2003) is the tendency for people with outcome knowledge to exaggerate the extent to which they would have predicted the event beforehand. Applying this to the threshold interview context, Shinners-Kennedy and Fincher state that students are asked to make a judgment of a situation with the outcome known to them: understanding the specific conceptual knowledge (or not). And "If hindsight bias is a phenomenon in education (as with historical, judicial and clinical judgments) then our choice of methods biased against the information we sought" (Shinners-Kennedy and Fincher, p. 13). Students would have difficulties remembering the details of not-understanding, half-understanding and misunderstanding. Hence, the use of retrospection is rejected by them.

Emotional recall (Blane, 1996) is defined as remembering events where emotions were important. Shinners-Kennedy and Fincher cite Blane, stating that research (e.g. in the medical domain of lifestyle habits) found that, in recall tasks, the type of information to be remembered matters. Perhaps counter intuitively, the

270

more emotions that were involved, the more difficult the task to remember details accurately. They also suppose that acquisition of threshold concepts is an emotionally laden event. Hence, in this case because of the associated emotions, it would be very hard to remember the details of the understanding process. And again, in this case applying the results of emotional recall research to the threshold interview context, retrospection is rejected.

ARGUMENTS IN FAVOUR OF INDIVIDUAL PCK AS A BETTER ALTERNATIVE

As Shinners-Kennedy and Fincher still believe in the reality of the threshold concept phenomenon in learning, but do not believe any more in retrospection tasks for students, they look for another source of information and choose for experienced teachers' expertise: PCK. Shulman's method of eliciting PCK is semi-structured group interviews. First the teachers are asked about the so-called 'Big Ideas' of a subject. For every Big Idea, the groups have to come up with shared answers to questions concerning students' difficulties, etc. Like some PCK investigators, Shinners-Kennedy and Fincher prefer to take interviews with *individual* teachers instead of groups. Using the PCK method is argued for because of its underlying body of research, its simplicity, and its production of concepts at the useful level of situated practice.

COUNTER ARGUMENTS

Our first argument is personal and maybe context specific, but still worth mentioning. We did research into CS threshold concepts and obtained interesting and opposite results to those of Shinners-Kennedy and Fincher.

Our second argument concerns the phenomenon of hindsight bias, that is its applicability to the threshold concept retrospection research. Shinners-Kennedy and Fincher state their criticism in conditional mode: "If hindsight bias is a phenomenon in education (as with historical, judicial and clinical judgments), then …". So, it is a question of transfer of one cognitive psychological domain to another. The transfer of results from one domain to another is not an open door in cognitive psychology and often requires more research into a specific domain and specific respondents. Whether this phenomenon holds true in education is an open question.

Thirdly, one could argue that in the case of asking for threshold concepts, most students understood the specific concept in the end, and the probability for that outcome was large: teachers and students did their best to reach understanding and those students that failed most of the time will not be in the sample. So the question is whether the retrospection task is really a hindsight situation as described in the literature.

Fourthly, if the students are not simply asked for difficulties in their learning but explicitly for understanding processes with threshold-concept characteristics, then they are not asked to judge a situation with known outcome, but to recognize a process, which again, is not a hindsight situation.

Finally, there is a considerable educational literature on the positive effects of reflection on one's own learning processes (see e.g., Ben-Ari, 2001, for the domain of CS education). If reflection because of hindsight bias would result in 'everything was easy and I reached understanding without much trouble', what would be the gain?

Concluding, we are not convinced that the phenomenon of hindsight bias is a threat to retrospective threshold research.

Our third counter argument concerns the effect of emotions on recall, especially, the argument that students don't recall accurately what their threshold concepts were, because of the distorting role of emotions. Typically these results come from people interviewed about traumatic events in their life (Blane, 1996). Can 'hard' learning, i.e. going through liminal space, be called traumatic? Perhaps if students do not reach the necessary level of understanding and have to end their study career. But these students are seldom respondents in threshold concept research. Most students, our respondents certainly were, are interviewed at the moment they successfully understood the concepts referred too, or if not, could continue with their study career as not-understanding the specific concept appeared not to be of crucial relevance. Thus we are not convinced that the phenomenon of emotional recall is a threat for retrospective threshold concept research. (Actually, at a certain point in their argumentation, p. 13, Shinners-Kennedy and Fincher seem to have the same opinion: "We had certainly expected the acquisition of a threshold concept to be an "emotionally laden" event and were surprised when recollections were closer to the 'hum drum' and 'background' events of everyday learning which our questions educed". However, they are not consistent in this observation in their final conclusion, as it appears to us).

What about individual PCK as a method? We do not think it is a good alternative method to group-level PCK. We have extensive experience with the PCK method and judge it as a fruitful but time consuming method to get pedagogical knowledge about specific subjects. We used the group interviews and replacing those with individual interviews does not take less time. You still need many interviews to transcend the local situation of a specific teacher and it will be harder to combine these isolated results compared to the group situation where the integrating work is done in the group session.

More seriously, we have doubts about the validity of the threshold information that would be obtained by interviewing university teachers. PCK is the combination of content knowledge and pedagogical knowledge in practice. Most PCK research has been done in the context of secondary education and rightly so. Experienced secondary teachers generally have good content knowledge as well as good pedagogical knowledge in practice. Experienced tertiary teachers possess very good content knowledge but, compared to secondary teachers, less practical pedagogical knowledge, due to less pedagogical training and less intensity as well as less frequency of interaction with students. For primary teachers it is the other way around. Thus, if you ask tertiary teachers for threshold concepts of their students, do you get what you want? We maintain that the direct information from students is more valuable than the indirect information from their teachers.

Our main conclusion is, that the retrospective methods of asking students for their threshold concepts should not be rejected, and that the individual PCK method of asking teachers is a worse alternative.

Next we will describe our threshold concept study within the domain of Computer Science, using the retrospective method and with students and teachers as respondents.

RESEARCH QUESTIONS

Our study within the CS domain is explorative and comparative. The research questions are the following:

- *Which threshold concepts do students mention?*
- *Are these concepts similar to what has been reported before?*
- *What is the applicability of the various characteristics of the threshold concept according to the students?*
- *Which concepts do teachers think their students mention most?*
- *What are the similarities and differences between the students' threshold concepts according to their teachers and the actual students' concepts?*

METHODS

Context

The study is carried out in the context of the three-year BSc programme Computer Science and Engineering at the Eindhoven University of Technology (TU/e). It is a CS programme with a focus on theory but also on practical experience in software engineering.

Respondents

Participants are students in the second semester of the third (last) year of the programme (N = 59) and the majority of their university teachers (N = 18).

Instruments

The students' task was part of a series of compulsory reflection assignments (digitally delivered). First the threshold concept was explained and the five characteristics

(Meyer & Land, 2006) were given: *transformative; irreversible; integrative; alien or counter-intuitive*; and *bounded*. Also four non-CS examples were presented. Then the students had to write down one or more threshold concepts from their experience and to indicate the applicability of the five characteristics. The students' texts were not graded, but only accepted if it was clear that the work had been taken seriously.

The teachers' task was partly similar to the students' task. Explaining the threshold concept construct was done in the same way as part of a plenary presentation at an educational meeting. The task had the individual paper-and-pencil format. The teachers were not asked about their own threshold concepts, but about which three threshold concepts they thought their students mentioned the most. Only concepts were asked for, no opinion about applicability of characteristics nor an explanation about the choice of concepts.

Analysis

The authors of this chapter possess various relevant skills and roles in relation to the programme. Bloo (B) has a CS background and occupied the function of lecturer in the programme as well as study advisor; Perrenet (P) has a combined mathematics and psychology background and occupied the function of educational advisor; Zwaneveld (Z) has a mathematics background and has organized the Dutch training programme for secondary CS teachers. The author with the greatest distance to the programme (Z) initially categorized the threshold concepts mentioned by students and their teachers. For the most part this process was unproblematic. Incidentally categorization was difficult because of differences in the level of specificity or because of text ambiguity. In these cases categorization was done in collaboration with the other two authors. B especially knew most of the students and teachers personally and could 'read between the lines'. The students' thresholds were compared to the most relevant lists of results mentioned in Shinners-Kennedy and Fincher (2013); the characteristics applicability was counted.

RESULTS

Students' Threshold Concepts

Almost every student mentioned 1 to 3 concepts. One student mentioned none. Seven concepts were mentioned without explanation. See Table 1 for all frequencies.

Table 1. Frequencies of threshold concepts mentioned by students (N = 59)

Threshold concepts	Number
number of threshold concepts mentioned	108
number of *different* threshold concepts	53

We present two student's response examples, translated from Dutch. Notice that most students constructed several of such examples. In the process of analysis, we added the italic terms for characteristics including an extension denoting the student's opinion on the applicability.

First example student response:

One of the threshold concepts in CS is 'object'. For the starting programmer hard to understand. One of the first assignments was 'Scanner' and I use the syntax of the example given during a lecture. But don't really understand what I was doing. It was strange that something simple as a scanner had such a complicated syntax. (*alien*+) Only at the end of my first year I fully understood the concept, during an assignment Pentomino (a puzzle). Then I defined objects/classes myself. The syntax was not any longer strange. During that year my view on this subject was dramatically changed. (*transformative*+) I started to connect concepts. (*integrative*+) Through this assignment a lot of things became fully clear (= vs equals(), pointers). 'Object' is a concept that is very typically for CS (but not for the related mathematics). (*bounded*+)

Second example student response:

The first threshold concept that comes to mind is also one of the first thresholds that I passed. This happened during the course of Logic and Set Theory, when the subject was truth-tables of logical operators. In fact, these operators all were clear and logical (and I had used those operators before) except for the operator of logical implication. I could not understand why a logical operator associated with that truth table had the name 'implication', a well-known term in English and Dutch. I passed the threshold (without an 'Aha Erlebnis') and after that I could not remember any more why this was not logical to me before (this confirms the second characteristic). I suspect it has to do with the tautology 'false => false', because I thought that if a proposition A is not true (false), this does not have to imply that proposition B is false as well (of course, this is the inverse interpretation of what it means to state that 'false => false' is a tautology.

Whether this is really a threshold concept, I don't know, as it is only a small one. I am not sure if characteristic 1 holds. (*transformative*?). My view of the subject changed, but it was a rather small subject and therefore probably not very important.

Characteristic 2 clearly is applicable because I cannot totally reproduce the problem I had with the concept. (*irreversible*+)

Characteristic 3 does not really apply because the subject does not contain many aspects. At the utmost the intuitive interpretation and the logical interpretation are taken together. (*integrative*–) Characteristic 4 does apply indeed, because it took quite some time before I accepted the operator. (*alien*+)

I have some doubts again concerning characteristic 5, because, as I stated before, it is such a small subject. However, it does demarcate the difference between logic within mathematics/computer science and everyday reasoning, because definitions become more clear and strict. (*bounded+*)

Applicability of Threshold Characteristics According to the Students

Table 2 presents the frequencies with which students associate a characteristic with a particular threshold concept. Clearly, all characteristics are present at more than 50% of the cases a concept is mentioned. *Transformative* is thought applicable the most, *bounded* the least.

Table 2. Percentages of thresholds characteristics judged applicable to the threshold concepts according to the students

Characteristics	Applicability (%)
transformative	88
irreversible	72
integrative	64
alien or counter-intuitive	78
bounded	55

Threshold Concepts Mentioned by Students

From the 53 different threshold concepts, some are mentioned by many students, some only by one. Only two threshold concepts are mentioned by 10 or more, 35 by just one student ('unique threshold concepts'). In Table 3, the percentages of the total of 53 concepts are shown.

Table 3. Variation in the students' concepts list

Number of times mentioned	Percentage of the list of 53 different concepts
10 or more	4
2–9	30
1	66

The threshold concepts mentioned by the students are shown in Table 4 with the number of students mentioning those. Notice that the maximal possible frequency is 59 (the number of students). There are few high frequency threshold concepts and many low frequency.

Table 4. Threshold concepts mentioned by students

Threshold concept	Frequency
object orientation	17
logic	12
undecidability	5
algorithm	4
induction	3
abstraction/structure layers	3
complexity	3
programming	3
programming methods	3
recursion	3
halting problem	3
pointers	2
data structures	2
race-conditions	2
functional programming	2
asymptotic running time	2
matrices	2
objects	2
other, unique concepts	35

Comparison with CS Threshold Concepts Reported in Literature

Shinners-Kennedy and Fincher give several lists of CS thresholds, mainly using the source of CS education experts. If we compare with our list, the most important difference is their prominence of programming concepts. For our purpose of comparison, the student perspective is best suited. Shinners-Kennedy and Fincher report the results of an extensive international study (Boustedt et al., 2007). They used the standard methodology mentioned in the beginning of the section 'Arguments against threshold concepts retrospection methodology'. The conclusions are that threshold concepts do exist and are useful; for instance, *object orientation* and *pointers* satisfy the conditions for being a threshold. Comparing with our results we see agreement on the first concept: *object orientation* is on top of our list. *Pointers* is mentioned by our students, but it plays a minor role. On the other hand, our second candidate would be *logic*, instead of *pointers*. Surprisingly *logic* does not appear in the list of Boustedt et al. Neither does 'our' *undecidability*. We conclude that there is some similarity (*object orientation*), but more dissimilarity.

Students' Thresholds According to Their Teachers

Almost every teacher mentioned 2 to 3 concepts. One teacher mentioned none. See Tables 5 and 6.

Table 5. Frequencies of thresholds concepts mentioned by teachers (N = 18)

Threshold concepts	Number
number of threshold concepts mentioned	49
number of *different* threshold concepts	21

Table 6. Variation in the teachers' concepts' list

Number of times mentioned	Percentage of the list of 21 different concepts
6 or more	10
2–5	29
1	62

In Table 7 we present all specific threshold concepts mentioned by the teachers and the frequencies. Notice that the maximal possible frequency is 18. There are few high frequency threshold concepts and many low frequency.

Table 7. Threshold concepts expected by the teachers

Threshold concept	Frequency
recursion	9
complexity	6
object orientation	5
undecidability	5
induction	4
logic	3
computability	2
variable	2
other, unique concepts	13

Comparison of the Students' List and the Teachers' List

What is striking is the similarity in frequency structure: few high frequency threshold concepts and many low frequency. Some concepts (10) appear in both lists, which means that teachers rightly expected students to mention certain concepts. However, more concepts were expected by the teachers, but not mentioned by the students (11) and many more concepts were mentioned by the students, but not expected by the teachers (43). See Figure 1 for the related percentages.

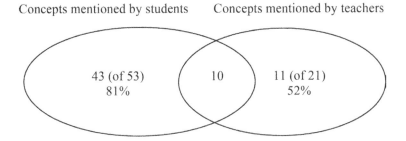

Concepts mentioned by students   Concepts mentioned by teachers

Figure 1. Numbers of the (non-) overlapping different thresholds mentioned by students and teachers and the percentages of the non-overlapping different threshold concepts

Figure 2 shows the relation between both lists in more detail.

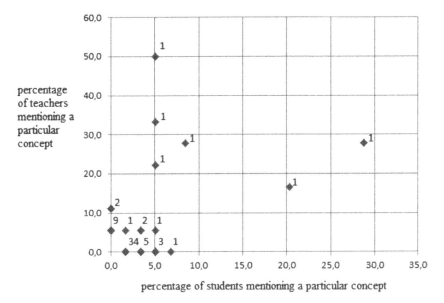

percentage of teachers mentioning a particular concept

percentage of students mentioning a particular concept

Figure 2. Percentage of students vs percentage of teachers mentioning a particular threshold concept

Point (20.3; 16.7) (1) represents that one concept (*logic*) is mentioned by 20.3% of the students and 16.7% of the teachers; point (3.4; 5.6) (2) represents that two

279

concepts (*functional programming, pointers*) are mentioned by 3.4% of the students and 5.6% of the teachers.

The scatterplot illustrates little relationship between the two lists (correlation $r = 0.47$).

CONCLUSIONS AND DISCUSSION

Conclusions

We performed a critical analysis of Shinners-Kennedy and Fincher's paper about the methodology of threshold research and performed our own study with retrospective methods. On various theoretical as well as practical grounds, we neither agree with Shinners-Kennedy and Fincher on the flaws of the retrospective methods in threshold research nor on the superiority of the alternative of asking teachers individually for their PCK. Our study into CS threshold concepts using a retrospective method proved to be fruitful.

Students mention a variety of concepts. Some concepts (*object orientation, logic*) have a much higher frequency than others; many concepts are only mentioned by a single student.

The list of concepts is only partly similar to other lists, reported in literature. *Object orientation* appears on many lists. *Logic* does not.

Students judge all five threshold concept characteristics (*transformative; irreversible; integrative; alien or counter-intuitive; bounded*) applicable to their threshold concepts most of the time. The judged applicability is lowest for *bounded* (55%) and highest for *transformative* (88%).

When teachers are asked for the threshold concepts their students would mention, they mention a variety of concepts. Some concepts (*recursion*) have a much higher frequency than others; many concepts are only mentioned by one teacher.

There is a partial correspondence between the lists of concepts mentioned by teachers to be expected of their students and the actual students' list. There is more dissimilarity than similarity. The top concepts of one list appear on the other and vice versa, but most of the time at a lower place. The correlation is 0.47.

Our use of a retrospective method with students and teachers brought forward interesting results.

Implications for Education

As few concepts are thresholds for many students and many concepts are thresholds for few students, what's the use for education? Of course, teachers should give extra attention to concepts mentioned by many students (*object orientation*), but many students clearly have a lot of other threshold concepts and often these concepts are unique. Teachers should be aware that 'every concept could be a threshold concept for someone'. After inventorying, students with specific unique threshold concepts could be partnered to others with different concepts and both should benefit from reciprocal explanation.

Our students proved, that if asked for, they could reflect on their learning processes. As reflection on one's own learning processes is good for learning itself and for the development of metacognitive skills (Ben-Ari, 2001), even if the retrospective method would be proven to be unreliable, then still giving students a retrospective task, such as our assignment, would be stimulating for their learning. At the Durham threshold conference Felton stressed this point also in his keynote.

Reliability

What is the quality of our measurement?

When analysing the data for a small percentage, categorizing was hard as related concepts were mentioned at very different levels of specificity and abstraction. Concerning specificity, students sometimes mentioned a whole subject or course whilst others mentioned a concept within the subject or course. Could this be a threat to the reliability of our results? For practical reasons we did not work with independent raters, so no inter-rater reliability coefficient could be calculated. However, as one of the authors was well acquainted with all respondents we could clear up any doubts. And because the percentage was small, our results would not have been very different in case of a different categorization.

Our students' as well as our teachers' task was compulsory. Probably in a less strict context the answers would be less reliable.

Validity

Did we measure what we wanted to measure?

We asked students for one or more threshold concepts. Maybe they could have mentioned more. We presume that they mentioned their most important ones. Also, there is not yet a final answer to the question, who to ask best for threshold concepts? Are students in the position to accurately reflect on their own learning? At the Durham conference Shinners-Kennedy presented another argument against the use of retrospection, i.e. the reconstructive aspects of memory processes (Shinners-Kennedy, 2014). Furthermore, if students state that eventually they understood a concept, are they correct? When we had our teachers' session and showed them – after they had done the task themselves – some examples of students' responses, a striking remark was: "This student clearly has not conquered the threshold". The student thought that he had. Furthermore, when we would ask the same students a few years later, would they come up with the same concepts? One thing is clear, when we ask teachers (or experts, or books) we get a partly different set of concepts. Which list is the true list? Our conviction is, that maybe the only but impractical way to get the true list, is to sit next to students during the whole learning process. The second-best way is asking the primary source: the student.

When one questions a respondent in a paper-and-pencil task, the wording matters. In our opinion, it is important to give a definition, including characteristics and non-CS examples. Higher education students can handle such information. Perhaps, in the assignment, it should be stated what level of specificity is expected. On the other hand, if a student says that a whole course is a threshold, then for that student that is the truth. Teacher respondents could be asked various questions. We asked teachers about what they thought their students would answer. Of course one should not ask teachers for their own thresholds, as the teachers probably as a sample are not representative for students in general. However, one could ask teachers for what students *should* answer. This is in fact the Shinners-Kennedy and Fincher's approach to gathering PCK.

Variety in Thresholds Lists

Our results differ partly from those in the literature and there are also many differences between students' threshold concepts. We suppose that two factors are important in what becomes a threshold concept. First, there is the curriculum. Especially in CS, as it is a rapidly developing field, the curriculum changes frequently. When a concept is not in a curriculum, it cannot become a threshold concept for the students concerned. As an example, Denning (2004) gives a list of core technologies in CS. One could expect threshold concepts within every core technology. One of the core technologies is artificial intelligence (AI). No student of our sample mentions an AI concept as a threshold. The explanation is not that AI is easy, but that AI is not part of the Eindhoven curriculum! At other universities, it is. So, we suppose that the top of the list is mainly determined by the curriculum.

Second, the individual learning history is a factor too. Constructivism (Ben-Ari, 2001) states that every student has his/her unique knowledge representation because of his/her unique learning path. We suppose that the bottom of the list is mainly determined by personal learning history.

Ideas for Further Research

We did not analyse the characteristics data further than establishing frequencies. Relating the characteristics applicability to specific concepts and concept frequency would be interesting. Just as including other characteristics mentioned by researchers such as *discursiveness*.

We considered the curriculum as a factor of influence. It would be interesting to investigate another domain with a more stable curriculum and compare the list patterns. As we are also experts in the mathematics education domain and mathematics' curricula are much more stable, this would be our candidate.

Another phenomenon asking for further research would be the different specificity/abstraction levels in the respondents' answers. What is the variation between the students' threshold concepts level? When students mention a whole subject, maybe they have many threshold concepts within that subject? When teachers mention concepts at a higher abstraction level, maybe they are thinking about their own threshold concepts after all? Related to this is the level theory of Van Hiele (1986) about the different thinking levels of students and teachers and the consequent problems in interaction. See also Perrenet on abstraction levels within learning CS (2009). Shinners-Kennedy and Fincher discuss the subject of response level too, in relation to Rosch's research on cognitive categorization and levels of concept representation (Rosch, 1978).

Honours

Although we disagree with Shinners-Kennedy and Fincher concerning the unsuitability of retrospective methods and the suitability of the individual PCK method, we would like to stress that their paper is interesting and relevant and that it has importance for threshold research in all disciplines. It discusses, with reference to general literature, many relevant aspects. We hope to read more from them!

ACKNOWLEDGEMENTS

We thank teachers and students from Computer Science and Engineering at TU/e for their participation. We are grateful to Mara Saeli for her constructive remarks on an earlier version of this chapter.

REFERENCES

Ben-Ari, M. (2001). Constructivism in computer science education. *Journal of Computers in Mathematics and Science Teaching, 20*(1), 45–73.

Blane, D. B. (1996). Collecting retrospective data: Development of a reliable method and a pilot study of its use. *Social Science and Medicine, 42*(5), 751–757.

Boustedt, J., Eckerdal, A., McCartney, R., Moström, J. E., Ratcliffe, M., Sanders, K., & Zander, C. (2007). Threshold concepts in computer science: Do they exist and are they useful? *ACM SIGCSE Bulletin, 39*(1), 504–508.

Denning, P. J. (2004). Great principles in computing curricula. *ACM SIGCSE Bulletin, 36*(1), 336–341.

Felton, P. (2014). *On the threshold with students*. Keynote presented at the Durham conference Threshold Concepts in Practice, Durham.

Fincher, S., & Petre, M. (2004). *Computer science education research*. London: Taylor & Francis.

Flanagan, J. C. (1954). The critical incident technique. *Psychological Bulletin, 51*(4), 335.

Henriksen, K., & Kaplan, H. (2003). Hindsight bias, outcome knowledge and adaptive learning. *Quality and Safety in Health Care, 12*(2), 46–50.

Meyer, J. H. F., & Land, R. (Eds.). (2006). *Overcoming barriers to student understanding: Threshold concepts and troublesome knowledge*. New York, NY: Routledge.

Perrenet, J. (2009). Levels of thinking in computer science: Development in bachelor students' conceptualization of algorithm. *Education and Information technologies, 15*(2), 87–107.

Rosch, E. (1978). Principles of categorization. In E. Rosch & B. B. Lloyd (Eds.), *Cognition and categorization* (pp. 27–48), Hillsdale, MI: Lawrence Erlbaum Associates Publishers.

Saeli, M. (2012). *Teaching programming for secondary school: A pedagogical content knowledge based approach* (Dissertation). Eindhoven University of Technology, The Netherlands.

Saeli, M., Perrenet, J., Jochems, W., & Zwaneveld, G. (2011). Teaching programming in secondary school: A pedagogical content knowledge perspective. *Informatics in Education, 10*(1), 73–88.

Saeli, M., Perrenet, J., Jochems, W., & Zwaneveld, G. (2012a). Pedagogical content knowledge in teaching material. *Journal of Educational Computing Research, 46*(3), 267–293.

Saeli, M., Perrenet, J., Jochems, W., & Zwaneveld, G. (2012b). Programming: Teachers and pedagogical content knowledge in the Netherlands. *Informatics in Education, 11*(1), 81–114.

Shinners-Kennedy, D. (2014, July 9–11). *How NOT to identify threshold concepts.* Paper presented at the 5th International Biennial Thresholds Concepts Conference, Threshold Concepts in Practice, Durham University, England.

Shinners-Kennedy, D., & Fincher, S. A. (2013). Identifying threshold concepts: From dead end to a new direction. In *Proceedings of the ninth annual international ACM conference on International computing education research* (pp. 9–18). New York, NY: ACM.

Shulman, L. (1986). Those who understand: Knowledge growth in teaching. *Educational Researcher, 15*, 4–14.

Van Hiele, P. M. (1986). *Structure and insight: A theory of mathematics education.* Orlando, FL: Academic Press.

Bert Zwaneveld
Open Universiteit (of the Netherlands)

Jacob Perrenet
Eindhoven University of Technology

Roel Bloo
Department of Mathematics and Computer Science
Eindhoven University of Technology

MARIANNE DICKIE AND ILONA VAN GALEN

21. NAVIGATING OUR THRESHOLD CONCEPTS TO ENABLE STUDENTS TO OVERCOME THEIRS

INTRODUCTION

The advantages of reaching students across geographic and temporal boundaries have seen online teaching transition from the unusual and quirky to conventional practice in Higher Education. In the past twenty years, a wealth of literature around learning and teaching online has made it possible to select specific approaches to curriculum and pedagogy. However, the actual design of online course sites is an area that has not been afforded the same consideration by academics.

Online courses are usually conducted in Learning Management Systems (LMS) such as Moodle; systems designed on the premise that academics with little technical expertise can easily load documents, create discussion forums and mark papers. Yet without adaptation, the fundamental 'design' of most LMS platforms is a skeletal structure that, used in its most basic form, can leave students baffled, confused and worst of all uninspired.

The ANU College of Law has taught the Graduate Certificate in Australian Migration Law and Practice (GCAMLP) online in Moodle since 2009. Our curriculum design has evolved over time, and our pedagogy rests solidly upon a constructivist approach that considers students as active participants in their learning, who create knowledge within a specific context and community (Ally, 2008).

Past research into online study has identified that it is the 'method not the media that matters most in learning effectiveness' (Rovai, 2002; Shea, Sau Li, & Pickett, 2006). We used this as our starting point for development, focusing on constructivist and pedagogical principles to teach and engage with our students. Ultimately our commitment to achieving positive student outcomes led us to the troubling, transformative, integrative and irreversible realisation that, for online study, the media also matter.

ONLINE KNOWLEDGE CONSTRUCTION

Online education has two specific characteristics differentiating it from on-campus teaching. These are the temporal nature of engagement and the role of the individual within a community of inquiry. Both result in a unique learning experience for student (Coates, 2007). In particular, the asynchronicity of online education means that students must be more self-directed learners than their classroom contemporaries.

R. Land et al. (Eds.), Threshold Concepts in Practice, 285–297.

To construct their own knowledge (Tavangarian, Leypold, Nölting, Röser, & Voigt, 2004), students must understand their own learning style and determine for themselves how and when to most effectively engage with course content, classmates and teachers (Bocchi, Eastman, & Swift, 2004).

Meyer and Land (2005) define threshold concepts as 'portals' that lead to a transformed internal view of subject matter, subject landscape or even world view'. The requirements for self-direction and collaboration imposed upon students by online learning transforms the ways learning is experienced and understood and the ways that teaching is practiced (Kligyte, 2009). Some online students adapt easily to this new understanding, whilst others struggle to refashion preconceptions of how they can learn and access knowledge.

In seeking to assist students navigate this ontological transformation, our pedagogical approach and our online site design centres on the three elements of social, teaching and cognitive presence identified by Garrison (Garrison, 2007) and others (Joo, Lim, & Kim, 2011) as essential to learner engagement and satisfaction. When we first ventured into the online space we studiously avoided any pressure to create artificial avatars or 'second life'. Instead, our course design intent was to create a community of learning, practice and inquiry (Garrison, Anderson, & Archer, 2001; Moisey & Hughes, 2008; Wenger, 2002).

Within this community, our mature graduate students encounter a curriculum that for many exhibits the troublesome discipline 'conceptual gateways' so clearly described by Land et al. (Land, Cousin, Meyer, & Davies, 2005). The majority of our students have professional backgrounds and past academic experiences in areas other than law. Therefore, online study in a completely new discipline presents a series of challenging adjustments to new and 'previously inaccessible ways of thinking about something' (Land et al., 2005).

Over six years of online teaching we have implemented an action research methodology for evaluating teaching quality and the online design of our courses. We use this collaborative evaluation model across three teaching sessions each year to investigate the effectiveness of student learning and teaching in individual courses and across the program of study. Gathering a broad range of sources of information about participant learning, the experience of teachers and qualitative student evaluation data, has allowed us to implement incremental improvement to the curriculum design. In particular, we have been able to edge progressively closer to an understanding of the best ways to assist students to negotiate the shifts in awareness that characterise crossing a conceptual threshold (Akerlind, McKenzie, & Lupton, 2011).

However one of our most significant program delivery improvements has come from an unexpected insight into our own, rather than our students, conceptual understanding of online study.

In late 2012 a casual conversation led us to consider that we might be looking at online learning from the wrong vantage point. In reviewing our approach we found that what we had considered to be a threshold concept for students was in fact a threshold concept we were facing as an academic and educational developer. The changes we made in response to this insight, together with the discussion of the positive impacts of those changes, is the subject of this chapter. It is our own navigation through liminality (Land et al., 2005) that has enabled us to better equip students to navigate the disciplinary thresholds of migration law, including legal reasoning (Akerlind et al., 2010), statutory interpretation and the role of policy in administrative law.

THE PATH TO A PROFESSION

Because the GCAMLP provides the necessary qualification for registration as a migration agent working in this complex area of Australian law, we strive to use teaching methods considered to be best practice in professional course work, including reflective practice to encourage students to monitor and appreciate their own gains in knowledge and experience across their time of study (Fisher, 2003; Schon, 1987).

The challenges confronted by our students differ from those of the average postgraduate. Our students are predominantly first generation Australians, or migrants themselves. Many are middle aged professionals seeking a career change. Few have a legal background: most have not studied for a number of years. And importantly, they have not studied online. To address their specific needs we engage with behaviourist, cognitive and metacognitive learning theories (Ally, 2008) in the ways we teach and introduce problems.

LOST IN THE ONLINE LANDSCAPE

Between 2009 and 2012 our evaluations showed us that our 'action research' (McKernan & McKernan, 2013) approach to teaching and curriculum improvement worked for most students, once they settled into the rigours of postgraduate study. However, these same evaluations also revealed ongoing student frustration about technology, as students described 'experiences of being confused, lost, or generally unable to maximise the opportunities the platforms were meant to offer' (Darwin, 2010). This type of commentary gelled with our day-to-day observations of student interactions during their online study.

Moodle allows us to track student interactions and determine how students look for, and engage with, their course materials, teachers and fellow students. Our analysis found that certain students found engaging in the online environment challenging. They searched in a haphazard way, clicked the same links multiple times and became lost, particularly within the foundation course. This was despite thoughtful site design that had focused on minimising common LMS flaws, including the notorious Moodle 'scroll of death' that generates so much discussion amongst Moodle developers and Moodle users on the web.

We had designed our course sites intending to make it easy for students to work immediately on their studies. Wanting them to forget that they were in an LMS, we had taken design inspiration from website principles, hoping to ensure users could navigate their courses on a computer, phone or tablet. We had avoided gimmicks and concluded that our design was slick, simple and clear. Certainly our course sites were unlike other ANU online courses.

In the early years, we accepted initial student evaluations describing difficulties in completing activities as an indication that new students were not engaging with essential aspects of the course because they were unfamiliar with working online. But we had expected, over time, to see a difference in the capacity of new students: the exponential increase in the use of social media and the need to engage online in most areas of life (Wallsten, 2013) should have led to a familiarity in working in an online environment.

Initially we believed the problem was predominantly one-sided. Student evaluations highlighting the complexity of studying law online appeared to confirm that students' own attitude to study was impacting on their ability to grasp essential legal concepts: 'A proportion of students comment on the stress of finding significant information when they are unused to law and to study' (Dickie, 2010, 2011).

We analysed comments by students who struggled to find resources and keep up and found that these students often complained that they were not 'lawyers' and it was the imposition of 'legal concepts' and online resources that made their study too hard. This was a baffling complaint, considering they had enrolled to study a postgraduate program in law (Dickie, 2011).

We had used threshold concept theory (Meyer & Land, 2005) to address specific concepts that relate to migration law such as the statutory interpretation that relates to differentiation between a valid visa application vs the grant criteria. Once again we felt this could provide new approaches so we looked at concepts which students consistently found counterintuitive and implemented changes to the course content and resources to assist them overcome these barriers to their learning (Meyer & Land, 2013). These included animations to explore key issues and special class discussions. Whilst insight into these particular legal concepts increased amongst students, the complaints raised by student cohort appealing results or withdrawing early did not change.

Once again we reviewed student comments and found that it was not just legal concepts that were confusing and frustrating them, nor was it the shift to self-management and online collaboration. Students appeared to be using these explanations because they were overwhelmed within the online environment. Simple things such as the locations of discussion forums, timetables, study guides, resources, due dates for assessment and the appeals process were getting in their way and preventing them from engaging with specific course work (Van Galen, 2012).

Our program comprises four subjects (courses). Each has its own site with distinct subject related resources and teachers engaging with students in subject specific activities. However the program itself relies on program wide policies and procedures, such as expected volumes of learning, methods of communication between students and ANU staff, assessment protocols, study deadlines and academic progression. We had consolidated all this information into a single Program site, accessed through links from each individual course. Students' unwillingness to follow these links to find what they needed, perplexed us.

Because we had followed best practice in web design we thought our sites presented clarity, simplicity and accessibility, but it was clear we continued to confuse our students. It seemed that the central site for the program wide information and resources had become a nightmare for some students who, after following the links, could not 'find their way back' to their courses.

In mid-2012 our review coincided with an ANU Moodle upgrade that made maintenance of the central site administratively awkward. We accepted the task of taking all the common program information and duplicating it on each course site. We added a Frequently Asked Questions section intended to enhance student understanding.

We anticipated that this new design would make things simpler for students because they no longer needed to move between two sites to access information. However we saw no change in the degree of, or reasons for, student confusion.

A third qualitative review of student comments combined with analysis of site interactions found that what we had considered to be a threshold concept for students – a transformation of how they viewed their role as learners – was in fact caught up in a threshold concept we ourselves needed to navigate: 'Some students attribute their failure to participate in key activities and/or to observe assessment deadlines to the complexity of information in the Wattle sites' (Van Galen, 2012).

CROSSING THE THRESHOLD

The notion that we might be looking at the students' experience of online learning the wrong way was made during a casual conversation between the authors of this chapter. This conversation canvassed my own experiences as a geographically challenged academic living in Canberra; a city well known for its plethora of roundabouts and awkward street formation. Similarly, the design of Australia's Parliament House is notoriously complex, yet as a past staff member, I had never been lost while working there. The explanation was twofold:

1. On each internal wall corner of Parliament House there is a directional sign explaining where you are in a simple graphic.
2. All new staff participated in an orientation exercise, similar to the O-week students experience at university.

As conversations often do, this one turned our minds back to work and we considered the components of the on-campus orientation week student experience. Even though our students were engaging online, we forced ourselves to think about their student experience as distinct from their online experience. This counterintuitive nature of troublesome knowledge is a feature of a threshold concept and alerted us to the fact that we may have been facing a need to transform our own concepts of the online experience (Meyer & Land, 2005).

We discussed the vast difference between the experience of the new online student and that of a new student on campus. Online students inevitably miss out on the physical and personal orientation to a new study environment and the introduction to the wider community of the university. In order to create a connection to the university learning community for online students, we needed to embrace some aspects of the ways people behave in the physical world and infuse these into our site design and student experience.

Our view of the LMS changed from that of a website to an environment students inhabited. This realisation, so contrary to the notion that it is the 'method, not the media, that matters most in learning effectiveness' (Rovai, 2002) radically transformed our view of site design and our engagement with online learning. We now understood that students who were bewildered by the online environment were like students asked to navigate a physical campus with many geographically dispersed buildings and activities, but without any directional signage. Without clearly signposted navigational clues, these students would not find their lecture rooms, libraries, teachers or fellow students.

This sudden comprehension made us consider our online site design through the prism of an alternate discipline: we realised that the very nature of online learning required us to become architects of the environment in which our students learn, to begin thinking of the course sites as physical spaces where activities could take place. They became for us a campus that students needed to enter and navigate in order to engage with their learning experience.

WAYFINDING

The discipline we drew from was not education, or web or software design but urban design: here was the guidance we needed to draw our students into the environment. Utilising the urban design principles of wayfinding, we reinvented physical spaces and activities in a virtual world, treating the online space not as a portal for learning but as a 'space' for learning.

In his 1960 work, 'The Image of the City' architect and urban planner Kevin Lynch discussed his observations of the way people form mental maps of cityscapes, relying on five elements – paths, edges, districts, nodes and landmarks – to attach identity, meaning and structure to their surroundings (Lynch, 1960). His definition of wayfinding focused on the participant's experience of interpreting an urban environment through the visible external cues.

Later exponents of wayfinding as an urban navigational methodology note that this is particularly important in 'dense and stimulus rich environments' (Passini, 1996). There is little doubt that the content and activities that form an online postgraduate program contribute to an environment that is particularly 'dense and stimulus rich'.

Wayfinding involves both cognitive and behavioural abilities 'to reach spatial destinations' that rely upon environmental clues that situate the destination within space and allow the traveller to make specific decisions along the way. In turn these decisions rely on recognition of these clues (Passini, 1984).

Using wayfinding principles my co-author redesigned the four course sites. The redesign focussed on strengthening the identity of groupings of similar activities into clearly defined, strategic entry 'nodes' (Lynch, 1960). Although the term 'node is also used in discussions about web navigation, its more traditional understanding in that field is a destination, rather than an entry point (Farkas & Farkas, 2000).

Quite purposefully, each course now contains a maximum of seven nodes, to minimise Moodle scroll and cognitive load for students. Each node links 'pathways' to specific activities or resources, all clearly signposted and all logically consistent with the overarching groupings. As the course progresses week-by-week, new content is added to the destinations at the end of these paths.

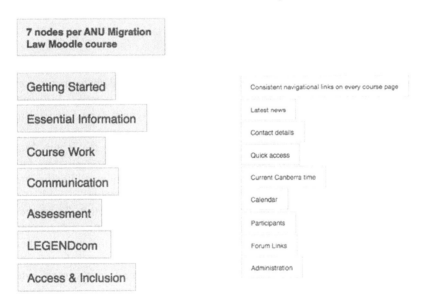

Figure 1. 7 Nodes per course

For example, a node called 'Course work' contains a link to a destination called 'Required reading', a folder that grows as new readings are added each week. This means that students, once they have learned to navigate to this virtual 'library' can reliably find what they are looking for, without having to make new navigational choices (Foltz, 1998). There is no need for students to scroll to find the most recent resource or activity because they are always available at the end of the original pathway.

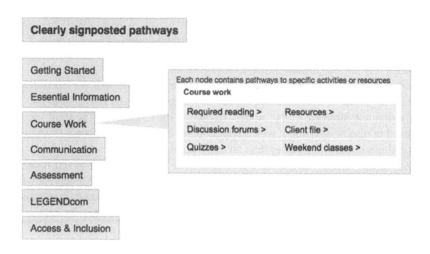

Figure 2. 7 Clearly signposted pathways

Four of the seven nodes emulate on-campus activities: Getting Started; Communication; Course work; and Assessment. The final three nodes contain consistent pathways to information and services: Essential Information; LEGENDcom (an online legal database) and the university Access and Inclusion centre.

Between each node there is a distinct 'edge' formed by the inbuilt Moodle demarcation between topics. Lynch proposed that the breaks in continuity formed by edges between areas of activity contribute to the formation of effective mental maps (Lynch, 1960) by making an environment more manageable.

Full time students take on two courses (subjects) simultaneously. To ensure that they maintain navigational confidence and recognition (Passini, 1984) from one course to the next, each course in the program has exactly the same wayfinding design: the positioning of each node is the same in each course. This consistency provides program coherence whilst creating risk full-time students might become 'disorientated' and work within the wrong course site, particularly if they have two windows open at the same time. To address this risk, we considered each course as a district (Lynch, 1960) with a distinct identity (Arthur & Passini, 1992) creating this identity through the use of individual colour coding for each course.

Each course is also equipped with a series of consistent landmarks: Moodle 'blocks' positioned on the right hand side of each page. These blocks contain handy hyperlinks to course news, teacher contact details, calendar, a clock showing local Canberra time (significant for assessment deadlines). We take particular care to establish blocks so that they appear in a strict and consistent order on every course page 'anchoring' each page to form a stable environment (Sorrows & Hirtle, 1999).

This stability reassures students that no matter what they click, they have not accidently 'left' their primary course site.

The redesign of the course sites was only one facet of our conceptual transformation. We had redesigned the sites as if they were a built environment, a campus complete with classrooms and areas for practice. Now we considered how we could introduce the students to that environment.

ORIENTATION

A key principle of urban design, architectural design and campus life is orientation. The ability to know where you are situated is a fundamental spatial, psychological and cognitive need (Carpman, 2002; Passini, 1984; Spiers & Maguire, 2008). During 'O week', on-campus university students engage in social activities, learning to navigate the campus, meeting their teachers and fellow students. We wanted our students to discover their campus in the same way, free of the tensions that actual study would bring to this experience.

Whilst orientation for online students is not a new concept and there is substantial evidence that orientation can be a critical element for an online students success, there is also evidence that students who are new to online learning have a very different attitude from those who begin study on campus (Stacey Ludwig-Hardman, 2003).

We felt that orientation should be an introduction to serious study, and a way to assist students to understand that they belonged to the broader university community where their contributions would be valued and their studies would require the same level of commitment as that of an on-campus student postgraduate law student.

We introduced an orientation period into the program, which runs from the Friday prior to the course beginning, to the Wednesday of the first week of study where students are presented with a limited view of their course sites. Like on-campus orientation week, there are no classes or lectures, but there are opportunities to explore the environment in which they are working, opportunities to meet their fellow students, and chances to 'rehearse the role of student' without the time pressures imposed by their real study schedule.

When students enter a course site during orientation,the only visible nodes are: 'Getting Started' and 'Essential Information'. The Getting Started node, which is based on past student questions about navigation difficulties, contains two specific activities. One is a self-guided lesson that informs students how to deal with practicalities like uploading a profile photo, redirecting their email and accessing a student card. The lesson allows students to track their own progress, to return to the lesson and to move through chapters of the lesson in different order. It also contains links to the actual actions themselves, so that students can, while they are completing the lesson, upload a photo, redirect their email or download a student card application form. The lesson closes with a hyperlink to a forum where students introduce themselves to their fellow students.

The other Getting Started activity is a game called 'Navigating This Course', a type of factual treasure hunt which challenges students to find, read and 'report' on the 'Essential Information' (assessment, study schedules, academic progression) needed to successfully engage with coursework and with other students.

Students present their 'finds' in a dedicated forum where they engage with each other and their teachers on a social level until the course begins. Each action a student completes during orientation represents a rehearsal for future online study, allowing students to practice opening documents, checking references, looking for answers, posting responses, and entering into online communication with other students and with their teachers. By completing these activities, which have no academic consequence, students gain confidence in working in the interface, developing an understanding of where and how they must work within the learning community.

Once coursework begins, the remaining entry nodes are introduced. The navigational strategies to move from these entry nodes to individual activities and resources have already been established: there is no need to learn them anew (Guenther, 2006).

The changes to our design are simple yet they cannot be underestimated for the impact they have had on students and their ability to access education online. They have transformed our teaching practices as well as the way we design our course sites.

NEW TEACHING PRACTICE INSPIRED BY NEW TEACHING SPACES

Whilst we had encompassed new online teaching techniques such as scaffolding, moderating, communicating effectively to build a social and cognitive presence, viewing a site through a wayfinding lens also resulted in new ways of interacting with our students. We now include wayfinding techniques such as 'signposts' in all written communications with students on discussion forums. This assists students to understand the intent of messages and ensures they can find critical information. We encourage teachers to engage with students individually, patiently answering what may seem to be the same question multiple times, and to be disciplined about where particular facets of engagement occur.

In this way we treat the site as both a physical environment and an interactive space. Students know where to locate specific interactions such as *Questions for the Convenor* and *Chat with other students*.

This new approach to communication and course design led to an innovative approach to teaching migration law through problem based learning. Prior to this we had struggled to understand how it would be possible to provide students with practical experience where they could apply the knowledge they were learning.

In order to address this we have created, within the course sites, virtual 'offices' where teams work on problems they then take to the 'Directors office' for feedback.

We include elements of authentic experiences (Brown, Collins, & Duguid, 1989; Lave & Wenger, 1991; Savery, 2006) including group work in 'virtual offices' where students interview professional actors as 'clients' and prepare complete client files.

Teachers within the virtual offices adopt roles as firm directors or firm managers. As managers they no longer 'teach' students but guide them to complete tasks within a group. Teachers and students interact in a safe place, based on mutual trust. The 'firm director' provides feedback on the legal artefact created by the team. In this way up to 250 students at one time can interact and gain practical experience.

The virtual office enables us to build in both flat and hierarchical structures. Participating in different structures allows students to grasp the hierarchical nature of the workplace, and to understand the need for differing types of deference, demeanor and the expectations of the 'client', 'firm director' and 'office colleagues'.

The work done in the virtual office is a central component of both summative and formative assessment which has built substantially on the constructive alignment of the curricululm (Biggs, 1996; Walsh, 2007). The practical application of disciplinary specific provisions such as the legislative definition of a valid visa application, and the implementation of legislative bars on applying for further visas, has assisted students to navigate those threshold concepts (including legal reasoning (Akerlind et al., 2010), statutory interpretation and the role of policy in administrative law) considered fundamental to the disciplinary practice of migration law.

CONCLUSION

There will always be a proportion of students who do not adapt to online study as readily as the majority. However, since crossing our own liminal threshold we have found that the reliance on a 'help forum' for daily work has dropped dramatically. Students readily assist each other to settle down and begin working and questions posted to the help forum now focus on IT matters associated with students own technology, rather than questions related to navigation within our courses.

Whilst ethical considerations mean we cannot include student evaluation comments, we can confidently report on our evaluations and Moodle log statistics. In the most recent teaching session of the 206 students enrolled in the first course, more than 90% had read the critical 'Essential Information' documents which include their important 'Study Schedule' during their orientation period. This is in sharp contrast to the same session in 2012 where our logs show that 30% of new students had not read the Study Schedule by the time the course concluded. More importantly, the feedback on student engagement and problems in our evaluations no longer include the perceptions we had seen in previous years or the complaints about working online.

For the majority of students the only threshold concepts they must navigate now reside firmly in the complex arena of migration law. However we feel we have crossed one of many in the world of course design and online teaching. We look forward to others revealing themselves.

REFERENCES

Akerlind, G., Carr-Gregg, S., Field, R., Houston, L., Jones, J., Lupton, M., … Treloar, C. (2010). *A threshold concepts focus to first year law curriculum design: Supporting student learning using variation theory.* Paper presented at the 13th pacific rim first year in higher education conference, Adelaide, Australia.

Akerlind, G., McKenzie, J., & Lupton, M. (2011). *A threshold concepts focus to curriculum design: Supporting student learning through application of variation theory.* Sydney, Australia: Office for Learning and Teachning.

Ally, M. (2008). Foundations of educational theory for online learning. In T. Anderson (Ed.), *Theory and practice of online learning.* Athabasca: Athabasca University.

Arthur, P., & Passini, R. (1992). *Wayfinding: people, signs, and architecture.* Ontario: McGraw-Hill.

Biggs, J. (1996). Enhancing teaching through constructive alignment. *Higher Education, 32*(3), 347–364.

Bocchi, J., Eastman, J. K., & Swift, C. O. (2004). Retaining the online learner: Profile of students in an online MBA program and implications for teaching them. *Journal of Education for Business, 79*(4), 245–253. doi:10.3200/JOEB.79.4.245-253

Brown, J. S., Collins, A., & Duguid, P. (1989). Situated cognition and the culture of learning. *Educational Researcher, 18*(1), 32–42. doi:10.2307/1176008

Carpman, J. R., & Grant, M. A. (2002). Wayfinding: A broad view. In R. Bechtel & A. Churchman (Ed.), *Handbook of environmental psychology* (p. 722). Hoboken, NJ: John Wiley & Sons Inc.

Coates, H. (2007). A model of online and general campus-based student engagement. *Assessment & Evaluation in Higher Education, 32*(2), 121–141. doi:10.1080/02602930600801878

Darwin, S. (2010). *Evaluation and course development report graduate certificate in migration law and practice* (Semester 2). Acton, ACT: ANU College of Law.

Dickie, M. (2010, Spring). *Migration law program Brisbane review day.*

Dickie, M. (2011). *Migration law program review day April 2011 – Changes to Program.*

Farkas, D. K., & Farkas, J. B. (2000). Guidelines for designing web navigation. *Technical Communication, 47*(3), 341–358.

Fisher, K. (2003). Demystifying critical reflection: Defining criteria for assessment. *Higher Education Research & Development, 22*(3), 313–325.

Foltz, M. A. (1998). *Designing navigable information spaces.* Cambridge, MA: Massachusetts Institute of Technology.

Garrison, D., R., Anderson, T., & Archer, W. (2001). Critical thinking, cognitive presence, and computer conferencing in distance education. *American Journal of Distance Education, 15*(1), 7–23.

Garrison, D. R. (2007). Online community of inquiry review: Social, cognitive and teaching prescence issues. *Journal of Asynchronous Learning Networks 11*(1), 61–72.

Guenther, K. (2006). Wayfinding on the web. *Online, 30*(1), 54–57.

Joo, Y. J., Lim, K. Y., & Kim, E. K. (2011). Online university students' satisfaction and persistence: Examining perceived level of presence, usefulness and ease of use as predictors in a structural model. *Computers & Education, 57*(2), 1654–1664. doi:http://dx.doi.org/10.1016/j.compedu.2011.02.008

Kligyte, G. (2009). *Threshold concept: A lens for examing networked learning.* Proceedings of the ascilite 2009 Conference, Aukland, New zealand, 540–543.

Land, R., Cousin, G., Meyer, J. H. F., & Davies, P. (2005). *Threshold concepts and troublesome knowledge (3): Implications for course design and evaluation.* Paper presented at the Improving Student Learning–equality and diversity, OCSLD, Oxford.

Lave, J., & Wenger, E. (1991). *Situated learning: Legitimate peripheral participation.* Cambridge, England; New York, NY: Cambridge University Press.

Lynch, K. (1960). *The image of the city.* Cambridge, MA: MIT Press.

McKernan, J., & McKernan, J. (2013). *Curriculum action research: A handbook of methods and resources for the reflective practitioner.* London: Routledge.

Meyer, J. H. F., & Land, R. (2005). Threshold concepts and troublesome knowledge (2): Epistemological considerations and a conceptual framework for teaching and learning. *Higher Education, 49*(3), 373–388.

Meyer, J. H. F., & Land, R. (2013). *Overcoming barriers to student understanding: Threshold concepts and troublesome knowledge*. London: Routledge.

Moisey, S. D., & Hughes, J. A. (2008). Supporting the online learner. In T. Anderson (Ed.), *The theory and practice of online learning* (2nd ed., pp. electronic text.). Edmonton: AU Press. Retrieved from https://anulib.anu.edu.au/tools/generic_revproxy.html?url=http://search.ebscohost.com/login.aspx?direct=true&scope=site&db=e000xww&AN=309173https://anulib.anu.edu.au/tools/generic_revproxy.html?url=http://site.ebrary.com/lib/anuau/Top?id=10290419.

Passini, R. (1984). Spatial representations: A wayfinding perspective. *Journal of environmental psychology, 4*(2), 153–164.

Passini, R. (1996). Wayfinding design: Logic, application and some thoughts on universality. *Design Studies, 17*(3), 319–331.

Rovai, A. P. (2002). A preliminary look at structural differences in sense of classroom community between higher education traditional and ALN courses. *Journal of Asynchronous Learning Networks, 6*(1), 41–56.

Savery, J. R. (2006). Overview of problem-based learning: Definitions and distinctions. *Interdisciplinary Journal of Problem-based Learning, 1*(1), 3.

Schon, D. (1987). *Educating the reflective practitioner*. San Francisco, CA: Jossey Bass.

Shea, P., Sau Li, C., & Pickett, A. (2006). A study of teaching presence and student sense of learning community in fully online and web-enhanced college courses. *The Internet and Higher Education, 9*(3), 175–190. doi:http://dx.doi.org/10.1016/j.iheduc.2006.06.005

Sorrows, M. E., & Hirtle, S. C. (1999). The nature of landmarks for real and electronic spaces. In C. Freksa & D. M. Mark (Eds.), *Spatial information theory. Cognitive and computational foundations of geographic information science* (pp. 37–50). Berlin: Springer.

Spiers, H. J., & Maguire, E. A. (2008). The dynamic nature of cognition during wayfinding. *Journal of environmental psychology, 28*(3), 232–249. doi: http://dx.doi.org/10.1016/j.jenvp.2008.02.006

Stacey Ludwig-Hardman, J. C. D. (2003). Learner support services for online students: Scaffolding for success. *International Review of Research in Open and Distance Learning, 4*(1).

Tavangarian, D., Leypold, M. E., Nölting, K., Röser, M., & Voigt, D. (2004). Is e-learning the solution for individual learning. *Electronic Journal of e-Learning, 2*(2), 273–280.

Van Galen, I. (2012). *Evaluation and course development report graduate certificate in migration law and practice 2012.*

Wallsten, S. (2013, March 8). *What are we not doing when we're online.* Paper presented at the Economics of Digitization, Stanford University, CA.

Walsh, A. (2007). An exploration of Biggs' constructive alignment in the context of work-based learning. *Assessment & Evaluation in Higher Education, 32*(1), 79–87.

Wenger, E. C., McDermott, R., & Snyder, W. (2002). *Cultivating communities of practice* (Vol. 1) Cambridge, MA: Harvard Business Review Press.

Marianne Dickie
ANU College of Law
Australian National University

Ilona van Galen
ANU College of Law
Australian National University

ANDREA S. WEBB

22. THRESHOLD CONCEPTS AND THE SCHOLARSHIP OF TEACHING AND LEARNING

INTRODUCTION

When studying for a career in academia, most graduate students are trained in the methodologies and discourses of their discipline, however there is an inherent mismatch between the responsibilities that most faculty members undertake on a daily basis and the training that they have received (Shulman, 2000). Research-intensive universities around the world increasingly have to demonstrate innovations in teaching and learning in order to deliver high quality student learning experiences in diverse program contexts. National and institutional organizations are emphasizing the importance of scholarship to support program and policy changes (Probert, 2014).

Threshold concepts can work as a lens with which to investigate the scholarship of teaching and learning (SoTL) and as a frame to consider curriculum for SoTL programmes. Curriculum and pedagogy informed by threshold concepts encourages participants to stretch outside of their institutional cultures and cross disciplinary boundaries.

THE SCHOLARSHIP OF TEACHING AND LEARNING

The scholarship of teaching and learning is an important international movement, coming into maturity in the 21st century, which contributes to the quality of teaching and learning in higher education, as well as a growing body of educational literature (Hubball, Pearson, & Clarke, 2013). With a focus on student learning in diverse educational contexts, it encompasses a broad set of practices that engage educational leaders in examining pedagogical practices in a methodical and rigorous way in order to improve their programmes, criteria shared with quality scholarship (Glassick, Huber, & Maeroff, 1997; Hutchings, Huber, & Ciccone, 2011).

Providing a literature informed, peer reviewed justification for programme and policy changes, SoTL is a practical and complementary undergirding for research in teaching and learning; offering methodological flexibility applicable to the diverse educational contexts across research-intensive universities. Utilizing evidence based approaches to practice and rigorous research design can provide strong justification for programme reforms or adoption of specific pedagogical practices.

R. Land et al. (Eds.), Threshold Concepts in Practice, 299–308.

However, many institutions lack internal SoTL expertise and the available time to effectively develop and evaluate curriculum and pedagogical practices (Hubball, Lamberson, & Kindler, 2012). Unfortunately, administrators and faculty development professionals have struggled with incentives to encourage and prepare academic staff to do this type of scholarly work (Richlin & Cox, 2004). There are a number of barriers to the adoption of SoTL including: tenure and promotion policies and practices that incentivize SoTL (Boyer, 1990; Hubball & Pearson, 2010; Webb, Wong, & Hubball, 2013), accountability for programme review to be supported by evidence based practice, the challenge of the meaning of SoTL and the discourse of the scholarship of teaching and learning (McKinney, 2002), allocation of time where research, teaching, and learning are seen as competing rather than complementary initiatives (Dobbins, 2008), movement outside of disciplinary cultures (Bunnell & Bernstein, 2012), and the problematic relationship between SoTL and educational research (Kanuka, 2011; Svinicki, 2012). There is a need for better and more integrated theoretical work in the scholarship of teaching and learning (Gurung & Schwartz, 2010; Hutchings, 2007) and the ultimate purpose of this chapter is to identify the threshold concepts in the Scholarship of Teaching and Learning in order to facilitate the adoption and wide-spread use of the scholarship of teaching and learning. An understanding of SoTL that includes threshold concepts (Meyer & Land, 2003, 2005, 2006) will help to facilitate the requisite cultural shift within departments and institutions.

THRESHOLD CONCEPTS

Threshold concepts have generated a great deal of interest evidenced by the wealth of literature that continues to develop and the idea has resonated with a range of disciplines in higher education. As such, threshold concepts have arisen as part of a drive to improve the quality of teaching and learning environments within higher education (Kandlbinder & Peseta, 2009; McLean, 2009; Meyer, 2012; Moore, 2012).

A common starting point in discussions of threshold concepts is a set of five key characteristics identified by Meyer and Land (2003, 2006): threshold concepts are transformative, irreversible, integrative, often, but not necessarily bounded, and often troublesome. For the purposes of this chapter, I place emphasis on the transformative[1] nature of troublesome[2] knowledge in threshold concepts as learners navigate the liminal space.

The dimensions of Threshold Concepts are more than just building blocks towards understanding within a discipline or field (Lucas & Mladenovic, 2007). Often acting as gatekeepers of the field and facilitators of enculturation, they need to be negotiated as portals, spaces, relationships, or periods of time (Land, 2012). This invites curricular designers to investigate the sources of epistemological barriers and free up the blocked places by redesigning course sequences and activities. As well, they have proved useful for initiating cross-disciplinary discourses (Carmichael,

2010; Irvine & Carmichael, 2009); these conversations are a starting point for curriculum making (Carmichael, 2012).

Threshold concepts highlight the shared elements of a community's knowledge and the point around which identity and membership are conferred (Irvine & Carmichael, 2009). Therefore, mastering threshold concepts opens portals through which learners may engage and participate in community with experts. These open portals act as entry point in to the 'big tent' of scholarship in teaching and learning, and the engagement with a community of scholars.

WHY THRESHOLD CONCEPTS WITH THE SCHOLARSHIP OF TEACHING AND LEARNING?

Threshold concepts provide an emergent theoretical framework to reconsider research and practice in higher education (Lucas & Mladenovic, 2007). This framework implies demanding and promoting forms of dialogue about educational research and practice that may not be taking place within disciplines, but this type of work is taking place in the scholarship of teaching and learning. Glassick, Huber, and Maeroff (1997) apply the construct of scholarship (a way of thinking and practicing) to an area (teaching in higher education) previously undefined in this way. Both SoTL and threshold concepts are focused on the broad context of teaching and learning experience.

Finding and smoothing 'stuck places' in disciplinary knowledge is a familiar task for SoTL scholars, as it is foundational to pedagogical content knowledge (O'Brien, 2008; Shulman, 1987). Ways of thinking and practicing (WTP) include subject specific thinking processes and skills that are purposefully applied to engage learners. Similar to Shulman's pedagogical content knowledge, WTP suggests a concern with pedagogy in discipline specific contexts. There is great value in dialogue between instructors, within a discipline, who possess the normative expectations about what a learner should understand, and the student who is going/has gone through the learning experience. When connected with SoTL, threshold concepts can offer a multilayered approach to collaborative investigation (McLean, 2009); emphasizing a cross-disciplinary community of practice.

Barradell (2013) and Cousin (2008) suggest that threshold concepts can provide a comfortable bridge between disciplinary expertise and pedagogical practice. This transition into a new educative environment may be destabilizing and challenging to the faculty member's sense of identity. Learning requires making a shift to reinterpret the constructed nature of what was previously held as truth. The same could be said of those entering into the SoTL. Heeding Boyer's (1990) call for a scholarship of integration, "doing research at the boundaries where fields converge" is important at "forcing new topologies of knowledge" outside of confining disciplinary cultures (1990, p. 19). As SoTL scholars investigate the educative practices within their disciplines, they are engaging this boundary-crossing discourse and stimulating instructor reflection on practice.

Ultimately, given the varied understandings of threshold concepts, it is not surprising to see a diverse set of research approaches, methods, and analytic tools (Irvine & Carmichael, 2009). Incorporating the ways of thinking and practicing in multiple disciplines requires a certain level of flexibility, much like scholarship in teaching and learning. The discursive nature of threshold concepts makes it difficult to apply a universal standard, however conceptions of rigorous scholarship may prove useful. This breadth has already proved useful as a means of structuring data collection and analysis for participants new to enquiry into teaching and learning. Openness invites scholars to engage in enquiry without concern for their novice ability/status (Bunnell & Bernstein, 2012).

A scholarship of teaching and learning focus brings rigor to enquiry into practice in higher education. Provoking and managing a threshold concept framework can be a powerful pedagogic strategy to achieve that aim. In exchange, threshold concepts have the potential to locate troublesome aspects of knowledge and assist curriculum developers in identifying and navigating conceptual thresholds.

THE STUDY

Begun in 1998, the UBC Faculty Certificate Program in the Scholarship of Teaching and Learning Leadership (UBC SoTL FCP) is a learning-centred, leadership programme for educational leaders with a focus on collaborative intra- and interdisciplinary practice. The nature of the programme creates an environment in which faculty engage in SoTL through scholarly study of their educative practices and ongoing critical reflection.

The UBC SoTL FCP is situated within a unique context, with supportive university governance and long standing institutional initiatives both supporting the development and sustainment of SoTL across the university. And while it is locally situated, the model is generalizable to other institutions wanting to transform their institutional initiatives through systematic, cyclical enquiry (Hubball et al., 2012) and support their faculty members as they move from personally relevant scholarly teaching to the scholarship of teaching and learning.

Educational leaders previously enrolled in the UBC SoTL FCP were invited to be participants in the study. A questionnaire was sent via email to all past graduates of the UBC SoTL FCP in the Fall of 2013. The questionnaire was based around four key questions[3] which attempted to highlight what the participants saw as the challenging topics in the scholarship of teaching and learning, in order to identify the key learning concepts and 'stuck' places (Kandlbinder & Peseta, 2009; Kiley & Wisker, 2009).

The thirty-two questionnaires provided the foundation and organizing framework for the interviews, where impressions and reflections were discussed in greater depth. Interviews are the most common method of data collection used in higher education threshold concepts research with subject matter experts (Irvine & Carmichael, 2009; Humphrey & Simpson, 2012; Kiley, 2009; Kiley & Wisker, 2009). Therefore, thirteen interviews, conducted in January and February of 2014, were employed to explore participants' ways of experiencing the scholarship of teaching and learning in the UBC SoTL FCP context. Recognizing that the goal of the constructionist interview is to examine how the participants have experienced particular aspects of SoTL, I developed a few guiding questions, but otherwise focused on exploring the participant's experience through conversation. Further, the constructionist interview (Rubin & Rubin, 2005) collaboratively generates knowledge; therefore both the participant and myself are creating the concepts and ideas raised through the questionnaire.

Ongoing data collection and analysis of the study was informed by van Manen's (1990) interpretive phenomenology and endeavoured to be rigorous, while remaining flexible and capable of interpreting complex phenomena within socially constructed experiences (Charmaz, 2005; Jones & Alony, 2011). Each data source was summarized and then the essential themes developed using thematic analysis. Four key characteristics have been highlighted for identifying the threshold concepts this study, troublesome, liminal, transformative, and bounded. Constant comparative methods were used to incorporate and strengthen the description of the threshold concepts.

FINDINGS AND DISCUSSION

Throughout the questionnaires and interviews, participants consistently identified three threshold concepts as central to their learning in the Scholarship of Teaching and Learning.

Threshold Concept I, Conceptions of Research

One of the thresholds includes how new SoTL scholars envision research, the research questions they ask, and what they consider valid data collection for study. This was articulated through specific reference to language, readings, research projects, and feelings of insecurity (referred to by participants as 'imposter syndrome').

In many cases, participants spoke of new research methodologies and methods helping them move from intuitive knowledge through the "complete sea changes" into social science research. The "exposure to the academic side" of teaching and learning brought with it a new discourse of SoTL. Almost all of the participants highlighted their disconnect with the new language as a major barrier to engaging in SoTL research. However, once one masters a new language, they become cultural insiders and are able to translate for colleagues the "jargon of the expert".

The driving force behind a shifting conception of research included acknowledgement of participants' epistemology and ontology as drivers for their approaches to research. This acknowledgement of their 'subject position' opens reflection, not just on teaching and learning, but on the development and design on such research. I speculate that the long-standing enculturation into disciplines, and the associated ritual knowledge (Perkins, 1999), may impede a novice SoTL scholar's deep understanding. Once they acknowledges that there are alternate views of scholarship within different disciplines, then there is a possibility that they will recognize alternative ways of conducting research.

Threshold Concept II, Permeability within Institutional Cultures

Permeability assumes a broad view of higher education; moving between the ways of thinking and practicing in different fields. Adopting what you learn in one place and applying it in another. Institutional culture in higher education, has figured prominently throughout the project. It is a barrier, something to work around, and a challenging factor within SoTL development. Many participants spoke about trying to balance their disciplinary scholarship and the SoTL work.

In the interviews, it became clear that while many participants saw teaching as part of their job description, the SoTL FCP extended their conception of professional responsibility. The current methodological openness of SoTL invites faculty members, previously sceptical of social science research qualitative methodologies to begin engaging. Similarly, the tension between disciplinary culture norms, jargon across disciplines, unfamiliarity with social science research methods, and human subjects ethics review protocols has proved to be a challenge for the scholarship of teaching and learning (Hubball, Clarke, & Poole, 2010). The innovation required here is to invite faculty members, and not only education specialists, to see this kind of enquiry as an aspect of their work as instructors in a research-intensive university.

Threshold Concept III, the Novice to Expert Continuum

New SoTL scholars are in continuous oscillation between expertise, in their discipline, and being novices in the scholarship of teaching and learning. Liminality can be scary but it can also be tremendously generative. In this study, the UBC SoTL FCP provides a space/place/time, physically and intellectually, outside of disciplinary cultures; where innovation does not need to be constrained by previously held assumptions and conventions.

Exemplifying high stakes learning in higher education, faculty members require support as they pass through the liminal state. There are times during their induction into SoTL when they will begin to demonstrate ontological and discursive shifts. The transition to 'studentness' (Cousin, 2012) can propel faculty members into insecurity as they are oscillating on the continuum. This can be highly intimidating, especially to educational leaders in higher education who often are charged with making high stakes decisions about curriculum at research-intensive universities.

Embracing liminality means that a learner knows that navigating threshold concepts can be emotionally taxing, then the adoption or encouragement of particular dispositions would help learners mitigate the negative aspects of the liminal experience. A support network is key. While all the participants have experienced working through a challenging learning process, they have also activated collegial networks. Support from a community of practice, self-efficacy, optimism, hope, and resilience could provide a personal foundation for the negotiation of the liminal space (Land, 2012). Externally, the relationship between instructor and learner is key to navigating the threshold (Cousin, 2012). In accepting the position of 'studenthood', a learner accepts an implied apprenticeship of enculturation into new or changing knowledge.

Over the seventeen years of the UBC SoTL Leadership FCP, change was not uniform, with some participants become more active in SoTL (institutionally & nationally), while others have confined the effects to their classrooms. Some participants suggested that they came to the UBC SoTL Leadership FCP with an interest in change (both personal and professional) and consciously put themselves in intellectually and ontologically challenging positions. But, almost all recognize that their experience changed their whole approach to learning; seeing the programme as "an enlightening experience" and "a stepping off point" that opened their eyes.

CONCLUSIONS

Investigations into threshold concepts have lead to their current conception, where they have much to offer the scholarship of teaching and learning. I have identified three threshold concepts that are of particular importance to curriculum developers in the scholarship of teaching and learning: conceptions of research, permeability within institutional cultures, and embracing liminality.

The increasing theorizing of threshold concepts within curriculum development (Carmichael, 2012; Land, 2012) could help faculty developers consider how the scholarship of teaching and learning could be useful to educational leaders. Therefore highlighting these threshold concepts within the scholarship of teaching and learning could serve to 'discipline' educational leaders, new to the field, in the nature of SoTL as a field.

ACKNOWLEDGEMENTS

The author of this chapter would like to express her sincere thanks to the past graduates of the UBC Scholarship of Teaching and Learning Faculty Leadership Program for their critical contributions to this research.

NOTES

[1]   The transformative nature of threshold concepts involves an ontological shift as well as a cognitive one. Learning to think within a discipline is characteristic of the transformative agenda, which demands that learners 'rework' their prior knowledge in the light of the new concept.

[2]   Threshold concepts often challenge a learner's existing knowledge or beliefs. The fragmentation of all or part of the self in these 'stuck places' represent traces of cultural, social, and educational influences which need to be transformed in order to lessen the emotional discomfort.

[3] The questions from the questionnaire included (1) What are 5 ideas or concepts about the scholarship of teaching and learning in higher education that are the most important to you? (2) What readings, lectures, discussions, etc. helped you understand these key concepts or ideas? (3) What topics or themes were challenging for you to learn? (4) What helped you overcome these challenges?

REFERENCES

Barradell, S. (2013). The identification of threshold concepts: A review of theoretical complexities and methodological challenges. *Higher Education, 65*(2), 265–276. doi:10.1007/s10734-012-9542-3

Boyer, E. (1990). *Scholarship reconsidered: Priorities of the professoriate*. Princeton, NJ: Carnegie Foundation for the Advancement of Teaching.

Bunnell, S. L., & Bernstein, D. J. (2012). Overcoming some threshold concepts in scholarly teaching. *Journal of Faculty Development, 23*(3), 14–18.

Carmichael, P. (2010). Threshold concepts, disciplinary differences and cross-disciplinary discourse. *Learning and Teaching in Higher Education: Gulf Perspectives, 7*(2), 53–71.

Carmichael, P. (2012, June 28–29). *From this curriculum to that which is to come*. NAIRTL Conference 2012, Trinity College Dublin. Retrieved July 10, 2013, from www.nairtl.ie/index.php?pageID=634

Charmaz, K. (2005). Grounded theory. In J. A. Smith, R. Harre, & L. van Langenhove (Eds.), *Rethinking methods in psychology* (pp. 27–49). Thousand Oaks, CA: Sage Publications Ltd.

Cousin, G. (2008). Threshold concepts: Old wine in new bottles or new forms of transactional curriculum inquiry? In R. Land, J. H. F. Meyer, & J. Smith (Eds.), *Threshold concepts within the disciplines* (pp. 261–272). Rotterdam, The Netherlands: Sense Publishers.

Cousin, G. (2012, June 28–29). *Threshold concepts as an analytical tool for researching higher education*. NAIRTL Conference 2012, Trinity College Dublin. Retrieved July 10, 2013, from www.nairtl.ie/index.php?pageID=633

Dobbins, K. (2008). Enhancing the scholarship of teaching and learning: A study of factors identified as promoting and hindering the scholarly activities of academics in one faculty. *International Journal for the Scholarship of Teaching and Learning, 2*(2). Retrieved July 5, 2013, from http://www.georgiasouthern.edu/ijsotl/v2n2/essays_about_sotl/_Dobbins/index.htm

Glassick, C. E., Huber, M. T., & Maeroff, G. I. (1997). *Scholarship assessed: Evaluation of the professoriate*. San Francisco, CA: Jossey-Bass.

Gurung, R. A. R., & Schwartz, B. M. (2010). Riding the third wave of SoTL. *International Journal for the Scholarship of Teaching and Learning, 4*(2). Retrieved March 15, 2013, from http://academics.georgiasouthern.edu/ijsotl/v4n2/invited_essays/_GurungSchwartz/index.html

Hubball, H. T., & Pearson, M. (2010). Grappling with the complexity of undergraduate degree program reform: Critical barriers and emergent strategies. *Transformative Dialogues: Teaching & Learning Journal, 3*(3). Retrieved August 11, 2013, from http://kwantlen.ca/TD/TD.3.3/TD.3.3_Hubball&Pearson_Undergraduate_Degree_Program_Reform.pdf

Hubball, H. T., Clarke, A., & Poole, G. (2010). Ten-year reflections on mentoring SoTL research in a research-intensive university. *International Journal for Academic Development, 15*(2), 117–129. doi:10.1080/13601441003737758.

Hubball, H. T., Lamberson, M., & Kindler, A. (2012). Strategic restructuring of a centre for teaching and learning in a research-intensive university: Institutional engagement in scholarly approaches to curriculum renewal and pedagogical practices. *International Journal for University Teaching and Faculty Development, 3*(2), 95–110.

Hubball, H. T., Pearson, M., & Clarke, A. (2013). SoTL inquiry in broader curricula and institutional contexts: Theoretical underpinnings and emerging trends. Invited Peer-reviewed Essay for inaugural issue. *International Journal for Inquiry in Teaching and Learning, 1*(1), 41–57. doi:10.1353/iss.2013.0009

Humphrey, R., & Simpson, B. (2012). Writes of passage: Writing up qualitative data as a threshold concept in doctoral research. *Teaching in Higher Education, 17*(6), 735–746. doi:10.1080/13562517.2012

Hutchings, P. (2007). Theory: The elephant in the scholarship of teaching and learning room. *International Journal for the Scholarship of Teaching and Learning, 1*(1). Retrieved August 8, 2011, from http://www.georgiasouthern.edu/ijsotl/2007_v1n1.htm

Hutchings, P., Huber, M. T., & Ciccone, A. (2011). *The scholarship of teaching and learning reconsidered: Institutional integration and impact.* San Francisco, CA: Jossey-Bass.

Irvine, N., & Carmichael, P. (2009). Threshold concepts: a point of focus for practitioner research. *Active Learning in Higher Education, 10*(2), 103–119. doi:10.1177/1469787409104785

Jones, M., & Alony, I. (2011). Guiding the use of grounded theory in doctoral studies. *International Journal of Doctoral Studies, 6*, 95–114.

Kandlbinder, P., & Peseta, T. (2009). Key concepts in postgraduate certificates in higher education teaching and learning in Australasia and the United Kingdom. *International Journal for Academic Development, 14*(1), 19–31. doi:10.1080/13601440802659247

Kanuka, H. (2011). Keeping the scholarship in the scholarship of teaching and learning. *International Journal for the Scholarship of Teaching and Learning, 5*(1). Retrieved August 8, 2011, from http://www.georgiasouthern.ed/ijsotl/v5n1/invited_essays/Kanuka/index.html

Kiley, M. (2009). Identifying threshold concepts and proposing strategies to support doctoral candidates. *Innovations in Education and Teaching International, 46*(3), 293–304. doi:10.1080/147032909030690001

Kiley, M., & Wisker, G. (2009). Threshold concepts in research education and evidence of threshold crossing. *Higher Education Research and Development, 28*(4), 431–441. doi:10.1080/07294360903067930

Land, R. (2012, June 28–29). *A closer look at liminality: Incorrigibles and threshold capital.* NAIRTL Conference 2012, Trinity College Dublin. Retrieved July 10, 2013, from www.nairtl.ie/index.php?pageID=627

Lucas, U., & Mladenovic, R. (2007). The potential of threshold concepts: An emerging framework for educational research and practice. *London Review of Education, 5*(3), 237–248. doi:10.1080/14748460701661294

McKinney, K. (2002). *The scholarship of teaching and learning: Current challenges and future visions.* Remarks presented at the ceremony to install the Cross Chair in the Scholarship of Teaching and Learning at Illinois State University, Normal, IL. Retrieved March 15, 2013, from http://sotl.illinoisstate.edu/crossChair/sotlFuture.shtml

McLean, J. (2009). Triggering engagement in SoTL through threshold concepts. *International Journal for the Scholarship of Teaching and Learning, 3*(2). Retrieved from http://www.georgiasouthern.edu/ijsotl

Meyer, J. H. F. (2012). Variation in student learning as a threshold concept. *Journal of Faculty Development, 26*(3), 8–13.

Meyer, J. H. F., & Land, R. (2003). Threshold concepts and troublesome knowledge: Linkages to ways of thinking and practising within the disciplines. In C. Rust (Ed.), *Improving student learning: Improving student learning theory and practice–Ten years on.* Oxford: Oxford Centre for Staff and Learning Development.

Meyer, J. H. F., & Land, R. (2005). Threshold concepts and troublesome knowledge (2): Epistemological considerations and a conceptual framework for teaching and learning. *Higher Education, 49*(3), 373–388. doi:10.1007/s10734-004-6779-5

Meyer, J. H. F., & Land, R. (2006). Threshold concepts and troublesome knowledge: An introduction. In J. H. F. Meyer & R. Land (Eds.), *Overcoming barriers to student understanding: Threshold concepts and troublesome knowledge* (pp. 3–18). London: Routledge Falmer.

Moore, J. L. (2012). Designing for transfer: A threshold concept. *Journal of Faculty Development, 23*(3), 19–24.

O'Brien, M. (2008). Threshold concepts for university teaching and learning: A study of troublesome knowledge. In R. Land, J. H. F. Meyer, & J. Smith (Eds.), *Threshold concepts within the disciplines* (pp. 289–305). Rotterdam, The Netherlands: Sense Publishers.

Perkins, D. (1999). The many faces of constructivism. *Educational Leadership, 57*(3), 6–11.

Probert, B. (2014, May). *Why scholarship matters in higher education.* Australian Government Office for Learning and Teaching, Sydney, NSW.

Richlin, L., & Cox, M. D. (2004). Developing scholarly teaching and the scholarship of teaching and learning through faculty development communities. *New Directions for Teaching and Learning, 97,* 127–135.

Rubin, H. J., & Rubin, I. S. (2005). *Qualitative interviewing: The art of hearing data* (2nd ed.). Thousand Oaks, CA: Sage.

Shulman, L. S. (1987). Knowledge and teaching: Foundations of the new reform. *Harvard Educational Review, 57*(1), 1–22.

Shulman, L. S. (2000). Inventing the future. In P. Hutchings (Ed.), *Opening lines: Approaches to the scholarship of teaching and learning.* Menlo Park, CA: The Carnegie Foundation for the Advancement of Teachning. Retrieved July 3, 2013, from http://www.carnegiefoundation.org/elibrary/inventing-future-opening-lines-approaches-scholarship-teaching-and-learning

Svinicki, M. D. (2012). Who is entitled to do SoTL? *International Journal for the Scholarship of Teaching and Learning, 6*(2). Retrieved December 15, 2012, from http://www.georgiasouthern.edu/ijsotl/v6n2/invited_essays/Svinicki/index.htm

van Manen, M. (1990). *Researching lived experience.* Albany, NY: State University of New York Press.

Webb, A., Wong, T., & Hubball, H. T. (2013). Professional development for adjunct teaching faculty in a research-intensive university: Engagement in scholarly approaches to teaching and learning. *International Journal for Teaching and Learning in Higher Education, 25*(2), 231–238.

Andrea S. Webb
Department of Curriculum & Pedagogy
Faculty of Education
University of British Columbia

DAVID MORONEY, EUGENE MCKENDRY AND ANN DEVITT

23. KNOWLEDGE, BELIEF AND PRACTICE IN LANGUAGE TEACHER EDUCATION

Integration and Implementation of Threshold Concepts over a Teaching Career

INTRODUCTION

This chapter is framed around the notion of adaptivity (Hammermass et al., 2007) as the crucial characteristic for teachers throughout a teaching career whereby in order to remain expert, teachers must adapt to external and internal prompts for change. Teacher cognition, "what teachers think, know and believe" (Borg, 2006, p. 1), underlies professional practice and it is all these dimensions of theoretical and empirical knowledge and beliefs which may be subject to change. Threshold Concepts offer a powerful lens to explore this conception of teacher professional knowledge and development, from student to veteran teacher, for two reasons. Firstly, the integrative nature of the theoretical framework for threshold concepts facilitates the generation of insights through the juxtaposition of key theories in teacher professional learning such as transformation (Mezirow & Taylor, 2009), and Communities of Practice (Wenger, 1998). Secondly, the potential of threshold concepts as catalysts in the restructuring of not only learners' knowledge systems but also their beliefs and even identity resonates with this model which views deep and unsettling learning as a cyclical component of professional development for teachers.

The chapter presents a qualitative case study in two phases of professional development of language teachers in Ireland using the lens of Threshold Concepts. The first phase explores conceptions of threshold concepts for language teaching in the personal narratives of eight in-career language teachers.[1]

The second phase follows a group of three student language teachers over the course of their year-long programme of initial teacher education, charting their personal development within the context of the concepts identified by the professionals in phase 1. This work provides the subject-specific focus of modern language teaching, which expands on previous work on teacher professional development within the field of Threshold Concepts (Cove, McAdam, & McGonigal, 2008; Atherton, Hadfield, & Meyers, 2012; Devitt et al., 2014). The next section sets out the theoretical framework of teacher professional development which underpins this work and the interactions between this and the literature on threshold concepts.

R. Land et al. (Eds.), Threshold Concepts in Practice, 309–319.

The chapter goes on to present the methodology and findings of the two study phases separately and concludes with an integrated discussion.

TEACHER PROFESSIONAL LEARNING AND DEVELOPMENT

As noted above, the teacher as an adaptive expert (Hammerness et al., 2007) is considered the goal of teacher professional learning within the framework of this study. Hammerness et al. in their definition distinguish between 'routine experts' and 'adaptive experts' where they state that both continue to learn throughout their lifetime but, whereas "routine experts develop a core set of competencies that they apply throughout their lives with greater and greater efficiency," adaptive experts 'are much more likely to change their core competencies and continually expand the breadth and depth of their expertise' (2007, p. 360). In the context of a teacher's career, adaptivity entails reflective practice, the capacity to reflect on experience and adopt critical insights into practice (Schön, 1983). The process of change may not be an easy one and may be emotionally painful, as in Heifetz et al.'s (2009) model of adaptive change which entails changes to belief systems. At its most profound, adaptive change can be transformative, in the sense of Mezirow and Taylor (2009), engaging not only knowledge and beliefs but even an individual's subjectivity.

The trajectory and phasing of the journey from novice to expert teacher has been the subject of much research over many years (e.g. Fuller, 1969; Richardson & Placier, 2001). Earlier staged models of teacher professional learning have given way to a more gradual developmental process. Such a view of teacher development is holistic, not focusing only on competencies and knowledge. Borg's conception of teacher cognition encompassing "what teachers think, know and believe" (2006, p. 1) integrates with this view of teacher development. Woods and Çakir (2011) contend that teacher cognition is composed of at least the two dimension from personal beliefs to impersonal "truths" and from experiential to theoretical knowledge. In this context, the interaction between knowledge and belief is integral to teacher development, as articulated by Borg (2011, p. 370): 'it is widely recognized that teacher education is more likely to impact on what teachers do if it also impacts on their beliefs'. Similarly the tension between the personal and the abstract and the need to bridge the theory-practice divide is also a key issue in teacher education.

In the context of such complexity, threshold concepts as they have been articulated in the literature offers a means of integrating multiple dimensions within one framework. The teacher as adaptive expert entails a career path which contains limitless thresholds opening onto limitless "previously inaccessible ways of thinking" and acting (Meyer & Land, 2003, p. 414). These thresholds may be troublesome and marked by emotional turmoil and possibly culminating in transformation. Furthermore, it is the individual's complete epistemological and ontological system (knowledge, beliefs and identity) which may be implicated in the integration of new concepts. Barradell and Peseta (2014, p. 2) echo this by noting that grasping a threshold concept itself has the 'potential to create a change in knowledge, and importantly a change in self…the learning becomes part of the very fabric of the learner'. Cove et al. (2008) and Atherton et al. (2012) have explored possible threshold concepts for teaching and contexts for their integration. Devitt et al. (2014) drew on the perspectives of students, academics and professionals to explore teacher development using the threshold concepts lens of troublesomeness and transformation. This chapter builds on these studies focusing in on the subject-specific dimensions of language teaching.

STUDY PHASE 1: IN-CAREER TEACHERS

Methodology

This study phase was conducted as an exploratory qualitative case study in 2013 with practicing language teachers in Ireland. The study set out to explore a broad concept of teacher knowledge, such as that outlined in the previous section, moving away from a competencies-based approach to teacher education, and building on the findings of Devitt et al. (2014). The key research questions are outlined below:

- What do experienced teachers articulate as threshold concepts (TCs) underlying good language teaching?
- Is the enactment of these concepts dependent on the policy context within which teachers work?
- What are the conditions and encounters that facilitate or challenge the integration and practice of these TCs over a teaching career?

In order to address these questions, participants took part in interviews exploring their personal narratives as teachers and learners of language and within this were asked to consider what they consider were the fundamentals of good language teaching. There were 8 teachers from the Republic of Ireland. The sampling for this study was purposeful drawing from teachers with at least 5 years experience teaching in different school types and teaching at least one of the main curricular languages (Irish, French, German, Spanish and Italian). The sample size is in line with indications of appropriate theoretical sampling for qualitative research with expert participants (Guest, Bunce, & Johnson, 2006). Interviews were transcribed and a thorough thematic analysis of participant interviews was conducted. The analysis was driven by a priori themes derived from the literature on language teaching (e.g. Long & Doughty, 2009) and threshold concepts and was also open to themes identified in the data.

Findings

The two concepts of language use and learner autonomy were identified by language teachers as both critical to good teaching of languages and in some cases transformative in their own experience of teaching. These concepts could be considered as threshold concepts for language teacher education.

Real language use. The first concept articulates a belief as to the purpose and nature of language teaching: the need to generate opportunities to use language meaningfully as both an end and means of the language learning process. A number of sub-themes were identified here that relate to the literature on language learning, for example focusing on meaning rather than form in teaching, authenticity of materials, tasks and communication inside the classroom and promoting interaction with the language outside the classroom. The dominant sub-theme however which was articulated by all teachers was the use of the target language (TL) in the classroom. The majority of the teachers expressed maximal TL use as an article of faith, part of their belief system for what it means to be a language teacher. The source of this belief was different for different teachers but for these teachers it seems fundamentally grounded in experience and belief. For some it derived from professional experience in the context of teaching English as a foreign language (TEFL) where the use of the TL in the classroom is required as there is no alternative lingua franca. The personal experience of enacting this practice and observing its effectiveness embedded the belief such that it would be enacted in other contexts. One teacher (MET) recounted the transformative experience during Initial Teacher Education (ITE) of coming to believe that using the target language in the classroom could work:

MET: But it was an amazing experience to watch somebody teach a very unusual language to a group of people and have them speak it within an hour

AMD: And what did you get out of that?

MET: Oh it completely transformed my way of thinking about languages. I would speak the language, but I didn't really believe that you could teach a language through the target language at that stage.

AMD: And how did that affect how you taught?

MET: It radically changed it!

For another teacher (LBA), this principle was based on a core belief, not related to teaching:

LBA: I should say that, this was for me sort of holy cause because I am a great believer in the necessity for the Irish language … and the implication of that was that in teaching in the classroom I would never, almost never use English.

Fostering learning autonomy. The second concept relates to the notion of student-centred learning and student accommodation identified as a threshold concept for teaching in Devitt et al. (2014). This concept for language teachers could also be framed as part of the developmental process outlined by Fuller (1969) as a move from concern with the self to a concern for the learners. Within the context of language teaching, this translates as learner empowerment to manage their own learning goals and activities. This is summarised as learner autonomy and is a major research area in the field of language education (Little, 1991). The related sub-themes consistently maintain a learner focus on topics such as learner confidence, motivation, strategy use and goal setting. Teachers identified this as part of prolonged experience of working with learners but also as a result of interaction with peers and theory as in the example below:

MFE: And I studied the work of Leni Dam in Denmark and I suppose that was a huge moment for me because eh I hadn't heard of the concept of the autonomous learner before that. And it was something, because while I was studying I was also teaching at the same time, I tried to introduce, you know, some of the methods that she spoke about. And I think that is crucial to have an autonomous learner.

Contexts and catalysts for change.   The teachers in this study noted explicitly and implicitly a number of factors that contributed to their learning and integration of new concepts in relation to language teaching. Professional dialogue with like-minded peers was identified by several participants as vital to maintaining an adaptive perspective and conversely the challenge of trying to develop new ways of working in the face of an unsupportive professional environment was also a common theme. The context of practice to generate change was also considered essential, as in the example above where the catalyst for change is theory but the availability of a context to practice these changes allowed its integration. These two points are very important in the context of initial teacher education where programmes are intended to provide optimum conditions for teacher development.

STUDY PHASE 2: PRE-SERVICE TEACHERS

Methodology

The follow-on study was conducted during the academic year 2013–14 with three pre-service language teachers of French undertaking a one-year Initial Teacher Education (ITE) postgraduate programme in Ireland. As noted above, previous work with a number of stakeholders in ITE (students, teachers and teacher educators) had indicated that the key learning for pre-service teachers at ITE was "a learner-centred perspective generating positive relationships in the classroom" (Devitt et al., 2014, p. 130). This study aimed to investigate the subject-specific dimensions for pre-service language teachers focusing on the learner perspective but also the language teaching concepts identified in phase 1. The sampling in this instance was opportunistic with 3 pre-service teachers of French on one ITE programme volunteering to participate for the year. The participants were engaged throughout the year in both teaching practicum and University modules, teaching 2.5 days a week and attending University for 2.5 days. The data in this phase involved a reflective journal of professional learning sent by email every 2–3 weeks over the 7 months of the ITE programme. Participants were asked to articulate in these emails the challenges they were facing at that time in their teaching and aspects where they felt they had made progress. At the end of the year, individual semi-structured interviews were conducted with each participant to discuss the participants' sense of progression and factors contributing to this over the course of the year. After the interviews were transcribed, a thematic analysis was conducted of the full data set.

Findings

Liminality. The sense of the liminal space of Initial Teacher Education is very powerfully evoked by participants with the theme of impostorship (Brookfield, 2006), praxis shock (Kelchtermans, 2002), or mimicry (Land et al., 2010) leading ultimately to a reconstitution of the self as teacher:

ST1: I spent the entire first week in constant shock …Learnt to deal with it quickly because if you don't you are left like a lamb to slaughter

ST1: I kinda turned the corner with it [teaching] just in the last couple of months. I feel really confident now and looking back to the very first class that I had, I kinda felt like I was winging it, just going in there pretending I was a teacher and now actually I feel like I am a teacher

ST2: I am finding it hard to remember I am just a student teacher and that I am not expected to set the world alight!

Threshold concepts for language teacher education. In terms of the specific concepts which were identified in phase one, the student teachers maintain a focus on target language use specifically which reflects a strong emphasis in the ITE programme. They discuss it in operational terms, how to achieve maximal use and how this is progressing, rather than as an article of faith.

ST3: By and large all year groups have retained most of our interaction phrases, especially those we were able to enact such as putting their hands up, opening copies and turning on the lights. The repetition of the phrases week-on-week is also helping to re-inforce the work we did on the phrases. I've also done quick spot checks where I ask someone to enact an instruction to see if it is indeed being retained.

However, similar to the in-career teachers, it is the realisation of the effectiveness and feasibility of this strategy in their experience which embeds this in practice:

Interviewer: You mentioned in the beginning that one of the key challenges was use of the target language. In the second email or something like that. Is it still…

ST3:   No. Not at all.

Interviewer: It's gone now?

T3:   I am much more comfortable. I don't even think it was myself or my ability to use the French. It was their [the students] ability to accept that's what it was going to be like.

The broader aspects of creating opportunities for meaningful interaction with and in the language which the in-career teacher noted are not addressed. Using the TL in the classroom constitutes a routine that must be mastered in order to free up the teacher's attention for other matters, consistent with current theories of skill acquisition, from novices where skill execution requires full attention to experts where skill execution, is procedural or automated (Beilock et al., 2002). The participant data reflects this incremental progress towards mastery of a routine which still requires their conscious attention to maintain.

The notion of learner autonomy is not explicitly addressed but the shift in orientation to a more student-centred perspective is in evidence in the data. The participants note on different occasions specific efforts to adapt their teaching to the specific needs of individuals in their classes.

Unlike previous studies which mentioned that pre-service teachers often encountered classroom management and discipline issues in their ITE programs in Ireland (Clarke et al., 2012, p. 148), the three respondents did not mention any major disciplinary issues that arose throughout their teaching year, except that some students were chatty and this only in the context of how she constrained her routines in order to overcome the issue:

ST2:   Ya more creative. Ya I kinda felt like the beginning of the year I tried more things with them and I had a lot of discipline issues with them to begin with so I had to pare back and tried to be a little more in control of the class. And then tried to limit the group activities that I did until I got them behaving in an acceptable way.

Contexts and catalysts for change.   In terms of the contexts or catalysts for change, professional dialogue emerged as a key driver, as in phase 1. In this case though it is the university placement tutors as well as peers who provide impetus for change. The visits of the tutors constituted turning points for students by drawing their attention to aspects of their practice:

ST1:   That was because [TUTOR] told me twice …

Interviewer: You didn't see it yourself for example?

ST1:   No

Int: Then you saw it or you agreed or disagreed?

ST1:   No, she told me and I thought about it a lot. She told me in the first inspection she came to … I'm really aware of it which is good so all the time in the back of my mind.

Daloz's notion of mentors as both "gatekeepers" and "guides" (2012, p. 96) is articulated clearly in one participant's response to their first tutor visit:

ST2:   I was so nervous beforehand but am looking forward to the next one now so I can keep on improving.

Interaction with peers is also noted as a catalyst for development. These interactions take place on the course as both unstructured informal encounters and structured collaborative on-line reflections, although this distinction is not drawn by participants.

As might be expected, all discussion of professional development on the course is framed in terms of practice. The structure of the programme with pre-service teachers split between school and university every week fosters the contextualisation and implementation of professional learning in practice, not always successfully however from the participants' perspective:

ST1: College has been a struggle just because of time management and trying to balance school, home and college has been hard. And then like I said to you before I found lots of the course impractical and I find it quite frustrating having to sit through a lecture and I'm going I could be doing my laundry, picking up the kids from school or whatever.

DISCUSSION AND CONCLUSIONS

The findings of the two studies represent two very different points on the trajectory of adaptive experts but they share much in common. The pre-service teachers have not yet achieved the status of routine experts and are still automatizing language teacher routines such as target language use. Although it is too early to posit whether the pre-service teachers will become adaptive experts, they do exhibit an openness to learning and adaptation. This is structured to a certain extent by the constraints of the teacher education programme that scaffolds for progression. Within this, the role of the placement tutor is key as a driver of change. The in-career teachers interviewed also expressed a similar openness to change. At the time of interview, there was a major curriculum change on the horizon for lower post-primary schools and the teachers were excited by the opportunities this would afford them. They had almost uniformly expressed the exam system as a major constraint on ability to teach in accordance with their beliefs about good teaching, in particular in relation to use of the target language. The curriculum change should deliver much greater flexibility in content and assessment choices for teachers. In terms of Woods and

Cakir's (2011) cognition dimensions, the curriculum change offered the possibility of better alignment of knowledge, belief and practice.

Both groups of participants point to the value of professional dialogue in the learning process. As in Hammerness et al. (2007), a community of practice offers support for teachers tackling new problems and interpreting experiences that may lead to change. In the case of the pre-service teachers, the role of the more knowledgeable other in the form of the placement tutor is vital in directing the teacher's focus to aspects of experience that need consideration. Given the role tutors play in assessment, it is not surprising then that previous studies have noted that some pre-service teachers adapt strategically by complying with their placement tutor's personal perspectives (Vonk, 1993, cited in Clarke et al., 2012). In this context, Daloz's dual characterisation of tutors is particularly telling:

> It is characteristic of the journey metaphor that mentors may be seen as gatekeepers as well as guides. They stand at the boundary of the old and new worlds, and as such they hold the keys for successful passage. (Daloz, 2012, p. 96)

They also value opportunities for discussions with peers to develop practice in structured or unstructured settings. In the case of the in-career teachers, this dimension has immense value and is seen as a valuable resource for maintaining focus and energy over the career. Some of the teachers have used both traditional (e.g. subject teacher associations) and non-traditional (e.g. social media) to engage with colleagues, particularly where the immediate community is not conducive to new learning. In this sense, adaptivity is as much a product of a community as of the individual, following on from Hammerness et al.'s (2007) discussion of learning communities.

In this pursuit of the threshold concepts for language teacher education, it would seem that student-centred teaching is a concept which continues to develop in varied and sometimes subject-specific ways over a teaching career. The findings here suggest that a threshold concept, such as maximal target language use, may not be irreversible in the context of constraints on practice imposed by external factors such as in this case subject curricula and assessment methods. Finally, if adaptivity is the essential characteristic of an expert teacher, perhaps the only really essential concepts for teaching are how to identify and implement necessary change, as with these tools and within a strong community of practice the other concepts will fall into place.

NOTE

[1] This phase was part of a study funded by SCOTENS (the Standing Conference on Teacher Education North and South) on threshold concepts in language teacher education in Ireland, North and South, as reported in Devitt and McKendry (2014). This chapter focuses on the Republic of Ireland data within this study.

REFERENCES

Atherton, J., Hadfield, P., & Meyers, R. (2012). *Troublesome thresholds and limiting liminality: Issues in teaching in vocational education.* 4th Bienniel Conference on Threshold Concepts: From personal practice to communities of practice, Trinity College, Dublin.

Barradell, S., & Peseta, T. (2014). Promise and challenge of identifying threshold concepts: A cautionary account of using transactional curriculum inquiry. *Journal of Further and Higher Education,* 1–14.

Beilock, S. L., Wierenga, S. A., & Carr, T. H. (2002). Expertise, attention, and memory in sensorimotor skill execution: Impact of novel task constraints on dual-task performance and episodic memory. *The Quarterly Journal of Experimental Psychology Section A, 55*(4), 1211–1240.

Borg, S. (2006). *Teacher cognition and language education: Research and practice.* Norfork, AR: Continuum.

Borg, S. (2011). The impact of in-service teacher education on language teachers' beliefs. *System, 39*(3), 370–380.

Brookfield, S. (2006). *The skillful teacher: On technique, trust, and responsiveness in the classroom.* San Francisco, CA: Jossey-Bass.

Clarke, M., Lodge, A., & Shevlin, M. (2012). Evaluating initial teacher education programmes: Perspectives from the Republic of Ireland. *Teaching And Teacher Education, 28,* 141–153.

Cove, M., McAdam, J., & McGonigal, J. (2008). Mentoring, teaching and professional transformation. In R. Land, J. Meyer, & J. Smith (Eds.), *Threshold concepts within the disciplines* (pp. 197–211). Rotterdam, The Netherlands: Sense Publishing.

Daloz, L. A. (1999). *Mentor: Guiding the journey of adult learners.* San Francisco, CA: Jossey Bass.

Devitt, A., Kerin, M., & O'Sullivan, H. (2014). Threshold concepts and practices in teacher education: Professional, educator and student perspectives. In C. O'Mahony, A. Buchanan, M. O'Rourke, & B. Higgs (Eds.), *Threshold concepts: From personal practice to communities of practice* (pp. 129–133). Cork. NAIRTL.

Devitt, A., & McKendry, E. (2014, April 3–7). *Threshold concepts in language teacher knowledge: Practice versus policy.* Annual meeting of the American Educational Research Association, Philadephia, PA.

Fuller, F. F. (1969). Concerns of teachers: A developmental conceptualization. *American Educational Research Journal, 6*(2), 207–226.

Guest, G., Bunce, A., & Johnson, L. (2006). How many interviews are enough?: An experiment with data saturation and variability. *Field Methods, 18,* 59–82.

Hammerness, K., et al., (2007). How teachers learn and develop. In L. Darling-Hammond & J. Bransford (Ed.), *Preparing teachers for a changing world: What teachers should learn and be able to do.* San Francisco, CA: Wiley and Sons.

Heifetz, R., Grashow, A., & Linsky, M. (2009). *The practice of adaptive leadership: Tools and tactics for changing your organization and the world.* Boston, MA: Harvard Business Press.

Kelchtermans, G., & Ballet, K. (2002). The micropolitics of teacher induction. A narrative-biographical study on teacher socialisation. *Teaching and Teacher Education, 18,* 105–120.

Land, R. (2012). *Keynote: A closer look at liminality: Incorrigibles and threshold capital.* 4th Biennial Conference on Threshold Concepts, Dublin, Ireland.

Land, R., Meyer, J. H. F., & Baillie, C. (2010). *Threshold concepts and transformational learning.* Rotterdam The Netherlands: Sense Publishers.

Land, R., Meyer, J. H. F., & Baillie, C. (2010). Editors' Preface: Threshold concepts and transformational learning. In R. Land, J. H. F. Meyer, & C. Baillie (Eds.), *Threshold concepts and transformational learning* (pp. ix–xlii). Rotterdam, The Netherlands: Sense Publishers.

Little, D. (1991). *Learner autonomy 1: Definitions, issues and problems.* Dublin: Authentik.

Long, M. H., & Doughty, C. J. (Eds.). (2009). *The handbook of language teaching.* Chichester, UK: Wiley-Blackwell.

Meyer, J. H. F., & Land, R. (2003). Threshold concepts and troublesome knowledge: Linkages to ways of thinking and practising. In C. Rust (Ed.), *Improving student learning – Theory and practice ten years on* (pp. 412–424). Oxford: Oxford Centre for Staff and Learning Development (OCSLD).

Mezirow, J., & Taylor, E. (Eds.). (2009). *Transformative learning in practice*. San Francisco, CA: Jossey-Bass.

Phipps, S., & Borg, S. (2009). Exploring tensions between teachers' grammar teaching beliefs and practices. *System, 37*, 380–390.

Schön, D. (1983). *The reflective practitioner, how professionals think in action*. New York, NY: Basic Books.

Wenger, E. (1998). *Communities of practice: Learning, meaning, and identity*. Cambridge: Cambridge University Press.

Woods, D., & Çakir, H. (2011). Two dimensions of teacher knowledge: The case of communicative language teaching. *System, 39*, 381–390.

David Moroney
School of Education
Trinity College Dublin

Eugene McKendry
School of Education
Queen's University Belfast

Ann Devitt
School of Education
Trinity College Dublin

LEIF M. HOKSTAD, GRO RØDNE, BJØRN OTTO BRAATEN,
STEFFEN WELLINGER AND FREDRIK SHETELIG

24. TRANSFORMATIVE LEARNING IN ARCHITECTURAL EDUCATION

Re-thinking Architecture and the Education of Architecture

INTRODUCTION

In this chapter, we will present TRANSark, an ongoing project on the development of architecture and the education on architecture at NTNU, the Norwegian University of Science and Technology. We will present a two-fold challenge to the profession and its education. On the one hand, the trade itself is challenged by changes in economic realities, changed demands and needs from the public, users and authorities. On the other hand, the schools of architecture report difficulties in developing and maintaining meaningful learning trajectories where the learners manage the transition from pupil to student, from novice to "expert". Putting more emphasis on what the learner experience actually is, the student voices, seems to be a necessity. To frame these challenges, the project draws upon the threshold concept framework as the main pedagogical perspective to develop a teaching and learning environment that may provide a transformational learning experience, not only for the students, but for their teachers as well. To gather and analyze student perspectives to inform the design of new learning trajectories, the 'decoding the discipline' approach is applied. The chapter also presents four focus areas, organized in work packages that this development project on architecture education will undertake. Finally we will argue in favor of developing a perspective on the education of architects that calls for developing the dual professional; a professional equally at home in the professions of architecture and teaching and learning.

CHALLENGES TO THE ARCHITECTURE PROFESSION AND ITS EDUCATION – THE BIG RETHINK

Many modern challenges, in engineering, medicine and environmental issues to name but a few, are increasingly of an interdisciplinary character. This implies that the solutions to these highly complex and sometimes ill-defined modern challenges need to be found by crossing discipline borders and defining new and emergent ontologies and epistemologies. These emerging knowledge domains are characterized by either *bridge building* (exchange between complete and firm disciplines) or *reconstruction*

R. Land et al. (Eds.), Threshold Concepts in Practice, 321–333.

(detaching parts of several disciplines to form a new and coherent whole) (Gasper, 2004; Klein, 2010).

Architecture is a highly interdisciplinary field, where understanding and practice occurs in the highly complex intersection of aesthetical, ethical, technical, economical, functional challenge. Architecture is a knowledge domain where aesthetic, tactile experience is crucial, and creative practice is a way of thinking and a way of understanding.

Several sources within the field of architecture describe the challenges and constraints of the profession and consequently to the education of architects. To this particular context, suffice it that we primarily refer to the seminal essay series in The Architectural Review, collectively called 'the Big Rethink' by Peter Buchanan, where many of the challenges to the field of architecture have been explicitly discussed (Buchanan, 2012). Among these, Buchanan points to issues spanning from "the proliferation of ever more materials and modes of manufacture, assembly and construction management" to the need to "collaborate with a widening array of consultants in multidisciplinary design teams in which even the architect component is made up of individuals of differing expertise" (Buchanan, 2012). The context of the education and of practice takes place within the confines of economic and ecological challenges. The field of architecture is in some instances increasingly interdisciplinary, in the sense that the profession may be seen as a hub, where several disciplines need to interact. In addition, the field of architecture is in other instances increasingly transdisciplinary, where the need to transcend disciplinary boundaries is urgent. Consequently, among the challenges is to prepare the students for multiple possible frameworks and competing values, ill-defined problems and open-ended situations, an educational challenge described in the perspective of complexity (Qvortrup, 1998; Barnett, 2000; Luhmann, 2000; Rasmussen, 2004; Mason, 2008). The field of architecture and the education of architects is thus faced with what Klafki has termed "key issues of the times", that need a re-description of the following categories: intention, subject matter/content, media, methods, student background and context (Klafki, 1998; Heimann, 1976).

Such challenges will indeed call for learning trajectories that are transformational, and requires learning experiences that shape the learner and produce significant impact, a paradigm shift, which affects the learner's later learning experiences (Mezirow, 2000; Clark, 1993).

STUDENT VOICES

As stated above, the second strand of this project is the need and wish to incorporate more clearly the student voices. Over the years, the Department of Architecture and Fine Arts have gathered evaluation materials from the students. In line with the threshold concept framework, the perspectives of the learner provides an important basis to TRANSark, in that the world of the learner is brought more into focus of the learning trajectory. That which is troublesome to a learner is sometimes difficult to see for teachers and course designers, since they already have passed through the portal. Its additional value, to the teachers, is that student voices provide an opportunity to refocus attention and recall how we 'got there' ourselves, how we "got it" when we learnt these things. In turn, this leads the attention to aspects of tacit knowledge in a discipline and amongst professionals and practitioners in that discipline. As a methodological approach, this is in line with the "decoding the disciplines" methodology applied in several threshold concept research and development projects in several disciplines (Millendorf & Pace, 2004; Shopkow, 2010).

These data sets are now being analyzed, and will provide the basis for a more thorough methodology based on the principles of 'decoding the disciplines' (Shopkow, 2010). This material is rich and suggestive, and gives abundant insight into the world of the learner. Based on the existing material, a preliminary list of potential threshold concepts has been established in the TRANSark project.

An introductory comment to the context of the architect students may also be necessary. These students are among the best-qualified applicants to our university, and architecture (along with medicine and nano-technology) has the highest entry score at our university. These students are highly qualified and have a previous school experience in which success and being among the best is their main point of reference. Equally important is that their previous experiences in the educational system is largely rooted in a monodisciplinary ontological and epistemological framework. Obviously, they expect university studies to give the same experience. The samples from the data material, however, gives an insight into the constraints and affordances of their transition away from a monodisciplinary perspective.

First, a few samples of the findings that may well introduce us to the 'world of the learner'.

In a looking-back exercise in the 6th semester of study, the following sample is symptomatic and representative for how learners perceived their situation in the first year:

Sample 1

> In the beginning we were thrown into something completely new and unknown that has been difficult to deal with. The feeling of not being clever enough, and not having control of what you are doing, have resulted in a lot of frustration and stress, and this has influenced the process to the extent that I have become exhausted and depressed, and I wanted to quit.

In this sample the issues of uncertainty and lack of confidence to challenge is articulated. The experience of being in a liminal space is clear. The extract also suggests the pain experienced by this learner, as well as an escape urge.

Sample 2

> Eventually it became clear that the project was about examining the edge/ridge, the exciting state of mind where meaningful and many faceted places may emerge. ... The architecture here on the edge/ridge is rich on senses, a delicate point of balance. It *is* senses.

The sample here refers to a student project where the building site was in a slope, so the edge/ridge reference is simultaneously direct and concrete as well as metaphorical, and, willingly and consciously or not, sheds interesting light on the learner experience. This sample condenses a threshold experience; we see the learner in the midst of a liminal zone, and who is in the process of coming to grips with central aspects of architecture. The experience is truly transformational; in the sense that a previous understanding is left and a new one emerges: architecture is about senses, about perception. Indeed, an ontological shift is taking place. The student in question also shows that s/he is finding meaning in the liminal state, and that it is not altogether a negative experience.

Sample 3

> I have experienced that it is better to take one idea and explore that one, rather than spending weeks on developing several. When you got something concrete to work with, it is easier to explore it and to work towards a result.

Sample 4

> The process is slowing down. I will take the time to embrace this. ... Want to gather the material I have, to see what it is. Slowly. This semester I will not run over myself, and be embarrassedly left behind. Then I must quit.

In these samples, also reflective comments in 6th semester, the students reveals a more mature understanding of their own learning trajectory. Here, they accept that 'time on task' and staying in the liminal zone is not only necessary, but also fruitful.

Sample 5

> "Will it be architecture, eventually? I don't know."

The aspect of uncertainty and doubt as to being cut for becoming an architect is expressed here.

Sample 6

> In the course of this process I noticed that I worry all the time about the work that is ahead. It is easy to forget to be present in the work to be done here and

324

now. I worry about what is to come, and I worry that I will not succeed, that it won't turn out the way I wanted, that I do not get far enough in the process. … but, I noticed a greater calmness once I did something physical, and could see a result of this by the end of the day.

Sample 7

"With regards to how I (work) I think it is more difficult to put into words and identify how I work now."

This sample points to the fact the learner is on his or her way out of the liminal zone and is seemingly becoming oblivious to what it was like to be there. This also coincides with a phenomenon described in several contexts by the involved teachers regarding a teacher's ability to remember what it was like to be there, and the struggles and tribulations this implied. The sample exemplifies the necessity for the teacher to be able to make that move back in one's own learning trajectory.

In sum, the student voices examples from this sample material give an important insight into what it like to be a student of architecture, their challenges, their fears and their expectations.

CANDIDATE THRESHOLD CONCEPTS

Cousin suggests that the threshold concept framework is neither teacher-centred nor student-centred, and resists this traditional binary (Cousin, 2010). Rather, the framework encourages a partnership between educationalists, students and discipline specialists, with an emphasis of developing a dialogue between the three. More so than traditional educational research, this framework is focused on the study *with* rather than a study *on* learners and teachers (Cousin, 2010). To follow this approach in a TRANSark setting, the candidate threshold concepts are developed through a triangulation of data collected from students (questionnaires, observations of student work, interviews with students, analysis of artefacts (drawings, constructions, built objects), interviews with teachers, and collaboration for analysis of data with an educational researcher external to the Faculty of Architecture and Fine Arts.

Based on the material the samples above extracted from an existing data collection give a preliminary picture of what potential or candidate threshold concepts that will be pursued in the TRANSark project period. We propose the following as the candidate threshold concepts:

TC1: Liminality

The data gathered and analyzed so far in this project suggests that *liminality* is an overarching threshold concept, which is expressed in a number of related and partly nested sub-categories that points to liminality.

'Liminality' refers to the state the learner finds himself or herself in, before passing over or coming through. Within the threshold concepts framework liminality has attracted attention, because liminality describes the most difficult part of the learning trajectory. At the same time, the liminal stage also represents also an opportunity for transformation and change. The term stems from anthropology and is first introduced by Van Gennep in his highly influential *Les Rites de passage* (van Gennep, 1909). Here, van Gennep introduces the notion of a three part structure for a rite of passage: *separation, liminal period*, and *reassimilation*. The ideas of liminality were adopted and made known through several studies by Victor Turner in his studies of, amongst others, the 1960s counter cultures (i.e. Turner, 1969). To Turner, persons in a liminal state are neither here nor there; they are "betwixt and between the positions assigned and arrayed by law, custom, convention, and ceremony" (Turner, 1969). The liminal state is one of unrest, disorder, but also of affordances and dynamism. This process may also be seen in terms of an initiation process, where the learner is passing from a stage of innocence to a stage of insight and belonging in a group sharing the same kind of insight. Liminality thus represents a middle position in the transition from being an outsider to becoming an insider, and contains both an individual as well as a social aspect. For both van Gennep and Turner the notion of liminality is part of a wider theory of socialization.

The state of liminality may be experienced by the student or learner as being *stuck*, a feeling associated with failure, defeat and loss of self-confidence (Kiley & Wisker, 2009). The transition through the liminal state may not be seen as sequential or as a linear process. On the contrary, it is clear that the process is characterized by oscillation, of false victories and defeat, of "messy journeys back, forth and across conceptual terrain" (Cousin, 2006). It follows from this that the processes are time consuming, iterative and recursive, and for most learners certainly painful. Recalling Buchanan's description of the challenges in architecture, the wide span of areas in the truly interdisciplinary field of architecture opens itself readily to liminal experiences for the learners. In the material collated and analyzed so far, there is a suggestion that the liminal stage is characterized by the students' lack of ability to oscillate between different perspectives, or insights from different disciplines that can be gathered in an overarching understanding. A sub-theme we perceive here is the lacking ability to zoom in and out of a problem, from detail to the big picture.

TC2: Living With and Thriving From Uncertainty

Most of the literature consulted that describes the liminal zone in the threshold concept framework, suggests that the liminal zone is a place learners want to leave and be done with it. However, there are suggestions in this material that a learner who is maturing in his or her learning approach becomes more relaxed about the liminal zone and actually finds the tension stimulating and a necessary part of the learning trajectory. This we may see in samples 3, 4 and 6. In these samples, we see an emergent ontological shift in the way the learner perceives himself or herself and his own learning trajectory. We here perceive an extended view of the liminal zone as a complex, suggestive and many faceted. This ambiguous perspective of the liminal zone is certainly a topic of future research.

The notion of *dealing with defeat* is related to the threshold of living with uncertainty. The teachers at this architecture school report extensively and independently of each other how many of these students strive to understand and accept that failure is a necessary and fundamental part of their learning trajectory. The present samples also contain this concern. We suggest that this aspect is related to factors of the students learning trajectory. On the one hand, this reflects the learner's understanding of himself or herself, as being successful and clever. On the other, this reflects an understanding of a learning trajectory as being linear and continually moving forward, again based on previous experiences from primary and secondary school.

TC3: Confidence to Challenge

In this material, we find clear indications that the *'confidence to challenge'*, first suggested as a threshold concept in the work by Jane Osmond (Osmond, 2014), represents a threshold concept to these learners. Given that most of these students are highly gifted with the highest entry grades at our university, they have expectation of success, progress and mastering the assignments given. However, since assignments throughout the courses are increasingly open-ended and devoid of a predefined "correct" learning outcome, these learners find it much harder to solve the assignments satisfactory, both for themselves and for their teachers. Their previous experience in the educational system has taught these students certain recipes, for how to deal with assignments that now are of no use to them anymore. They are thus in need of unlearning these approaches, and the replacements are yet unclear. We suggest that this implies an ontological challenge not yet mastered by these learners.

The lack of confidence to challenge on the behalf of the students is frequently expressed in criticism towards the teachers and their assignments as being "unclear", and "without a precise enough recipe" as to the assignments given, and consequently to "what architecture is about". Sample 8 below from a teacher evaluation report reflects this kind of criticism. Perhaps more interesting is the fact the reflections such as this one points to the mismatch between what the students expect of their teachers and what the teachers expect of the students. In the threshold concept literature, it is often commented that teachers may well have forgotten how they "got it" and "got there". Sample 8 points to "the no-mans-land" of mismatched expectations:

Sample 8

Concerning the "lack of architecture" and the expectations of a "clearer purpose", this is something that we need to look more carefully into. Clearly, there is a mismatch between the staffs' expectations and of where the students are, and the students' own expectations of the course. It is a difficult task to make use of/translate what one has learned (up until now in the study) into new situations. We, as tutors, were unprepared for the possibility that architect students would stop thinking as architects when given other/unusual assignments.

In sum, we may argue that grasping the underlying game, the episteme the second overarching threshold concept in the present material. To the students, the underlying game is not clearly in sight and does not have a clear content or structure. To the teachers, the underlying game is partly implicit and part of their tacit knowledge. Allwright's sigh as to 'why learners don't learn what teachers teach' comes to mind here (Allwright, 1984). This also implies that in a redesign the teachers will have to look back into their own learning trajectories to recall how they "got it" at the time.

The highly interdisciplinary nature of the profession and its education suggests that the learners find it challenging to integrate into one unified understanding and develop the ability to oscillate effortlessly between the "big picture" and details. Connected to grasping the episteme, the underlying game of architecture, and is connected to the transformation of 'thinking like an architect'.

DESIGNING FOR TRANSFORMATIONAL TEACHING AND LEARNING ENVIRONMENTS

The present project of rethinking architecture acknowledges that the challenges are two-fold; the changes in the profession itself, and thereby its education, and the need to develop a learning trajectory that takes into account the realities of the learners. The TRANSark project seeks to meet the two-fold challenges by organizing the research into four work packages that represent overarching perspectives.

WORK PACKAGE OVERVIEW

The research and development activities will be organized in work packages, and the collective effect of the work packages is to enable a research based redesign of courses given at the faculty. The following courses are targeted for this project: Architecture 1 and the Master course Making is Thinking, the "Live Studio" projects and Master course in architectural design (deep structures in architecture "dealing with complexity"). The work packages are chosen because they are already in a process of development at NTNU and are having a mutual impact on each other. The figure below illustrates the relationship between the different work packages. WP 1 emphasizes an individual aspect of the learners trajectory, intends to address two important aspects of becoming an architect: to enable students to integrate the cognitive and the performative aspects of the profession, as well as giving an understanding of scale as early as possible in their education. WP 2 addresses aspects of the "architect in the world". WP 3 addresses issues of complexity, stemming from the interdisciplinary nature of the profession. WP 4 will apply the overarching perspective of the threshold concepts framework, and based on data collected in the three work packages provide a feedback for development of the three work packages.

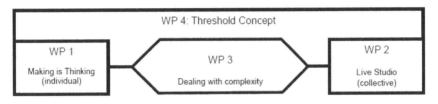

Figure 1. Overview of workpackages

WP 1: Making is Thinking

Acknowledging that architecture belongs to the "making disciplines" and the connection between mind and body, we emphasize to give the students an embodied experience by working in full scale from the very beginning of the study. Full-scale building projects continue in several assignments throughout the curriculum. This has been the result of an intentional priority area especially on wood as a building material for the last 10–12 years. By working in scale 1:1, they will gain a knowledge that not only covers professional and academic skills, but also remains as tacit knowledge (Polyani, 1966). It is also building their self-confidence to later implement projects on their own. Full-scale building projects continue in several assignments throughout the curriculum and our students carry out high quality full scale building projects on their own, throughout the world. In rethinking the contents of WP1 it will be an aim to make use of the experiences from WP2, WP3 and especially the research in WP4, in the further development of didactic tools. This way of learning by doing could have impact on other assignments and courses at our Faculty and possibly be useful also within other disciplines.

WP 2: Live Studios

Live Studios, a PBL based "in situ" methodology, are conducted to challenge the students; to bring them out of the "academy" and into real-world situations that enable them to gain insights, skills and understandings that cannot be academically "taught". By "being in the situation" where solutions are sought both physically and socially, they not only learn much more efficiently by having to engage all their senses, but they acquire a much wider understanding of what architecture is and what it does. Being outside the academy the problems students confront are embedded in real-world constraints, social and material, that trigger ingenuity, innovation and creativity all according to the principles of problem-based-learning. The experience we have gained so far shows that the students acquire a capacity to improvise, to communicate effectively, and to respond architecturally within a responsible social setting. The Live Studio approach is grounded in the recognition that architecture is a deeply practice based and social endeavor aside from being rooted in the arts and in technology. Hence, it is rooted in the writings of Freire and Lakoff & Johnson as well as on the doings of Rural Studio of Auburn University and the Mass Design Group (Freire, 1987; Lakoff & Johnson, 1980).

WP 3: Dealing with Complexity and Change

One of the characteristics of the field of architecture is to deal with complexity. Not only technology becomes more and more complex, but the overall context of the design – and building processes are developing into still higher levels of complexity. Even more challenging is this situation, because it is also continually changing. To deal with high levels of complexity and change calls for new ways of thinking, both about the role of the architect and the role of architectural education. This work-package will focus on developing pedagogical tools for dealing with high levels of complexity and change. The Integral Approach, as it is formulated by Ken Wilber, provides a map and a method (Integral Methodological Pluralism) that can be used as a tool of orientation in complex matters. As an interdisciplinary field, the architectural perspective in itself is a kind of integral approach. In a time where specialization and fragmentation is a main trend, it is crucial to develop understanding of the relationship between the details of things and the whole picture.

The other aspect of dealing with complexity and change is to be grounded in basic knowledge and experience of the field. For an architect to deal with high levels of complexity and change, it is crucial to master the simple fundamentals that make architecture into something more than mere production of buildings and physical manifestations of system logic. Architecture deals with the meaning-aspect of our built environment. This starts with the embodied experience of space, the tactile and physical quality of materials, constructions, light and space. The physical, emotional, structural and artistic aspects are the fundamentals for making meaningful buildings. This work-package will focus on developing methods that corresponds to these fundamental aspects of architecture.

WP 4: Threshold Concepts

Although the threshold concepts framework in the last few years has been introduced into a large number of pedagogical settings and research initiatives in higher education (Flanagan, 2015), little research has been conducted as of yet in the field of architecture.

The TRANSark project will frame the challenges described previously in the redesign of courses with a particular focus on the threshold concepts framework, and will focus on how the identified threshold concepts is expressed and experienced. A redesign of courses and content will focus on how patterns and integration may be made accessible for the students, and how to make "the underlying game" accessible for the learners (Perkins, 2006). The preliminary work has been referred to in the section of student voices.

The focus is, from the point of view of designing a learning trajectory, on the world of the learner, and the effort to grasp what the world looks like to a learner who is entering into a new ontological and epistemological terrain. They represent deep aspects of a discipline and are frequently associated with tacit knowledge. Students from Bachelor to Master level, and their teachers, will be the target of research. A methodology based on seminal work in the field (Meyer & Land, 2006; M. Flanagan, 2015; Davies & Mangan, 2010; Shopkow, 2010), will be appropriated to the context of architecture. The activities taking place in WP 1, WP 2 and WP 3 will provide the basis of study.

In this project, the data will be collected from the students and teachers taking part in the work packages described above. The threshold concepts work package, then, intends to provide an overarching perspective on the education of architects, and findings will be used to provide a loop back to the development of the courses.

DEVELOPING THE DUAL PROFESSIONAL

The challenges presented above, from the profession and its education as well as the challenges experienced by the learners, call for a rethinking of how we perceive the role of the teacher, and the components of his or her competence. Teachers of architecture has a variety of entry routes into HE teaching, and may thus have a dual identity, one as part of a profession of architects, but also an identity as teachers of that profession. The teacher identity need to be developed more fully. To meet the dual nature of the challenges described above, the project intends to investigate into the notion of a 'dual professional'. This implies a professional skilled in the profession of architecture, as well as in the profession of teaching in higher education. By focusing on the aspects of liminality, the learner's main experience, and the underlying game, that which the teacher already has arrived at, the threshold concept framework opens for developing a methodology that is targeted at the 'no-mans-land of mismatched expectations'. The notion of a dual professional also aligns with the emerging focus on professionalism in higher education. From an emphasis on teacher qualification programs, the focus on professionalism of higher education has developed into an emerging research discipline, the 'scholarship of teaching and learning' (Hutchings, Huber, & Ciccone, 2011). In this project, we will draw upon the threshold concepts framework as one possible lens to arrive at a clearer understanding of the components of a dual professional, and acknowledging that transformational learning also implies transformations for the teachers as well as for the learners.

REFERENCES

Allwright, D. (1984). Why don't learners learn what teachers teach? The interaction hypothesis. In D. M. Singleton & D. G. Little (Eds.), *Language learning in formal and informal contexts*. Dublin: IRAAL.

Buchanan, P. (2011–2012). *The big rethink*. 12 Essays. Retrieved from
  http://www.architecturalreview.com/home/the-big-rethink
Cousin, G. (2006, December). An introduction to threshold concepts. *Planet* [online], *17*, 4–5. Retrieved
  from http://www.gees.ac.uk/planet/p17/gc.pdf
Cousin, G. (2010, February). Neither teacher-centred nor student-centred: Threshold concepts and
  research partnerships. *Journal of Learning Development in Higher Education*, Issue 2.
Davies, P., & Mangan, J. (2007). Threshold concepts and the integration of understanding in economics.
  Studies in Higher Education, *32*, 711–726.
Flanagan, M. T. (2015). *Threshold concepts: Undergraduate teaching, postgraduate training and
  professional development. A short and bibliography*. Retrieved from http://www.ee.ucl.ac.uk/
  ~mflanaga/thresholds.html
Freire, P., & Macedo, D. (1987). *Literacy: Reading the word & the world*. London: Routledge and Kegan
  Paul Ltd.
Gasper, D. (2004). Interdisciplinarity. Building bridges and nurturing a complex ecology of ideas. In
  A. K. Giri (Ed.), *Creative social research* (pp. 308–344). Delhi: Sage Publications, and Lanham, MD:
  Lexington Books.
Heimann, P. (1976). *Didaktik als Unterrichtswissenschaft*. Stuttgart: Ernst Klett Vorlag.
Hutchings, P., Huber, M., & Ciccone, A. (2011). *The scholarship of teaching and learning. Institutional
  integration and impact*. San Francisco, CA: Jossey-Bass
Kiley, M., & Wisker, G. (2009). Threshold concepts in research education and evidence of threshold
  crossing. *Higher Education Research and Development*, *28*(4), 431–441.
Klafki, W. (1998) Characteristics of critical-constructive Didaktik. In B. B. Gundem & S. Hopmann
  (Eds.), *Didaktik and/or curriculum. An international dialogue* (pp. 307–330). New York, NY: Peter
  Lang.
Klein, J. T. (2010). *Creating interdisciplinary campus cultures. A model for strength and sustainability*.
  San Francisco, CA: Jossey-Bass.
Lakoff, G., & Johnson, M. (1999). *Philosophy in the flesh*. New York, NY: Basic Books.
Mason, M. (Ed.). (2008). *Complexity theory and the philosophy of education*. Malden, MA: Blackwell
  Publishing.
Meyer, J. H. F., & Land, R. (2006). Threshold concepts and troublesome knowledge: An introduction. In
  J. H. F. Meyer & R. Land (Eds.), *Overcoming barriers to student understanding: Threshold concepts
  and troublesome knowledge* (pp. 3–18). London: Routledge Falmer.
Middendorf, J., & Pace, D. (2004). Decoding the disciplines: A model for helping students learn
  disciplinary ways of thinking. In D. Pace & J. Middendorf (Eds.), *Decoding the disciplines: Helping
  students learn disciplinary ways of thinking: New directions for teaching and learning, No. 98*
  (pp. 1–12). San Francisco, CA: Jossey-Bass.
Mezirow, J. (2000). *Learning as transformation: Critical perspectives on a theory in progress*.
  San Francisco, CA: Jossey-Bass.
Pallasmaa, J. (2009). *The thinking hand*. Southern Gate: Wiley.
Perkins, D. (2006). Constructivism and troublesome knowledge. In J. H. F. Meyer & R. Land (Eds.),
  Overcoming barriers to student understanding: Threshold concepts and troublesome knowledge.
  Abingdon: Routledge.
Polyani, M. (1966). *The tacit dimension*. Gloucester, MA: Peter Smith.
Qvortrup, L. (1998). *Det hyperkomplekse samfund. 14 fortællinger om fremtiden*. København: Gyldendal.
Rasmussen, J. (2004). *Undervisning i det refleksivt moderne*. København: Hans Reitzels.
Shopkow, L. (2010). What decoding the disciplines can offer threshold concepts. In J. H. F. Meyer,
  R. Land, & C. Baillie, (Eds.), *Threshold concepts and transformational learning*. Rotterdam, The
  Netherlands: Sense Publishers
Turner, V. (1990). Are there universals of performance in myth, ritual, and drama? In R. Schechner &
  W. Appel (Eds.), *By means of performance* (pp. 1–18). Cambridge: Cambridge University Press.
van Gennep, A. (1909/2004). *The rites of passage*. New York, NY: Routledge.
Wilber, K. (2007). *Integral vision* (pp. 347–363). Boston, MA: Shambahala Publications Inc.

Leif M. Hokstad
Unit for Educational Development
Norwegian University of Science and Technology

Gro Rødne
Faculty of Architecture and Fine Art
Norwegian University of Science and Technology

Bjørn Otto Braaten
Faculty of Architecture and Fine Art
Norwegian University of Science and Technology

Steffen Wellinger
Faculty of Architecture and Fine Art
Norwegian University of Science and Technology

Fredrik Shetelig
Faculty of Architecture and Fine Art
Norwegian University of Science and Technology

ABOUT THE CONTRIBUTORS

Lorraine Anderson (née Walsh) is Head of the Centre for the enhancement of Academic Skills, Teaching, Learning & Employability (CASTLE) at the University of Dundee. She is also Deputy Chair of the QAA Scotland national Enhancement Theme: Student Transitions. Her main areas of practice and research are in continuing professional development and professional recognition for university teachers; issues of identity relating to professions, transitions and threshold concepts; collaborative working; and doctoral supervision. Her other publications include: Walsh, L. and Kahn, P. (2010). *Collaborative Working in Higher Education. The Social Academy*. Routledge: New York and London. Lorraine is a Fellow of the Higher Education Academy and of the Royal Society of Arts.

Bijaya Aryal is an Assistant Professor of Physics in the Center for Learning Innovation at the University of Minnesota Rochester. He received his B.Sc. and M.Sc. degrees from Tribhuvan University and M.S. and Ph.D. degrees in Physics from Kansas State University. He is active in physics education research and his ongoing major research areas focus on students' problem solving in physics and transfer of physics concepts and skills learning across physics and other disciplines. His research on student learning has resulted multiple papers, book chapters and conference proceedings. He has been frequently contributing paper and poster presentations to American Association of Physics Teachers, Physics Education Research Conference, National Association for Research in Science Teaching and American Physical Society meetings. His international presentations include his research efforts on integration of physics in interdisciplinary contexts.

Tom E. Baldock is a Professor in the School of Civil Engineering at the University of Queensland. He is a hydraulic and coastal engineer with a strong interest in Engineering Education. He has been Chair of the School Teaching and Learning Committee since 2007. His main research focus is surf zone and swash zone hydrodynamics and sediment transport, both experimental and field, for application to wave run-up and coastal inundation, tsunami, beach erosion and coral reef processes, and how these may change with projected sea level rise. With the assistance of a number of post-doctoral fellows, his Engineering Education research has focused on developing tools for peer assessment, e-learning and metacognition activities in large Engineering classes of over 250 students.

Mark Barrow is Associate Professor and Associate Dean (Academic) in the Faculty of Medical and Health Sciences at the University of Auckland. In this role he oversees the teaching programme of the faculty. Mark holds a Doctor of Education and has published work related to the role of student assessment in the formation of an educated identity, the application of quality assurance systems in tertiary education institutions and the links between the identity of doctors and nurses and their capacity to collaborate in interprofessional health care teams.

Terje Berg is an Associate Professor at the BI Norwegian Business School, Department of Accounting, Auditing and Law. His current research interests are the interplay between theory and practice within management accounting, as well as the important bridge between academics and businesses: textbooks and teaching, and more particularly how students learn. Within this context, he is taking part in several research projects on threshold concepts.

Jonte Bernhard is Professor in Engineering Education at Linköping University. He has a MSc in Engineering and a PhD in Solid State Physics both from Uppsala University. Before his appointment as full professor in 2012 he was an associate professor in Electronics. He has taught courses in Electrical Engineering and in Engineering Physics for 30 years as well as courses in Education for 15 years. He has been coordinator for the Nordic Network in Engineering Education Research (NNEER) funded by NordForsk (Nordic Ministerial Council) and is currently associate editor for the *European Journal of Engineering Education*. He has published extensively on topics related to Engineering and Physics Education Research as well in Material Science. He has been the principal investigator for several research projects funded by the Swedish Research Council and educational development projects funded by the Swedish Agency for Higher Education.

Roel Bloo studied mathematics at the Catholic University of Nijmegen. Subsequently he did a PhD in theoretical computer science at the Eindhoven University of Technology (TU/e). After being post-doc and assistant professor, both for one year, in 2001 he obtained a combined position as study counsellor, lecturer and assistant programme coordinator for the BSc programme of Computer Science and Engineering at TU/e, a position which he has held ever since.

Bjørn Otto Braaten has since 2001 been Associate Professor at the Department of Architectural Design and Management at the Faculty of Architecture and Fine Arts at the Norwegian University of Science and Technology (NTNU). He is currently head of the five year Master program in Architecture. His main field of research is deep structures in architecture and transformative learning. He has systematised and analysed a comprehensive empirical material of the individual work of first year students (2001–2006). What has been discovered are expressions of liminality and basic patterns of space connected to transformative learning processes. The work package 'Complexity & Depth', as a part of the TRANSark project concerning transformative learning, has been developed on the basis of this research. Bjørn Otto is also involved in teaching and research connected to full scale building courses dealing with wooden structures, managed by Professor Jan Siem at the Department of Architectural Design, History and Technology.

David P. Callaghan is a Senior Lecturer of Coastal Engineering, in the School of Civil Engineer at The University of Queensland, Australia. He researches in Engineering Education and in Coastal Engineering including statistics of extremes, beach erosion from extreme events, physical and biological interactions of salt marshes, coral reefs and seagrasses, lagoon dynamics, wave propagation. His Engineering Education research centres on trailing and refining sustainable teaching activities in large engineering classes (>350 students) that improve student learning, particularly towards thinking like an engineer.

Anna-Karin Carstensen is Senior Lecturer in Engineering Education at Jönköping University. She has a PhD in Engineering Education Research from Linköping University. She has taught courses in electrical engineering, control theory, mechatronics and computer science for thirty years. She is part of the Engineering Education Research group at Linköping University, where she has cooperated with Professor Bernhard for over ten years. She has been a member of the Board of Education and Research Education at Jönköping University (2008–2011).

Glynis Cousin was Professor and Director of the Institute for Learning Enhancement at the University of Wolverhampton. Prior to this she worked in adult, community and higher education, holding academic posts at Coventry and Warwick universities before being appointed Senior Advisor at the Higher Education Academy. She is the author of *Researching Learning in Higher Education*.

Jason P. Davies has, since 2003, held varied teaching and research roles at University College London in UCL's Centre for the Advancement of Learning and Teaching. These have included multiple roles in an interdisciplinary research project on a UCL-wide Evidence, Inference and Inquiry project, and being programme director of UCL's former MA Education. Previously he was a postdoctoral fellow at the Wellcome Trust Centre for the History of Medicine at UCL. He has taught widely across UCL over two decades. He currently teaches interdisciplinary courses and is part of the team that supports UCL's Arena programme for Higher Education Academy (HEA) fellowship. His abiding interest is in people's experience of interaction through different knowledge systems. He has published on interdisciplinarity, history of religion and constructions of belief. He is currently convenor of the Society for Research into Higher Education (SRHE) Academic

Practice Network and is a founder member of the Teaching and Learning Ancient Religion Network (tlarnetwork.org). He occasionally tweets (@JasonPtrDavies) and sometimes updates his webpage at http://tinyurl.com/bt6awuh.

Ann Devitt is Assistant Professor in Modern Languages at the School of Education in Trinity College Dublin and course director of the Initial Teacher Education programme in the School. Her research interests include second language teaching and learning, in particular Computer Aided Language Learning and the discourse of the classroom and textbooks. She also conducts research in teacher education, focusing on reflective practice and threshold concepts for Initial Teacher Education.

Marianne Dickie is the Director of the Australian National University (ANU) College of Law Migration Law Program. She has worked extensively in the migration field since 1993. She is a qualified migration agent, was a board member of The Rehabilitation Unit Survivors of Torture and Trauma at the Mater Hospital in Queensland from 1995 to 1996, and an immigration adviser to the Australian Democrats from 1998 to 2004. In addition to managing the Migration Law Program since 2007, Marianne works with the community providing pro bono migration advice in the legal advice clinic she established in 2009, under the Auspices of the Aids Action Council of the ACT. Marianne holds a Masters in Higher Education from ANU and is a Senior Fellow of the Higher Education Academy. She continues to research and write in her two areas of passion, education and migration.

Morten Erichsen is an Assistant Professor at BI Norwegian Business School, Department of Marketing. Erichsen lectures in subjects as marketing, strategy and management. He is taking part in several research projects within learning and leadership and has written a textbook about leadership in small and medium enterprises.

Peter Felten is Assistant Provost for Teaching and Learning, Executive Director of the Center for Engaged Learning, and Professor of History at Elon University, North Carolina. His publications include the co-authored books *Transforming Students: Fulfilling the Promise of Higher Education* (Johns Hopkins University Press, 2014) and *Engaging Students as Partners in Learning and Teaching* (Jossey-Bass, 2014). He is President-Elect of the International Society for the Scholarship of Teaching and Learning (ISSoTL), and Co-editor of the *International Journal for Academic Development*.

Michael T. Flanagan is a Teaching Fellow in the Department of Electronic and Electrical Engineering, University College London (UCL). Before his retirement he ran a bioelectronics group within the department and his pedagogic research is now centred on cross-disciplinary education at the postgraduate level. An earlier move from an industrial laboratory to a university led to an interest in the gap between academic and industrial perceptions of what a graduate entering industry should be. He was active in introducing an academic/industrial integrated programme, at both masters and doctoral levels, and in the development of technology enhanced learning for industrial continuing professional development. He maintains a website that provides a comprehensive reference list of current work on the Threshold Concept. (http://www.ee.ucl.ac.uk/~mflanaga/thresholds.html).

Aminul Huq is an Assistant Professor of Mathematics in the Center for Learning Innovation at the University of Minnesota Rochester. He received his B.Sc. degree from University of Dhaka and M.A. and Ph.D. degrees in Mathematics from Brandeis University with specialization in Combinatorics. He is active in undergraduate mathematics education research and his ongoing major research areas focus on interdisciplinary projects, critical thinking and curriculum design. He is a Project NExT fellow (Blue dot `10). Over the past several years he has been contributing papers and presentations to the MATHFEST, American Mathematical Society and international conferences on group work, interdisciplinary projects, calculus and statistics curricular changes.

Leif M. Hokstad is Professor in Digital Competence in Teaching and Learning at the Norwegian University of Science and Technology (NTNU). At the Educational Development Unit he trains newly employed faculty in the teaching profession. Among his assignments are to develop courses in supervision, the use of technology in teaching and learning environments, assist in course design at program and department level. His most recent project is the TransARK project at NTNU, a joint enterprise between the Unit of Educational Development and the Faculty of Architecture and Fine Art. This initiative aims at a rethinking of architecture and architecture education based on a threshold concept-centred methodology for curriculum design for the education of architects. His teaching experience includes the Norwegian School of Business (BI), where he currently gives courses in intercultural communication and negotiation. He also is a pedagogical advisor and researcher at the Centre for Medical Simulation at NTNU.

Dan Kaczynski is Professor in Educational Leadership at Central Michigan University where he teaches qualitative research, research methods and program evaluation. His publications and presentations promote technological innovations in research, curriculum reform, and doctoral education. Dan's current research is based in Australia where he is exploring threshold concepts in doctoral education and the methodological integration of data analysis software. He holds appointment as a visiting fellow at The Australian National University and adjunct professor at the University of Canberra.

David B. Knight is an Assistant Professor in the Department of Engineering Education at Virginia Tech (USA) and affiliate faculty with the Higher Education

Program, Center for Human-Computer Interaction, and Human-Centered Design Program. His research focuses on student learning outcomes in undergraduate engineering, learning analytics approaches to improve educational practices and policies, interdisciplinary teaching and learning, organizational change in colleges and universities, and international issues in higher education. He previously served as a postdoctoral fellow in engineering education in the University of Queensland's School of Civil Engineering.

Ray Land is Professor of Higher Education at Durham University and Director of Durham's Centre for Academic Practice. He previously held similar positions at the Universities of Strathclyde, Coventry and Edinburgh. He has been a higher education consultant for the OECD and the European Commission and has recently been involved in three European Commission higher education projects in Europe and Latin America. He is currently advisor to the Norwegian TRANSark project on architectural education. He has published widely in the field of educational research, including works on educational development, learning technology, threshold concepts and quality enhancement. His latest book (with George Gordon) is *Enhancing Quality in Higher Education: International Perspectives* (Routledge 2013). He is a Fellow of the Royal Society of Arts and a Principal Fellow of the Higher Education Academy.

Linda Martindale is a Lecturer in the School of Nursing and Health Sciences at the University of Dundee. Her main areas of interest and practice are: dissertation supervision for taught postgraduate programmes, including supporting dissertation supervisors as part of her dissertation co-ordinator role; teaching evidence-based practice and research methods across undergraduate and postgraduate programmes; and supporting students and staff to develop skills in online teaching and learning. She is her School's lead for e-learning and co-leads the University's Distance Learning Forum. Her PhD focused on threshold concepts in research and evidence-based practice for undergraduate nursing students and Linda is also involved in setting up a special interest group for threshold concepts in healthcare. Her other research interest is in online distance learning programmes for Masters students in developing countries and she currently leads a longitudinal study of the effectiveness of online distance learning for healthcare students in Kenya and Eritrea.

Julie McCredden is a cognitive psychologist with a background in working memory limits to human reasoning and in models of analogical reasoning. She has been working in the applied areas of engineering education and educational design for 6 years. Julie has worked in promoting the use of helpful technologies for improving learning outcomes for students, and in assisting lecturers to adopt these technologies. She has an interest in understanding what makes complex concepts hard to learn, and in methods such as metacognition, situated cognition, metal models and analogies for helping students to grasp difficult concepts and be able to apply them in the real world.

Daniel McGill is Program Manager with the Department of Engineering at Macquarie University. He has an extensive background in working with Engineering Departments at Macquarie and, previously, Murdoch University. Daniel has had a key role in developing the Department's Learning and Teaching program and, in this context, has been closely involved in the strategic review of the Department's curriculum. He has taken a lead in the development and rollout of the modularisation of the Engineering program incorporating the implementation of Threshold Concepts as the feature of this approach to pedagogy. This ongoing curriculum development project has led to publications detailing the mapping and implementation of the Department's program of study and fundamental alignment with the requirements of both the University's Learning and Teaching strategy as well as the Stage 1 Competency requirements of Engineers Australia. Daniel has been an active participant in Australasian Association for Engineering Education.

Susannah McGowan works in CALT at University College London. As a researcher, one of her current projects explores the impact of the scholarship of teaching and learning across the UK. In addition to working in London, she continues to serves as a consultant on technology enhanced learning and research methodologies to the Association of Jesuit Colleges and Universities in Washington DC (US) and the Center for Engaged Learning at Elon University in North Carolina (US). Prior to receiving her PhD in learning, culture and technology studies at the University of California, Santa Barbara, she served as the assistant director of curriculum design at the Center for New Designs in Learning and Scholarship (CNDLS) at Georgetown University in Washington D.C. While at CNDLS, she directed projects and programmes aimed to support professional development in learning design, student engagement, and technology-enhanced learning.

Eugene McKendry Dr. Eugene McKendry is Senior Lecturer at the School of Education in Queen's University Belfast where he coordinates the Modern languages PGCE and is director of the Northern Ireland Centre for Information in Language Teaching and Research (NICILT).

Jan H. F. Meyer is a Professor of Education, in the School of Civil Engineering at The University of Queensland, Australia. He has two symbiotic research interests: in university teaching, and student learning wellbeing. In order to inform teaching, much of his earlier research activity concentrated on the quantitative modelling of individual differences in students' learning. This modelling work has, in turn, been used since 2004 as the basis for further research in developing mechanisms to help students develop their metalearning capacity (awareness of, and control over, their learning). The more recent development of the Threshold Concepts Framework integrates these modelling and metalearning interests and extends them into new research domains as reflected in his most recent publications.

Ahmad Thamrini Fadzlin Syed Mohamed is a Senior Language Teacher, an eager educationist, and an inspiring hockey coach at the National Defence University of Malaysia. He is currently pursuing his PhD at Durham University, undertaking research on threshold concepts and its application in the education and training for future officers. His other research interests include Second Language Teaching and Learning and Post-Colonial Literature.

David Moroney is a PhD candidate in the School of Education at Trinity College Dublin exploring how Threshold Concepts can enable teacher transformation in Initial Teacher Education. He has a MA in TESOL from the University of Birmingham where he is also a distance learning tutor for their MA in TESOL and Applied Linguistics programs. Currently, he is a lecturer in the English Department in the University of Cologne.

Marcia D. Nichols is Assistant Professor in the Center for Learning Innovation at the University of Minnesota Rochester where she teaches literature and medical humanities and engages in learning research. In addition to work on pedagogy, she has published on Charles Brockden Brown, Edgar Allen Poe, early modern erotica and eighteenth and nineteenth-century medicine and midwifery. Her current book project analyzes the constructions of gender, sexuality and masculine identity in midwifery manuals and other medical texts in the long eighteenth century.

Anne O'Callaghan works as a palliative care specialist and is clinical director of the Auckland Hospital Palliative Care Service. She has an interest in medical education and in particular how learning can best be facilitated in the postgraduate clinical environment, given that transfer of learning from medical school into this environment is not always effective. She has trained as a learning facilitator of communication skills and is involved in teaching at undergraduate and postgraduate levels. She is currently enrolled as a doctoral candidate with the Faculty of Education, The University of Auckland and is using grounded theory methodology to investigate how junior doctors engage with communication challenges in the hospital environment. As a result of this she is constructing a theory of medical voice.

Taimi Olsen is the Director of the Tennessee Teaching and Learning Center at the University of Tennessee, Knoxville, having joined the center in the fall of 2009. She holds her doctorate in American and Twentieth Century Literature, with literature publications on E. E. Cummings, including *Transcending Space:*

Architectural Places in Works by Henry David, Thoreau, E. E. Cummings, and John Barth. Regarding faculty development and teaching, she has been published in the Academic Commons, New Directions in Teaching and Learning, and Talking Matters. Her workshop/presentation topics include issues of assessment, visual learning, threshold concepts, and flexible classrooms.

Liza O'Moore is a Senior Lecturer in the School of Civil Engineering at the University of Queensland. She teaches into first and second year engineering and leads the final year capstone design project. Liza has research interests in the areas of transition and preparedness for first year, graduate competencies and large class teaching. In 2011 Liza was awarded an Australian Learning and Teaching Council Citation for Outstanding Contribution to Student Learning. She was a project team member on the OLT funded "Get set for success: using online self-assessments to motivate first year engineering students". Liza has undertaken interdisciplinary research in the areas of competence assurance and the use of simulators for CRC – Rail. Liza has also provided advice on accreditation of VET sector Associate Degrees, and in the curriculum development for new BE (Civil) programs at tertiary level.

Jacob Perrenet has a background in mathematics and educational psychology. He has worked as a mathematics teacher for several years. Next he did didactical research in mathematics at several universities and got his PhD in Social Sciences on a dissertation about collaborative learning. He worked as an educational advisor and as an innovator in the context of technological education at several universities. Since 1997 he is affiliated to the Eindhoven University of Technology and, although formally retired in 2013, he is still involved in teacher training, development of academic competencies, and educational research in both mathematics and computer science education.

Anthony Parker is Professor of Electronics and Director of Learning and Teaching in the Department of Engineering at Macquarie University, Sydney, Australia. His research interests are primarily in microwave electronic, where he has contributed pioneering developments in transistor modeling and nonlinear analysis of radio circuits and systems. His work is in collaboration with many international industry partners, where his work is being applied to real world problems and has experience in commercial workplace environments. Prior to his present position, Parker was foundation Head of Engineering for over a decade, and has led the top-down design and introduction of the new program. He has been pursuing a research approach for the curriculum design, which involves threshold concepts, outcome based assessments, and improvement and management of student experience. He is a member of Engineers Australia, Australasian Association for Engineering Education, and a Senior Member of IEEE.

Julie Rattray is Director of Postgraduate Taught Programmes (PGT) and Lecturer in Education and Psychology in the School of Education at Durham University. Her research interests include the affective dimension of liminality within threshold concepts, teaching, learning and quality in higher education, and conceptual development. In particular she is interested in the ways in which students might experience and cope with troublesomeness as they encounter it in their learning. She is a Senior Fellow of the UK Higher Education Academy (SFHEA) and is currently working on projects exploring aspects of postgraduate student transition and induction.

Gro Rødne is an architect and Associate Professor at the Department of Architectural Design, Form and Colour, at the Faculty of Architecture and Fine Art at the Norwegian University of Science and Technology (NTNU). She is the Project Manager of TRANSark (Centre for Transformative Learning in Architectural Education: http://www.ntnu.edu/transark) and responsible for the work package 'Making is Thinking' which seeks to investigate the transformative aspects of the students' experience through direct learning by making. Gro has been Programme Lead for the first year of the Master program in Architecture for six years and is responsible for the master course *Making is Thinking*. The course objective lies in hands-on experiences and in the overlap between artistic and architectural methods. Gro is founder, partner and member of the board at Agraff Architects.

Michelle Salmona is a PMI certified Project Management Professional, a Senior Fellow of the Higher Education Academy, UK and Vice President, Research at the Institute for Mixed Methods Research. Her research agenda is wide and varied and promotes inter-disciplinary approaches to issues of culture and access. Recent research includes exploring the changing practices of qualitative research during the dissertation phase of doctoral studies and investigating how we bring learning into using the technology during the research process. Michelle works internationally as a consultant program evaluator and trainer in research methods and qualitative data analysis software.

David W. Schumann is Emeritus Professor and Founding Director of the University of Tennessee Teaching and Learning Center. Previous to retirement, he held the William J. Taylor Professorship of Business in the Department of Marketing and Supply Chain Management. He has previously served in the roles of department head, senior associate dean, and co-founder of the Global Leadership Scholars Program (college honors). As an applied psychologist, his research has been published in numerous elite scientific journals in advertising, communications, consumer psychology, marketing, social psychology, and teaching and learning in higher education. He is the former President of the Society for Consumer Psychology and is a Fellow of the American Psychological Association.

344

Fredrik Shetelig is Professor in Architecture and Dean of the Faculty of Architecture and Fine Art at the Norwegian University of Science and Technology (NTNU). He was the initial 'mover' for establishing TRANSark (Centre for Transformative Learning in Architectural Education, http://www.ntnu.edu/transark) as a centre where passion for teaching architecture could combine with cutting edge research on learning processes. Fredrik is a former founder and partner of Pir II arkitektkontor.

Dermot Shinners-Kennedy is a lecturer in the Department of Computer Science and Information Systems at the University of Limerick and an early adopter of the concept of threshold concepts. His research interests focus on the teaching and learning of programming and the difficulties experienced by novices attempting to acquire programming knowledge.

Julie A. Timmermans is the Instructional Developer – Consulting and Research at the Centre for Teaching Excellence at the University of Waterloo. She supports faculty and staff with designing, implementing, and disseminating results from pedagogical research projects and manages the Learning Innovation and Teaching Enhancement (LITE) Grants program. She also chairs the institution-wide teaching and learning conference which annually bring together faculty and staff from across the university to discuss pedagogical research and wisdom of practice. Recently, she has had the opportunity to do educational development work in France and Japan. Her research interests explore the intersections between threshold concepts, the development of epistemic beliefs, and educational development.

Virginia M. Tucker is on the faculty at the School of Information at San José State University, where she teaches and coordinates curriculum development for courses in information retrieval, database design, and search; she is recipient of the Outstanding Lecturer Award. She is also a part-time public law librarian and committed to providing access to justice and legal information. Dr. Tucker previously worked as an information architect and client training manager in Silicon Valley; she started out in the information profession as the physics librarian at Stanford University. Dr. Tucker's current research interests include information experiences, search interface design, curriculum development, and online learning environments. She has a PhD in information systems from Queensland University of Technology, an MLS from the University of California at Berkeley, and a BA from Stanford University in music composition.

Ilona van Galen is a skilled communicator who has worked in online educational design and development at the Australian National University (ANU) College of Law since 2008. She brings to this rewarding and challenging higher education role an extensive career in public communications and community consultation and engagement, particularly in the controversial arena of urban renewal and redevelopment. This multidisciplinary background has enabled Ilona to explore innovative online educational design approaches integrating best practice in written communication, visual communication, web design, and the urban design principles of wayfinding. Ilona is committed to making the experience of learning to navigate their online campus as effortless as possible, freeing them to focus on engaging with difficult subject matter, with fellow students, and with their teachers. She has a BA in Communications from the University of Technology in Sydney (UTS) and a Master in Professional Studies from the University of Southern Queensland (USQ).

Andy Wearn began his academic career whilst GP training in Birmingham (UK), later working as a GP principal and a clinical lecturer. He came to New Zealand in 2001 to set up a clinical skills centre for the University of Auckland's health professional programmes. He is involved in the design, resourcing and delivery of early skills curricula in the Faculty of Medical & Health Sciences. He has a range of roles within MBChB, other faculty undergraduate programmes and the postgraduate Clinical Education programme, and he continues to practice clinically. Among external roles, he is currently editing the journal FoHPE (Focus on Health Professional Education). Andy has collaborated broadly and has an eclectic mix of publications in education and primary care.

Andrea S. Webb received her Ph.D. in Curriculum Studies from the University of British Columbia. She taught high school Social Studies and English for many years before taking a position in Teacher Education at the Faculty of Education, University of British Columbia. Her current research interests lie in the scholarship of teaching and learning and educational leadership, particularly within the context of higher education.

Steffen Wellinger is an architect and Associate Professor at the Norwegian University of Science and Technology (NTNU) in Trondheim, where he mentors the student-initiated Live Projects. Live Projects in Norway and the global south are used to trigger social entrepreneurship, learning and a new professional culture. The combination of hands-on production, applied user insight and working in challenging contexts opens up new approaches to sustainable planning. In 2010 Steffen received the SINTEF award for outstanding teaching at NTNU. As leader of the work package 'Live Studio' in TRANSark (Centre for transformative learning in architecture education) he is responsible for research and development and Live Activities for students of Architecture and Fine Arts at NTNU. Steffen is a partner in Bjørke Arkitektur.

Beth A. White is Program Coordinator of the University of Tennessee Teaching and Learning Center. Prior to joining the TennTLC, she was in counseling practice for seven years before transitioning into higher education where she has taught courses in psychology for the past twenty years. In addition, she has done extensive work as a freelance editor for both Pearson and Worth publishers and recently wrote an instructor resource manual for Macmillan. Beth has published in the areas of faculty development and teaching psychology. Her areas of interest include threshold concepts and new faculty development.

Gina Wisker is Professor of Higher Education & Contemporary Literature at the University of Brighton and Head of Brighton's Centre for Learning and Teaching. She is also a Visiting Professor at the University of Johannesburg. Her research interests are in learning and teaching, postgraduate study and supervision and she has published *The Postgraduate Research Handbook* (2001, 2008) *The Good Supervisor* (2005, 2012) and *Getting Published* (2015) (all Palgrave Macmillan). Gina teaches, supervises, researches and publishes in twentieth-century women's writing, particularly postcolonial, Gothic and popular fictions and published *Postcolonial and African American women's writing* (2000), *Key Concepts in Postcolonial Writing* (2007), *Margaret Atwood, an Introduction to Critical Views of Her Fiction* (2012, all Palgrave Macmillan) and *Horror* (2005, Continuum). Gina has been chair and co-chair of the Heads of Education Development Group, is chief editor of the SEDA journal *Innovations in Education and Teaching International*, chair of SEDA Scholarship and Research committee, and the Contemporary Women's Writing Association. Gina is a Principal Fellow of the HEA, a Senior Fellow of SEDA , and a National Teaching Fellow.

Leigh N. Wood is Associate Dean Learning and Teaching and Professor in the Faculty of Business and Economics at Macquarie University. Leigh contributes to university-wide policy formation, sets the direction for learning and teaching at Macquarie in conjunction with other stakeholders, and implements learning and teaching strategy across the faculty.

Bert Zwaneveld began his professional career as a secondary mathematics teacher. As a part-time job he was then also math teacher trainer. After some years as one of the vice-principals of the school where he was math teacher, he became math course developer in the department Computer Science of the Open Universiteit (of the Netherlands). In that period he got his PhD in math education on a dissertation about structuring mathematical knowledge by students. Since 2004 he is professor in the professionalization of teachers in math or computer science. Since 2011 he is emeritus professor, still doing research in both math and computer science education.

INDEX

Lightning Source UK Ltd.
Milton Keynes UK
UKOW06f1059080516

273774UK00001B/32/P

9 789463 005104